The
NOIR
FORTIES

ALSO BY **Richard Lingeman**

Drugs from A to Z: A Dictionary

*Don't You Know There's a War On? The American
    Home Front, 1941–1945*

*Small Town America: A Narrative History,
    1609–The Present*

*Theodore Dreiser: At the Gates of the City,
    1871–1907 (Vol. I)*

*Theodore Dreiser: An American Journey, 1908–1945
    (Vol. II)*

*Theodore Dreiser: An American Journey
    (abridged edition)*

Sinclair Lewis: Rebel from Main Street

Double Lives: American Authors' Friendships

The Nation Guide to the Nation

The NOIR FORTIES

The American People from
Victory to Cold War

RICHARD LINGEMAN

NATION
BOOKS
New York

Published by Nation Books, A Member of the Perseus Books Group
116 East 16th Street, 8th Floor, New York, NY 10003

Nation Books is a co-publishing venture of the Nation Institute
and the Perseus Books Group.

Books published by Nation Books are available at special discounts for bulk pur-
chases in the United States by corporations, institutions, and other organizations.
For more information, please contact the Special Markets Department at the Perseus
Books Group, 2300 Chestnut Street, Suite 200, Philadelphia, PA 19103, or call
(800) 810-4145, ext. 5000, or e-mail special.markets@perseusbooks.com.

Every effort has been made to secure required permissions for all text and
images reprinted in this volume.

The author acknowledges the contribution of a grant from Furthermore, a program
of the J.M. Kaplan Fund.

Design by Pauline Brown
Typeset in 11.5 point Dante Std by the Perseus Books Group

Library of Congress Cataloging-in-Publication Data

Lingeman, Richard R.
    The noir forties : the American people from victory to Cold War /
Richard Lingeman.
        p.   cm.
    Includes bibliographical references and index.
    ISBN 978-1-56858-436-2 (hardcover : alk. paper)—ISBN 978-1-56858-690-8
(e-book) 1. United States—History—1945–1953. 2. United States—Politics and
government—1945–1953. 3. United States—Intellectual life—20th century.
4. United States—Social conditions—1945–55. Social psychology—United States—
History—20th century. 6. Social change—United States—History—20th century.
7. Film noir—Social aspects—United States—History—20th century. 8. Film
noir—United States—History and criticism. I. Title.
E813.L56 2012
973.91—dc23
                                                                      2012024868

10 9 8 7 6 5 4 3 2

This book is dedicated to my friend
Mitchell Winn (1931–2011).

CONTENTS

AUTHOR'S NOTE

THIS BOOK COVERS ROUGHLY the five years between the surrender of Japan in World War II and the Korean War, which I lived through as a young man. I wrote it in hopes of constructing a narrative of *how* America got from victory to cold war, weaving together a historical enlargement of my smaller personal memories. The Korean conflict was the flash point of the long cold war, that "twilight struggle" that President John F. Kennedy romantically evoked in his inaugural address. And in 1953 I found myself enlisted as a common soldier in that war.

As I worked on this book, I began thinking of it as a "memoir in the form of history." The personal history aspect serves as a footnote, so to speak, to the main narrative. Most of our lives are obscure footnotes in history; most of us are bit players, supernumeraries in the crowd scenes. But still we try to look outside and beyond ourselves and perceive the larger currents of history in which we were swept along.

The narrative here is more political and cultural history than social history. I realize that things like ballpoint pens, Aureomycin, tail fins, and teenagers got invented during those years, give or take; and the grander issues such as the causes of the cold war are still debated in the halls of academe. But in this inquiry I've assigned myself, I try to tell what Americans thought in those five momentous years when their country went from peace to war, a war that changed my life and the lives of my contemporaries.

A note on the title: I devote a large chunk of the book to what I've dubbed "noir culture," after the body of crime films known as film noir, which flourished between 1945 and 1950.[*] I believe films noir are a key for unlocking the psychology, the national mood during those years.

For all the joys of homecomings and for all the hopes of prosperity of those years, looking back, they seem quite dark at times, a hangover of the war, in which nearly four hundred thousand Americans died and more than 30 million worldwide. How could these things not have affected each of us bit players, however remotely? They were branded on our unconscious. The times saw rising tensions with the Soviet Union and with the intrusion of demagogic anti-Communism into domestic politics. Those years saw the death of Franklin D. Roosevelt, the twilight of the New Deal, and a conservative counterattack on the communal ethos that had carried the United States through depression and war. They were also a time of chances missed, choices made, roads not taken; a time of change and fear of change. And so this book is an exercise in alternative history.

Many of the writers and directors who made the films noir were on the political left, so their movies reveal the hopes of those on the left and their fears that their ambitions for a better world were closing down. In the best of these films, artists' perceptions of the postwar world were transmuted into cinematic dreams—or nightmares. These tell us something about the movies flickering inside people's heads during those years.

CARL BROMLEY, MY EDITOR AT NATION BOOKS, encouraged me in developing this book. Thanks to my longtime *Nation* magazine colleagues Victor Navasky and Katrina vanden Heuvel for their support and for reading and critiquing a much longer version. I am grateful to the Furthermore Foundation for a timely grant that enabled me to add essential material on New York noir (see Chapter Seven). The interviews with the people of Red Oak, Iowa (see Chapter One), were arranged by Jacky Adams, keeper of the town's World War II memory. Special thanks also to George Maher,

---

[*] Definitions of film noir differ. The movies I discuss in this book under this rubric have all been denominated as such by a majority of film critics and scholars. They have also been called "crime melodramas."

a civic-minded citizen of that beautiful small town. And thanks above all to the people of Red Oak who shared their memories and stories of the war, which hit their town so hard. Gratitude is also due to Rich Sternberg, who proposed the trip to Red Oak out of the blue. It was financed by a grant he received from the New Jersey Principals Association. He was my companion on the road and collaborator in the interviews. This book is a synthesis of the work of many scholars, whom I hope I have cited adequately in the text or notes. The interpretations of their facts and commentary is my own unless otherwise indicated. Thanks to Daniel LoPreto for his valuable help in tracking down song publishers. A much different kind of help was provided by Jenna Baynes, of Columbia Orthopaedics Sports Therapy in New York City, and Dr. Craig Rubenstein, also of New York, who helped me deal with shoulder and back problems that were slowing me down. Finally, as usual, thanks to Anthea Lingeman, for care and feeding and all manner of support, including technical.

The author (right) in Japan, ca. 1955, with a fellow counter-intelligence agent. In the Jeep is a recovered "weather balloon" gondola. Unbeknownst to them, the downed balloon actually carried a CIA spy camera. *Author photo*

Prologue

CONFESSIONS OF A COLD WARRIOR (I)

I HAVE A RECURRING MEMORY OF JAPAN. I am in Fukuoka, driving a car. Kelly, a fellow agent, is beside me in the front seat. Rabbit is hunched over in the backseat. Kelly's yelling, "Faster!" I jam the accelerator and swing the wheel on the Chevy; we go careering down dark streets. Something is after us, and I'm lost in a foreign place . . .

Two years, from 1954 through 1956, I served in Japan as a Special Agent with the Army Counter Intelligence Corps. I had enlisted in the CIC with my friend Mitch, who sold me on it, because of the Korean War and the draft. All of our class of '53 had avoided the worst of the war with college deferments, but graduation meant you had to choose. Go to graduate school, which meant choosing a career, which I was not ready to do. Or be drafted. Or enlist in the service of your choice. We opted for the third and joined the Army on July 14 (Bastille Day, Mitch, a Francophile, reminded me). This was two weeks before the truce was signed, ending the Korean War without peace.

We had several months of training at the CIC school at Fort Holabird, Maryland ("the Bird"). Before graduation, about twenty of us (but not Mitch, as I'll explain later) were told we were going to Japan. First, though, we were ordered to take a six-month crash course in Japanese at the Bird. It was too short a time to develop fluency in the language, of course, but I emerged able to speak rudimentary sentences. Still, in my work I had to use an interpreter.

In July, with a dozen other replacement agents, I boarded a troopship in Oakland. After a two-week voyage, we steamed into Yokohama harbor. I could see Fujiyama looming against the soft blue sky like a woodblock print by Hiroshige, its peak capped by a white crown of snow shading lower down into gray-blue.

Disembarking I was dunked into a maelstrom of alien sights and sounds and smells, drowning in the *foreignness* of it all.

An Army bus took a group of us to CIC headquarters in the middle of Tokyo, where we would stay for six weeks of indoctrination. It was a large four-story brownish-yellow, glum-looking building with a porte cochere over the main entrance. The site housed the main offices of the 441st Army Counter Intelligence Corps Detachment and also served as a barracks.

This building, located directly across the street along the moat surrounding the vast sprawling grounds of the Imperial Palace, had been the headquarters of the Kempei Tai, the Japanese military police. Supposedly, some of Gen. Jimmy Doolittle's fliers who were captured after the audacious US 1942 bombing raid on Tokyo were tortured in the basement cells here. No doubt Japanese were tortured as well by the secret police. During the American occupation, the CIC took it over and renamed it Norton Hall, after a CIC agent killed in the Philippines in World War II.

I had little interest in the history of the building. Compared to the Army barracks life we were used to, it was a luxury hotel. We attended classes by day, and at nights and on weekends we explored this strange humming city.

In late summer, after the end of the rainy season, Tokyo was a semitropical city. A blanket of humidity lay on it, sodden and heavy like a great sponge. Exploring, we wandered off into narrow twisty side streets, not knowing where we were going, ambling past low wooden shops with sliding doors and latticework windows overhung by blue curtains covered with cabalistic characters and flanked by bright red paper lanterns, the clopping of hundreds of wooden *geta* in our ears. People sat in bars and cafes over fruit drinks or tea, mopping their brows and exclaiming, *"Ahhh atsu-u-u-ii!"* ("It's hot!"), drawing out the word like a sigh. Office workers hurried along the streets, fanning themselves and dreaming perhaps of the beaches at Kamakura, a nearby resort where Tokyo people went to dip in the sea. *Ahhh atsu-u-u-ii!*

IN THE SODDEN HEAT, laborers worked stripped down to *furoshiki*— loincloths with bright-colored sweat rags tied around their foreheads. Visitors arriving hot and dirty on coal-burning trains hurried to inns, where they shed their business suits or kimonos and donned starched blue and white *yukata,* then moved to the common bath and soaked in the rising steam and afterward sluiced their naked bodies with wooden buckets of cold water. Refreshed, they returned to their rooms to relax, sitting crosslegged on the tatami around the low table, catching a faint breeze from the garden through open sliding doors, and sucking the juice from orange wedges or drinking glasses of Nippon beer from cold quart bottles and munching seaweed crackers.

There were a few Western-style hotels in the city, the main one and crown jewel being the Imperial, built by Frank Lloyd Wright in the 1920s and designed to be earthquake-proof. Low-lying, it sprawled over a large area, a reddish-brick sprawling structure, crouched like a great toad in the middle of the city.

Once, while walking along a public corridor of the Imperial, I ran into a man from my hometown, Ben. A West Point graduate wearing a major's oak leaf insignia, Ben was a sharp soldier, tall and ramrod straight. I was wearing my uniform with a private's insignia, so I reflexively saluted before shaking hands. We were both very stiff and rank-conscious.

Neither of us said what he was doing. We CIC agents had been instructed not to tell anyone about our status, except when on official business. In the field we wore civilian clothes and flashed identification cards designating us as Department of Army Civilians—"dacs." Our mail even came to a cover address—Detachment A, 5th Service Group, or some such.

So in the corridor of the phantasmagoric Imperial, with its red bricks and bits of colored glass around the windows, we called to each other across a gulf of rank and secrecy, exchanging news about our parents, who moved in the same circles in our mutual and very distant Indiana hometown. Those topics exhausted, we engaged in a cryptic dialogue like in a Samuel Beckett play, with little said about our work, where we were stationed, what we were doing there. (Much later I discovered from Ben's obituary that he served in the Central Intelligence Agency. Possibly he was in it even then, which would explain his reticence with me.)

Ironically, when I was a working agent I discovered a case file on "Suspected CIA Agents" or some such rubric. Apparently the CIC was supposed to keep track of CIA spies in our territory—I was never told why, of course. In pursuit of this particular one, I spent days in a fruitless stakeout looking for a Catholic priest who was said to be working undercover (under cassock?) for the Agency. I don't know if the spy priest was ever located; I never knew for a fact that he even existed, for I never learned the results of this or any other investigation.

"The first charm of Japan is intangible and volatile as a perfume," wrote Lafcadio Hearn, regretting he had not written down his first impressions of the country as soon as he arrived in 1890. Mine, though faded by time, flicker dimly in memory: The kamikaze taxi drivers. The haughty policemen in smart uniforms starched to a knife-edge directing traffic at intersections with flowing ritualized gestures like kabuki actors. The Ginza crowds at night. Neon signs with twisty snakelike characters luridly glowing pink, blue, white. The bars, nightclubs with "hostesses" eying you, yakitori counters with dripping birds (chickens, sparrows, or songbirds) on spits over charcoal braziers. The sushi restaurants where you sat at a counter that had a channel in which water flowed over a bed of smooth white stones and watched the chef's agile fingers shape the sticky rice like a magician performing a sleight-of-hand trick and produce ovoid morsels of rice topped with gleaming orange, red, or white slices of fish. The noodle shops with vats of seething pork broth, which countermen ladled into bowls over swirls of noodles, meat, and vegetables, and placed before hungry lunchtimers who slurped their soup with noisy appreciation. The Pachinko parlors where men in identical short-sleeve white shirts stood transfixed before rows of machines, watching with glazed eyes as the little steel balls caromed about behind the vertical glass.

At night, lying in my bunk at Norton Hall, I could hear the sounds of the street. Punctuating the muted noises was the reedy wail of the noodle vendor's *shakuhachi* flute, curling sinuously into the air like cigarette smoke, a sound I'll forever identify with the Japan I remember.

As far as I know, our field office at Camp Hakata, near Fukuoka on the island of Kyushu, never caught any spies. I do know that I never saw the Soviet courier we were ordered to find and watch. He was said to be contacting a spy in our city (something like that; I don't remember the details). Instead, I spent nights staked out at a bar looking for a thin man with a scar on his cheek who never appeared. Did he exist? If he did, I never knew for a fact.

According to later histories, the 441st CIC did break up some Soviet spy rings during the Korean War. In my day it seemed to be spending most of its time tracking the overt, legal political activities of the militant Japan Communist Party, the Socialist Party, and the labor unions—though I'm speaking only from my own parochial experience.

In any case, I had no part of that mission; I was assigned the ultranationalist beat, keeping track of myriad fractious "patriotic" groups with exotic names like Black Dragon Society and Imperial Chrysanthemum Society. Some were direct descendants of the fanatical movements of the 1930s that had agitated for war and assassinated government officials who opposed their hot-blooded ideas. Their historical predilection for violence was the main reason for our coverage of them, I assume. And they did have some influence with certain right-wing Japanese politicians. Much later, some of them cultivated ties to wealthy business leaders, conservative politicians, and the Yakuza, although in my time their mob connections were not objects of investigation.

In my work, I met with an informant known as I-37, a private investigator we called Rabbit for some reason I've forgotten. Maybe it was because he was a furtive little man. He made his living checking out the character references and bank accounts of future brides and grooms in arranged marriages. He also had contacts in local ultranationalist organizations and a willingness to sell us the inside dope on their activities—

meetings, plans, pamphlets, demonstrations. I took his neatly written reports, had them translated, and wrote them up.

"Make it like Hemingway," the Major, a literate man, used to tell us. "Short declarative sentences." Those reports were a good training ground for a terse style that told only the facts. I'm afraid, however, that American taxpayers didn't get many facts in return for the money I paid Rabbit. The groups he reported on never seemed to do much beyond talking and quarreling with one another, coining disdainful epithets for their rivals like "a harmless society for moon viewing." The "inside" information I-37 gave us was impossible for me to verify except with the police, and you had to be cagey with them; if you told them too much you might reveal the identity of your informant, and these identities were our most secret secrets.

During my stint in Japan I engaged in clandestine investigations in which hard facts had a way of melting into the shadows of ambiguity. Apart from the daily routine of writing and filing reports and paying occasional calls on the police, a lot of my work took place at night, meeting informants and taking their handwritten reports or jotting down what they told me.

I suspect (though I don't know it for a fact) that the police officials with whom we swapped bits of information had an ambivalent attitude toward our clandestine poking about in their now-sovereign country. Not that they were unfriendly; possibly they regarded us with the same ambivalence they must have had toward those cases of C-rations we gave them at Christmastime, a tradition going back to the hungry years after the war. The rations in the boxes probably helped feed their families, but by 1954 Japan was producing ample rice, vegetables, and fish, and one wonders if our friends truly relished Army OD shade 7 green cans of franks and beans, chicken and noodles, beef stew, and other staples that were intended to be eaten by GIs in the field (and which we agents, who didn't eat with the rest of the troops in the mess hall, subsisted on when we'd come up short before payday).

The job was, well, interesting. It was like being an investigative reporter for a paper with a very limited circulation. Norton Hall in Tokyo never responded to, commented on, criticized, or praised my reports—

except for one time. Many years later, going through my service files, I came across a letter from headquarters commending my field office's "efficient and timely execution of your phase of Project 119L." By then I had completely forgotten what Project 119L was. But I did remember reading in the *New York Times* about a CIA surveillance operation, publicly described as a meteorological experiment, that had sent balloons bearing a gondola with a camera over China to take high-altitude photographs of Chinese military sites. That, I'm sure, was the Project 119L I (or rather, we) had been commended for: I remember well going to pick up one of those "weather balloons," which we were told had been netted by a Japanese fishing boat.

The boat was moored in a tiny fishing village in Saga Prefecture, the neighboring one to ours. I set out in one of our black jeeps, accompanied by another agent, a quiet Nisei man from California named Tom, who would be my interpreter. All we were told was that a large weather balloon floated over the China Sea by the US Air Force to record meteorological information had fallen into the sea and been netted by a crew of Japanese fishermen. Our job was to bring back the gondola. We drove miles over flat back-country roads, skirting hills and rice paddies, to a tiny, isolated fishing village.

When we arrived the boat's crew was quickly assembled. They turned out to be a group of wiry men with seamed faces tanned nut-brown by sea and wind. They were angry, we soon sensed after the traditional courtesies, though Japanese manners prevented them from saying so outright. After much indirection and "*sa-a-a-a-hs*," Tom pinned down the origin of their distemper: they had been led to expect a reward of ten thousand yen for returning their odd catch to American authorities. That was news to us: we had brought no funds. Somehow, we talked our way out of this impasse by extravagant promises of greater riches to come, and escaped with our hides and our prize, a yellow plastic portholed gondola about the size of a small refrigerator, in the back of the Jeep. (See picture on page xii).

Lack of response to my work from headquarters may explain why I still remember the Major's words praising a report I had submitted: "a superior job of investigation." That one reported on interviews with some paratroopers who'd been POWs in Korea. The case involved an American prisoner who had defected to North Korea. At the time the POWs were widely believed to have been brainwashed by the Chinese. Why else would they choose Communism over Americanism? The case's eye-catching heading impressed me most: TREASON.

We all liked the Major, a lean man whose shoulders were stooped from a war wound. He took a vicarious and intelligent interest in our work, which we appreciated. He loved to argue with us college-boy liberals about Senator McCarthy's latest revelations, constantly reminding us after his fourth or fifth VO and water that "Dean Acheson said, 'I won't turn my back on Alger Hiss.'" (Hiss, a suspected Soviet spy, was a protégé of Acheson who had been convicted of perjury during a congressional hearing at which he was confronted by alleged coagent Whittaker Chambers.)

One of the pluses of my work was that it gave me a chance to travel into the surrounding countryside, driving one of our vehicles—either a Jeep painted black or a Chevrolet painted blue—as a cover. On some outings I drove past rice paddies with green sprigs protruding from watery black rows, the fresh spring air redolent of night soil. Other junkets took me to Saga City in neighboring Saga Prefecture, where we met ordinary Japanese people as well as police and government officials.

The police in Fukuoka City were tough but genial guys who went in for coarse joshing and after-hours sake. We usually became friendly with the detective we dealt with and entertained his superiors at "liaison parties" in restaurants or inns, with geishas pouring the sake and playing childish table games, laughing at our jokes and singing children's or drinking songs. After the cops got to know us, they reciprocated by inviting us to their homes, where we met recessive wives who dominated the home and wide-eyed children with bowl haircuts. We also paid New Year's Day calls, observing a Japanese holiday tradition of toasting one another with cup after cup of sake and eating the seasonal sweet red-bean cakes.

Although these relationships were friendly, the cops were professionally nosy. Conversing with them through an interpreter, I had time to think up an evasion to touchy questions. But that did not always save me. Once, a detective sergeant who handled ultranationalist cases—Tanizaki,

I'll call him—suddenly asked me point-blank if (giving Rabbit's real name) was a CIC informant. I felt my face prickle and redden; Christ! I was blushing! Lying so blatantly was a challenge to a small-town boy raised in the code of the Boy Scouts and graduated from a Quaker college that took pride in its honor system. Furious with myself, I stuttered a denial, but Tanizaki, a shrewd guy, may have guessed he had hit a nerve. (I suspect he had the same informant, whom we were thus double-paying—though of course I don't know it for a fact.)

One day, the Major suggested that I add Tanizaki to our roster of paid informants. I vaguely promised to try. I might have also objected, but didn't, that Tanizaki and I had a good, friendly relationship and that I saw no point in putting it on a different plane, meeting him secretly in a parked car at night and handing him cash. I never did make the approach; I couldn't even think how to go about it, what to say, given the linguistic obstacle course one had to traverse when asking a favor of a Japanese person.

But my reluctance ran deeper than that. I felt such an arrangement would amount to *bribery,* in which I had absolutely no experience but which I didn't approve of. Tanizaki, who had a family and did not make a munificent salary, might have been grateful for some extra income. Who knows? We might have moved beyond the hints, the fencing, to a franker, more open relationship. I might have learned what he knew about what we knew and about the CIC and our informants. But I couldn't do it, even though it meant disobeying what was kind of an order from the Major. Fortunately, he forgot about it, as happened with a lot of his big ideas.

Later, I recruited a better informant—a veteran ultranationalist leader who had risen to a high post in his organization after surviving the immediate postwar days, when many of his youthful comrades committed seppuku on the Yoyogi parade grounds in Tokyo (so he told us) to protest the emperor's surrender. This informant, whom I'll call Shimura, was missing the tip of his little finger. He boasted that he had cut it off and sent it to a rival gang member who was pressing him on a gambling debt. Shimura said it was the traditional samurai way of shaming someone who had wronged you; like many ultranationalists, Shimura fancied himself living by the medieval code of Bushido, the code of the samurai. He regaled us with gossip about his comrades and their drunken misadventures in brothels sharing the same woman.

I recruited Shimura in collaboration with Captain Whitestone, a veteran agent who spoke shamelessly bad Japanese, talking so loud that he gave an illusion of fluency. At least he was facile enough to flatter Shimura for his selfless devotion to the emperor and, more to the point, to offer him a large monthly retainer, which he agreed to take. I suspect those thousands of yen he collected went a long way toward financing the desultory activities of his organization that he duly reported to us.

Much later it struck me that in a sense, Tanizaki had been using me—or trying to—as an unwitting informant, subtly probing me. One of his obvious goals in our regular information exchanges, I realized, was to find out what we—the CIC—knew and try to guess how we knew it. For if he could deduce who our informant was (and I think he succeeded in doing that—see below), he could lean on the man and possibly disrupt the organization. Putting these groups out of business was, after all, his job.

But I don't know that for a fact.

THE REASON I CAME TO BELIEVE—though it may have been just the paranoia that went with the job—that Tanizaki had discovered Rabbit was working for us was because of an incident that occurred at one of our meetings. We were parked on a wide dirt road leading to a giant *tori* at the entrance to the city's main Shinto shrine. Kelly, a fast-talking, round-faced Hawaiian Nisei agent, was interpreting for me that night. Suddenly, he looked back and jerked a thumb at a car that had pulled up behind us.

"The cops! Bug out! Scram!" he hissed, ordering Rabbit to duck down in the backseat. I started the motor and we roared off, primed by the fear that if we had stayed the inquisitive cops would have sauntered up to our parked car, shined a flashlight on our informant, grilled him, maybe arrested him.

Glancing in the rearview mirror I saw the lights of the other car. "Faster!" Kelly said. I jammed the accelerator and steered wildly along a boulevard on the outskirts of the city, careering between three-wheelers and cyclists like a Pachinko ball. Luckily, it was late and there wasn't much traffic. I felt the Chevy leaning as we screeched around a corner, Rabbit cringing in the backseat.

"Goddamn, he's still coming! Faster!" Kelly yelled. I saw in the rear-view mirror two headlights like the glowing eyes of some big cat relentlessly hunting me down.

I speeded up and roared along a boulevard that led into a large park, cut the wheel and skidded into a side road lined with trees, swerved down another dark street. Eventually, after turns and double-backs, our nemesis was no longer in view. We stopped on a deserted street and let Rabbit out. He scurried off without a word. It was a strange game of cat-and-mouse. Later, I half-wondered, Was there *really* a pursuer? Was it really the cops? Had Kelly jumped to a conclusion too fast? Or was it the usual paranoia?

After we'd met our informants late at night, Kelly and I sometimes went drinking in small bars and hotels that he knew. Japanese places, though, not the cabarets that the GIs in their short-sleeve Hawaiian shirts and khakis frequented, drinking quart bottles of Nippon beer and watching the girls on the dance floor mamboing with each other to "Cherry Pink and Apple Blossom White," last year's American hit just arriving in Japan after crossing the International Date Line. They'd later bargain with the mama-san for a hostess they liked and take her to her tiny room or a shabby hotel. Occasionally, we stopped at one of those GI places, the Akadama, where we "shared" a hostess named Akemi . . .

Sometimes we entered places with signs saying "Japanese Only," where Kelly (who got around) might have known the manager or the mama-san. Sometimes, I heard a hissed *"gaijin!"* (foreigner) slit the smoky air. One night, very late, while we were ordering food at a noodle cart, a drunk walked up to us and started yelling that Kelly had called him a *baka* (jerk); I remembered when it happened. He was driving us and had yelled out of the car window at a man on a bicycle who was blocking our way. Now I glanced at the man and saw he was extracting from under his shirt a very long, slender, silvery knife, all the while muttering harshly. Instinctively, driven as much by booze and dislike of fist fights as courage, I stepped in and managed in my limited Japanese to joke him out of it. That seemed to be a fairly frequent role for me on late-night rambles—mediating fights, usually between drunk soldiers. The pacifist in me coming out.

There was a certain brothel, known as the Shakuhachi House, where the GIs went and every perversion under the moon was said to be available. Once, a group of agents raided it—or maybe "crashed" it is the word—in search of an AWOL GI who had made off with thousands of dollars in payroll money he was transporting from one base to another. He was rumored to be hiding out in the place, living it up. The Major probably got a tip from headquarters, mobilized his troops, and struck in the dead of night. The operation quickly turned into a bedroom farce of opened and slammed doors, with GIs emerging in their skivvies, angry at being expelled from warm beds. At one point I saw an EM roughing up the Major (who was in civilian clothes). I intervened, pinning his arms back, not knowing what the hell to do next. I think some of my comrades took charge of the GI and calmed him down.

Kelly and I continued the search. Then we burst into a room and met a scene I can never forget: a woman wearing only panties and bra was spraddled on a low bed, her arms and legs tied to the posts. A smiling guy was jabbing her with a lighted cigarette, while she writhed and shrieked. Seeing us, she cried, "Hey, you want to burn me? I like, I like it." I saw her body was spotted with red sores. We quickly backed out the door.

WORKING IN THIS SHADOW WORLD, I developed a taste for the night city, with its louche back-alley bars and hot-bed hotels, the exhilarating dangers, the sense of living on the edge (in my imagination at least). The night got to me. Going through some diaries I kept in Japan while writing this account, I came across a kind of prose poem, probably written after a late night of drinking at the Akadama. Reading it sent my thoughts hurtling back to Fukuoka nights.

14 November. . . . Dark silhouettes weaving on the dance floor—the jarring, irrelevant rhythms of the orchestra—the street at night—a lone figure ahead, shadow reflected and lengthened on the dimly lit pavement—the black still waters

*of the canal—the street lights glowing alone and separate in the night like indi-
vidual souls—pinpoints in the black night of Existence*

Sometimes, night makes you look into yourself. Sometimes, I didn't
like what I saw.

Many years later, I came upon films noir, a theme in this book. Those
dark crime films—mainly those made in the late forties—spoke to me.
Whenever the Film Forum, that temple of cinema on West Houston
Street in Greenwich Village, offered a program of films noir, I would sit
through them daily, alone in the dark, watching double and triple features.
Those films seemed to catch the paranoia, the deception, the mendacity
of the cold war—that "long twilight struggle." I have never talked about
my rather unremarkable adventures in Japan, since everything we did,
down to eating at the PX, was classified, strictly speaking. The films served
as divining rods for subterranean memories.

I started reading the many books about film noir; the concept fascinated
me. I later happened upon a study of German films from the Weimar era,
From Caligari to Hitler, by Siegfried Kracauer, who used Expressionist films
as a way of understanding the collective mind of the German people and
their progress from Weimar to hell. It suggested a way for me to probe
the subconscious of postwar America, those years just after the war when,
I think now as I look back, many dark currents swirled under the surface
of life . . .

These noir films seemed to evoke the mood of the time better than any
other movies made during the years leading up to the Korean War. The
Korean War had changed my life and my plans and the lives and plans of
many of my friends, and killed others a few degrees of separation from me.
How did it come about? Why did it happen? The films expressed subconscious reactions to the growing tensions between the United States and
the Soviet Union, to the Red Scare, the blacklists, the loyalty investigations. Of particular interest were the symbolic expressions of despair at the
decline of New Deal liberalism and the rise of the red-baiting that led to
McCarthyism and the growing fear of Communism at home and abroad,
a tide of fear that ultimately carried us into the Korean War. Trends were

set in motion that culminated in the war, almost as though it was fore-ordained. Those movies provide an insight into that psychology.

The hedyday of films noir also bracketed the fall of the liberal left right after the war, because many of them were conceived and made by the writers and directors who would be interrogated by the House Un-American Activities Committee, which descended on Hollywood like a storm cloud in 1946 and left behind in 1950 the wreckage of careers and artistic freedom, and a blacklist that authorized studios to fire any per-former who had been accused by anyone of being a Communist or sym-pathizer, never mind the lack of evidence. The downfall of the idealistic hopes invested in the war, the rebirth of our wartime hatred of the enemy, recycled against the Soviet Union, the threats of a common enemy packed into the portmanteau "Communism"—all these (along with a lingering death consciousness from World War II) were subtexts of these films, or at least the best of them. They grew out of the same general subsoil of emotion in which germinated the political culture of those short years from the Dionysian revels of VJ Day to June 25, 1950, when North Korean troops crossed the 38th Parallel and the cold war began.

Voices

There'll be love and laughter
And peace ever after
Tomorrow when the world is free.

—Nat Burton and Walter Kent, "(There'll Be
Bluebirds Over) The White Cliffs of Dover"

Tzena, Tzena, join the celebration.
There'll be people there from ev'ry nation.
Dawn will find us laughing in the sunlight
Dancing in the city square.

—Issachar Miron and Yehiel Haggiz
(English translation by Mitchell Parrish),
"Tzena, Tzena" (1941)

Oh leave the dishes in the sink, Ma,
Leave the dishes in the sink.
Each dirty plate will have to wait
Tonight we're going to celebrate.
Leave the dishes in the sink.

—Milton Berle, Gene Doyle, and Spike Jones,
"Leave the Dishes in the Sink, Ma" (1944)

"We shall not soon purge ourselves of the
feeling of guilt which prevails among us. . . .
What a precedent for the future we have furnished to other nations even less concerned
than we with scruples or ideals! Surely we
cannot be proud of what we have done. If we
state our inner thoughts honestly, we are
ashamed of it."

—David Lawrence, columnist (1945)

You remember two great cities in a
distant foreign land
When scorched from the face of earth the
power of Japan
Be careful, my dear brother, don't take away
the joy
But use it for the good of man and never to
destroy.
Atomic power, atomic power
It was given by the mighty hand of God

—Fred Kirby, "Atomic Power" (1946)

We came from behind and we came up fast.
We got together and spotted 'em aces and
spades and beat 'em at their own game.
Showed 'em how to pull off what
Napoleon and Hitler never even dared to
try—invasion across the Channel;
Showed 'em how to flank a flank and blitz
a blitz;
Showed 'em that when you *get together* and
conquer, it works out better than divide-
and-conquer;
Showed 'em how to wage a war and work and
plan and sing songs, all at once . . .

—Norman Corwin, *Untitled and
Other Radio Dramas* (1947)

I'll get by as long as I have you
Though there be rain and darkness too
I'll not complain
I'll see it through.

—Fred E. Ahlert and Roy Turk, "I'll Get By (As Long As
I Have You)" (1928), *Billboard's* No. 1 hit in 1944

Blue Skies, a formula show biz musical, was Paramount's biggest box office hit of 1946. *Everett Collection*

1

VICTORY DREAMS

ON AUGUST 14, 1945, *the day Japan surrendered, the day the war ended, I was at summer camp. We were in our tents for rest period. Suddenly shouts bounced from tent to tent:*

"The war's over!"

"The war's over!"

"The war's over!"

"Yay! My dad can come home!"

Early in the afternoon, Americans started hearing news reports from all over the world that Tokyo had accepted the Allied terms. Minutes after 7 p.m. Eastern War Time, President Truman, broadcasting from the White House, announced that the Japanese had surrendered unconditionally, which was not quite true, and declared a two-day holiday.

That same night the War Department dispatched 37,300 telegrams to war contractors canceling 83,000 uncompleted munitions contracts worth $17.5 billion ($209 billion in 2009 purchasing power), thus saving the last possible defense dollars.

A raucous crowd, mostly servicemen and -women who had been waiting in Washington's Lafayette Square for official word, quickly swelled to fifty thousand when the news came. They climbed on top of streetcars; they formed a conga line; they yelled, "We want Truman!" A thin rank of military policemen stood by the White House fence to hold back the mob. The dapper president, in office little more than three months, accompanied by his retiring wife, Bess, finally emerged flashing the V sign. He broadcast remarks to the crowd: "This is a great day, the day we have been waiting for." He asked everyone to help him make a lasting peace. He then approached the high iron fence bordering the White House lawn, waving until his arm grew tired.

In New York the cork popped, and animal spirits foamed up. A laughing, screaming, yelling, dancing, singing, drinking, kissing crowd of more than 750,000 people packed Times Square. By Wednesday it would grow to 2 million—the largest since the 4 million people who had welcomed home General Eisenhower, hero of the Normandy invasion. The din became earsplitting, the air torn by car horns, whistles, and the throaty boom of the *Queen Elizabeth*'s horn. The city had shuttered bars for the day, but people carrying bottles were ubiquitous, drinking their way to the "biggest hangover in history," wrote *Yank*'s New York reporter. A Brooklyn war wife described the scene:

> First of all the [streets] were jammed with people, mostly servicemen, packed in tightly from curb to curb—some walking eight and ten abreast, singing, laughing and blowing horns. Confetti and streamers were ankle deep and were being sold at every street corner. . . . Policemen and M.P.s . . . took no heed of the goings on like the sailors and soldiers . . . grabbing every woman and girl in their arms and passionately kissing them in spite of kicking, screaming, and protesting. People sat on the curbs of Broadway and Times Square right in front of the cops and necked—but most violently!

A nurse named Edith Shain heard the official announcement on the radio while on duty at Doctors Hospital on the Upper East Side. Without changing out of her white uniform, she and a coworker hurried to Times Square.

She didn't get very far down Broadway before a sailor grabbed her and mashed his lips on hers while bowing her back in a dance-floor dip. A week later she saw her picture on the cover of *Life* magazine, locked with the sailor in the famous photograph by Alfred Eisenstaedt.

Shain never saw the sailor again. Fifty years later, some publicists and New York officials staged a "reunion" between her and a man who had been arbitrarily designated her kisser, out of more than twenty claimants to the title.

The photo recorded traditional male dominance, but many women were as aggressive as the guys. Wilding bands of women planted smacks on the lips of surprised men. A Boston reporter described a "kissing fest" in that city, in which servicemen were kissed so often their faces were smeared with lipstick. A young flyer named Robert Billian, who came to Times Square with some buddies, described the scene:

> The girls were grabbing the service men and kissing them, you know, and all this business. And we were kind of standoffish on this, to be honest with you. And so, I guess, this group saw us and they thought, well, they'd have some fun with us. So, a couple of good looking gals came up to us, and they said, "Now close your eyes we want to give you something that . . ." you know. So, we closed them, expecting to be kissed, and with this, they grabbed our hand and stuck some screws in our hand and closed our hand around them and ran.

There were reports, none fit to print in the *New York Times*, of couples doing it in the road. Simon Greco, a religious CO, had expected "some great religious feeling to take over" the city on VJ Day. Instead, "a bunch of people gathered in Times Square, some gals getting laid."

Times Square on VJ Day saw an orgy that far surpassed New Year's Eve's traditional revelry. But it was not only sex that broke out; it was also an orgy of good feeling, a communion of release and happiness, an expression of unity. It was as if the young, who had borne the risk of death in this war, were celebrating in primal ways their own and others' emergence from the Shadow, cheering the victory of Eros over Thanatos in the most public of squares.

In Washington the reckless, orgiastic mood swept through a crowd swollen to five hundred thousand revelers. Thomas Emerson, a sober New Deal lawyer who had just taken over as general counsel of the Office of War Mobilization and Reconversion, which was charged with planning the nation's transition to a peace economy, caught a streetcar downtown, where he witnessed mass hysteria on a scale such as he had never seen be-fore or would ever see again: "Ordinary manners were completely aban-doned, at times the scene approached a sort of orgy. A girl stripped off all her clothes on the corner of 14th and F streets. . . . Another girl and man stripped off all their clothes and exchanged clothing . . . some people en-gaged in public acts of sexual intercourse."

Four years of war had transformed the slow-moving pre-war capital into a boomtown of brass hats, dollar-a-year men (businessmen who do-nated their services to wartime economic agencies), civil servants, and government girls. They all joined soldiers and sailors in a "screaming, drinking, paper-tearing, free-kissing demonstration." People passed around bottles. Officers shared them with enlisted men. "We're all civil-ians now!" cried a soldier, extolling the spirit of fraternization after years when some 14 million men and women in uniform had lived under the military caste system.

One block from the White House, at the venerable Willard Hotel, Washington's grandest hostelry, the marble-columned lobby was chock-ablock with generals and admirals, lobbyists and dollar-a-year men. A bald-headed man tried to slide down the grand main staircase but fell off and tumbled down the stairs ass over teacup.

There were islands of sobriety in the turbulent sea. A solemn group sang "The Star-Spangled Banner." A man told a *Yank* correspondent, "You know, soldier, it's a nice celebration, but I lost two sons—two sons. It might be a joke to some . . ." He shook his head sadly and walked away, head bowed.

Down in pleasure-loving New Orleans, there were premature celebra-tions all through Tuesday afternoon, with office workers throwing confetti from windows. When five o'clock came without official word, the crowd along Canal Street was still waiting for a sign that the big one could begin. At last, the *Times-Picayune*'s extra announcing peace hit the streets. All copies were gone in three minutes.

"No Mardis Gras was ever as gay or as wild as the celebration that fol-lowed," a *Yank* reporter claimed. Ironically, Bourbon Street, the epicenter of Mardis Gras, was quiet. That was because the police had ordered all bars closed for twenty-four hours. But the drinkers had armed themselves with portable potables, and the party snaked through the cars on Canal Street, the city's broadest thoroughfare. As it became packed, traffic slowed to a glacial ooze. Men clambered up the sides of streetcars to kiss women inside. One gang hijacked a stalled truck loaded with watermelons and tossed them to the crowd. Amid the pandemonium other New Orleanians crammed the Jesuit cathedral, crossed themselves, and knelt to say their prayers.

In San Francisco, officials may have regretted not closing the bars. Soldiers and sailors broke into liquor stores, liberating bottles of whiskey. The mixture of booze with the exuberance of young soldiers and sailors released from the prospect of death was highly volatile.

Initially, the mood was mellow. A sybaritic *Chronicle* columnist reveled in the thought of the end of wartime shortages and the return of peacetime pleasures: nylon stockings, Oxford cloth shirts, joy rides in the country, voyages to faraway places on a tramp steamer, Scotch whiskey, cartons of cigarettes. In keeping with the jubilant public mood, the police early in the day received orders to "let the people do anything within reason and keep property damage down." Firecrackers hoarded by residents of Chinatown exploded like a firefight. Soldiers and sailors held a tug-of-war with a fire hose and climbed on top of the streetcars. A voluptuous redhead danced naked at the base of the Native Sons fountain. Two young women stripped off their clothes and frolicked in the lily pond near the Civic Center. A sailor offered his coat to the redhead and escorted her to parts unknown; soldiers offered towels to the two naiads to shield their emergence on dry land.

As the day reeled by, Market Street became littered with bottles. Groups turned into mobs, and the celebration exploded in a wild melee, as aggressive instincts were released. Many of the drunk soldiers and sailors were slated to ship out to the Pacific theater. Some 1.6 million troops passed through the ports around San Francisco during the war. Now the last wave had been reprieved. They went wild.

"A looting, smashing crowd" stampeded into the streets, wrote a *Chronicle* reporter. Nothing, he said, could stop them but tear gas or fire

hoses. But the police were unprepared, and the mob raced around smashing windows. The rioters—a quarter of them "falling down drunk"—ram-
paged along Market Street, attacking women, smashing windows,
wrecking thirty of those famous streetcars before the night was out.

Finally, at 11 p.m., the cops moved in. Deputy chief Michael Riordan,
in a booming voice, ordered the mob to disperse. No one heeded him. It
would take police two days to get the city buttoned down.

When it was over, there was a grim tally: eleven dead, more than one
thousand hurt. Among the dead was Marine Pfc. James Prim, thirty-four,
who'd survived the brutal South Pacific campaign. He died of a fractured
skull after falling down stairs. A couple of newlyweds, Stella and John Morris, died the same day, smashed by a drunk driver.

Not everyone welcomed the noise. Lt. Thomas Richard Mathews,
who'd survived hard fighting in Italy, was aboard a packed troop train
heading to California. When it stopped in Helper, Utah, to pick up a
booster locomotive, VJ celebrants in the streets were firing every weapon
they had. The combat-jangled GIs hit the floor in unison.

For many, though, the celebration meant gathering quietly with
friends to have a few drinks. The churches were open and well attended
by people who offered up prayers of thanks. Those who had drifted away
from religion returned to pay their respects. A woman in Salisbury, Connecticut, who called herself "not much of a churchgoer," said the church
bells rang and everyone dropped what they were doing and "went to
whatever their church was. And those who didn't have a church went to
any church. They came in overalls, they brought children and babies.
Some just came to say a few words and sing a hymn . . . it was one of the
most moving, simplest services I ever heard."

In Red Oak, Iowa, about 900 folk crowded into a memorial church service. Hundreds of others gravitated to town or jumped in their tired jalop-
ies, said goodbye to gas rationing and barreled around the town square
honking their horns. People leaned out their windows, waving and shout-
ing at the drivers, who waved back.

In neighboring Villisca, people hurried downtown. A fire alarm blared
for half an hour and church and school bells rang. The Methodist church's

PA system broadcast patriotic airs, and American Legion vets led the townspeople in a parade, accompanied by noisemakers of all description. This was followed by community singing, a flag-raising, and an ecumenical service of thanksgiving held at the church.

These two towns had been hard hit by the war. National news organizations reported that Red Oak (population 5,763) and surrounding Montgomery County (15,698) suffered the highest number of casualties *per capita* of any place in the nation. This sad distinction made Red Oak the subject of myriad stories in national publications. *The Saturday Evening Post,* which published one of them, calculated that if New York City had suffered proportionately to Red Oak, it would have lost more than 70,000 instead of the 16,106 it ultimately did. New York City (population 7.4 million) sent 850,000 young men and women into service.

To Red Oak people it seemed only yesterday that Companies F (Villisca boys) and M (Red Oak boys) of the Iowa National Guard had marched in uniform around the town square and on to the Burlington Northern station. There they formed up and boarded a train that took them to basic training at Camp Claiborne, Louisiana.

After completion they shipped out, becoming among the first American troops to fight the Nazis in the 1943 invasion of North Africa. Capt. Bob Moore of Villisca won a Silver Star for rallying his men when they hit the shore and came under fire. The landing was a farrago of muddled leadership and bad planning. Matters didn't improve in the ensuing campaign. Slammed hard by Gen. Erwin Rommel's seasoned, well-equipped, and armed tank divisions, the under-armed and poorly led Iowa National Guard units suffered heavy casualties. Some 900 troops from the 168th Battalion were trapped by the Germans, including many of the Iowa boys. Moore, now a major and second in command, led them out of the trap, marching silently through the German lines at night until a sentry challenged them and they broke and ran as Moore had told them to do. Many, however, were shot or captured. On February 16, the exhausted remnants straggled into American lines. A count showed that of the original 900, fewer than half came through. Moore, who was among them, would win a Distinguished Service Medal for his bold escape. But as Rick Atkinson writes in his Pulitzer Prize–winning *An Army at Dawn,* "For all ordinary intents and purposes, the 168th Infantry Regiment—Iowa's finest—had been obliterated." The survivors of Companies F and M (whose origins dated back to the Civil and Spanish American wars) would be reassigned to other units.

The news hit Red Oak like a tornado. Telegrams from the War Department began arriving at the Western Union office in Red Oak, Iowa, early on March 8, 1943. Rex Holmes, the regular delivery boy, was alone in the office when suddenly he heard the teleprinter urgently dinging. This was a signal that the Des Moines office had traffic for Red Oak. He flipped the switch and told them to go ahead. The clattering machine began spewing out tape that piled up in the basket like spaghetti in a bowl. They all carried the same message: "The Secretary of War desires me to express his deep regret that your son _____ has been missing in action in the North African area since February ___. Additional information will be sent you when received." Each was signed by the adjutant general of the Army.

Rex telephoned his boss, who had gone out for coffee, then hopped on his bike and started pedaling around town. His recollection is that he delivered sixty telegrams over the next few days. He knows for sure he was on the go mornings, nights, and weekends, pedaling down streets lined with trees stippled with hazy green, climbing up steps onto front porches, knocking on doors with blue star service flags. In a day or so, after the news had ricocheted through the town, the women began to dread his arrival. With shaking hands they tore open the envelopes, extracted the rectangles of yellow paper, and read the message. Some collapsed in hysterics. Rex or a family member would help them to a chair. Some were considerate with the young boy in his olive green cap with the brass WU insignia, as though trying to protect him from this adult tragedy.

On that first day one delivery took him only as far as the next door, where he handed Mae Stifle separate wires informing her that her sons, Dean and Frank, were missing. Mrs. Stifle was a widow who worked as a housekeeper at the Hotel Johnson, where the telegraph office was located. For fourteen years she had made beds and cleaned toilets at the hotel while raising eight children. She fainted when she read the news, and Rex called a doctor. Later the same day, another message arrived announcing that her son-in-law Sgt. Darrell Wolfe was also missing. Rex couldn't go back and asked his boss to take it.

"It was hard to call on people," he recalled. "I knew damn near all of them. I got to the point where I hated to go up to a house, but somebody had to do it." Those first days townspeople congregated on the wide, pillared veranda of the Hotel Johnson and waited for the casualty lists to be read. Typical of small towns, everyone knew the boys named, at least by sight or reputation.

The *Red Oak Express* published on its front page daily reports of casualties and pictures of every one of the missing soldiers as a rivulet of details steadily flowed in, ready or not:

"Missing in Action!"

Those were the crisp words that the telegraphic ticker carried to the homes of seventeen Montgomery county homes today

BULLETIN

At four o'clock this afternoon nine additional Red Oak boys were listed as missing in action in Africa.

Red Oak's List Advances to 25

None Officially Reported Dead; S.W. Iowa Is Hit Hard

Summary of County's Casualties Shows

56 Missing, Prisoners, Dead

War consciousness mounted hourly in Red Oak, stunned by the flood of telegrams this week informing nearest of kin of the national guard soldiers missing in action on the Tunisian front.

Rosie Nelson, who grew up on a farm outside Red Oak, remembered the day the telegrams arrived. She was teaching school at a nearby town. The superintendent opened the door of her classroom and motioned to her. Out in the hall he told her, "Your brother is missing in action. I'll take over your class. You go home." When she reached her parents' house, the table was already laden with covered dishes of food brought by the neighbors. "The whole town was in mourning," she said. People anxiously exchanged scraps of news: "What did you hear?" She had said goodbye to her brother at the depot with the other members of Company M, including the young man she would marry.

Wilma Palmquist remembered her future mother-in-law telephoning her and saying, "There's good news and bad news." Her fiancé, Bernard, was alive, but he had been wounded.

Months later, letters started trickling in from the missing men being held in German POW camps. Most asked their folks to send food or chocolate. On Mother's Day the War Department confirmed to Mae Stifle that her missing sons were in one of the camps. "Never once did I give up hope," she told a reporter. "Maybe it was just intuition." Even though they were POWs, it was the "happiest day of her life."

Dorothy Schrage, who lived in town while her husband, Gil, was away in the Navy, remembered the casualty lists being read out on the white-pillared veranda of the Hotel Johnson. After the bad news struck, she said, "a pall settled over the town. The news made you realize what war was about. People were very stoic. But they were bewildered, they couldn't really believe it. It was hard, but the town pulled together."

These were "stoic but hopeful" people, wrote a reporter from the *New York Herald Tribune* who came to town to do a story on how Red Oak was taking the news. At that moment, by chance and bad luck, Red Oak had the painful distinction of coming "as close to any town in America to knowing what the war was all about," a local historian said.

To the generation that fought the war, the dream that it would be followed by a lasting peace became palpable on VJ Day—an entitlement, almost, or a reward for their uneven sacrifices, like the return of steaks, nylons, and Scotch whiskey. A social worker named Eileen Barth spoke for many: "I was hopeful. I thought that democracy and progress could be endless. The good times would come and there would be lasting peace. I really believed it." She knew that most people of her generation looked forward only to material progress, she later reflected, but "these were people who lived through the Depression. . . . Perhaps they concentrated a little too much on the material life. The war did it. The hope was there: the end of all wars."

Many felt suspended between two worlds—the blessedly receding war and the nebulous future. Mary Irwin wondered what the postwar world held for her. She decided: "People would be free to go on with their lives, though I had no idea what that would mean. It was sort of like being in a state of suspension . . . . The war was always a big part of my life. It shaped me in a lot of ways."

Some who survived took satisfaction in their role in the war effort, large or small, whether as an atomic scientist working on the Manhattan Project in New Mexico or as an air raid warden in Manhattan. One of those Los Alamos scientists, Robert Wilson, looked back on the national effort: "It was a good time in America. It was a good time to be an American. It was a time when the whole country was pulling together." A time when common enemies gave people a collective purpose.

A few days after VJ Day, Marjorie Haselton wrote her husband, John, that she'd been to church and the pastor had spoken movingly of world peace and inner peace. But she wrestled with questions about the meaning of all the sacrifice. Some had done more in the war than John had, some less, but "I know I would rather feel in my heart and I know you would too— that you did more than your share rather than less." This was a moment "when we can be truly great. . . . It isn't easy to be great, but therein lies the greatness and the beauty of your character, in facing the hard things."

A SOCIOLOGICAL STUDY published as *Children of the Great Depression* by University of North Carolina professor Glen H. Elder Jr. analyzed the generation that lived through both the Great Depression and World War II, drawing on a survey of 167 Oakland, California, children born in 1920 and 1921, with data from other studies for comparison. The cohort Elder analyzed could be called the "crisis generation," which spent its formative years in the Great Depression, then entered World War II. Elder found that his subjects were "drawn into the nation's struggle for survival in both crises; the struggle became their civic obligation and their personal hardships part of the nation's experience." They were faced with "nation-saving" challenges, exhorted by their government to submerge their own identities in the larger group, to make sacrifices for the common good. The central message was "the forging of national solidarity through appeals and coercion which subordinated personal and group interests to the higher cause, mass mobilization of citizen talents and contributions in the national effort, and the pride that came from participation in a collective effort that eventually prevailed."

The lives of these Depression-raised kids were marked by what the historian Caroline Bird calls "the invisible scar" of the economic crisis. The shrinking economy had narrowed the life choices of many—who didn't start out with any great expectations. College was still pretty much for the rich, impossible for the overwhelming majority. The years in high school could be cut short by the need to work to help out a family whose father was sick or laid off. Securing a steady long-term job was a long shot. Marrying and buying a home had to be postponed. Having children was on hold or their number limited. The birthrate during the Depression was the lowest in US history.

This generation had been raised on the language of wars, even in peacetime. Roosevelt had used martial rhetoric in mobilizing the country against the invading Depression.

Many young men joined the Civilian Conservation Corps for lack of regular jobs. In Red Oak this was not uncommon. In the CCC you got paid a dollar a day planting trees and conserving soil. Many a young man "got his first pair of shoes," as the saying went, in the CCC. The Corps became accustomed to a military command structure. In the late forties it expanded military training among its "tree army." The CCC provided the virtues of military service without the evils of war, its forms of cooperation without its ugly substance.

The CCC also bolstered the country's war readiness by taking on the refurbishing of crumbling arsenals, army camps, naval stations, and other military facilities, restoring them at a time when defense spending was parsimonious. In addition, the workers on these projects were a source of trained labor for the war effort.

The Corps drew on World War I precedents in fighting the Depression (as did the National Recovery Administration). According to Elder, "Mobilization under the New Deal developed techniques and resources that prepared America for the emerging fascist threat in Europe." One of the objectives of the Civilian Conservation Corps was to instill "martial virtues in the nation's youth. . . . CCC recruits convened at army recruiting stations; traveled to an army camp where they were outfitted in World War I clothing; were transported to the woods by troop-train; fell asleep in army tents to the strain of 'Taps' and woke to 'Reveille.'" After the draft was started in 1940, the CCC was phased out.

During the Depression a goodly number of young men from Montgomery County joined Iowa's National Guard in order to collect the pay for weekend drills and two weeks' training every summer. Still, money wasn't the only reason to sign up. Some enjoyed the socializing the Guard offered.

New Deal programs and the Popular Front produced a culture based on respect for the needs and aspirations of the common people that went beyond the party-lining proletarian novels of the day. Morris Dickstein catches a sense of its ubiquity in the lives of ordinary Americans in his history of the Depression, *Dancing in the Dark:* "For my parents who had come to the United States as immigrants when they were young, the Depression and the New Deal remained daily facts of life, fueling their anxieties and influencing their life choices." Americans living through the Great Recession of 2008 got a taste of what it was like back then—how a paralysis of fear gripped the nation as the stock market crash widened and deepened, as one-quarter of the labor force was unemployed and without hope. The programs identified with the New Deal—some frankly improvised and experimental, a few boondoggles, most more enduring—provided a social safety net where once had been an abyss of despair, raised morale, and put the country on a path toward economic recovery and full employment, though those did not fully arrive until the hyper-Keynesianism of World War II spending kicked in.

The Works Progress Administration (renamed the Works Project Administration in 1939), attacked as a giant boondoggle, was, in retrospect, a valuable and effective pump-priming program. According to Nick Taylor's history of the WPA, *American Made,* the agency built "650,000 miles of roads, 78,000 bridges, 125,000 civilian and military

buildings, 800 airports (built or improved), and 700 miles of airport run-
ways. It also served almost 900 million hot lunches to school children, and
operated 1,500 nursery schools. It presented 225,000 concerts to audiences
totaling 150 million people, performed plays and circuses before another
30 million, and created 475,000 works of art." When FDR declared WPA's
termination on December 4, 1942, he said,

> By building airports, schools, highways and parks; by making huge quan-
> tities of clothing for the unfortunate; by serving millions of lunches to
> school children; by almost immeasurable kinds and quantities of services
> the Works Project Administration has reached a creative hand into every
> county in this nation. It has added to the national wealth, has repaired the
> wastage of depression and has strengthened the country to bear the burden
> of war. By employing eight millions of Americans, with thirty millions of
> dependents it has brought to these people renewed hope and courage. It
> has maintained and increased their working skills; and it has enabled them
> once more to take their rightful places in public or in private employment.

The government-sponsored cultural initiatives primed the pump of historical writing and reporting, and fed and clothed numerous artists who
might otherwise have gone under. Popular Front culture of the time inspired a burst of art—murals, sculpture, photography, architecture,
movies, books, and plays.

The heartbeat of the WPA's muse was a documentary impulse that
inspired writers, photographers, artists, playwrights, and historians, each
in ways appropriate to his or her medium. Collectively, writes Alfred
Kazin, it unleashed "a thundering flood of national consciousness and self-
celebration . . . a swelling chorus of national affirmation and praise" that
strengthened the nation's sense of identity on the eve of World War II.

In the novels of the period, there was another motif that could be called
the "democracy of suffering." In John Steinbeck's *Grapes of Wrath,* the outcast Joads are granted their dignity as human beings deserving of decent
treatment. And so too were the Tennessee mountain people celebrated in
James Agee and Walker Evans's *Let Us Now Praise Famous Men.*

That spirit of equality of sacrifice instilled by New Deal culture would become a national ideal during the war, appealed to through propaganda, however far from that spirit were real life and a war effort that unequally apportioned sacrifices with its for-profit, cost-plus economy. As radio bard Norman Corwin and other propagandists chorused, it was a war that would be won by teamwork, collective effort, mass production—men, women, and minorities working together on the line, backing up the selfless service of the common soldier, sailor, or marine (or WAC, WAVE, SPAR, or nurse) at or behind the front. The central theme of the Office of War Information (OWI) was that this was "a people's army, fighting a people's war." The universal name for the common American soldier became "GI," standing for government issue, as if the men and women comprising the armed services were a standardized product. GI Joe became the generic hero of the time; this image rationalized the process by which the military die-cast civilians into interchangeable parts. His plainspoken Homer was Ernie Pyle; *The Story of GI Joe,* based on Pyle's columns from the front, was the best "war movie" of the 1940s.

Elder writes that in their postwar lives many of the children of the Depression "did better than expected from the perspective of their social origins." Those who'd grown up poor and lacking in self-confidence turned their lives around after the war. The novelist Clancy Sigal recalled the war's impact on families:

Suddenly, in the army, what Eleanor Roosevelt called her "lost generation" of depression kids had enough to eat, clothes that were replaced when torn, free of charge, a bed to sleep in, a job with a military occupation specialty number (mine was 745). . . . The great depression drilled us in a different sort of courage, cowardice and stoicism. You shrug off what's happening around you, keep your mouth shut, move ahead one step at a time, don't ask questions or make waves, just do it, and keep repeating the proto-infantryman's mantra, "Better you than me."

For the men in the unit I later joined, the Fourth Division, scaling the heights of Normandy's Point du Hoc cliffs under intense fire was a nasty but logical extension of what they'd experienced as "economic casualties" back home. My boyhood friend, Jack, who spent 112 days in frontline combat with the 103rd in wartime Europe, said it best:

"They call us guys the 'greatest generation'. So much crap. Your mother and mine spent more time on a combat line than any soldier, only it was an undeclared war in our homes. You and me, too, we've been at war all our lives."

The most pressing postwar question for the members of the Crisis Generation was, Would peace bring prosperity or another depression? The scars were still too fresh. A Gallup poll showed two-thirds of the respondents cautiously optimistic. But they were willing to forecast only five to seven good years down the road. They hoped for such bounties of better times as a steady job, a family, and a new house (15 million said they planned or hoped to spend $5,000 on one).

A vague internationalism mingled with hopes for peace floating about in the zeitgeist. Most Americans invested tentative hopes in the embryonic United Nations. In July 1945 a plurality of 44 percent answered yes and 36.4 percent no to the question "Do you think it will be possible for the UN to work out a peace that will last at least 50 years?"

Still, people did not entirely believe that the destruction of imperial Japan and Nazi Germany would bring peace. A 1947 Gallup poll showed 60 percent still feared Germany would start another war. As late as 1949, 36 percent thought Japan would fight against the United States in the next war. As for the Soviet Union . . .

Wartime propaganda movies planted in American minds two ideas, write Clayton Koppes and Gregory Black in their book *Hollywood Goes to War*. One was the "division of the world into slave and free" representing either the forces of evil or those of righteousness. And the other was a "universalized version of the idea of regeneration through war," which united Americans in patriotic oneness, unmarred by class, race, or other social barriers. War would bring "internal and international harmony," the films taught. This propaganda "coincidentally helped prepare America for the cold war" (as we'll see in future chapters).

The nation's war aims, beyond defeating the enemy, were never clearly defined, making "victory" (which usually connoted military supremacy and unconditional surrender of the Axis powers) an end in itself rather than a stepping-stone to a new political order in the war-torn areas replacing the fascist and imperial ones.

Bruce Catton, later a Pulitzer Prize–winning historian, complained in a 1948 memoir about his public relations work with the War Production Board that the nation's war aims were too narrowly focused on military victory rather than on the challenge of defining and building a better world. "This was to be a purely military war, a straight exercise in strategy, tactics, and logistics, a strictly military war in place of the all-out *people's war* we thought we were fighting."

The closest the government came to giving "victory" some political content was the OWI's "people's war," which, as the historian Gerald D. Nash summarizes, was "a war to create a brave new world. An Allied victory would bring the peoples of the world jobs, better health and housing and social insurance. It would benefit minorities, and also women around the world." A global New Deal, with TVAs rising everywhere, was a model for some—including President Truman, who evoked it as an inspiration for his Point Four program of technical assistance.

Catton's complaint was that people would emerge from the war with little sense of what their GIs had fought against or for: What was the nature of fascism? Was it confined to a few aberrant nations in the Old World? Did it have homegrown equivalents? What was the antidote-ideology? How could it be nurtured and expanded at home and abroad? How could a durable peace be secured? What would be America's geopolitical and military role in securing the peace? The nation faced those questions whether it wanted to or not.

President Roosevelt seemed wary about setting up Americans for the disillusionment that followed World War I and the failure of Woodrow Wilson's Fourteen Points. The farthest he would go in enunciating the nation's war aims was to call World War II a "war of survival." He conspicuously refused to issue any blueprints as detailed as Wilson's. Mainly FDR invoked the Four Freedoms, which he had identified in his third inaugural address in January 1941, and the concept of a United Nations organization, which would punish future aggressors before their conflicts metastasized into World War III.

As the pundit Max Lerner wrote, "Roosevelt had committed himself only to conservative formulations of war ideals. . . . Wilson was largely martyred by creating expectations he could not fulfill. . . . Roosevelt, on the other hand, has let others do the talking about postwar ideals—[Vice President Henry A.] Wallace, [Wendell L.] Willkie, [Sumner] Welles, [Cordell] Hull—he himself has stuck close to the need of inter-Allied cooperation for the war itself and the immediate transition period. . . . In short, where Wilson tried to create the new world, Roosevelt has been content to stand by and help midwife it."

FDR's liberal supporters might have recalled World War I, when prominent progressives like the philosopher John Dewey endorsed Wilson's aims and assurances that American entry into the war would advance progressive goals. From the betrayal of these aims, they might have—should have—learned the lesson that wars can thwart the advance of undesirable ideological visions (e.g., Nazism ruling Europe), but they do not bring into being any better alternative vision of government. Wars in themselves accomplished nothing positive; whatever gains were made were achieved at the peace table or by democratic legislatures implementing a postwar agenda. Or by citizens demonstrating against racism, an incarnation of Nazi doctrines of "Aryan" (white) supremacy, which the war effort had tacitly endorsed by maintaining segregation in the Armed Forces and which the New Deal coalition had tolerated in the South.

Willkie wrote a best-selling book envisioning the postwar era called *One World*. The title was widely adopted as a shorthand expression for a more peaceful globe. (Unfortunately, the world was far from one.) Willkie, a utilities lawyer and 1940 GOP presidential candidate, had rejected the isolationist wing of his party, led by Senator Robert Taft, to embrace the Roosevelt administration's internationalist program. In 1942 he toured the world on a special mission for Roosevelt (who privately entertained the idea of making Willkie his 1944 running mate on a national unity ticket—which, of course, he did not do, choosing Harry Truman and dumping the incumbent, Henry Wallace, to the dismay of hard-core New Dealers and the delight of Democratic bosses, who had been reading polls saying Americans wanted a middle-of-the-roader like Postmaster General and former Democratic Party chief Jim Farley as his next running mate). Willkie's *One World* told Americans that they must choose among three courses after the war: "narrow nationalism," "international imperialism," and "a world in which there shall be an equality of opportunity for every race and every nation." (He preferred number three.)

These sentiments were too heady for most Americans, but they appealed to a lot of idealistic folks who were imbued with a vision of a world in which those thirty-three allied nations—and the emerging new ones casting off the shackles of colonialism—would live peacefully ever after. They bought Willkie's message that internationalism guaranteed peace, without thinking much about the concessions America and other nations would have to make to achieve it.

Vice President Wallace shouldered the New Deal guidon and preached the necessity of a program to rebuild the postwar world. His earliest utterances on the subject were aimed at *Time* chief Henry Luce (a critic of the New Deal), who had proclaimed an "American century" that envisioned a world dominated by American capitalism. Wallace called instead for a "century of the common man," which entailed an international New Deal administering programs designed to solve the age-old problems of hunger and economic development. "The object of this war," he famously said, "is to make sure that everybody in the world has the privilege of drinking a quart of milk a day. . . . Peace must mean a better standard of living for the common man." Aside from milk being considered the sine qua non of a healthy diet, Wallace's dream was anticolonialist and antifascist: "No nation will have the God-given right to exploit other nations."

Conservatives like James Witherow, president of the National Association of Manufacturers, mocked Wallace's program as "milk for Hottentots and TVAs on the Danube," while Connecticut representative Clare Boothe Luce, Henry Luce's beautiful, acid-tongued spouse, labeled it "globaloney." Even within the administration, there was opposition to Wallace's rhetoric. Secretary of State Cordell Hull chastised Wallace and

OWI chief Elmer Davis, propagator of "people's war" ideals, for stirring up "worldwide revolution even at the danger of producing revolution in the United States." When Wallace suggested to Commerce Secretary Jesse Jones that part of the higher prices the United States was paying for Bolivian tin could go to feeding hungry miners there, Jones told him, "We ought to avoid any action that would make people think that we were engaged in social reforms of any kind."

Roosevelt also feared that specific plans would be politically divisive. Sumner Welles, a close foreign policy adviser, explained that if Roosevelt "spoke to the American people . . . of postwar problems, they might be distracted from the cardinal objective of victory and controversy might develop which would jeopardize national unity."

Lacking any higher motivations, let alone a vision of a postwar world order beyond FDR's sketchy picture of the United Nations, most Americans reverted to the personal and parochial. What many of these Depression- and war-scarred people wanted was "security" at home, in terms of jobs and prosperity, and abroad, in terms of safety from future aggressors. This priority held for soldiers as well. A *Fortune* poll reported, "The American soldier is depression conscious and . . . worried sick about postwar joblessness." President Roosevelt addressed Americans' economic anxieties in his 1944 State of the Union address, in which he called for a "Second Bill of Rights." His fireside chat on January 11 of that year celebrated the concept of security: "The one supreme objective for the future, which we discussed for each nation individually and for all the United Nations can be summed up in one word: security. And that means not only physical security, which provides safety from attacks by aggressors. It means also economic security, social security, moral security—in a family of nations."

Two popular films of 1946, *Blue Skies* and *The Blue Dahlia,* similar in titles but opposing in genre, caught the ambivalent public mood of the times, which more or less oscillated between faith in the future and worry about problems that lay ahead. *Blue Skies,* a musical, was realistic in its way. The plot hinged on marital troubles vaguely reflecting the real-life ones of returning vets. Jed (Fred Astaire) and Johnny (Bing Crosby) are song-and-dance men who vie for the love of Mary (Joan Caulfield, a placidly beautiful blonde). Crosby wins her, but they have marital problems. It seems he has an allergy to settling down and a penchant for opening nightclubs in faraway places like Cleveland, selling them and moving on. They reunite after he returns from the war service with the USO. To women of the time, Johnny symbolized the abandoning male—all their servicemen who went away. The characters face the same marital readjustments that contemporary women were going through.

A grimmer take on this theme was *The Blue Dahlia,* definitely not a musical but one of a series of crime dramas in which returning veterans figure as killers or righteous avengers. In the script by crime novelist Raymond Chandler, Lt. Cmdr. Johnny Morrison (Alan Ladd) comes home angry and violence-prone to find his wife has been cheating on him. When he calls her out on her infidelities, she shrugs, reminding him that the war's over, soldier.

Blue Skies, The Blue Dahlia: two films that offered an almost manic-depressive vision—one, skies of blue (following a light rain); the other, stormy weather. They were templates of the ideology of the postwar cinema, but *The Blue Dahlia* presaged a series of crime films, later dubbed films noir, that would more deeply echo the American unconscious between 1945 and 1950.

Voices

It was while wandering through the many graves, away from noise and distracting thoughts, that I began to really sense the dead. They spoke in a soft, almost undetectable manner, like gentle ocean swells that pass beneath a vessel at sea.

—MICHAEL SLEDGE, *SOLDIER DEAD* (2005)

If a country is worth living in, it's worth dying for.

—EUGENE SLEDGE,
WITH THE OLD BREED AT PELELIU AND OKINAWA (1981)

Because hope and possibility and illusion had begun even then to vanish and more and more he had let the idea of his own extinction become part of the way he lived and part of the way he felt and all the values he put on everything were part of the knowledge and certainty that he would occupy such a grave as he had passed himself so many times since: earth no higher than the surrounding earth and the crossed sticks planted in the earth and a helmet on the crossed sticks, and under the helmet the dog tags, hanging, and the rain falling on all of it.

—ALFRED HAYES,
THE GIRL ON THE VIA FLAMINIA (1949)

"What did the lieutenant do before he got out of the Army?" . . .
"He was a businessman. He worked in an office."

"You kill me. He'll be a businessman in 1958 when we're fighting the Battle of Tibet. I got the facts down cold. They put him on a nice hospital ship and take him home and give him his walking papers. Then he'll go back to business while we fight the Battle of Tibet."
"Maybe he'll die."
"Nobody dies."

—HARRY BROWN, *A WALK IN THE SUN* (1944)

There are some things so bad and so careless that you wish to God they didn't pretend to be good-intentioned so you couldn't [put] in a holler without making a heel of yourself. I've felt pretty much the same way looking at newsreels of ceremonies at the tomb of the Unknown Soldier. The bands playing and the people singing, all in their own way, the right way, and the generals, the statesmen, and the club ladies all speaking a little piece for themselves. And they all mean so goddamn well—I guess—and no one is responsible any more than I was responsible for her.

—JIM THOMPSON,
NOTHING MORE THAN MURDER (1949)

"You're telling me I am dead. You're explaining my life away. I don't even know you. You're crazy."
"I don't think you fully understand, Mr. Bigelow. You've been murdered."

—*D.O.A.* (1950)

2

D.O.A.

ONE HUMID AND PARTICULARLY MISTY Sunday morning in October, the *Joseph V. Connolly* sailed through the Narrows and entered New York Harbor, escorted by two destroyers and a flock of smaller craft. The *Connolly* was a low-slung standard-issue military transport, painted a utilitarian gray and tan.

As it hove into dock, spectators on land could see that its decks were lined with sailors standing at attention. Displayed on the boat deck was a gray steel coffin.

For this voyage the *Connolly* had been drafted as a mortuary ship, its cargo of servicemen killed in the European theater being transported to America for reburial. This was the first of many such shipments to cross the Atlantic. In its hold were 6,248 coffins identical to the one on deck, each containing shrouded remains dug up and officially identified, sometimes after lengthy forensic investigations. The name of each was listed on the ship's passenger manifest as "[Name] Deceased." This touch suggests that the military was respectfully in denial: that is, transporting slain soldiers as if they were live "passengers" rather than cargo.

Another ship, the *Honda Knot,* had arrived on the West Coast on October 10, with 3,012 flag-draped coffins aboard—remains from the Pacific theater. Parting a shroud of gray mist, the ship sailed under the Golden Gate Bridge and into the Port of San Francisco. Forty-eight fighter planes (one for every state) flew over and dipped their wings in salute, as Naval and Coast Guard vessels closed in to escort the *Honda Knot* to its berth. A

D.O.A. is the story of a walking dead man: Edward O'Brien learns he has ingested a slow-acting poison. *Everett Collection*

crowd of 5,000 was waiting on the dock; there was no parade, but the next day six of the coffins, representing five service branches and a civilian, were displayed in the City Hall rotunda, and thousands filed by to pay their respects.

Like the bodies aboard the *Connolly*, those debarked in San Francisco were being returned under a War Department policy that allowed the next of kin to choose whether they wanted their slain service person buried in the United States or to lie in one of the 360 US military cemeteries around the world.

The single coffin displayed on the *Connolly* contained the body of an unnamed Medal of Honor winner killed in the Battle of the Bulge. The soldier chosen to receive the city's tribute represented those 6,247 other coffins aboard and more than 230,000 soldiers who would eventually be returned to the United States for reburial. *New York Times* reporter Meyer Berger, a veteran feature writer, used the most somber tones in his palette to transform New York into a great necropolis: "Down in the lower harbor the vacant towers of Manhattan rose in the haze like white and gray tombstones towering skyward. Richmond-bound ferryboats glided in silence to port of the marine procession, their flags at half mast. Crowds on the decks were bareheaded and the passengers bowed as in prayer."

The *Connolly* docked at Pier 61, at West Twenty-first Street, where many troopships had been recently arriving packed with grinning GIs waving at cheering loved ones on the docks. This time there were no cheers. Berger saw women weeping and men doffing their hats and looking away as the coffin was placed on a gun caisson.

Escorted by 4,000 soldiers, veterans, city officials, and others, the caisson, drawn by an armored car, moved east across Twenty-third Street. At Fifth Avenue, the cortege turned north and proceeded to Central Park. Spectators lined the route. "The silence was awesome," Berger wrote. "Nobody spoke, not even the children. Eyes were moist and lips moved in prayer as the flag-draped bier passed."

A crowd estimated to be more than 150,000 had assembled in Sheep's Meadow, parted by a grassy lane lined with flags leading to a platform on which stood a catafalque draped in purple and black. Behind it were seated some 200 politicians, church officials, and foreign dignitaries. As a dirge played, a woman in the crowd keened: "There's my boy, there's my boy!" Eight pallbearers placed the coffin on the catafalque. "Now the sobbing was even more general. Men hid their faces. Women shook with emotion," Berger wrote.

The city's official greeter, Grover Whalen, called for two minutes of silence, and a Catholic chaplain delivered the invocation. Then came speeches by politicians: Mayor William O'Dwyer, Governor Thomas E. Dewey, Army Secretary Kenneth Royall, Albert A. Crew of the American Legion, other service representatives, and a Protestant and a Jewish chaplain.

Then the pallbearers placed the coffin back on the caisson. Mothers were sobbing, and one of them keened: "Johnny, my Johnny. Where is my boy?" The caisson lumbered away to the strains of "The Vanished Army."

The next day the *Connolly* carried its cargo to the Brooklyn Army depot, where the coffins were off-loaded by tough longshoremen "with tears streaming down their cheeks," according to reports. The coffins, each accompanied by an escort of equal rank to the soldier inside, were eventually shipped by rail to towns all across America for burial.

By most estimates, 405,000 American servicemen and -women died in World War II. For each of them there were, according to authorities in such matters, at least four grieving people. There were also the 607,096 wounded, some of them permanently disabled, and more than 200,000 mentally scarred. In addition, between 1942 and 1945 some 5.6 million "normal"—i.e., civilian—deaths occurred in America.

Some 183,000 American children lost their fathers in the war. According to Charles Tuttle's study of home-front children, *"Daddy's Gone to War,"* the loss of a father or older brother was the most devastating event in their lives. He quotes one of them on how the war "totally" changed her life: "It took away two brothers I never got to know, brought *great* grief to my parents and changed our whole family structure." For Henrietta Bingham, the war had initially meant patriotic enthusiasm when her sixteen-year-old brother, Gerald, lied about his age to join the Air Corps and trained as a turret gunner on a B-24. In 1943 he was killed in a training accident. His body was escorted home by a close buddy, whom the family "adopted" as a kind of surrogate for Gerald. Henrietta watched as her parents turned into old people almost overnight.[*]

Henrietta was eleven when she lost her brother. Children's reactions, of course, varied according to their age. Pediatricians say that children do not begin to understand the finality of death until eight or nine. The older children, from ten to fifteen, "are the ones most frightened" by thoughts of death and the ones who suffer from symptoms like insomnia, which stems from conflating death with sleep: "I'll go to sleep and not wake up."

In her novel *Rumors of Peace*, about a girl growing up in wartime California, Ella Leffland shows her heroine trying to come to grips with the images of death she sees in *Life* magazine and newsreels, along with fears of Japanese planes coming to bomb them fueled by panicky news stories early in the war. She has an epiphany one day about images that stick in her memory—a Polish family killed in the fields, bombed-out Rotterdam, soldiers lying dead in the snow, their frozen arms grotesquely protruding. She imagines that the boy from her town who was killed in the Japanese attack on Pearl Harbor must have hated to die. "They all must have," she thinks, "and it was too much to know, too painful, too pitiful, too huge and boundless, and why should I have to see such a thing now, just when I knew we were safe [from bombs], and I had found happiness again. I pressed my hands to my ears, as if that would squeeze me back into my happiness, but I felt like a pond when a stone has been dropped, and ripples spread out as though set in motion forever. For those terrible ripples would be with me forever, even if my own yard were never bombed, even if only good things happened to me for the rest of my life."

---

[*] This fantasy of denial was a common phenomenon. The family in William Saroyan's wartime novel *The Human Comedy* achieves some consolation in this manner. The story centers on the impact of the loss of a cherished older brother on a young Western Union boy who has already seen firsthand the effects of death on the living while delivering War Department telegrams. The family absorbs the brother's Army buddy. Saroyan had written *The Human Comedy* as a film script and grandiosely wanted to produce and direct it, but L.B. Mayer and others eased him out. His biographer, John Leggett, comments on the resulting movie: "They had made his screenplay into sleazy propaganda that sought to persuade Americans to accept the loss of their sons in this war. It was an outrage to its author."

The Office of War Information's Bureau of Motion Pictures urged studios to slip into films a lesson on how to cope with the loss of a serviceman. The well-meaning propaganda came out hollow, tinny. Take the *March of Time* semi-documentaries. Produced by *Time* magazine and shown in movie theaters during the 1930s and '40s, they combined film clips and reenactments to discuss problems in the news. One of them, which appeared right after the war, addressed the general question "Is everybody happy?" One of the unhappy ones, a woman on a radio show, apologetically tells a solemn man with a mustache that ever since her fiancé was killed in the war she has felt, well, down. He scolds her: "Many of us have had people killed in the war." She should buck up, think of the good things of life—sunshine, flowers, trees in bloom, and the like.

In *This Republic of Suffering,* her book on the Civil War dead, Drew Gilpin Faust explains that during the war Americans became disturbed at the crude way battlefield remains were treated "more like animals than humans." As a result, they "worked to change death in ways that ranged from transforming the actual bodies of the dead through embalming to altering the circumstances and conditions of interment by establishing what would become the national cemetery system and a massive postwar reburial system." This was a recognition that the soldier dead were not just the responsibility of their families, that "they, and their loss, now belonged to the nation." Their remains, repositories of their "selfhood" and "surviving identity," "deserved the nation's recognition and care."

The duty of properly interring the dead, zealously guarded by organized veteran groups that provided firing squads at reburials, was passed down the generations. By World War II and its aftermath, the task had become bureaucratized, a national effort lavishly funded by Congress and carried out by military burial units and a vast clerical staff. The official policy was "no man left behind." (Or woman, we presume.)

In late 1946 the families of soldiers, sailors, and marines killed in action and buried in temporary graves near the sites of fierce battles began receiving a notification from the US Army Quartermaster Corps. It read: "'Tell me about my boy' is the request most frequently sent to the Quartermaster General of the Army by next of kin who want additional information on the progress of the War Department's program for the return and final burial of those who died overseas in World War II." Recipients were informed that they could leave their boy's remains in a military burying ground overseas or have them shipped home and interred at the government's expense. The bodies would be exhumed from temporary cemeteries, most located near sites of battles in the Pacific and Europe, transferred to a permanent site, or shipped home. The operation would take place in stages; some military cemeteries would be "evacuated" before others, the brochure explained. Thus one mother might receive a questionnaire about disposition of her son's remains months before her neighbor did. Obviously, this was an attempt to deter the anguish and worry accompanying the surge of remains arriving across America.

Over the return of the World War II soldier dead hung memories of World War I, when there were reports of disrespectful handling and coffins dumped without notice on grieving parents' doorsteps. Congress's appropriation of money to recover all the missing and the dead and bring home those whose next of kin wanted them was an attempt to do better by the slain. But in this war the rolls of the dead were far longer than in World War I; the battlefields farther flung; and the logistics of finding, identifying, and preparing them more daunting. And the military bureaucracy was prone to lapses and errors.

First, there might be a long delay in locating the missing, which left parents and wives to stew in uncertainty. Until the return of the remains or other confirmation, a dead son remained alive in his parents' memories, and it was hard to find the peace of resignation and forgetfulness. Even where there were witnesses to a death (such as of prisoners shot or starved in a prison camp) and the military changed the status "missing in action" to "killed in action," next of kin still would not give up hope until the body was returned to them. The vigil was not always futile; bones turned up in fields and forests many years after the war, their identity confirmed by forensic tests. Even those families whose dead had been recovered had to wait three, four, five years. Consider the four Borgstrom brothers, all killed in 1944. Each had served in a different branch of service, each had been killed in a different place. Their coffins did not arrive in their hometown

of Tremonton, Utah, until July 1948. The military tried to make amends
by having the dead brothers lie in state guarded by sentries from each of
their service branches, followed by an elaborate military funeral.

There are stories of people who waited years to learn the fate of a missing son and died before the final notification arrived. And of families that
never received their son's remains. Even confirmation of the death did not
ease the pain of some. Benjamin McKeeby, a paratrooper with the 82nd
Airborne, was killed in France. His brother Richard E. McKeeby recalled,
"I remember the first telegram that came to our home when he was missing in action, and the hopes and fears of my parents and the rest of the family and friends. Then came telegram two, [saying] where he had been
killed. My mother became very depressed, cried a lot and stayed in bed,
and lost her interest in the world around her. She underwent treatment at
Greystone [Psychiatric Hospital] in New Jersey for several years. I lost a
brother and a mother."

The desperation of parents or wives of the missing is apparent in pa-
thetic letters received by chaplains, military officers, and Red Cross workers during the war:

> You realize, I am sure, how awful the suspense is when you are not able
> to do one thing about it. If only I could know that he is alive. I thought
> perhaps you could tell me something about what happened and if you
> think he could be a prisoner of war.
>
> We would like to know if you could find out anything about what
> happened to him for us. Maybe you could find one of his friends who
> might know something about him. Could you tell me if many prisoners
> were taken from the 79th Division that day?

Sometimes a commanding officer or a buddy would send news about
how their son died and add comforting words. A mother who received
such a message took months to reply, saying she was "so broke up I have
not had the strength or ambition to write." When she was able to, she
begged for tangible details of the manner of his death and burial: "Could
you tell me just where he was wounded? I mean the place. If you are not

allowed to now, would you be so kind as to bear this in mind and tell me later when it is not a military secret. Also just where he is laid to rest and if it is a permanent burying place or he will be moved later."

After the war some parents, wives, and buddies found consolation visiting an overseas grave. John Palmquist of Red Oak, Iowa, had been a tail gunner on a B-17. He was wounded during a raid, and while he was in the hospital, his plane was shot down, all of the crew killed. For years he stayed silent about his war experiences, tormented by survivor guilt. Then, after their children were grown up, he and his wife, Wilma, traveled to England to visit the cemetery where his fellow crew members were buried. After they got home, Wilma noticed that every night he would go down to the basement and stay there for hours. When she finally went down to ask him what he was doing, he told her he was writing an account of his war experiences. It was his way of purging the war.

Military policy required the return to the next of kin of all personal effects recovered from the body. The unit commander was supposed to collect the remnants of a life—wallet, cigarette lighter, money, photographs, letters, pocketknife, souvenirs, Bible, lucky pieces, and so on—and forward them to the nearest Effects Depot run by the Quartermaster Corps, where they were sorted, filed, packaged, and forwarded. In 1945 the European depot was located in a former glass factory near Folembray, France. It also temporarily stored the effects of wounded, captured, interned, and missing soldiers. The facility, enclosed by stone walls and high fences, consisted of eleven main buildings, and 1,250 people made up the assembly line processing and shipping the paltry leftovers to the Army Effects Bureau in Kansas City. By the end of 1945 the effects quartermaster had received more than 300,000 packages of personal property and had sent out some 235,000 packages to next of kin. The depot also handled more than $2 million in currency or Finance Department receipts, which went to soldiers' families.

For workers from the Army Graves Registration Service (GRS), a division of the Quartermaster Corps, handling the personal effects was more stressful than preparing remains for burial. Sorting through and perusing letters or photographs or other tangible memorabilia made the loss that much more vivid. Sometimes, the item would compromise a soldier's privacy, an obvious example being an address book listing girlfriends or a sheaf of love letters from a girl other than the wife he left behind. Regulations specified that "pornographic" or "embarrassing" materials were not to be sent; also items "that are contaminated, mutilated, burned, blood stained, damaged beyond repair, or unsanitary." A GRS worker exhuming bodies in Belgium unearthed an airman still clutching a rabbit's foot.

A valuable item, such as a watch or jewelry, might expose the effects worker to temptation. And valuables could be lost in transit or misfiled, causing further anguish among loved ones. On the other hand, some parents gained some comfort from receiving their boy's effects, like the architectural critic and social philosopher Lewis Mumford, whose son, Geddes, was killed in Europe:

> Yesterday a small parcel came from the Army's distributing depot in Kansas. Within it was a small manila envelope, and out of it came the following items: two rusty cigarette lighters, a cheap automatic pencil, a dozen fragments of paper money, including a part of a ten dollar bill, grimy pieces of paper marked with sweat and blood; a combat rifleman's badge . . . an Italian Theater ribbon with a bronze star in the middle, the ribbon stained with blood, his social security card, preserved by scotch tape, three little photographs. . . . All this was found on Geddes's body; it tells little and it tells much. These were the last tokens of his life and all that one shall over know, beyond conjecture or fantasy, of what his death was like.

The Quartermaster Corps, in conjunction with other service branches, was charged with the mission of locating, identifying, and transporting those soldier dead whose next of kin had requested they be shipped home at government expense and buried on American soil. The government would pay for the reburial. No remains were shipped until the fighting was ended, meaning that the 2,300 service personnel killed at Pearl Harbor on December 7, 1941, waited six years before returning to the mainland (more than 700 were interred in Hawaii's Punch Bowl military cemetery).

Some 78,000 soldiers who had gone missing in World War II have never been found, but remains still turn up in jungle villages or rural French or Italian cemeteries. One French family had tended for years the grave of a GI who'd been hastily buried on their farm.

The massive effort to locate, identify, and return the remains of the dead started in 1946 and was terminated in 1951. The work was onerous, especially in the Pacific theater, where some of the bloodiest battles had been fought on small atolls. Mass graves had been bulldozed out of brittle coral, and there was often no clear delineation between the burial ground and the battlefield. Sailors killed aboard ships attacked or sunk at sea by submarines and kamikaze planes would be committed to the ocean or interred in military cemeteries ashore, of which Honolulu's Punch Bowl is the largest permanent one.

The GRS men were the specialists, the supposedly detached professionals in this grisly but necessary task, but even they sometimes broke under the strain of handling the dead—a job they mostly performed with respect and devotion. By the time of the Korean War, the dead were transported to GRS facilities in country, embalmed and shipped back to the States. But the emotional toll on GRS personnel was just as severe.

Another group, the undertakers, also took a professional interest in the disposition of the dead during World War II. The sales manager of a cemetery complained to a US senator that the military policy of giving a free burial to dead soldiers who had been returned to the States "interferes with organized business and free enterprise."

After the war the GRS continued locating and digging up more bodies, embalming and identifying them, shipping them home for reburial. Some of the remains were not in what the GRS delicately termed "viewable" condition. In such cases, according to Michael Sledge's informative *Soldier Dead,* "the remains are wrapped very carefully in plastic sheets, covered by a muslin cloth, and then wrapped in a green wool blanket. Then a uniform decorated with all appropriate medals and designations is pinned to the blanket"—a kind of respectful euphemizing of the body's state.

GRS teams conducted a massive four-year search for the missing in the European and Pacific theaters after the war. As the cold war settled in,

search teams in East Germany were harassed by Soviet occupying authorities. Eventually 16,649 remains were discovered there. By March 1946,
246,492 soldiers killed overseas had been identified but 40,467 were still
among the unknowns. Since that date 18,461 more remains have been
found. Remains of 21,286 have not been located.

Reburial was a tough, grim task. A New Zealand reporter watched a
US team exhuming the occupants of a temporary military cemetery near
Auckland in July 1946:

> Sweating American soldiers were dragging soggy corpses out of the ooze
> at Vaikumete Cemetery, Auckland, last week. Thus, 113 dead Americans
> began their last ride to a permanent resting place. . . .
>
> In a tree-lined plot were opened graves. Coffins lay around to receive
> the decomposed dead. Shovels were rammed into mounds of mud piled
> beside the holes, and desolate white crosses stuck askew in the ground. In
> dungarees and gum-boots, the grave-gang worked. They were an average
> looking crew. . . . There were city men and smalltown boys. In green-
> cloth denims, rubber gloves and heavy boots, they pried from the sticky
> earth reluctant bodies which had lain there for two and three years.
>
> They were obeying orders. The U.S. Congress had ordered all military
> dead buried abroad be repatriated.

The remains unearthed by this GRS unit were from Samoa, the Fiji Islands, and New Zealand. They were transported to Hawaii, where they
were reburied between April 26 and September 9, 1946.

In its "Tell Me About My Boy" directive, the US War Department offered next of kin the option of leaving their son in a grave in one of the
official military cemeteries established during the war and improved afterward. Many chose to do this; as a result, more than 97,000 remains eventually were interred in military cemeteries, along with 10,000 unknowns.
In time, twenty-four cemeteries sprouted overseas, green and immaculate,
with marble walls silently intoning the names of the missing. Some 10,000
GIs lie in the cemetery at Lorraine, 9,000 in the one near Normandy. In
the Punch Bowl near Honolulu rest 13,000 from the Pacific theater; the

walls list 18,000 missing and dead. The Congress provided generously for these necropolises.

At first, because permanent memorials had fallen out of style—and in some courthouse squares of city centers there were already monuments to the fallen of previous wars—official monuments to the World War II dead were put on hold. But pressure on legislators mounted, sometimes with the political objective of publicizing a particular branch of the service. As a result, several prominent World War II monuments were built that were designed less to mourn the dead than to proclaim the nation's military might and its readiness to face new wars if necessary.

Such was the case with the first big World War II memorial, the grandiose Marine Corps War Memorial at Arlington National Cemetery, which features one of the largest bronze statues in the world, weighing 100 tons. It was inspired by Joe Rosenthal's iconic photograph of marines raising the flag on Iwo Jima, which was later revealed to have been staged for the camera in order to create a more patriotic image than the original taken by a combat photographer. Three of the marines in the tableau survived the war but not the peace; unable to handle the publicity tours, two of them died prematurely from alcoholism.

The dimensions are bombastic, like one of those heroic Soviet statues; the rifle carried by one figure is sixteen feet long. As Michael Sherry writes, the tableau "promoted military preparedness, and loomed as mammoth and aloof, inspiring rather than approachable." He quotes Ann Marlin and John Wetenhall: it "betokened military might, the new doctrine of armed deterrent, [and] the global ambitions of American foreign policy after World War II." John Bodnar writes that the Marine Corps "sought to reinforce their image as a group of patriotic and skilled warriors but worried that in the postwar era more government support might go to the Air Force and the Navy." So it hired the advertising agency J. Walter Thompson to mount a fundraising campaign for the memorial, with the result that it became "the definitive collective memory of the war." And, it might be added, a monument to the military-industrial complex as well.

It took the government until 2004 to complete the much-debated World War II Memorial on the Washington Mall. In contrast to two

nearby memorials to the fallen in the Korean and Vietnam wars, the former composed of a life-size ghost patrol of soldiers in combat and the latter slabs of black granite set in a hillside on which are inscribed the
names of every one of the dead, the World War II Memorial is a classi-
cally proportioned, precisely laid-out oval site at the opposite end of a
reflecting pool to the Lincoln Memorial. The deaths of more than four
hundred thousand Americans in the war are abstractly symbolized by
four thousand gold stars; classical columns "substitute a sense of national
harmony and grandeur for the sordid reality that was the war itself,"
Bodnar writes. "This memorial contributes to the process of myth making by simplifying the history of the war and concealing the complex set
of attitudes and emotions that haunted the wartime generation." The
text set in stone speaks abstractly of liberation from America's selfless sacrifice. The human factor is absent.

This stony finality contrasts with a body of dissent just after the war, the
voices warning against the growing militarization of society. Among
the most eloquent was Edgar J. Jones's caustic "One War Is Enough," in
the February 1946 *Atlantic Monthly*. Jones worried about people talking re-
signedly about the possibility of another war, as if it was as inevitable as
the morning sunrise. He asked, "Has everyone in this country lost faith in
peace?" While those who fought understood the savage nature of war,
Americans at home were shielded from it and thus considered their country exceptional, more decent and high-minded than the rest of the world.
Jones trashed those illusions of American exceptionalism:

> What kind of war do civilians suppose we fought, anyway? We shot pris-
> oners in cold blood, wiped out hospitals, strafed lifeboats, killed or mis-
> treated enemy civilians, finished off the enemy wounded, tossed the
> dying into a hole with the dead, and in the Pacific boiled the flesh off
> enemy skulls to make table ornaments for our sweethearts, or carved
> their bones into letter openers. We topped off our saturation bombing
> and burning of enemy civilians by dropping atomic bombs on two nearly
> defenseless cities, thereby setting an all-time record for instantaneous
> mass slaughter.

The literary critic Edmund Wilson remarked in 1945 that the vast, incomprehensible number of wartime deaths had left many Americans more callous than concerned. "No one pretends to give a damn anymore—unless they are one's close friends or relatives—whether people are killed or not," he wrote of casualty reports. He wondered if this callousness was being paid for "by repercussions, the spitefulness and fear and stifled guilt, in our immediate personal relations." During World War I, he recalled, some "humanitarian feeling survived and continued to assert itself." But in that war civilians had not been killed in great anonymous masses as had been done by World War II area bombing of cities and the atomic bomb.

As he mourned his son, Lewis Mumford was reminded of Americans' cultural evasion of death, which endured in wartime. As a result, "despite massive efforts at repression, the daily imminence of violence and death in our lives poisons our happiest moments; so that in sheer self-defense we anesthetize our feelings in advance." That deadens our humanity. For "he who has not accepted death or lived with grief has not fully encountered human experience—as I would find for myself only in middle life." In an unpublished column on VE Day called "And So It Is Over," which was found among his effects after he was killed in the Okinawa campaign, Ernie Pyle wrote of his weariness at seeing so many dead men "in such monstrous infinity that you come almost to hate them." He continued:

> These are the things that you at home need not even try to understand.
> To you at home they are columns of figures, or he is a near one who went
> away and just didn't come back. You didn't see him lying so grotesque
> and pasty beside the gravel road in France.
>
> We saw him, saw him by the multiple thousands. That's the
> difference . . .

Paul Fussell writes in *Wartime* that people in America hadn't been told about even 10 percent of the horror of this war: "The real war was tragic and ironic, beyond the power of any literary or philosophic analysis to suggest, but in unbombed America especially, the meaning of the war seemed inaccessible. As experience, thus, the suffering was wasted. . . . America has not yet understood what the Second World War was like and has thus been unable to use such understanding to re-interpret and re-define the national reality and to arrive at something like public maturity."

Yet something remained even for us on the home front. I still recall, sixty-five years later, reading an article about the death camps, with drawings meant to show their factory-like efficiency. This article, conflated in my mind with newsreel images of stacks of pale, grossly naked corpses plowed into graves, inspired nightmares of human bodies being processed like animals on a slaughterhouse assembly line. At the time, because I was so young and distant from the real war, I could never truly move beyond the images of horror, for I had no frame of meaning, philosophical or political, to shape it, try to understand it, take action on it. The fascist racial doctrines—the monstrous cruelty of war itself—that inspired these scenes were beyond my limited horizons of comprehension.

IN 1944, THE BLOODIEST YEAR of the war for American forces, a new trend in Hollywood movies was marked by the release, in April, of *Double Indemnity*. Directed by the German-Jewish émigré Billy Wilder, adapted by Raymond Chandler (the screenwriter of the aforementioned *Blue Dahlia*) from James M. Cain's hard-boiled novel, and starring Barbara Stanwyck and Fred MacMurray (both cast against their usual wholesome type), it was immediately hailed as a new kind of crime film. It also caused an unusual stir in the industry: even before the war was over, executives had been trying to identify what kinds of films might appeal to postwar audiences, and the critical and box-office success of this kind of crime film seemed to point the way.

Reviewers praised *Double Indemnity* as a fresh take on the murder genre. The film, peopled with recognizable contemporary American types who spoke of death in callous, calculating language and shot with dark chiaroscuro lighting, told an unedifying tabloid-style story of greed, lust, and murder, in which MacMurray, an insurance agent, falls for Stanwyck, and devises a plan to murder her husband and collect twice as much under the double indemnity clause of his policy.

The Hollywood Reporter called the movie "realistic," "grim and grizzly [*sic*]," one of the most "gripping and exemplary crime films ever screened." It was "exemplary," the reviewer insisted, because it showed the folly of attempting to carry out the perfect crime, a coded way of saying that the Breen Office, which enforced the Motion Picture Code (MPC) was justified in ignoring the film's violations.

Under the headline "Crime Certainly Pays on Screen," the *New York Times*'s movie writer reported that the box-office success of *Double Indemnity* had inspired Hollywood studios to launch a procession of "homicidal films"—"lusty-hard-boiled, gat-and-gore crime stories" featuring a "plausibly motivated murder and studded with high-powered Freudian implication." It was reported that a second wave of such stories was in the works and that "within the next year or so movie murders particularly with a pathological twist will become almost as common as the weekly newsreel or musical." These films—*Laura, Murder My Sweet, Phantom Lady*—were dubbed hard-boiled or "red meat films" because of their violence (shown or implied). They were becoming popular, according to the *Times,* because they offered a "violent escape in tune with the violence of the times." Psychologists testified, the reporter wrote, that as a result of the war, "the average moviegoer has become calloused to death, hardened to homicide and more capable of understanding a murderer's motives." The story closed on this note: "These are times of death and bloodshed and legalized murder; these are times when, if an audience can stomach newsreels of atrocities, it can take anything."

Writing in the leftish *Film Quarterly,* John Houseman, a New York producer and director who had worked with Orson Welles at the Mercury Theatre, insisted that what he called the "tough" movie (referring to private-eye films) was no lurid Hollywood invention because "its pattern and its characteristics coincide too closely with other symptoms of our national life. A quick examination of our daily and weekly press proves conclusively, whether we like or not, that the 'tough' movie, currently projected on the seventeen thousand screens of this country, presents a fairly accurate reflection of the neurotic personality of the United States of America in the year 1947."

Houseman observed that marketing pressures drove Hollywood to choose stories that reflected "the interests and anxieties of its hundred million customers." As the producer, most recently, of *The Blue Dahlia,* a murder story, he should know.

Some critics commented that the increase of screen violence followed after government censors eased up on their wartime restrictions against showing dead and wounded American soldiers to shock apathetic Americans on the home front into working harder and giving more support to the war effort. The Breen Office had contributed to this trend by relaxing its taboos against graphic scenes of torture and death in fictional war movies as well as shots of American dead and wounded in combat documentaries. (Although filmmakers were free to ignore its recommendations, they were subject to a $30,000 fine if they released a film without the MPC seal of approval.)

When studios made films about the war, they emphasized patriotic propaganda and glossed over the central fact of war, which was death. In Hollywood war films death was usually noble or heroic, though at times sad. What the films concealed, the film historians Clayton R. Koppes and Geoffrey D. Black write in *Hollywood Goes to War,* was "what everyone knew but found hard to voice aloud—that death was random and success only partly related to one's desires"—practically the obverse of the Hollywood credo—that death, if acknowledged, was noble and the portal to an afterlife, and that success always rewarded the virtuous with a happy ending to their suffering.

This reticence had applied even in the war movies. Films like *A Guy Named Joe* (a dead flyer comes back to guide invisibly his successor at the controls and with his girl) and *The Human Comedy* (a family's beloved son is killed in action, and they adopt his buddy who comes to tell them about his death) seemed to be trying to defeat wartime death by denial. Just after the war MacKinlay Kantor, who had been commissioned to write the novel that was the source of *The Best Years of Our Lives,* published a beautifully crafted magazine story about a soldier and his British girlfriend: the reader gradually becomes aware that the soldier is dead, that the girlfriend was killed in London by a bomb, and that he is leading her into the afterlife.

"Nobody dies" is the ironic mantra chanted by the GIs in *A Walk in the Sun* (adapted from a 1944 novel by war correspondent Harry Brown). Here it was a case of repeating a thing that you know is not true. Several men die in the firefight that climaxes the novel and the movie.

During World War I, Sigmund Freud wrote an essay called "Thoughts on Death in Wartime." Freud, who would formulate his profoundest theories of Eros and Thanatos after that conflict (and who had three sons at the front), wrote that in war the layers of civilization are shed, and men revert to their natural instincts. He did not venture to analyze what men in combat thought, but contended that people like him on the home front, with loved ones at risk, were exposed as never before to the phenomenon of mass death, albeit from afar; and this spectacle reminded them of their own mortality.

Overcivilized moderns, Freud suggested, repress the idea that death must come to each of them, and "at bottom no one believes in his own death . . . in the unconscious every one of us is convinced of his own immortality." In peacetime death intrudes in our lives—the deaths of parents, relatives, friends, victims chronicled in the media, ourselves—but we attribute it to "normal causes" (contingencies such as accident, disease, infection, and so on), and muffle its impact in stylized rituals and religious consolation. We do this to "modify the significance of death from a necessity to an accident." But in war "death comes in great numbers, overwhelming our emotional defenses"; thus we think about war deaths as "exceedingly terrible." They hold our attention.

In the crime films violent deaths provided a symbolic equivalence to the lingering reality of wartime deaths—for those who had been in the thick of the war; for civilians who had lost loved ones; and for ordinary people who had experienced them only vicariously in the battlefield reports, casualty lists, newsreels, and photos.

Consider *D.O.A.*, which on its surface appears to be a murder film with a gimmicky plot twist but which symbolically represents the inexorable nature of death. As the plot has it, the hero (Edmund O'Brien), in the big city for a convention, wakes up after a night of revelry feeling seriously ill. He goes to the hospital, where tests are taken, and the doctors tell him that he has somehow ingested a slow-acting poison that will kill him in a matter of days. "You're telling me I am dead!" he protests. "You're explaining my life away. I don't even know you. You're crazy." And the doctor replies: "I don't think you fully understand, Mr. Bigelow. You've been murdered." It turns out that his drink was switched at a bar by someone who has it in for him and whom he spends the rest of the film hunting for before meeting his death foretold.

The movie's first-person narrator is a "dead man walking," which echoes the fatalism of soldiers in combat, who sometimes feel that they are under a death sentence. As the novelist and World War II veteran James Jones put it, a soldier is virtually a walking dead man because he "knows and accepts beforehand that he's dead, although he may still be walking around for awhile." In *Double Indemnity* Walter Neff feels a sense of his own doom, telling the insurance investigator who suspected him: "As I was walking down the street to the drugstore, suddenly it came over me that everything would go wrong. It sounds crazy but it's true, so help me. I couldn't hear my own footsteps. It was the walk of a dead man."

Another analogue to death in war was the gratuitous, arbitrary, and coldly calculated violence that became a hallmark of the new wave of crime films. As the sinister agents of this fate, psychopathic killers came into vogue. The type was unforgettably played by Richard Widmark in *Kiss of Death* (1947). Widmark shockingly portrayed Tommy Ugo as a giggling sadist who pushes an old woman in a wheelchair down a stairway to her death. The film historian David Thomson describes Widmark's performance: "The sadism of that character, the fearful laugh, the skull showing through drawn skin, *and the surely conscious evocation of a concentration-camp degenerate* established Widmark as the most frightening person on the screen" (italics added).

The violence in these films was not always measured quantitatively in terms of literal gats or gore. *Double Indemnity* contained no violent scenes beyond the half-bungled murder (by strangulation) central to its plot. But the cold calculations of the perpetrators, their middle-class ordinariness (dramatizing the potential killer inside any normal-looking, respectable man or woman), their cool greed, the clumsily brutal way the murder is carried out, the familiar urban settings—had a cumulative shock effect on contemporary audiences.

These films seemed to appeal to a new state of mind among postwar audiences, whose numbers were swelled by veterans. Audiences of all ages had become cynical about the phony heroics of the propagandistic war movies, especially after seeing hints of the real thing in newsreels or the combat documentaries shot by Hollywood pros like John Huston (*The Battle of San Pietro*) and William Wyler (*The Memphis Belle*). Fictional war films seemed phony because they competed with the real war in magazines and newsreels, while in the hard-boiled crime films death was more real because it was shown in an unidealized, unheroic way in a fictional context.

The "red meat" trend in Hollywood launched in 1944 was so distinctive it was seized on after the war by French film critics, who were suddenly exposed to a deluge of American films made between 1941 and 1945, which were simultaneously released in France after the lifting of a wartime embargo. They were struck by how these crime films stood out from standard Hollywood fare with the routine happy ending or patriotic message. They conferred on these films a more elegant name—*film noir*. In a 1946 article in *French Screen,* the critic Nino Frank writes about being struck by the "radically different" vision of life in America found in these films, which depicted it as rife with "greed, criminality, violence, anomie." All film noir, Nino Frank concluded, was concerned with the "dynamism of violent death."

The French cinema scholars Raymond Borde and Etienne Chaumeton, who would write a seminal book, *Panorama du film noir américain 1941–1953 (A Panorama of American Film Noir 1941–1953),* published in 1955, seized on this description as a defining trait. "Few cycles in the entire history of film have put together in seven or eight years such a mix of foul play and murder," they declared. "Sordidly or bizarrely, death always comes at the end of a tortured journey. *In every sense of the word a noir film is a film of death.*"

It's fair to say that what the French critics discerned in these crime films reflected the postwar mood in their own country, which seethed with recriminations for France's defeat and charges of war crimes. Intellectuals, particularly the existentialist philosophers, had a sense of being bound to the past with no clear idea of how to free themselves. They saw in film noir, as James Naremore writes, "a world of obsessive return, dark corners, or *huis clos*" ("no exit"—the title of a play by the existentialist philosopher Jean Paul Sartre). Similarly, the astute contemporary reviewer Barbara Deming, in her study of American films of the forties, saw the "no exit conclusion" as a recurring motif: whenever the hero and heroine try "to escape a condition of life in which [they] no longer believe . . . helplessness overwhelms them."

Speaking for American filmmakers, the writer/director Abraham Polonsky agreed that a preoccupation with violent death was common among crime films, which were always about a "general sense of jeopardy of life," and this was a "correct representation of the anxiety caused by the system." In other words, the capitalist economic system generated anxiety, and film noir more accurately portrayed this state than other kinds of films. As a Marxist, Polonsky preferred to attribute the sense of jeopardy, uncertainty, to capitalism. French critics like Frank, Borde, and Chaumeton, writing more from an aesthetic or philosophical perspective, tended to see it as a surreal or existential state of humankind.

The war's psychological shocks reverberated through the popular culture, most prominently in the films noir that proliferated in the late forties (and it should be noted that Hollywood continued to turn out familiar, more popular genres, from Westerns to musicals to family films). Preoccupation with violence and death and a mood of disillusionment, uncertainty, and cynicism were the most prominent symptoms of the war's lingering aftermath in the culture. A tributary to the crime film trend was the public's fascination with abnormal psychology springing from stories about unpredictable psychoneurotic vets. Closing the circle, psychoanalysis was in vogue in Hollywood.

Death in war had been directly communicated to the home front in telegrams from the War Department and indirectly through newsreels and photographs. The impact of these, along with the uncertainties and insecurities of the postwar period—the faded "victory dreams," the loss of the sense of common purpose war imposes, the fears of giving up financial gains achieved in the war boom, the pressure to grab security, the materialism and consumerism, the readjustment pains of 14 million veterans (some with combat neuroses) and their families (comprising nearly a quarter of the entire population), the glitches and slowdowns in reconversion to peacetime production, the persistence of wartime austerity measures like rationing, the strikes and labor-management tensions that had erupted, the mourning for the dead, the rising tensions with the Soviet Union, the chronic dread instilled by the horrors of the atomic bomb and the Holocaust—all these moods merged into a vague sense of gloom and pessimism, the reverse image of traditional American optimism and faith in the future. It tempered the victory dreams of postwar abundance, which seemed ephemeral to a generation scarred by the Great Depression. It produced the popular mood of those early postwar years, 1945–50, which I call "the noir forties" and other historians have labeled "the age of anxiety," "the age of doubt," "postwar blues," "triumphalist despair." These moods and emotions were the mass psychological subsoil in which sprouted the nation's politics and culture at the time.

Voices

Seldom, if ever, has a war ended leaving the victors with such a sense of uncertainty and fear, with such a realization that the future is obscure.

—EDWARD R. MURROW, 1945

In a quaint caravan
There's a lady they call The Gypsy
She can look in the future
And drive away all your fears.

—BILLY REID, "THE GYPSY" (1945 HIT SONG)

Detour, there's a muddy road ahead.
Detour, paid no mind to what it said.
Detour, oh these bitter things I find.
Should have read that detour sign.

—PAUL WESTMORELAND, "DETOUR," PERFORMED BY
SPADE COOLEY (NO. 2 ON *BILLBOARD* CHART IN 1946)

3

RECONVERSION
JITTERS

UNLIKE IN THE YEARS immediately after World War I, there was no political sloganeering about a "return to normalcy." Nor was there a backlash by the soldiers against wartime lies and patriotic propaganda. (Any backlash was against those who didn't fight—and made out like bandits.) There was no flamboyant hedonism and rebellion (beyond the usual), no sad young men, no Jazz Age, no prohibitions and taboos to defy. Nevertheless, normalcy, which meant the way things were before the war, was what people wanted to go back to—quietly, with no big fuss, no flag-waving, parades, or marching bands. This was a war people wanted to *get over with;* a war in which, to those who served in it, the overriding objective was making it home.

Recovering the pre-war past seemed more attractive than the uncertain future. Hence, the operative prefix of 1945–46 was "re"—as in "*re*conversion" (changing over war plants to production of peacetime goods), "*read*-justment" (returning vets relearning civilian ways), and so on, down through "*re*integration," "*re*conditioning," "*re*naturalization," "*re*habilitation." All these words denoted a sort of orderly process of getting back to doing what you were doing before the war—i.e., leading a normal life. The process encouraged looking backward, not forward. Even popular music was saturated with nostalgia. And, conversely, workers looking ahead and worried about the future—about earning less money (or not having a job

Frustrated pianist Tom Neal thumbs to California for a new life;
fate and Ann Savage shunt him on a *Detour*. *Everett Collection*

at all) in peacetime than they were during the war—were said to be suffering from "conversion jitters" (as we'll see in Chapter Five).

The road ahead seemed pocked with uncertainty. People were feeling what the press labeled *"reconversion jitters."* An obscure, low-budget B movie released in 1946 called *Detour* inadvertently caught the unsettled mood. It was directed by the German émigré Edgar G. Ulmer (who had learned filmmaking during the post–World War I Weimar era in Germany before fleeing the Nazis) for a Poverty Row studio, Producers Releasing Corporation, and was later anointed a *film noir* classic.

Al plays piano in New York bars. He is sustained by fading dreams of Carnegie Hall; torn between high art and low pop, he likes to sneak in a Chopin polonaise between the vulgar boogie-woogie numbers he reels off for tips. He decides to hitchhike to the West Coast to join his girlfriend, a singer trying to make it in Hollywood. En route, fate grabs him by the neck: "Until then I had done things my way," says Al's voiceover, "but from then on something stepped in and shunted me off to a different destination than the one I'd picked for myself." Along his journey a rich man picks him up, then has a heart attack and dies. Al, figuring he'll be under suspicion if he reports the man's death and needing money, appropriates the man's identity—clothes, wallet, money, Cadillac convertible. Tooling along fate's bypass, he picks up a hitchhiker named Vera, who reveals herself to be a vixen. Turns out she fought off the same guy whose identity Al has assumed (and who had shown Al the fingernail scratches she left on him). She blackmails Al with threats of exposure, and when she reads in the paper that the dead man was on his way to collect a large inheritance, she orders Al to impersonate him and collect the dough, which they will split. He refuses and they argue. Again fate sticks out its foot, this time upending Vera. She gets drunk and threatens to call the police. When Al tries to stop her she retreats into her room, where she somehow gets the cord around her neck before collapsing into a stupor. Al jerks on the cord, unwittingly strangling her to death. In the final scene, he hits the road to hitchhike, but fate's noose has coiled around him. A police car comes along, picks him up, and drives off. His essential innocence in the two deaths is known only to himself. As Al's voiceover comments: "Whichever way you turn, fate sticks out a foot to trip you. Fate, or some mysterious force, can put the finger on you or me for no good reason at all." In the Kafkaesque universe evoked by Ulmer, as in other films noir, guilt is arbitrary, the sentence is death, and there is no appeal.

The film was Ulmer's adaptation of a novel by Martin Goldsmith: "I was always in love with the idea," he said, "and with the main character—a boy who plays piano in Greenwich Village and really wants to be a decent pianist. He is so down on his luck that [his girlfriend, a singer] who goes to the coast is the only person he can exist with sex-wise—*The Blue Angel* kind of thing [i.e., she has a career and will support him when he joins her]. And then, the idea to get [him] involved on that long road of fate—where he's an absolute loser—fascinated me. And the boy who played the leading character, Tom Neal, wound up in jail after he killed his own wife; he did practically the same thing he did in the picture." Ulmer shot *Detour* in six days and brought it in at a rock-bottom $36,000. (When he made *The Wife of Monte Cristo* he took two weeks, "because it was a *big* picture.")

Detour evoked the sense of drift millions of returning veterans and redundant war-plant workers felt in that first postwar year. Uncertainties loomed: fears of another Depression, of the Soviets, of the A-bomb too. You'd lost agency; fate was in the driver's seat.

William S. Graebner describes this existential angst in his cultural history *The Age of Doubt:* "In the absence of accepted moral and ethical principles of conduct and belief, an infinity of actions and beliefs became possible and the anxiety of choice unavoidable." In an overload of choices, sometimes people drift, letting fate or chance take the wheel. Graebner describes a pervasive sense of "loss of the sense of self [which] led to totalitarianism, mass alienation, loneliness, rootlessness and superfluousness." For many in such a state, a job and family, "settling down," security, and repose became the driving goals. Politically, those more vulnerable to the symptoms might have cast a favorable eye on strong, conservative leaders like the new senator from Wisconsin, Joseph McCarthy, who'd been elected in the 1946 midterms. Many among the wide swath of people who during the Depression and war had supported Franklin Roosevelt felt a vacuum of leadership after his sudden death in April 1945. And with the "Japs" and the Nazis gone, who was there to hate? Where was the great national purpose that had been drummed into their ears?

Al had been dreaming of a new life with his girl, playing the music he wanted to play, but he was shunted off on a detour. A song by Tex Williams, which reached No. 2 on the country music charts in 1945, was coincidentally titled "Detour":

> *Trav'lin down life's crooked road*
> *Lots of things I never knowed . . .*
> *Spent the next five years in jail,*
> *Should've read that detour sign*

The great coordinated industrial and military effort of war gave way to the frustrating problems of reconversion as various companies that had cooperated in that effort switched to the competitive civilian economy. Divisive rivalries and prejudices that had been patriotically suppressed resurfaced. In his 1946 best seller *Inside USA,* the journalist John Gunther described the national mood in negative terms:

Yet once the war is over its backwash smears over us, and the nation succumbs to greed, fear, ineptitude, fumbling of the morning hopes, shoddy dispersal of the evening dreams. That in late 1946, the two most painful and pressing shortages in the land should be of the most primitive necessities of life, food and housing, is evidence enough of the disintegration, no matter how temporary these shortages may turn out to be. . . . Does [this] show that to become efficient this country needs the stimulus of war? Does it mean that 295,000 [*sic*] Americans have to be killed in order to give us true effectiveness as a nation?

Of course, not everybody saw it that way. According to *Time*'s Washington correspondent, writing right after the war ended: "There's a lush feeling of satisfaction, of relaxation, of happiness abroad in the land, much of it is traceable to the man in the White House." That actually seems to

be a reference to the new president, Harry S. Truman, whom the magazine praised for his businesslike, hardworking efficiency. According to the
first Gallup poll after he took over in April 1945, following Roosevelt's
death, his approval rating was a dizzying 87 percent, which topped even
FDR's summit of 84 percent. (Truman's approval among low-income
people, FDR's most devoted constituency, sagged to 57 percent, however.)
More relevant, a poll showed 85 percent of Americans were worried about
economic problems.

Certainly, 1946 was a year of flux and transition. After Pearl Harbor
some 17 million people of all ages had moved from their native counties,
on the way to military service or war jobs. After VJ Day some 10.5 million
pulled up stakes, many heading back to where they came from. Sociolog-
ically, America looked like a giant ant farm under glass, streams of people
on the move.

THE CULTURAL AND PSYCHOLOGICAL effects of the migrations of the
hill people to the centers of war production were profound. Harriette
Arnow, whose naturalistic novel *The Dollmaker* chronicles the experiences
of a Kentucky family that moves to Detroit, where the husband has a job
in a war plant, explained in an interview that she too had moved to Detroit
during the war with her husband, a journalist. "I began writing [*The Dollmaker*] during the depression, which had sent hill people back home
again," she said. "And then, as I was still writing during the Second War, I
witnessed the permanent move the men made by bringing their wives and
children with them to the cities. With that last migration, hill life was
gone forever, and with it, I suppose, a personal dream of community I
had since childhood."

In those days the voice of "hillbilly" popular music was the Grand Ole
Opry, broadcasting live from Nashville every Saturday night over station
WSM. Before the war country music was mainly doleful laments reflect-
ing traditional values of family and faith. Under the strains of migration
to cities up north the hold of the old-time values was loosened. As Robert
Oermann, coauthor of *Finding Her Voice: The Saga of Women in Country*

Music, said, "After World War II, country music topics broadened considerably. Prior to the war, country was very much home and hearth and religion. After the war came drinking songs and what are called cheating songs, which are songs of adultery." One of the pioneering female country stars, Kitty Wells, who overcame the traditional prejudice that pushed women singers to the background, began performing songs about women demanding their right to their independence. In "Release Me," her most popular number, a woman confesses to her husband or sweetheart that "I have found a new love, dear./And I'll always want him near."

Of course, most of the cheating songs were recorded by male singers, since that was considered a male prerogative. Hank Thompson was one such performer who sang about straying men in songs like "Soft Lips" and "The Grass Is Greener Over Yonder" (1949). He had a hugely popular hit in which a young man is drawn to the bars and dancehalls in the war towns that were crammed with country people making good money. Called "The Wild Side of Life" (1952), with a tune based on the old Carter Family song "I'm Thinking Tonight of My Blue Eyes," it contained the line "I didn't know God made honky tonk angels./I might have known you'd never make a wife." Wells fired back at this blame-the-woman game with her hit "It Wasn't God Who Made Honky Tonk Angels."

Country music's changing values to accommodate looser secular morals was part of a larger trend in popular music whereby all the ethnic and regional styles achieved a breakout to more widespread appeal. For example, after the war "race music" styles like boogie-woogie and blues, considered somewhat disreputable and risqué, began making the pop charts. As a sign of this broader tolerance, the music magazine *Billboard* replaced the term "race music" (meaning music popular with African Americans) with "rhythm and blues." "Western" (cowboy) music merged with "country" to become "country and western," and country stars like Eddy Arnold tailored their styles to sound more like Frank Sinatra and other pop crooners.

The postwar rise of race music and country, which led eventually to their merger into rock and roll, was the result of cultural cross-fertilization engendered by accelerated social mobility, as different racial, ethnic, and class groups moved to the centers of war industries, bringing their music with them. With the war economy providing decent paychecks—after years of poverty and rural austerity—these people, or some of them, sought out new pleasures. In bars, juke joints, and honky tonks, they spent their earnings on Saturday night drinking and dancing to "their" music played live or on a jukebox. They tuned in to it over the radio. Two powerful 50,000-watt stations in Nashville—WLAC and WSM— blasted out a steady diet of race and country music, respectively. Because these stations had loyal fans, advertisers who were targeting these audiences poured money into the station's coffers. (Hair straighteners and cosmetics, for example, were marketed to African Americans.) Finally, record stores sprang up to sell the songs people heard on the radio and jukeboxes. Because the Big Three record companies (RCA Victor, Decca, Columbia) dominated mainstream pop, jazz, and classical, independent labels, more attuned to country and R&B tastes, proliferated to make the "hillbilly" and "race" records that the fans would buy. Some became majors in their own right: King, Mercury, Capitol, Excelsior, Chess, Atlantic.

What's more, white people were listening in and finding the new music, especially R&B, exciting. Soldiers heard in off-duty dives what they didn't hear at home and liked it. And so the hard-driving, happy music called boogie-woogie or swing or jump blues or country swing began hitting the pop as well as the R&B charts.

Of course, country and western and race music had been around for years, and major record labels had issued some hits in these genres. And there were subgenres like blues, which had a long history among African Americans, as did jazz, which the major labels had been pressing since the 1920s. But during and after the war, leading jazz musicians like Charlie Parker, Dizzy Gillespie, and Charles Mingus (who used to stop playing and lecture audiences who were talking instead of listening to him) moved into bebop, a more cerebral, avant-garde form that appealed to the cognoscenti (that is, the seriously hip). When jazz players wanted to reach the masses they played dirty blues, swing, or jump music—the kind of music people could dance to, revel to—or music with a hard urban beat that reflected the taste of young blacks, and soon white teens were emulating them.[*]

Country music also moved toward a contemporary, raunchy, bluesy sound played by artists like Hank Snow and, preeminently, Hank Williams. Williams, arguably country's greatest composer-performer, had actually learned to play the guitar from a black street musician, and he injected some bluesy licks into his playing. One of his first big hits was the twenties standard "Lovesick Blues," which he sang in hillbilly style, yodeling—thus not straying too far from his fan base. In another reinterpreted blues hit, "Move It On Over," he mixes in sly country wit, as the singer bemoans being consigned by his wife to the doghouse after coming home late. In a series of verses Williams rings changes on "move" as he tells the dog to make space for him: "Slide it on over," "ease it on over," "drag it on over," "sneak it on over," "shove it on over," etc. (A later version adds "rock it on over," showing why the song has been called a predecessor to the first rock hit, "Rock Around the Clock.")

Some R&B artists—notably Louis Jordan, known as the king of R&B—initially appealed to GIs in California just back from the Pacific who were hitting the dives and juke joints on weekend passes. They liked to drink and dance to the hard beat of jump blues and boogie-woogie. This music extolled hedonism and served as a reaction against the puritanical austerity and denial that was preached, if not rigidly practiced, during the war years. After the war, a wave of pent-up consumerism was unleashed that crested in the fifties and powered the economy, including the record business, to rising prosperity. The *Journal of Retailing* would offer a quasi-religious

---

[*] My Army service exposed me to a wider musical universe. There I got to know a lot of men from Kentucky and West Virginia. Those of us from other parts of the country argued with them over music they played on radios in the barracks. They were fanatically devoted to country, of course, and despite being force-fed, I grew to like Hank Williams, whose untimely death in a car crash at age twenty-nine the country boys were still talking about with hushed reverence. I found the hillbilly genre was in some ways closer to reality because it produced several songs about the Korean War (e.g., "Dear John" and "Missing in Action"). We Easterners and college boys favored pop standards. As for rhythm and blues, I recall listening to boogie-woogie on some long-range radio station late at night in the forties. It was regarded as a kind of forbidden music, with its pounding sexy beat meant for jitterbugging.

vision of the consumption society: "Our enormously productive economy demands that we make consumption our way of life, that we convert the buying and use of goods into rituals, that we seek our spiritual satisfaction, our ego satisfaction in consumption."

What expressed this philosophy better than Louis Jordan's big 1946 hit "Let the Good Times Roll"?

> *Hey everybody, let's have some fun*
> *You only live but once*
> *And when you're dead you're done . . .*
> *If you want to have a ball*
> *You got to go out and spend some cash*

Let's not leave scx out of the picture. The biggest R&B hit of the first postwar year was Joe Liggis's "The Honeydripper," the No. 1 race record from September 1945 through January 1946. As Jim Daws and Steve Propes write in a history of pre-rock, the song was heard in record stores, fried chicken shacks, and shoeshine stands along LA's Central Avenue, the beating heart of African American culture on the West Coast. GIs prowling for sexual release heard it. It achieved 2 million sales, a large number for the time, and the purchasers included whites who boosted it to No. 12 on the mainstream pop charts, the highest position achieved by a race record up to that point.

The song was pressed by Exclusive Records, one of the numerous independent labels to start up after the war, many of which were black-owned and located along Vine Street, which became known as Hollywood's Tin Pan Alley. Others proliferated along Tenth Avenue in Midtown Manhattan. The small labels specializing in race or R&B music had first call on a large cohort of emerging black artists, whom the major record labels ignored.

Postwar race and country music exploited American roots music— blues, gospel, Appalachian Scotch-Irish folk ballads. The R&B sound was spread by the radio stations, their ranks swelled by local broadcasters who catered to black audiences. The stations increasingly used disc jockeys because they provided cheap programming, filling the time with chatter and records. Nashville's WLAC was the powerhouse for this kind of music. As historian John Broven writes in *Record Makers and Breakers,* the station "was a major factor in exposing R&B and gospel records to new audiences in the South and beyond. It was this listener crossover movement from the southern black communities to (mainly) white teenagers over a large swathe of the country, that would help to stoke the rock-n-roll revolution."[*]

"The Honeydripper" was such a song: it had a sexy, good-time message. In black lexicon a "honeydripper" was a smooth talker, a hep guy—maybe a zoot-suiter—who appealed to women. As the lyrics purred, "The honeydripper, he's a killer / The honeydripper . . . he's a solid gold cat / He's the height of jive . . . / He's a riffer, the honeydripper."

Joe Liggis, the musician who wrote the song, capitalized on its success by forming a six-player group called the Honeydrippers. This was in keeping with the trend in R&B music toward small bands, which were popular with bars and clubs because they were cheaper than the big swing orchestras. By then the music of Glenn Miller (killed in the war), Tommy Dorsey, Benny Goodman, Harry James, and other big bands, which had its heyday in the thirties and early forties, was on the way out. (Stan Kenton was one of the last survivors, with his new, dissonant jazzy sound). Tastes had changed; people weren't going out dancing as much, and the costs of touring were becoming prohibitive. The jump groups like Louis Jordan's Tympany Five and the Honeydrippers featured a raucous good-time sound, dominated by a pounding beat and the honking saxophone sound pioneered by jazzman Illinois Jacquet and popularized by Jordan, also a sax man. This sound caught the ears of black and white teens, and was later

---

[*] Growing up in Indiana, we heard WLAC playing the forbidden black music we called boogie-woogie. Sometimes teens would park outside town and play it on their car radios while dancing in the road. To Midwestern white kids, black music had the allure of forbidden fruit: the prejudice of the times was a factor, as was the sexy innuendo; but mainly it was the down-and-dirty beat, so different from the big-band swing tunes.

parlayed by one of the founding fathers of early rock, Bill Haley and His Comets, into the hit "Rock Around the Clock" (1955).[*]

The future emergence of rock was foretold in the noir forties by a plethora of songs with "rock" in their titles and lyrics, signifying everything from action and excitement to sex. Typical was "Good Rockin' Tonight," classified as a jump blues. Written and recorded by Roy Brown, it was not a success until the popular black singer Wynonie Harris recorded it, injecting it with a booster shot of gospel-style hand-clapping and ending with a loud refrain of "hoy, hoy, hoy," a repeated nonsense hepcat word that Joe Liggis had used in "The Honeydripper." Brown followed with the sequel "Rockin' at Midnight," which had a short reign atop the R&B charts.

"The Honeydripper" had a biracial appeal, one suspects, to young black and white men. It articulated what they aspired to be: ladies' men, smooth operators. The wartime shortage of men had also made young women hungry for this kind of charmer; the loosening of sexual mores added to his irresistibility. Those slow, yearning, I'll-be-faithful-to-you wartime ballads that dominated the popular Saturday night radio program *Your Hit Parade,* like "I'll Walk Alone," "Miss You," "You'll Never Know," "Don't Get Around Much Any More," and "Saturday Night Is the Loneliest Night of the Week," as sung by teen-heartthrob crooners like Sinatra and Dick Haymes, became passé overnight. Young people, especially young servicemen and their girls, wanted to have fun, forget the war, bury the pledges of monogamy, and enjoy the sexual freedom that followed the relaxing of Victorian morals under the pressures of transient wartime encounters.

The new sounds and voices slithered their way into the pop mainstream. They differed in style from bland hits by artists like Patti Page, Jo Stafford, Perry Como, and Les Paul and Mary Ford (who introduced a fresh sound in their overdubbed take on the jazz-inflected "How High the Moon"). Pop still dominated the record sales, but its songs were growing more eclectic, which is to say out of touch. For example, the 1898 song

---

* Before he was famous, we used to catch him in a Baltimore nightspot. He seemed so touchingly eager to please his audience that we mock-cheered him on as he took off in honking sax flights, which we lovers of Dixieland snobbishly thought over the top. A couple of years later, he had honestly cheering audiences.

"When You Were Sweet Sixteen" was a hit for Perry Como, as was the more recent 1931 Russ Colombo throbber "Prisoner of Love." They lacked the American roots of race and country music; some had an ethnic flavor, which gave them novelty but lacked follow-ups. To be sure, folk songs achieved a surprising popularity, as Popular Front groups like the Weavers (until the red-baiters got them blacklisted) made hits out of folk and ethnic songs like Huddie Ledbetter's "Goodnight, Irene" and "Tzena, Tzena."

Even the rock revolutionary Elvis Presley needed to cultivate a clean-cut image to appeal to teenage fans. Standing as an example was the fate of Frank Sinatra, whose career veered into a detour in the fifties after his personal life blew up (then recovered after he won an Academy Award for his performance in *From Here to Eternity*). The African American greats like Billie Holiday were segregated out of the mainstream, tainted in the eyes of moralists and disc jockeys by their skin color and their association with jazz and drug use. Some R&B artists were too mature for wholesome teens because they played mildly sexy music. This they primarily performed before black audiences on the Chitlin' Circuit, a chain of venues mainly in the South but stretching across the country, where rising black artists could try out their acts, make their names, perfect their techniques, and move on to broader acceptance. Louis Jordan was a prime example of a black artist who learned how to appeal to wider audiences on the Chitlin' Circuit.

The successful black groups felt the stigma of race prejudice, necessitating their playing to all-black audiences at first; but their music slowly caught fire with white teen audiences looking for more exciting sounds than what was featured on *Your Hit Parade*. Similarly, country musicians bore the "hillbilly" stigma, which had intensified during the war, when people from Kentucky and elsewhere who migrated to work in the war plants of Detroit and California were resented as dirty and uncouth by local prudes. Thus the more modern style of a Hank Williams or the blander one of an Eddy Arnold (who moved on to the popular "Nashville Sound" in the fifties) appealed to a broader audience.

The music business itself had a kind of shady image—associations with drugs and race-mixing, so hated by ideological thought police like J. Edgar

Hoover. Also, the jukebox industry, which devoured 46 million records annually, was controlled by mobsters who had branched out from slots and pinball machines, which were similarly coin-operated and thus perfect for money laundering.

The war's ethnic migrations had an emulsifying effect on pop music taste, gradually opening it up to previously excluded subcultures. The contemporary pop music industry badly needed rebarbitizing. Its hits mainly emanated from Broadway musicals, movie soundtracks, and Tin Pan Alley songwriters in Hollywood and New York. The songs were given weekly airplay on *Your Hit Parade,* a Saturday night ritual for teens. The Big Three record companies profitably disseminated these hits on ten-inch acetate records, confining themselves to conservative genres like pop, jazz, and classical. Nobody, of course, really could predict whether a new song would catch on with the volatile teen market, so the Big Three played it safe by sticking to records by established white artists.

The wartime "faithful forever" ballads duly gave way to a more cosmopolitan mix of foreign and ethnic songs (reflecting the global scope of the war's battlefields) as well as clinging ballads like "To Each His Own." Abel Green, an editor at the showbiz weekly *Variety,* identified two trends in postwar pop: nostalgia, which reflected a search for emotional security amid the anxieties of the après-guerre world; and ethnic and folk numbers, which also offered a sense of security. As Green and coauthor Joe Laurie Jr. write in *From Vaude to Video:*

> If the threat of Communism the world over was distressing all hemispheres, at least in their native habitat the Americans seemed to yearn for the simple and romantic. . . . From a dispersed people [Jews] America borrowed and accepted "Tzena, Tzena"; from Huddie Ledbetter ("Leadbelly"), with an assist by musicologist John Lomax, they borrowed "Goodnight, Irene." From Italian and Germanic paraphrases came "There's No Tomorrow," "Forever and Ever" and "You're Breaking My Heart." . . . The British, too, contributed their quota of international hits with "Galway Bay, "Cruising Down the River," "Hop Scotch Polka," and "Now Is the Hour." Love songs set to melodies by classical composers like Tchaikowsky, Chopin and Grieg

were already a staple and Perry Como's big hit of 1945 was "Till the End of Time," set to a Chopin melody. A current joke told about a refugee whose first impression of America was that "the people here are all so classical-minded—they whistle the masters and sing and dance to fine old melodies."

But this heavy borrowing from the classics was a warning that Tin Pan Alley standard composers had no infectious beat for the restless young postwar audiences, who were becoming the chief record buyers, and little idea where their craft was headed. (The Broadway musical comedy writers like Rodgers and Hammerstein were an exception, placing some romantic songs on *Hit Parade* when recorded by popular artists.) What was lacking on the *Hit Parade* lineups was an authentic and fresh American voice generating the contagious energy that would vibrate in tune with prosperous postwar teens, becoming a subculture and a lucrative market. Its beginnings could be discerned in the fringe genres: Race, R&B, country, blues, even calypso.

Other popular arts had their own postwar reconversion problems. In the comics pages, as a historian Maurice Horn writes, the artists who emphasized humor discovered that "after a conflict that had cost 30 million human lives," it was hard to be funny. And the authors of adventure strips learned the hard way that their characters' outsize exploits seemed "contemptible, futile, and almost unseemly."

The rise of 25-cent paperback books was boosted by their pre-sold appeal to veterans who had read their favorite titles in Armed Forces Editions. The motion picture industry underwent similar soul-searching, as studio bosses tried to figure out what peacetime audiences would buy tickets for after a heavy war diet of combat, love stories, and escapist musicals.

POSTWAR UNCERTAINTY FUELED anxieties about another depression. GM, which had lost $2 billion in war contracts literally overnight, handed pink slips to 140,000 United Auto Workers union members, leaving 180,000 survivors. Labor economists predicted a $35 billion drop in total wages because of slashes in military spending. In September 1945 the *New York Times* reported that workers were close to rebellion in the Detroit

auto plants. A Gallup poll showed that 62 percent of the public feared a serious depression in the next ten years.

The economic barometers oscillated between inflation and deflation.
Wall Street was nervous, and its anxiety spread to the more conservative
Midwest, as revealed by this report from Chicago: "The business community here is considerably more optimistic about the economic future than
the financial experts in New York and the economists in Washington. But
business is beginning to be frightened in this area also, especially in the
large cities."

Professional economists issued downbeat forecasts of postwar unemployment running as high as 17 million. The economist Leo Cherne, later
a prominent conservative anti-Communist, predicted that unemployed
GIs would grow bitter and turn violent: "Occasionally you will see them
in strikes and riots. . . . The newly set up employment offices, particularly
at first, will grind slowly. . . . An occasional soldier will be found on a street
corner selling a Welcome Home sign. Others will start house-to-house
canvassing in their uniforms." Dire fears were packed into this headline
deck in the *New York Times* of August 20, 1943:

POST-WAR IDLE MAY BE 12,000,000
Labor Statistics Bureau Warns That Country Must Tackle the Problem at
Once Or Face Another War; Rapid Reconversion of Industry and Public
Works Among Proposed Remedies

The War Manpower Commission reported that 2.1 million defense
plant jobs had vanished as of August 31, 1945. Military spending plunged
from 42 percent of GNP in 1944 to just 4 percent in 1948. The armed forces
shrank from 12 million to 1.46 million over the same period. Secretary of
Commerce Henry Wallace, who had called for 60 million jobs after the
war, predicted that national income would fall by $20 billion by the spring
of 1946, which could mean 7–8 million unemployed. A 1946 Gallup poll
reported that 42 percent of respondents believed the state of the economy
to be the most significant problem confronting America. The gloomy economic forecasts, plus a determination to preserve the popular New Deal

safety net, influenced President Truman's decision to place a ceiling of $15 billion on the defense budget (later lowered to $12.5 billion) and bolster social welfare spending.

There were a few stubborn optimists like Fred M. Vinson, director of the Office of War Mobilization and Reconversion (OWMR), who forecast a peacetime world in which Americans would be "in the pleasant predicament of having to live 50 percent better than they have ever lived before." His postwar successor, Missouri banker and Truman crony John Snyder, however, conjured up a vision of 18 million people laid off from war plants and discharged from the armed forces scrambling for jobs, and 8 million not finding them.

The Pollyannas came closer to the truth than the Cassandras. Hoarded wartime business profits, war workers' savings, and pent-up demand fueled the boom that lifted off in 1947. Added to the mix were the bullish demographics—the spike in marriages and birth rates as GIs came home and set up households and had children. Government aid to businesses for reconversion, built into war contracts, helped provide the capital needed for retooling and expansion. Consumer demand for durable goods, from autos to washing machines, built up steam.

As production heated up to meet the growing demand, more civilian jobs opened up; average family incomes rose from $4,300 a year in 1945 to $6,000 by the early 1950s. The nation, though unaware of it, was embarking on nearly two decades of vigorous growth and higher wages, led by unionized industries. GNP increased at an average of 3.8 percent annually from 1946 to 1973; unemployment during those years hovered just below 4 percent; median household income grew by 55 percent, according to Census Bureau figures.

Still, the loss of war jobs had an immediate and visible impact on the economy. This was dramatically evident in Detroit when Ford shuttered its mammoth Willow Run bomber assembly plant, wiping out 20,000 jobs. For a time it looked like the world's largest bomber plant, built at a cost of $95 million, would become a white elephant. UAW vice president Walter Reuther called for the government to establish a TVA-like agency to take over the plant and make railroad cars or prefabricated housing.

Then, New Deal favorite Henry Kaiser, the prodigious fabricator of merchant ships in wartime, sprang to the rescue. He and his partner, Joseph Fraser, who had been head of Willys-Overland when it developed the Jeep (the most popular product of the war on four wheels), took over the plant to make cheap, all-aluminum "people's cars."

An added factor in the boom was the agility of the war industries in switching back to making and selling civilian goods. The New Deal economist Robert Nathan recalled being amazed at how fast the auto industry—which, along with housing and appliances, was a major engine of economic growth—actually brought this off. "After the demobilization," he said, "and war contracts were cut off, my God, the . . . industry was putting cars out in three or four months, not nine to twelve months. The ingenuity and the managerial capabilities of American industry really did a hell of a job of reconversion. It was much faster than expected. Unemployment got up around 4 million, as I recall, but nothing like 8 [that was predicted]."

Actually, joblessness in 1946 averaged roughly 2.5 million men and women per month; the unemployment rate for the year averaged 3.9 percent—far better than the 10 percent of the last pre-war year. In New York City, unemployment compensation claims leveled off at 240,000, compared with 635,000 in 1940. Nationwide the postwar peak was 2.7 million jobless; within a year's time more than half of those had found jobs.

Unemployment was low in part because fewer people were looking for work. Millions of married women departed the labor force to become housewives again, and weren't counted among the ranks of the jobless. About half of the 14 million veterans reentering civilian life would go to college or trade school on the GI Bill, removing themselves from the labor force.

Until civilian production got back up to speed, annoying shortages of consumer goods broke out like rashes. With too many dollars chasing too few goods, capital and labor fought about whether wartime wage, price, and material controls should be retained. The big corporations, small-business owners, middle-class professionals, white-collar workers—most of whom were traditionally Republican, even though they had voted for

FDR during hard times—favored doing away with controls. But polls also showed a majority of Americans fearing galloping inflation if controls were lifted.

It was mainly the largest organized economic interest groups that sought the end of controls. The National Association of Manufacturers, Big Business's lobbying arm, agitated for abolishing the Office of Price Administration (OPA), labeling price controls "regimented chaos." The NAM's efforts in 1946 were chronicled by its vice president in charge of public relations, Holcombe Parkes, in an address to a conclave of ad people in the spring of 1946. Parkes reported that 85 percent of the public had favored continuing price controls after the war. But an effective NAM advertising campaign reversed that support. Eight months later, asserted Parkes, only 26 percent of the public favored price controls. The PR blitz had included ads in 327 newspapers, twenty-six broadcasts on the NAM network radio show, sixty-two press releases, booklets and periodicals, and speeches by community leaders "by the hundred."

Whether the NAM alone slew the OPA dragon is debatable, but the well-funded group raised a loud voice against controls, as did other business lobbies, like the US Chamber of Commerce and trade associations. Farmer groups like the Farm Bureau, the National Grange, even the liberal Farmers Union—all weighed in against controls as well.

The OPA's chief, Chester Bowles, a former advertising executive, understood the NAM's campaign. When the OPA law came up before Congress for renewal, he adopted his own scare tactics, prophesying that the nation would embark on "an inflationary joy-ride—a joy-ride that will eventually result in the same wave of unemployment—the same epidemic of bankruptcies and foreclosures—that swept this country in 1920—and again in 1929."

A host of squealing piggies went to market (Congress) for relief from price controls. Truman was shocked by the spectacle of postwar greed unleashed; "The Congress are balking, labor has gone crazy and management isn't far from insane in selfishness," he wrote his mother back in Independence, Missouri. He believed in lifting controls gradually. Truman had come out of the war admiring the way the American people sacrificed

and pulled together in a communal spirit in line with the New Deal ethos.
Now he sensed a different spirit in the air: everyone for himself, greed in
the saddle. Those who could afford it bought rationed items on the black
market, while the great majority went without tires, steaks, and nylons.
As the historian James Boylan observed:

> The affluent went on a spree, spending freely for such available luxuries
> as liquor and restaurant meals. Many turned to the black market, willingly
> paying illegal prices for apartments, used cars, lumber and meat. A packing-
> house official in Chicago said the money that changed hands for meat
> alone made Al Capone's bootlegging look trivial. Although OPA initiated
> more than a thousand prosecutions a month in 1945 and 1946, the black
> market was scarcely dampened. The rampage of spending that it encour-
> aged could mean no good, either for OPA or for the majority who had
> emerged from the war with little cushion against inflation.

Several groups defended the OPA, including the Parent-Teachers Association and the League of Women Voters, which tended to be housewife-
and consumer-oriented. Its strongest champion was the labor movement,
which had a direct stake in the postwar fates of the National War Labor
Board (NWLB) and the OPA. The thing that unionists feared almost as
much as another Great Depression was runaway inflation that would
obliterate their wartime wage gains. Many progressive labor leaders favored policies that would *expand* the New Deal into a kind of social democratic America with collective bargaining conducted in the context of a
"broader labor-left agenda." That agenda would include a reinvigorated
OPA and NWLB to plan a postwar income policy that would rein in business profits through price guidelines and award a bigger slice of the pie to
workers through rising wages.

But a majority of Americans saw the OPA as another of those meddling
wartime bureaucracies, and were anxious to see the back of it. After Truman
vetoed a probusiness Republican bill that killed the OPA, Congress let it sink
into a coma. Prices shot up—sky-high by the Fourth of July. Steak nearly
doubled, butter rose 25 percent; decontrolled rents rose 1,000 percent in

some places. Big-ticket hard goods were in hot demand as production lagged because of strikes. A washing machine that cost $92 in 1942 cost $112 in 1946; electric irons zoomed from $4.35 to $8.68; refrigerators from $155 to $207.

The OPA limped along, supported by executive orders. In July 1946, Truman signed a renewal bill that Republicans could live with because it was riddled with exemptions demanded by special interests. It did, however, restore controls on meat, and in September farmers and cattlemen went on strike, withholding meat from the market rather than sell at the controlled prices. The packers ran ads predictably promising that if price controls were terminated, cheap and abundant meat would quickly follow.

An August 28 Gallup poll showed 49 percent approving the restoration of controls on meat and 43 percent opposing. A July poll found 43 percent agreed that "the former OPA was all right"; 20 percent favored the elimination of all price controls except on rents; and 23 percent supported junking the agency entirely. In October, with congressional elections looming, Democrats pleaded with the president to lift controls. DNC chair Bob Hannegan predicted a Republican sweep if controls were not dropped. And so, telling aides ruefully that he'd be damned whatever he did, Truman addressed the nation. On the morning of his speech, the Chicago *Tribune's* headline read, "3 Weeks to Go, No Meat, New Deal in Panic." Col. Bertie McCormick's paper, the voice of the conservative Midwest, let slip what was the Republican's larger target—the New Deal.

In his address to the nation, which drew a record radio audience, the president announced he was lifting controls on meat because he had no better alternative. He blamed "a reckless group of selfish men" for high prices, the same group that "has opposed every effort of this administration to raise the standard of living and increase the opportunity for the common man." He had been right in his prediction that whatever he did would win no credit with the public. His decision to remove price controls merely reinforced his image as a vacillating leader and undercut whatever legitimacy ceiling prices still had.

As Truman predicted, cattle prices climbed and "sucked livestock from grazing grounds like a vacuum," as *Newsweek* put it. Steak broke a dollar a pound, all but prohibitive for working people. By November the

Consumer Price Index had climbed to 150.7. By then, the OPA was on life support. As the conservative Washington *Times-Herald* crowed, "Even Democratic diehards admitted the New Deal concept of government was at an end . . . the planned economy of the past era is dead."

After a disastrous off-year election defeat in November 1946, Truman would abandon nearly all controls. He had become as isolated as Hemingway's old man in the sea, his presidency ripped to shreds in a special-interest feeding frenzy. Inflation accelerated. By December 1947, 48 percent of the public was calling for restoration of price controls and rationing, with 42 percent opposed.

A FRUGAL MIDWESTERNER who had known hard times firsthand, Truman was repelled by the voracious demands of businessmen, workers, and farmers. Perhaps his most sterling quality was an almost prudish honesty, which had stood him in good stead in the past, enabling him to emerge unsullied from a stint with Tom Pendergast's Kansas City machine; it had served him again in his wartime role as the chair of a committee investigating war contract corruption and profiteering. But he was not a natural politician like Roosevelt; nor did he project FDR's exuberant optimism, which had bucked up a nation through the thirties. He had the charisma of a bank teller; he spoke in the nasal drone of chronic sinusitis. Insecure (and ill-briefed) in his job, he procrastinated and wavered. Economics was his weakest subject. He had an explosive temper that stiffened his backbone in a crisis but on other occasions drove him to make rash statements that kept cooler-headed advisers in a constant state of damage control.

But in the postwar ideological wars with the GOP, he entered the lists as a longstanding New Dealer who had voted down the line for social welfare measures during his legislative career and favored extending them in the future. He remained at heart a small-business populist, antimonopoly, mistrustful of Big Labor and Big Business alike. Now he watched helplessly as interest groups overran controls like stampeding cattle. The year 1946 saw his approval rating go into free fall from that initial peak of 87 percent to 32 percent.

This lack of confidence in Truman's leadership contributed to the general sense of drift in the nation. It was as if some evil witch had transformed the prince into a toad. As John Fenton, head of the Gallup Company, whose poll tracked Truman's fall from grace, would charitably write: "It is questionable whether any Chief Executive could have stemmed the tide of reconversion resentment." Part of this mood, Gallup's polls indicated, derived from "a public disillusionment with the evaporation of their postwar dream world." This was blamed on a "collection of disenchantments": the slow pace of reconversion, rising prices, on and off (and on again) price controls, food shortages, and rising fears of the Soviet Union.

During the watershed years of 1945 and 1946—when Soviet diplomats obstructed the UN founding meeting in San Francisco and the London Council of Foreign Ministers, and Soviet atomic spy rings were uncovered— the public began to express to pollsters its growing fear of the Soviets. "The general tenor of U.S. public opinion in the years of the cold war," Fenton writes, "was set in those disappointing months in 1945 and 1946."

SOME FARSIGHTED BUSINESS LEADERS, however, saw the Soviet threat as a potential boon because it could reverse the postwar isolationism that wanted the boys brought home and defense spending slashed. In wartime, industrialists, worrying about postwar business uncertainties, had come to see that defense contracts after the war could be a cash cow. In a seminal 1944 speech to the Army Ordnance Association, Charles E. Wilson, president of GE, proposed a permanent collaboration between the Pentagon and private industry. Such cooperation, he said, should be "a continuing program and not the creature of an emergency. . . . The program must be insured and supported by the Congress in the beginning through resolution . . . later, by regularly scheduled and continuing appropriations. Industry's role in this program is to respond and cooperate. . . . Let us make this three-way [executive branch, Congress, and industry] partnership permanent and workable, not just an arrangement of momentary convenience." Wilson called for "a permanent war economy," which he justified as being in the interest of "preparedness" for future threats to US national security rather than because it would produce jobs and steady corporate profits. In that calculus, what would be called the military-industrial complex had its birth.

As defense spending began to revive in the late forties, foreshadowing the boom after the Korean War started, companies began looking to the Pentagon for injections of money, notably the aircraft industry, which practically went out of business at the war's end when military orders dried up and civilian demand for planes failed to materialize. The Pentagon, the five-sided architectural monstrosity built in September 1941 under the guidance of Army procurement chief Gen. Brehon Somervill, would become a synecdoche for the military-industrial complex and the source of lucrative contracts. According to Ruben Trevino and Robert Higgs, in the postwar years profit rates of the fifty largest defense contractors "substantially exceeded those of comparable nondefense companies."

Politicians like Texas representative Lyndon Johnson had grasped as early as the 1940 election that defense contracts could become a replacement for public works spending, which collapsed as Dr. New Deal gave way to Dr. Win the War. After VJ Day, with the rise of the rivalry with Russia, defense spending would "become as political as public works," writes New Deal historian Jordan Schwartz. Congress members would discover a new source of jobs for their districts and campaign funds for their personal war chests.

The power shift to the military and industrial alliance was foretold in 1944 when War Production Board (WPB) chief Donald Nelson resigned after attempting to put in place measures for an orderly transition to peacetime production. The big corporations hated his plan because it called for freeing small-business competitors that were no longer needed in the war effort to go back to making civilian goods. Nelson, a public-spirited executive (he had been head of Sears Roebuck), had challenged the two most powerful forces under WPB jurisdiction: large war contractors and the military. The two joined forces against him, and his authority was fatally weakened.

Nelson's successor was Julius A. Krug, who, according to a fellow New Dealer, began as a "liberal public servant" but was soon pushed into becoming "an apologist for big business." After VJ Day, Krug joined the "fast-conversion" advocates in government. From then on the voices of the moderates, those calling for selective, gradual phasing out of certain war agencies and controls, went unheard. On VJ Day there were 165 nonmilitary wartime agencies; by the end of 1946 there were none.

An example of how Krug's "fast decontrol" strategy served private interests was the housing sector. The need for shelter was desperate, especially among young working couples and veterans who were starting families. Ex–service people alone needed an estimated 2.7 million new houses. Those not in temporary housing like the Quonset huts for veterans mushrooming on college campuses were forced to crowd into overpriced rentals or double up with in-laws. Among 600 standing orders that Krug nullified was one called L-41, which awarded the highest priority in obtaining crucial building materials to companies engaged in new home construction.

A beleaguered rear guard of planning-oriented New Dealers working for the Office of Price Administration argued that L-41 should be retained to channel scarce materials into erecting houses for vets and their families rather than turning them over to the market, where they would flow to more lucrative projects like movie theaters, office buildings, and other public structures. The OPA warned that lifting controls on scarce building materials would bid up costs and put new homes out of the price range of those who most needed them.

Overcoming dug-in Republican and Southern Democratic opposition, Truman pushed through a watered-down housing act in 1950. It helped middle-class families but erected public housing projects for the poor that became dismal brick prisons.

Thomas I. Emerson, a New Deal lawyer working for the OWMR at the time of Krug's decision to drop L-41, flags this incident as "one of the first controversies between the remnants of the New Deal and the conservatives in the Truman administration." There would be many more.

Private contractors, recognizing a potential El Dorado in federally guaranteed housing loans for veterans, moved into the home-building market. The great bulk of the industry consisted of small contractors who threw up five or so units a year. Given the strong demand, new opportunities for mass production opened up. One builder who jumped in was the

New Deal's fair-haired boy, Henry J. Kaiser, the master shipbuilder who thought he could apply the same principles of mass production to this industry. In California he founded a company called Community Homes, which threw up hundreds of dwellings. But by 1950, Kaiser had decided that the decentralized housing market was too competitive for his liking. He preferred oligopolies like aluminum and steel.

Enter William Levitt, who had learned large-scale construction methods building airfields for the Navy during the war and was able to profitably adapt these techniques to large-scale home-building. In 1946 he started buying up Long Island potato fields and laying out suburban developments. For those who would populate them he designed a standardized prefabricated house with ready-made walls, which could be raised like a pioneer's barn on concrete slabs embedded on standard 60 × 100 foot lots. Swarms of semi-skilled workers performed repetitive tasks like assembly-line workers. The standard Levitt house came with a 12 × 16 foot living room, two bedrooms, one bathroom, and a kitchen located in the front of the house so moms could watch the kids playing in the front yard. The basic model sold for $7,990 (about $90,000 in 2010), nearly $3,000 more than the $5,000 at which Americans ideally priced their dream houses in a 1945 poll, showing how inflation was already outstripping victory dreams. Levitt required no down payments and promised no closing costs. He threw in a Bendix washer with the purchase price and an eight-inch TV set, which the resident paid for on the installment plan. There were other amenities, including plantings of apple and cherry trees, curved roads, swimming pools, playgrounds, and baseball fields—in short, the Great American Suburban Dream, subsidized by federally guaranteed mortgages and accessible by federally financed highways.

By 1948 Levitt's company was turning out 180 houses a week, or thirty-six a day. The first Levittown comprised 17,000 nearly identical gray-and-white Cape Cods capable of sheltering 82,000 people. In the beginning, the developments were regimented with company-trimmed lawns and maintenance, probably making veterans feel at home—just like a basic training camp. (The early Levittowns sold to veterans only.) It was forbidden to hang out one's washing on a backyard line.

Levittown is merely the most celebrated of the postwar low-density suburbs that encouraged the lemminglike desire to flee the troubled cities and expand into country air with a home of one's own. The overwhelming yen of vets (reacting against regimented service life) and others for private housing spawned tracts on former farm- or meadowland in the interstices between towns and villages. Demand was lubricated by federal programs guaranteeing mortgages like the GI Bill. Builders also received FHA and VA "production advances" to enable them to start houses. Another demographic fact: no African Americans allowed. In 1960 there were still no black residents in the Long Island Levittown. William Levitt proclaimed: "We can solve a housing problem, or we can try to solve a racial problem. But we cannot combine the two."

Of course, Levitt was going with the flow. Since the twenties suburbs had been havens for white families abandoning the cities. But after World War II, federal funding encouraged the trend. The price ranges also turned the suburbs into single-class enclaves and their denizens into long-range commuters, stimulating the auto and satellite industries but also expanding the nation's expenditure of carbon fuel.

"By the mid-1980s, three-quarters of the available housing stock of the nation had been built since 1940; of these, two-thirds were single-family detached homes," writes historian Caroll Pursell. Soaring demand for the cars to get commuters to work and back boosted auto production to new heights, reaching 7.6 million cars annually in 1963, plus 1.5 million trucks and buses. Within a decade, one in seven American workers was employed by the auto industry and its subcontractors. Freeways extruded their tentacles across California. The first one, completed just before the war, was only nineteen miles long. The freeway system grew after the state legislature authorized an additional 300 miles of roads in 1947, which were fully completed ten years later.

TRUMAN, DESPITE ASSURING HENRY WALLACE (one of the last of the New Dealers) that he was determined to carry on FDR's policies, harbored a personal hostility to the commerce secretary and the dwindling old guard, dismissing them as "professional liberals." Thus, he augmented his White House staff with his Senate aides Matthew Connelly and Gen. Harry Vaughan, and appointed Charlie Ross, a Pulitzer Prize–winning *St. Louis Post-Dispatch* reporter and high school friend, as his press secretary. Other Cabinet appointments followed, among them the Texan Tom Clark (architect of the attorney general's list of subversive organizations in 1947, which made guilt by association national security policy) to replace Francis Biddle, a strong civil libertarian, as attorney general; and Lewis Schwellenbach, a bland former senator from Washington, to succeed the veteran progressive Frances Perkins as secretary of labor. The South Carolina conservative James F. Byrnes, a wily Washington operator, became secretary of state, and John Snyder ended up running the Treasury. After the purge, only two New Dealers, Wallace and Interior Secretary Harold Ickes, sat in the Cabinet.

Snyder brought to the job the vision of a Midwestern small-town banker, but his friendship with Truman—they were both Missourians and poker-playing buddies, and their daughters were chums—made him a loyal servant. Robert Nathan, who worked in the OWMR, observed, "I've often said that if Truman had said to John Snyder, 'Look, John, if you don't jump off the Washington Monument we're in real trouble,' John Snyder would have jumped off the Washington Monument. He was a very loyal person but there wasn't the depth of conception, the grasp, not just theoretical understanding but policy aspects."

Rifts soon opened up between Snyder and the New Deal faction in the OWMR, who accused Snyder of subverting the office's mission. Thomas Emerson writes, "OWMR's mandated function was to deal with reconversion, and the underlying problem of reconversion was whether the economy could operate on a peacetime basis at as high or nearly as high a level as it had operated during the war." He recalled, "Whenever an issue arose in which one of the Roosevelt supporters took a view different from Snyder's the Snyder group would prevail and the other fellow would be fired."

Snyder's influence on Truman was mainly personal; the president followed his advice on hiring, in particular, which gave the administration team a more conservative face. For example, Snyder disliked ex-OPA chief

Chester Bowles, another New Dealer who in his postwar job as head of the Office of Economic Stabilization fought for continuance of price controls and other policies aimed at protecting the consumer. The office had been expanded in February 1946 to accommodate Bowles's clout as a wealthy advertising man, but Snyder undercut him with the president, leaving him, in a journalist's description, like a man who had parachuted into hostile territory "and was trying to defend a small clearing against the enemy."

The New Deal's last stands were sometimes made in the lonely trenches of postwar agencies like the OWMR. Often the reconversion issues boiled down to the fundamental argument about government's role in the economy. By the late forties, probusiness (meaning antiregulation) conservatives in government were becoming more assertive. In Washington the ideological fault lines broke several ways: regular Democrats vs. "Republocrats" (Southern Democrats and GOP conservatives); liberals and labor unions vs. small-government, probusiness conservatives; liberal Democrats and New Dealers vs. party regulars.

Worsening the plight of the left Democrats in government, conservatives were obsessed with rolling back the New Deal. They demanded an immediate return to the lost Shangri-La of free enterprise, meaning the twenties-style laissez-faire under Coolidge and Hoover, if not earlier. Their main weapon was propaganda bankrolled by large corporations and channeled through organizations like the American Enterprise Association (AEA), which was set up in 1943 by Lewis H. Brown, president of the Johns Manville roofing company. He had become exercised by what he regarded as the New Deal's slanders of the business community and wanted to restore its good name. For this task he hired bright young conservative intellectuals to grind out scholarly papers defending free enterprise, which he distributed to corporate leaders and members of Congress. On the other side of the fence, the Committee for Economic Development, a think tank for liberal businesspeople, was cranking out papers on the latest Keynesian thinking about full employment, social insurance, and labor relations.

AEA attracted big money from conservative corporations, which imperiled its tax-exempt status. In 1952 a GE executive, Alan Marshall, took over and hired a policy intellectual named William J. Baroody to run it. Baroody transformed AEA from a probusiness lobby into a scholarly probusiness think tank, well endowed by the DuPont brothers and other industrialists who yearned for another Gilded Age.[*]

The ideology powering these probusiness think tanks was that articulated by an Austrian economist named Friedrich Hayek. He and his Viennese mentor, Ludwig von Mises, who had immigrated to America before the war (Hayek arrived after it via England), produced twin "bibles" of the movement—Mises's more ponderous *Socialism* (1938) and Hayek's more accessible *The Road to Serfdom* (1946). Hayek's tome was a paean to the free market, which he regarded as the fount of human liberty. In prose darkened by his lingering trauma over the failure of the Western democracies to halt the rise of the Nazis, Hayek looked ahead to the postwar world and warned that socialism led straight to totalitarian Communism like that grinding down the Soviet people. Hayek claimed that National Socialism had been the end product of European social democracy; Communism was the same. Only free enterprise unbound could guarantee economic and political liberty.

The Road to Serfdom appeared in Britain in 1944 and was published obscurely in the United States that same year by the University of Chicago Press. The tome immediately picked up endorsements from Henry Hazlitt, a prominent journalist, and other conservatives; even John Maynard Keynes, a friend of Hayek's, called it "a grand book," though he obviously disagreed with the ideas contained in it. Spearheaded by a *Reader's Digest* condensed version, which sold more than 1 million copies and was distributed by GM as a pamphlet, it reached a mainstream audience. Actually, Hayek saw merit in certain government interventions in the economy, such as the antitrust laws and the minimum wage, but the popularizations hammered home a simple message that socialism led directly to totalitarianism.[**]

---

[*] Now known as the American Enterprise Institute (AEI).
[**] See Jennifer Schuessler, "Hayek: The Back Story," *New York Times Book Review,* July 11, 2010. The author reports that the 2010 endorsement of Hayek by a radical right-wing commentator, Glenn Beck, revived the dormant title with 100,000 in fresh sales.

Hayek's book chimed with a postwar antiauthoritarian mood among intellectuals, refocused from National Socialism and Hitlerism to Communism and Stalinism, of which the Communist Party USA was now considered the American quisling. The victory of Britain's Labour Party in 1945 galvanized American business conservatives, who became eager proselytizers of the Hayek gospel. They picked up Hayek's antitotalitarian dictum as a handy political cudgel in the battle to demolish New Deal social legislation and regulatory agencies, from the Wagner Act to the TVA on up to wartime agencies like the OPA. All were considered stepping-stones to postwar socialism, way stations to the United Soviet Socialist States of America.

In fact, there was little danger of that, as New Dealer Robert Nathan later chided:

> Many people had the crazy notion in the '30s that Roosevelt and the New Deal were all socialists. Some day, you know, they'd have the government owning all enterprise. My God, the war was the exact opposite of it. If ever a president had an opportunity [to adopt socialism] if he felt like socialism was better, it was Truman, at the end of the war. He could have done almost anything, you know, to have government-built plants stay [in government hands] and take back this and do this, but [they] went right back to private owners.

But probusiness lobbying and trade groups like the US Chamber of Commerce and the National Association of Manufacturers (NAM) had set themselves a real-time three-pronged postwar agenda: lifting wartime controls, rolling back the New Deal, and halting labor's wartime gains. To achieve these ends they redoubled their lobbying efforts in Congress, where they had eager allies in the conservative bloc of Republicans and Southern Democrats. (The foreign policy corollary—rolling back Soviet Communism and expanding markets for US-manufactured goods in Europe—would appear on the agenda in due course.)

Painting with a scarlet brush the causes of labor and social reform was another reliable method employed by the NAM and other business and management lobbies. As Kim Phillips-Fein writes in her book *Invisible Hands,* "The free market conservatives took the nightmarish fears inspired by anticommunism and turned them against the entire liberal state, making it seem as though the minimum wage and labor unions were about to usher in a new era of political enslavement."

By 1946 a tectonic conservative shift was under way in the country. To a significant number of Americans the term "New Dealer" now denoted a breed of remote, arrogant Washington bureaucrats who quoted Freud instead of the Bible. It was an easy step to dubbing them "socialists" (read: Communists). Historian Eric Goldman writes, "The joining of New Dealism and Communism in a troubled American mind was easy, almost axiomatic. Was it not the New Dealers, like the Communists, who talked of uplifting the masses, fighting the businessmen, establishing economic controls over society, questioning the traditional in every part of living?"

In October 1946, in the aftermath of the great labor revolt (discussed in Chapter Five), the Chamber of Commerce raised the issue of domestic Communism on behalf of the mainstream business community. The Chamber's Committee on Socialism and Communism, chaired by Francis P. Matthews—an Omaha lawyer and Democratic Party stalwart whom Truman would appoint as secretary of the Navy in 1950—issued a forty-page report: "Communist Infiltration in the United States: Its Nature and How to Combat It." This document, while admitting that the actual number of hard-core reds was comparatively small, nevertheless cried that their influence was frighteningly large. The party and its "fellow travelers" had "real success in forcing upon us a program contrary to the ideals of our nation." Examples, according to the committee, included State Department policies "forcing a harsh peace on Germany," opposing the fascist regime of Gen. Juan Perón in Argentina, and allowing the Soviets to take over Japanese-occupied Manchuria at the end of World War II. The report also condemned the Communist Party USA for infiltrating and traducing gullible unions.

Although the nation should adhere to its cherished ideal of freedom of speech, constitutional protections were never intended to authorize "sedition and treason," the document piously observed, thus injecting into the political discourse epithets that would remain loosely defined and poisonously emotive. The report recommended educational campaigns debunking Communist propaganda and called on the government to require the CP ("an agent of a foreign power") to reveal its membership, donors, and activities. Federal and state governments should be purged of party members and employees sympathetic to Communism through "a stringent but fair loyalty test." In its way, the report was a watershed, the first postwar call by a powerful business lobby to investigate Communist influences in and out of government; its recommendations would be reflected in a bill introduced in 1948 by Representatives Karl Mundt and Richard Nixon.

The Chamber's views were predictable but potent, for it spoke for wealthy American corporations like General Mills, Monsanto, General Motors, First National Bank of Chicago, and others. It summoned the business community to ally itself politically (and financially, of course) with the cause of anti-Communism as a means of obliterating the lingering New Deal. Its demand for exposure of red influences on American life and ousting Communists and fellow travelers in government gave impetus to the House Un-American Affairs Committee's investigation of Hollywood (see Chapter 6) and helped provoke Truman's executive order the following year commanding the discharge of federal employees whom security vetting had discovered to be "disloyal."

Of course, the Chamber wasn't the only group sounding off. GOP politicians had wielded the red brush in the 1944 election and would do so with an even heavier hand in the 1946 midterms. Dedicated anti-Communist groups were active, including the American Legion's Americanism Committee, which claimed to speak for some 3 million vets; the Hearst papers and their stable of right-wing columnists, like Westbrook Pegler and George Sokolsky; the rabidly isolationist, anti–New Deal *Chicago Tribune;* Southern segregationists; *Reader's Digest;* the America Federation of Labor; the Daughters of the American Revolution; the Catholic Church; Socialists; Trotskyists; lapsed Communists; and beyond-the-fringe rightist groups and liberal theologians. A galaxy of professional anti-Communists—like J.B. Matthews, Benjamin Mandel, Louis Budenz, and others—devoted their well-paid time to firing a barrage of wild charges at individuals and groups with leftist affiliations in their past. According to Ellen Schrecker, who traces the rise of the anti-Communist ideology in her book *Many Are the Crimes,* HUAC and the FBI started using such organizations as confidential informants in 1947.

Even the comics pages joined the counterrevolution. Harold Gray, who drew the daily strip *Little Orphan Annie,* led the way. Gray had been outspokenly anti–New Deal through the thirties. His benevolent capitalist Oliver J. "Daddy" Warbucks, the plucky little redhead's protector, espoused a doctrine of laissez-faire, individualism, success, and opposition to social welfare programs. In 1944 Gray threw in the towel and killed off Warbucks, saying the New Deal had broken even his stout heart. But in 1945 he resurrected Daddy. Asked by readers why he had wrought this miracle, Gray said, "The situation changed last April . . . Roosevelt died then."

Speaking for the American Legion in August 1948, national commander James F. O'Neill instructed Americans on how to fight the internal menace. "Moscow's strategy to sell its 'revolutionary products'" was to "disguise, deodorize and attractively package" them. The "salesmen and peddlers" of red terror were passed off as "twentieth-century Americans," "defenders of all civil liberties," "honest trade unionists," and "liberals and defenders of world peace." Such duplicity was all a "swindle and a con game," but the American Legion members could perform their patriotic duty by contacting "experts" in their communities—former FBI men and Army and Navy intelligence agents—who would be happy to help rid their towns of the plague. Drawing on fresh memories of wartime spy scares, he warned, "Never forget the fact that Communists operating in our midst are in effect a secret battalion of spies and saboteurs parachuted by a foreign foe inside our lines at night and operating as American citizens under a variety of disguises just as the Nazis did in Belgium and Holland."

Perhaps the official kickoff of postwar anti-Communism began when FBI director J. Edgar Hoover rasped out his influential testimony before HUAC on March 26, 1947. In it he advanced the Bureau's real goal, which was for the Justice Department to put the CP out of business by prosecut-

ing its leaders under the Smith Act. This statute banned teaching or advocating the violent overthrow of the US government. He also demanded
the exposure of Communists who had infiltrated the federal government,
the motion picture industry, and labor unions, encouraging the national
inquisition that would soon follow.

Since its creation in 1938, HUAC, under the clownish Martin Dies, had
kept the issue of reds in government and the union movement simmer-
ing. A conservative Texas Democrat, Dies became a nagging voice in the
campaign to discredit the New Deal by claiming that the Roosevelt administration was riddled with Communists and their sympathizers. His
headline-grabbing charges won him solid support among Republocrats,
and though he lost his seat in 1944, his committee was made a permanent
body of Congress in 1945, with ample funding and a staff of investigators.
The Dies Committee clandestinely exchanged information with the FBI and
publicized the Bureau's findings, unattributed, in its own hearings. With help
from HUAC, the Senate's internal security subcommittee, and congressional
conservatives, Hoover's well-funded FBI led the anti-Communism crusade
after the war.

The Chamber of Commerce went on to issue five ever-more-frightening
reports on the menace of domestic Communism. In January 1947, it called
on the Justice Department to publish a semiannual list of Communist-
controlled front organizations and labor unions. Later that same year Attorney General Tom Clark made public his heretofore secret list of "subversive"
organizations in America. Also in 1947, as a postscript to the great strikes
of 1946, the Chamber issued a report intended to expose the Communist
influence on the labor movement. This report included a recommendation
that Congress amend the Wagner Act to help employers stamp out the
Communist leadership of certain unions. That wish came true by way of
the Taft-Hartley Act, passed in June 1947, which required union officials
to state under oath that they were not members of the CPUSA. In 1948
the Chamber called for barring Communists from serving as teachers, li-
brarians, social workers, and book reviewers.

Soon the Chamber was demanding that all "pro-Communists" (unde-
fined but presumably obvious to the self-appointed authorities) be banned

from radio (presaging the corporate blacklists later in the decade) and that mildly liberal Social Gospel ministers be expelled from their pulpits.

Public opinion polls attested that big business's propaganda drive was effective. Its public image, which had fallen into ill repute in the thirties, had greatly improved. This was first the result of the war, which revived corporate America's economic and political fortunes. "The central role of business during the war," economic historian Harold Vatter writes, "terminated both the public disillusionment with business attendant upon the Great Depression experience, and the labor orientation of government under the New Deal."

As the public perceived it, corporate America had rolled up its sleeves and "got the job done." Big Business, through its well-funded publicists, claimed the credit for a munitions-production miracle. Early in the war the president of the Advertising Federation of America came up with what he deemed to be an appropriate name for World War II: "The War That Business Helped to Win." Cultivate the image of being a patriotic citizen, the ad man advised business executives, and you will collect postwar political dividends. It was highly important to impress the "common man" and his wife so that they, "and their boy home from the wars, will register that [probusiness] verdict at the ballot box." What, after all, could be better PR than helping to win a war?

One obscure yet telling measure of corporate America's image-buffing was the growing opposition to socialism. In 1942 the American public had evinced a surprising sympathy with it. To be sure, 40 percent were opposed to the concept of government ownership; but a significant 25 percent said they supported it, and another 35 percent said they had an open mind on the subject. Perhaps the conservatives were right: the New Deal had at least made Americans more sympathetic to the idea of state capitalism, industrial policy, and government intervention in the economy.

After the war, in the wake of developments traced above, that liberal 60 percent who were disposed to support or at least consider socialism had melted away to a puny 15 percent who said they favored moving "in the direction of socialism"; 65 percent, however, strongly insisted on moving the opposite way.

The upshot was that not long after Roosevelt's death, the anti–New Deal tide started rolling in. First, the Seventy-ninth Congress reversed sixteen consecutive years of higher taxes with a record cut of $5.9 billion. This was done in disregard of a predicted deficit of $30 billion for fiscal 1946. Individual taxpayers received $2.7 billion in concessions on their 1946 earnings, and businesses got $3.2 billion. Although the Revenue Act of 1945 dropped from the tax rolls 12 million low-income Americans who had been added during wartime, business clocked in as the big winner; its trophy was repeal of the excess profits tax, a wartime measure that docked 85 percent of corporate profits above a peacetime norm.

Later that same year, President Truman sent down his first legislative agenda. The unprecedented 16,000-word message enumerated a twenty-one point neo–New Deal agenda for Congress. Among the standouts were an increase in the federal minimum wage, a full employment bill, a permanent Fair Employment Practices Commission (FEPC), public housing programs, public works spending, and expansion of Social Security to cover more seniors and, most significant, provide them medical insurance. Agricultural measures included crop insurance, a school lunch program, and forest conservation. There were also a housing bill; a national science foundation, which would finance cutting-edge research; a TVA-style program for the St. Lawrence Valley; highway construction money; and appropriations for the United Nations Relief and Rehabilitation Agency, which was feeding the starving refugees in Europe.

This visionary program, Thomas Emerson states, "was designed to continue the New Deal." He and the others of the New Deal remnant at OWMR had helped draft the essential twenty-one points. This group also mapped out a strategy for passage by which each affected federal agency would lobby with key Congress members for its piece of the pie. Emerson also called for working through the Democratic National Committee to stimulate public awareness of the program—something not normally done.

That was only the first step. Then Sam Rosenman, FDR's speechwriter who had become Truman's, had to fight for inclusion of all the points, meeting strong opposition from Snyder and several other conservatives in Truman's inner circle.

In the event, Emerson relates, "The 21-point program was a complete failure." He attributes this setback to a change in the public mood. There was little popular support now for progressive programs. Such support, he decided, "is really 'crisis thinking,' without necessarily any awareness of the forces loose in the world, or even in the nature of the problems." In other words, people approved the New Deal when they feared hard times; but when happy days were back, well, let the good times roll! The liberal columnist I.F. Stone hit more or less the same note, writing in *The Nation* that the program was New Deal for the sake of New Deal: "Without an economic crisis and the public awakening it brings, little of this program can be enacted."

Judge Rosenman, however, was much more sanguine about it, perhaps because of his bruises from the fight just to keep the program in Truman's speech. He believed that Truman's decision to include it was momentous in itself—a victory for the pro–New Deal faction. He later told an interviewer:

> Personally, I think that the most important thing that I did for President Truman, and perhaps through him for the country itself, was to fight without let-up for that twenty-one point message. Although I believe that it really conformed with the President's general policy, and was wholly consistent with his prior senatorial voting record, it committed him publicly to the philosophy of the Fair Deal or its synonym, the New Deal. Carrying out that message to the extent he did was a great thing for him as well as for the United States.

As we shall see, Truman would campaign for reelection in 1948 on the program, which, as the presidential scholar Alonzo Hanby sums up, "laid out the agenda for the extension of the New Deal. His advocacy of national health insurance, federal aid to education, and, above all, civil rights largely defined the unfinished business of the Democratic Party and American liberalism for the next decade and a half."

Prominent on the Democratic Party's to-do list was government-financed health insurance later absorbed into a revised Wagner-Murray-Dingell bill, which the American Medical Association bludgeoned as a "monstrosity of Bolshevik Bureaucracy." AMA propaganda quoted Vladimir Lenin to the effect that "Socialized medicine is the keystone to the arch of the Socialist State." By calling for renewal of the FEPC, Truman also kept civil rights on the national agenda. All for naught: the door would clang shut on future New Deal measures in 1950 because of a different kind of crisis: the Korean War.

The full employment bill, which had been introduced separately but incorporated into Truman's package, did survive in a toothless version. In its original draft, the bill guaranteed every willing citizen's right to a remunerative job. This would be achieved by Keynesian stimulus spending: "To the extent that continuing full employment cannot otherwise be achieved, [the federal government should] provide such volume of Federal investment and expenditure as may be needed to assure continuing full employment."

As the historian James Boylan comments, "the bill offered clues to the liberal view of postwar society—an anti-business outlook in which prosperity would be counted in jobs, rather than profits, and in which free enterprise would not be left free to cause disruptive economic fluctuations." Such thinking, of course, was anathema to the high-riding business lobby.

Excised from the final version was the acknowledgment that the government had a *responsibility* to create jobs. The New Deal concern for the general welfare through public works projects, highways, dams, and the like remained in the toolkit, but Congress was expected to wield them on its own volition.

The defeat, Emerson writes, "was devastating to the morale of the New Deal element in the agencies. It indicated that the possibility of progressive action on the part of the government was ended for the indefinite future." The exodus of the old New Dealers accelerated. Emerson hung on at the OWMR through June 1946, when (as it happened) Snyder left the office to become Treasury secretary. Emerson resigned to teach at Yale Law School, and planned to devote his thinking to civil liberties issues and constitutional problems arising out of the relations between the individual citizen and the state, a field in which he would become a leading authority.

He thus recapitulated the postwar trend from economic-reform liberalism to civil rights–based liberalism.

And so the last measure of FDR's New Deal legacy would be the Servicemen's Readjustment Act of 1944, which would be expanded and popularly known as the GI Bill. Although the measure had a mixed parentage, its New Deal genes were dominant.

As Charles Bolte writes, the programs of the GI Bill, supplemented by others, were accepted as being in accord with "the beliefs of the generation which had grown up under the New Deal." Bolte was one of the founders of the American Veterans Committee, which represented World War II veterans with liberal views who regarded the American Legion as a reactionary group run by old World War I vets. This younger generation of soldiers was different, writes Dixon Wecter in a 1944 book on the coming veterans problem:

> Giving each soldier sixty dollars and a ticket home, in the manner of 1919 will no longer satisfy broader ideas of social responsibility which have sprung with the New Deal, under which most of these young soldiers grew up, which even conservatives now accept as part of the nation's structure. . . . For the first time we have a widespread fabric of social security, respecting unemployment and old age, in which the rank and file of the citizens participate. . . . The worst flaws in the preferential treatment of veterans qua veterans [will] thus be ended, by making social security the right of all and by grounding it upon the premium principle rather than the handout.

Roosevelt, who had opposed bonuses and special benefits for veterans, nevertheless believed in laying the foundation for a postwar economy unmarred by rampant unemployment, inflation, slumping farm prices, and feverish speculation like that in the twenties. His Economic Bill of Rights was supposed to foster a healthy postwar economy with jobs for returning vets. However, he was well aware that the conservative Congress elected in 1942 would never pass it. So he turned to a New Deal–inflected program for veterans. As FDR biographer James Mac-

Gregor Burns writes, "It was clear even with the anti-New Deal Congress of 1943, that many a progressive proposal that had failed in the face of the conservative coalition could muster support as a war or a veterans measure. Such was the case with the 'GI Bill of Rights.'" Because of fears of postwar unemployment, many Congress members feared another veterans' march on Washington—like the Bonus March of the early thirties, only much bigger and angrier.

According to Roosevelt's chief speechwriter, Judge Samuel Rosenman, the president did not believe that the government should pay bonuses to veterans as recompense for their giving the military the best years of their lives. Recalling the shabby treatment of the "Brother, Can You Spare a Dime?" World War I veterans, Roosevelt insisted that bonuses and handouts wouldn't do. In the thirties he had vetoed a bill to help ex-soldiers get early payments, saying, "The veteran who suffers from this depression can best be aided by the rehabilitation of the country as a whole." Similarly, he saw the postwar veterans problem as a matter of economic stimulation to bolster the peacetime economy.

Besides, Roosevelt said, bonuses couldn't begin to compensate these men and women for the lost years, when they might have gone to school or advanced in their jobs. What would most benefit these men and women vets would be the opportunity to make up for that lost time. The best way to provide this, he held, was to offer them education and job training.

Rosenman recalled that FDR became convinced of the need to step up federal aid to public education while traveling to his therapeutic retreat in Warm Springs, Georgia, where he observed the dilapidated state of schools in the South. He had seen for himself that children in the poorer areas were disadvantaged because their state or county could not afford good schools. He wanted to moderate these inequities by offering federal aid to education in the low-income states; but his ideas, like many New Deal measures, ran afoul of states' rights sentiments in the South, a smokescreen for the fear that equal education for blacks would undermine segregation.

On the assumption that even the most vehement states' rights politicians would not have a problem with helping veterans, Roosevelt decided to use educational assistance to them as a "kind of entering wedge," as Rosen-man called it, for broader federal aid to education. After the military draft was expanded to include eighteen- and nineteen-year-olds, in November 1942, a special committee appointed by Roosevelt to look into postwar benefits added a new priority to the Servicemen's Readjustment Act of 1944—education, on the theory that these younger GIs, who had not en-tered the labor force or started college, were owed vocational training or higher education in compensation.

The bill's educational benefits would become its most widely lauded feature. The benefits were fairly limited in the original bill, however, which had been drawn up by the American Legion. The Legion, the most powerful veterans lobby, had been loudly demanding improved care fa-cilities for wounded returnees, which were scandalously bad. It moved on to drawing up and backing the Servicemen's Readjustment Act. Congres-sional Republicans, eager to score points with the ex-soldier vote after the war, fully supported the Legion's bill. But their traditional opposition to welfare spending in general and to the New Deal in particular constrained them. And so when the drafters of the GI Bill enlisted New Deal agencies like the Labor Department and the Education Department to administer the program, GOP legislators sensed that Roosevelt the fox was working his sly tricks. Senator Bennett Clark claimed he had "never seen the veter-ans organizations of the United States so much wrought up" as they were about "the proposal to take the simple matter of veterans' rehabilitation and pitchfork it into a general scheme of social rehabilitation affecting all of the people of the United States."

Allied with the anti–New Deal Republicans were conservative South-ern Democrats, whose loudest voice on veterans issues was that of the fascist, racist anti-Semite John Rankin of Mississippi, who occupied the cat-bird seat as chair of the House Veterans Affairs Committee. Rankin made it clear in advance that he was damned if he would allow the same unem-ployment benefits to go to Mississippi blacks as were received by white vets. Better that neither group be corrupted by the dole. In the end he was narrowly outvoted by fellow members of the House-Senate conference committee drawing up the final bill.

Rankin was expressing the South's traditional hostility to New Deal measures like welfare, unemployment compensation, and Social Security, because they might empower blacks and poor whites, the traditional source of cheap and contented labor in the Southern mills. Also, Southern politicians claimed (with some reason) that the GI Bill's aid to colleges and universities would give the federal government increased leverage with state and local governments to promote racial integration.

The 1944 GI Bill soon proved inadequate, particularly in the area of loans and educational benefits, which targeted too few veterans for too short a time and provided too little financial aid. As a result of these short-comings, surveys in 1945 showed only a few returning vets enrolling.

And so New Dealers in Congress expanded the educational benefits in Title II to include *all* honorably discharged veterans with at least six months of service.[*] It also gave them four years to start their training and seven to nine years to finish, and raised tuition aid and living stipends from $75 to $90 per year for student vets with families. The revised law also boosted business and home loan guarantees and unemployment aid. But the important changes were in Title II.

All along, the bill had received the loud backing of the Legion's pow-erful lobbying operation in alliance with the high-volume Hearst press. But the New Dealers' contribution transformed a popular piece of special-interest legislation into something more—an "opportunity bill" that would potentially raise the educational and skills level of nearly one-tenth of the population.

Suddenly thousands more service members were eager to go to college or take a wide range of vocational training courses, from barbering to op-tometry to photography to ballroom dancing. That last frill was one of the inevitable mistakes that resulted from too much federal money flowing too fast, which resulted in money going to support frivolous or fraudulent programs. But those flaws were minor and in a way a testament to the virtues of farsighted beneficence. The important thing, as a presidential

---

[*] One group was discriminated against: those who had received so-called blue discharges, for homosexual "acts or tendencies."

commission later reported, was that to the extent the VA had made errors it had done so "consistently and perhaps often without justification . . . *in favor of the veteran*" (italics added). And most of those veterans paid the government back many times over in the higher taxes they paid on the higher earnings from the better jobs the GI Bill had prepared them for.

In the final months of his life, FDR devoted most of his fading energy to international problems and the looming peace. But he was too tired, too ill, too preoccupied with the war and the peace to devote any time to moving his Economic Bill of Rights through a hostile Congress.

The GI Bill was something of a legislative chameleon, a bona fide New Deal–style program that was acceptable to the American Legion, Northern Republicans, and liberal Democrats. It bolstered the prospects of a large segment of the population by giving them free education and vocational training, offered socialized medical care to the wounded and maimed, and gave federal loan guarantees to couples starting a home or individuals launching a business. By doing these things it fostered the economic well-being of the entire nation. Before the war only 6.4 percent of the labor force were college graduates; by 1970 the proportion stood at 13.8 percent. As the economy grew in those years, Americans invested their needed skills and prospered, and the relatively fewer—thus more in demand—unskilled workers prospered along with them.

It would be the nation's greatest investment in human capital in its history.

It was also the Roosevelt New Deal's last hurrah.

Voices

We kind of thought we were heroes doing a big job. When we came across a States-side magazine, all the articles were full of stories about GI's and what great guys they were. And all the advertising made us think all the cars and washing machines and electric toasters in the world were waiting for us. We got to thinking everybody at home was rooting for us and that all everything would be fine.

—WILLIAM McGIVERN, *HEAVEN RAN LAST* (1949)

There was a [period] of good feeling. The country felt it had done something worthwhile. The guys came back feeling they had accomplished something. Then they moved into a highly competitive society and immediately they had to go back to living routine lives.

—RAY WAX, STUDS TERKEL'S *THE "GOOD WAR"* (1984)

After the whole damn war, why am I scared now? I always thought peace would be peaceful.

—EX-PARATROOPER TOM RATH IN SLOAN WILSON'S *THE MAN IN THE GRAY FLANNEL SUIT* (1955)

He's stone cold dead in the market
He's stone cold dead in the market
He's stone cold dead in the market
I killed nobody but my husband

—LOUIS JORDAN AND ELLA FITZGERALD, "STONE COLD DEAD IN THE MARKET (HE HAD IT COMING)" (1946 HIT RECORD)

Momma's on the chair, Poppa's on the cot
Baby's on the floor blowin' his natural top
Sayin' Hey! Ba-Ba-Re-Bop (Hey! Ba-Ba-Re-Bop)
Ye-es, my baby knows

—LIONEL HAMPTON'S ORCHESTRA, "HEY BA-BA-RE-BOP" (NO. 1 RACE RECORD IN JUKEBOX PLAYS, 1946)

Myrna Loy coddles Frederic March on his first morning home from the war in *The Best Years of Our Lives*. *Everett Collection*

4

"HOME
STRANGE HOME"

WHEN DUANE R. "RED" JOSEPHSON came home from the war, his arrival caused hardly a ripple in Red Oak, Iowa: "Folks would say, 'Glad to see you,' and that was it," he remembered. "Things went right back to what they were." And he went right back to farming.

Harold Vest came back by train, got off at the Burlington station, walked home, knocked on the door, and announced, "I'm home." Then he went down to the square, deposited part of the $1,500 he'd saved from his Army pay in the bank, and went to a store to buy some civilian clothes. Then he called on his girlfriend and talked about getting married. Soon he went to work at the new Union Carbide plant and remained for "thirty-six years, eleven months, and nine days."

Veterans' homecomings varied widely, of course. Those arriving by ship at Pier 61 in New York City were welcomed by crowds of thousands. General Eisenhower was honored with a ticker tape parade on June 19, 1945, the largest in the city's history. More than 4 million citizens packed the parade route leading through the city to the Canyon of Heroes on lower Broadway. According to Richard Goldstein, "A General Electric noise meter calculated the roars of the crowd as the equivalent of 3,000 simultaneous peals of thunder." Police commissioner Lewis Valentine announced that this parade surpassed the delirious welcome in 1927 for Charles Lindbergh.

After months of delay, the pressure from people wanting the boys to come home goaded Congress into pressuring the War Department to speed up the discharges. The result was near anarchy. General George C. Marshall, chair of the Joint Chiefs of Staff, commented, "It was no demobilization, it was a rout." Starting in October 1945, an average of 750,000 men and women were mustered out every month; a total of 5.4 million had come home by the end of 1945. By June 1946, 12.8 million servicemen and -women had been discharged into civilian life, clutching papers and wearing a tiny lapel pin with an eagle in a circle (the "ruptured duck," intended to proclaim one's veteran status). Each one was richer by $300 in mustering-out pay (plus any winnings from the endless crap games aboard home-bound ships).

But after their arrival in the States and final processing, most returnees were on their own. No parades for them; perhaps the family had hung out a "Welcome Home George!" sign. The ex-GI cartoonist Bill Mauldin drew a picture of a homeless veteran sleeping under his sign. Transportation was often arbitrarily delayed from Europe and the Pacific, creating a large backlog; and plans changed so often that it was uncertain that a soldier, sailor, or marine would actually turn up on the announced day, while others would materialize as a complete surprise.

The 1946 movie *The Best Years of Our Lives,* a Sam Goldwyn production that was a box-office hit and won eight Academy Awards, is a self-conscious, earnest attempt to convey the truth about soldiers' release into civilian life. It relates the homecomings of three veterans, played by Frederic March, Harold Russell, and Dana Andrews. They meet on the plane on which they've hitched a ride to Boone City, their hometown. Reluctant to separate upon landing and finally break the male bonding they knew in the service, they have a few drinks together before, somewhat reluctantly, going home. March, playing a banker named Al, enters his well-appointed apartment, drops his bags at one end of the hall, and stares silently for a long moment at his surprised, teary wife, Milly, played by Myrna Loy. "I look terrible," she gasps. Thus did a modern Penelope greet her returned Odysseus. Milly spoke for many women whose plan to meet the homecoming husband dressed to the nines did not always work out.

The Best Years of Our Lives was the most credible of the wave of "veterans return" films that appeared after the war. The filmmakers tried very hard for surface veracity and social realism, while taking care to avoid raising any controversial political issues. Director William Wyler made the actors, for example, buy clothes suitable for their characters at a local department store rather than have the costume department run off new outfits. For the sake of authenticity, the character of Homer, a sailor who lost his hands in the war and uses prosthetic hooks, is played by Harold Russell, an ex-GI who'd lost his hands in a training accident. Russell was discovered by Goldwyn in a Department of the Army documentary about the rehabilitation of those who had lost limbs in the war. He won an Academy Award as best supporting actor and never made another picture (he went into veterans affairs work instead).

One strand of the film's intertwined plot lines deals with Homer's attempt to teach his fiancée, played by Cathy O'Donnell, and her family to accept his disability. He doesn't want their pity, but he does want them to understand that he's not the same man he was before the war.

Dana Andrews's character, Fred Derry, a decorated ex-bombardier, checks in to find his flashy blond wife, Marie (Virginia Mayo), is out partying with 4F friends. They reconnect, but Fred can't find work and resumes his old job as a soda jerk, only to be fired when he rebels against a promotion selling cosmetics. That displeases Marie even more, as does his refusal to wear his captain's uniform when they go out. He quickly finds out she'd been having an affair with a home-front profiteer. Rather than denying it, she taunts him about it, and their pre-war quickie marriage collapses. Helpfully informing him that "the war's over, soldier," Marie walks out.

Fred's back story dramatizes another aspect of service life: he's a poor boy who rose in the merit-based armed forces to the officer class. But once he returns to civilian life, he drops back into the lower class, to the displeasure of his mercenary wife. She insists that he cling to his higher military status by wearing his uniform to social functions, while he is trying to adjust to his comedown in life.

Al the banker, on the other hand, made sergeant during his GI career and was probably a good NCO, bonding with his buddies in combat—in contrast to his elevated small-town status as a banker. Back home, how-ever, he has his own readjustment problems, less to do with status than with his home life and his old job. He shows his high anxiety by drinking too much when he's alone with his wife. He is unhappy on the job because the bank is reluctant to extend small-business loans under the GI Bill to vets without collateral (a real-life issue, but the criticism of bankers would be taken as Communist propaganda by congressional red hunters a year or so later). The realities of civilian life are clashing with the nostalgic memories that kept him going in the Army. "I had a dream," he tells Milly. "I dreamt I was home. I've had that same dream hundreds of times before. This time, I wanted to find out if it's really true. Am I really home?"

Bill Mauldin had a dream of home, but when he got back he found the reality jarring, starting with the discovery that his wife had been seeing someone else in his absence. "Somehow a guy expects everything to be just like he left it," he wrote in the summer of 1945. It wasn't, though. There were housing shortages, meat shortages, and no shortage of black marketers profiting from them. Nor was there a shortage of well-meaning people pestering you with questions about what you were going to do next when you had no idea and needed time to think. Mauldin was a rarity, a wealthy ex-soldier, thanks to sales of a book of his *Yank* cartoons and commentary, *Up Front,* from which a movie was made. But he was not ex-empt from making the leap back into civilian life, and so he demobilized his much-loved GI characters, Willie and Joe, and drew caustic cartoons about their readjustment problems until he abandoned them as passé—forgotten figures receding into the past.

In *Best Years* the ex-sailor played by Harold Russell tries to make sure his sweetheart is aware that he needs someone to help him dress and un-dress and function in daily life. "I'm as dependent as a baby that doesn't know how to get anything except to cry for it," he tells her.

The women in *Best Years* play the traditional feminine roles of care-giver, wife, lover, sweetheart, companion, etc. The film and art historian Kaja Silverman writes that contrary to the usual macho males, the vets in the film have been, to varying degrees, deprived of their manhood—in or-thodox Freudian terms, castrated. The result, Silverman contends, is an "ideological unraveling—an unraveling which [*Best Years*] shows to be due in part to the massive exposure of the male populace to death and dissolution . . . and in part to the social contradictions of post-war America." As one example of this "unraveling," she mentions scenes in which the women, like good moms, tuck Al and Fred into their beds after that bibulous evening on their first night home. There is a subdued reversal of sexual roles in another scene in which Homer undresses to show his fiancée his stumps and she learns what kind of help he needs from others for even the simple task of going to bed. She ends up on her knees, promising she will never leave him. Silverman points out that in their marriage, they must adjust their sexual relationship so that he no longer plays the traditional male role: "He . . . has lost his hands—and with them his power to be sexually aggressive. . . . Every night, his wife will have to put him to bed, and then it will be her hands that must be used in making love. Beneath the pathos of the scene . . . one feels a current of excitement, in which the sailor's misfortune becomes a kind of wish-fulfillment, as one might actually dream it: he *must* be passive; therefore he can be passive without guilt."

One of the most formidable tasks a veteran faced was breaking with the all-male society that prevailed aboard ship or in the barracks (all-female in the case of women who served). As a marine, Eugene Sledge writes, "I realized that Company K had become my home. . . . It was not just a lettered company in a numbered battalion in a numbered regiment in a numbered division. It meant far more than that. It was home; it was 'my' company. I belonged in it and nowhere else."

This attitude came into play before the war's end, as seriously wounded men came home with early discharges. The marines in Sledge's company who got million-dollar wounds were last seen grinning and giving the thumbs-up sign as they were carried off on a stretcher. But after several months, their letters to their buddies "often became disturbingly bitter and filled with disillusionment," Sledge writes. A common thread running through the letters was "a feeling of alienation from everyone but their old comrades." They found civilians unaware of how easy they had it; they whined and complained about gas rationing or the shortage of meat.

There was also anger at the unfairness, the unequal sacrifices some of them had made, while others their age had amassed a lot of money in business or war work or dealing in the black market. Some who had gone into service had lucked out with stateside duty. Some felt guilty about surviving while losing close friends. Some even longed to be back in the old outfit as penance. Others considered volunteering for more overseas duty; a few actually did so.

Readjustment after the war was, no surprise, toughest for those who had been physically or mentally traumatized by combat. The overwhelming majority of these vets negotiated that challenge, but many combat soldiers carried memories too gruesome or simply too alien from civilian life to be easily communicated and thus purged. How could folks back home understand? Whenever they tried to describe their experiences, there came a point when the listener's eyes glazed over with denial. It was easier to say nothing and join the "Silent Soldiers Battalion"—an unofficial brotherhood comprising those who never spoke about the war, or did so only after many years.

In Red Oak, Harold Hughes's son, Bob, remembered his father was unable to stand war movies because they brought back bad memories. "We were under strict orders never to wake him up because he would react violently," Bob explained. "Mother would usually stand in the bedroom door and call to him. He'd always wake up tense. Once I forgot and woke him. He grabbed me. . . ." Bob was careful never again to wake his father; but his father never again hit him for any reason.

A Red Oak woman, Martha Heckert, who married her fiancé, Bob, after the war, said he didn't talk about his experiences for a long time. "It took him a while to feel he was part of the people at home," she said.

Duane Johnson, his son Steve recalled, was "in a different world" when he came home. He had undergone a Homeric odyssey getting there: after being captured in Italy, he made several escapes from German prison camps but always got caught. He felt it was his duty as a soldier to try to escape and harass the Germans. Finally, in 1945, he got away and hooked up with a Red Army unit in Germany. He left them after the captain, handing him a pistol, offered him the honor of shooting a captured Nazi officer.

Duane traveled in disguise through Europe. People were starving. He made it to Odessa on the Black Sea, where he'd heard he could get a ship to the States. After days of waiting he walked aboard a ship bound for Naples expecting somebody would shoot him. In Naples he caught an American ship that took him to New York. Back in Red Oak, there was no one he could talk to about the war. He said that civilians didn't know what it was like and so you couldn't talk to them. Finally he met a couple of German war brides who'd married Americans who had lived in bombed cities. He found he could talk to them. They understood what he'd been through.

In a different sense many wives had fought their own stressful war on the home front, which their husbands had trouble understanding. They had spent years alone, caring for small children, balancing the checkbooks, allocating scarce ration points, budgeting their husbands' meager allotments, holding down war jobs, doubling up with in-laws, moving into and out of boarding houses.

THE GAP BETWEEN civilians and combat veterans was shown in a Gallup poll in which half the respondents said their life had hardly been touched by the war. In another survey, two-thirds said they could not think of any real sacrifice they had made. A retired Red Cross worker told oral historian Studs Terkel, "The war was fun for Americans. I'm not talking about the poor souls who lost sons and daughters. But for the rest of us, the war was a hell of a good time."

Because of a flurry of sensationalized stories in the tabloid press, books, and movies, many civilians regarded veterans in general with wariness. They were seen as men who had been trained to kill and who might have combat fatigue (a Victorian-sounding euphemism for what is now called post-traumatic stress disorder) and go haywire.

The problem of combat fatigue was not helped by the lack of guidance to civilians. The Army censored photos showing soldiers who had mental breakdowns and suppressed John Huston's documentary on a psychiatric casualty ward, *Let There Be Light* (1946), because the film might harm recruitment. As James Agee, *The Nation*'s film critic, wrote, "After seeing this lesson in the costs of war, no young man with his full faculties would join up." Why, he asked, had the citizenry not raised an outcry against this act of censorship? He wondered if the nation's conscience had been numbed by patriotic propaganda.

Another movie, *I'll Be Seeing You* (1944), this one fictional, delivered a propaganda lesson to the home front on how to treat damaged soldiers. Its story brings together two wounded people: a young woman, played by Ginger Rogers, who is in prison for a minor crime, and a GI, played by Joseph Cotten, who is being treated for combat neurosis. They meet on a train: she is going to stay with an aunt and uncle in a small town; he is headed—well, he is really not sure where until he meets her and impulsively claims he has friends in the same town. They go out on a date, fall in love, are separated by misunderstanding, but reunite at the prison gate as she returns to finish her sentence. The mild-mannered Cotten experiences nightmares and hallucinations, but basically the film is a love story about two troubled souls who fortify each other.

There were a few honest pictures—like *The Men,* which showed a paraplegic veteran (Marlon Brando in his film debut) overcoming physical and psychological problems—but they did poorly at the box office. Problem films, fiction or nonfiction, breasted a tide of audience indifference and censorship by the service branches.

The most commercially successful kind of veterans' stories were those that took the form of a violent crime film. These most revealingly, though indirectly, expressed American society's combined wariness of and guilty feelings about veterans. The public attitude was an unstable compound of fear that vets would commit acts of violence, gratitude for their sacrifices, guilt because they had made them, and resentment of their special claims on society. As with any social group making such claims, people unconsciously wished they would go away, disappear into the civilian life. The movies of the time harbored this ambivalence, alternating between earnest expressions of society's duty toward veterans and a subconscious sense of fear or resentment.

As John Bodnar writes, postwar movies engaged in a kind of subconscious debate about whether vets were capable of fighting a war and coming home purged of the violence and aggression they necessarily learned to fight it: "To a surprising extent visions of virtue collided with fears of male aggression and insensitivity in many of these postwar films. Indeed, judging from the movies, the fears and anxieties of Americans in the early Cold War era were not only about Russians and bombs but about the makeup of the men who had just won the last conflict."

One type of returning-vet film justified the protagonist's violence as a necessary continuation of the fight against fascism. Typical was *Act of Violence* (1948), in which Frank Enley (Van Heflin) is pursued by Joe Parkson (Robert Ryan), who is bent on avenging the men of their bomber crew who were killed trying to escape from a POW camp. Enley, their commanding officer, had opposed the escape plot and tipped off the Germans. Parkson was badly wounded but survived; in his hospital bed he kept himself going with thoughts of vengeance: "I kept thinking back to that prison camp. One of [the men the Germans shot] lasted to the morning, you couldn't tell his voice belonged to a man. He sounded like a dog that got hit by a truck and left in the street." After the war Parkson tracks his former commander to a sunny suburb, where he is living a prosperous life. Enley, obviously shaken, confesses to his wife that he had ordered his men not to dig the escape tunnel and that when they went ahead, he told the camp commandant about the plan. His motives don't matter, he says. "I was an informer. I did it to save one life—me."[*] There are scenes at an architects' convention satirizing postwar prosperity—contrasting the partying civilians with the lone veteran's grim determination to close out his war with a violent act of retribution.

Other revenge pictures showed vets having to defeat the fascists one more time. In *Cornered* (1945), Dick Powell plays a veteran hunting the Nazis who killed his French girlfriend, a fighter in the Resistance. The trail leads to Argentina, where Nazis are alive, well, and hiding out.

---

[*] Several films about informers, pro and con but mostly con, were made during this period. Some of them were intended as a subtle comment on the anti-Communist blacklist. *Act of Violence* was probably one such film; it was directed by the German émigré Fred Zinneman, who in 1952 made *High Noon,* the classic parable of the blacklist.

More frequently in these crime pictures, the veteran is a wrongly accused man who must become a fugitive to prove his innocence, thus
restoring him to society's good graces. This symbolic figure reflected an
unconscious suspicion about whether a veteran really "belonged" in society after becoming a trained killer—an image sometimes interiorized by
the veteran, who views himself as somehow unfit for normal socializing.

The veteran-return pictures enacted a symbolic ordeal or test that the
returned hero must undergo before he can be reinducted into the tribe. He
must also show that he has purged or cleansed himself of the aggression
and violence that he needed as a warrior. This theme emerges in war novels as well. Sloan Wilson's best-selling *The Man in the Gray Flannel Suit* relates
the homecoming problems of Tom Rath, a former paratrooper, who says
in his modest way that he killed seventeen Nazis with his own hands. Now
he must adjust to the humdrum rhythms of family life and working for corporate bosses. In a relevant passage Wilson sums up Tom's problem:

> The trick is to learn to believe that it's a disconnected world, a lunatic
> world, where what is true now was not true then; where Thou Shalt Not
> Kill and the fact that one has killed a great many men means nothing, ab-
> solutely nothing, for now is the time to raise legitimate children and make
> money, and dress properly, and be kind to one's wife and admire one's
> boss, and learn not to worry, and think of oneself as what? That makes no
> difference, he thought, I'm just a man in a gray flannel suit.

These scenarios of maladjustment are acted out to some degree, and
in various ways, in nearly all the crime films about veterans. Sometimes,
the hero is not even identified as a veteran. Such was the case, Frank Krutnik argues, in the classic film noir *Out of the Past.* In it Robert Mitchum,
wearing the traditional militaristic trench coat in his role as an ex–private
eye, recapitulates the veteran's journey of return by trying to integrate himself into small-town life, only to be waylaid by his violent past. And Dix, the
small-time gunman in *The Asphalt Jungle,* also wants to put killing behind
him and come home to the green and peaceful Kentucky countryside—
but doesn't quite make it.

One of the key elements in classic noir is the idea of a man alone, out of step with the world, often vulnerable to a woman (or two) who may or may not have such good intentions. This solitary man represents the returning soldier, who was forced to do his murderous job during the war and now faces an alien America he can't quite fit into.

During the war there had been an explosion of illegal, or "wildcat," strikes—local job actions in which workers violated the no-strike pledge in defiance of their leaders because they believed they had to protest unsafe workplaces, inadequate pay, and other bad working conditions. The film historian Dennis Broe theorizes a link between postwar labor's pariah status and movies with fugitive outsiders as heroes.

The paradigmatic veteran-as-fugitive movie was *The Blue Dahlia* (1946), a crime melodrama starring Alan Ladd and Veronica Lake, who were a hot romantic duo at the box office. Ladd was due to report for military service, so the picture was a rush job to exploit his popularity one more time before he went off to war. The pressure thus fell on Raymond Chandler, who had cowritten the adaptation of James M. Cain's *Double Indemnity* with Billy Wilder and whose private-eye novel *The Big Sleep* was part of the postwar wave of crime films. *The Blue Dahlia* was his first original script, so the pressure was doubled. Chandler was a World War I veteran who had emerged with harrowing memories that he rarely talked about and never got over, according to his wife, Cissie. His forté was the murder mystery, so he wrote a standard-issue hard-boiled crime story about a returned veteran.

Chandler's unromantic "tough" hero is Lt. Cmdr. Johnny Morrison (Ladd), an angry and violence-prone man who comes home from the war to find a cheating wife who taunts him with her infidelity. When the wife turns up dead, he is the prime suspect and flees in order to clear himself of the rap. Lake picks him up hitchhiking, and they team up to find the real killer. The Navy Department objected to Chandler's script, which the studio had submitted in advance, as was customary—in particular the denouement, which reveals that Johnny's buddy Buzz (William Bendix) is the killer. Buzz has a steel plate in his head, the result of a war wound, and he goes into rages when he hears "jungle music" (boogie-woogie) on the jukebox. He shot Johnny's faithless wife out of misguided loyalty and then contracted total amnesia.

Faced with the Navy's threat not to cooperate in making the movie, the studio ordered Chandler to come up with a new ending. Rather than immediately going on a bender, as was his wont in times of stress, Chandler hatched a plan for a kind of working binge. He told the producer, John Houseman, that he could only write a new ending stimulated by alcohol. Houseman reluctantly agreed to an arrangement whereby Chandler would drink all he wanted and work at home. A doctor would make regular calls to administer vitamin shots (Chandler normally lived on bourbon and cigarettes during these sprees), limousines would be parked at the ready to fetch doctors or transport the maid to the stores, typists would be at their keyboards awaiting each new page of script, motorcycle messengers were on standby to bring it to them.

And so Chandler existed for weeks in a twilight world of inebriation: working, drinking, dozing off, waking, working. In this fashion he drafted a new conclusion and collapsed, his health damaged. But the film was made.

The Blue Dahlia was one of the earliest veteran crime films to hang its plot on their alleged potential for violence. An alternative approach to making a film about veterans' psychological problems was not to identify them as veterans. Consider Wilder's *The Lost Weekend* (1945), which features a writer named Don Birnam (Ray Milland) and his battle with the bottle. Wilder's harrowing depiction of alcoholism (probably inspired by Wilder's collaboration with Chandler) came at a time when it was recognized as a leading problem among returning servicemen and -women, and an ordeal for their families. (In real life, Iowa's hero Bob Moore was a closet alcoholic for much of his life after the war, as was his wife, Dorothy—and many other veterans, heroes or not.) The characters in *Best Years* routinely take multiple drinks to drown their anxiety about returning to civilian life.

Birnam, William Graebner writes, is a veteran in civilian garb who is "glad to be home from the war but curiously lacking in resolve and direction," a common malaise among returnees. When Birnam's loyal girlfriend chides him that "other people have stopped" drinking, he replies,

"They are people with a purpose, with something to do." She tells him he has talent and ambition and a project, a novel, in his typewriter, but he tells her his talent was drowned long ago and is "drifting around in the bloated belly of a lake of alcohol." When he's drinking he can imagine himself as a greater writer, fulfilling the promise of his college days. But when he is back to being Don Birnam, he loses his creative drive and his projects fizzle out.

Lori Rotskoff, in her study of alcoholism in the forties, *Love on the Rocks*, ties Birnam's state of drift to a general postwar letdown: "After the urgent, invigorating demands of war, many GIs and civilians felt listless in the face of the more mundane challenges of peacetime. After the victory celebrations ceased, an emotional pall of cynicism and passivity enveloped the nation as Americans groped for new sources of significance in their lives."

Although there were no murders in its story line, Wilder's film (based on the novel by Charles Jackson) was in look and attitude a true film noir. It was shot by Charles Seitz in the documentary style he had used in *Double Indemnity* mixed with subjective scenes of horror using expressionistic techniques. Harrowing shots of Third Avenue, which was then a drab street in the shadow of elevated tracks lined with pawnshops and sleazy bars, are used as a backdrop for Birnam's agonized odyssey to pawn his typewriter, in which he discovers that the shops are all closed for a Jewish holiday. Through the alcoholic's eyes, a walk on a city street becomes a journey through a grim urban battlefield. Birnam's alcohol-frayed nerves eventually trigger an attack of delirium tremens that unleashes terrifying little animals that are all in his delirious mind.

Another example of the veteran-problem genre, *Crossfire* (1947), a surprise financial hit, was also not "about" vets' problems. Rather, it focuses on a group of soldiers waiting to be discharged and trying to deal with the psychological residue of war. The story line dramatizes contemporary social problems—primarily anti-Semitism. The soldiers in the film and in *The Brick Foxhole,* the novel on which it's based, are seething with repressed violence. The implication is that society is as well, as people move from the unleashed hatred of the enemy in wartime to the sublimated violence of peacetime. "We don't know who we are anymore, we're just fighting and hating," Samuels (Sam Levene), the Jewish victim-to-be and a veteran himself, says while drinking with the soldiers at the bar. Plucking a peanut from a dish, he adds, "It's like we're focused on that one peanut, hating it; we've got to get back to loving life again." Few movies raised the toxic psychological effects of war's violence on the men who fought and, indirectly, on the country that had cheered them from civilian safety.

All of the veterans films, including *The Lost Weekend,* expressed resolute optimism that these characters would work through their problems with love, understanding, therapy, work, purpose, and the emotional support of the women in their lives. In *The Lost Weekend,* Don's girlfriend, Helen, sticks by him and in the end stops him from shooting himself. Her faith in him rather miraculously restores him to the novel he has been trying to write, and unlike in Jackson's novel he is cured.

As we have seen in his book *Film Noir: American Workers and Postwar Hollywood,* Dennis Broe focuses on a recurring film noir protagonist—the loner-outsider, whose plight matched that of labor right after the war. Wartime strikes were widely unpopular, and the postwar wave added to unions' unpopularity. The character of Joe in *The Long Night* (1947) counters the stereotype. The film, made by the liberal director Anatole Litvak, urged without preaching solidarity among veterans, workers, and common people. The enemy of the hero, Joe (Henry Fonda), is the Great Maxmillian (Vincent Price), a skillful deceiver who seduces Joe's girl (Barbara Bel Geddes) and filches his best chance for love and happiness. Lied to, falsely accused, and goaded into desperation, Joe shoots Maxmillian and barricades himself in his room. Although he is arrested at the end, he has not lost hope; the people in the square watching the drama of his arrest are sympathetic. As Joe is being taken away, a black man lights his cigarette, expressing a bond between this working-class guy and a minority—that is, with all members of the underclass. *The Long Night* is one of the few films of the time to touch on, however subtly, the goals of workers. (After the 1946 studio strike, the film companies were fiercely antiunion.) The 1939 French film on which it was based, *Le Jour se Lève,* directed by Marcel Carné in the style of poetic realism, has as its central theme the defeat of working people and the rise of fascism in France. Their defeat is symbolized by the hero's suicide at the end. *The Long Night* is fundamentally (if obliquely) optimistic.

Joe is shown very prominently to be a veteran; it is a proud part of his identity. (In the postwar strike wave, discussed in the next chapter, veterans often wore their uniforms on the picket lines.) But that identity buys him no respect in postwar America. After fighting for his country, he is rewarded with betrayal and trickery, so he fights back—violently. The film can't resolve the conflict between the wrongness of Joe's violence and the rightness of his cause; it is left in the air, though somehow, we are asked to believe, he will be redeemed and assimilated into America by joining in the progressive community of veterans, workers, and minorities.

In a middlebrow, noncrime drama like *Best Years,* the family is the haven for rehabilitation. After having severed his bonds to his military buddies, the veteran is briefly isolated and alone—until he recovers his place in family, job, and community, which requires that he compromise with the demands of civilian society while they adjust to his new identity as a returned veteran. Al's civilian family and his old job are waiting for him intact. The problem is that he sees them from a different perspective; now he identifies with the veterans (i.e., the borrowing class). His daughter is falling in love with his new buddy Fred Derry, a veteran who seems to have no future and who is married. The prospects for Al's readjustment to family life are better. True, he seems initially to be having trouble acclimating; but as he tells Milly, their long marriage has survived other rough patches.

Homer must carve out a new place for himself in his fiancée's family as well as in his own; he must teach them that he has come home a *radically different* man, a disabled person. It's up to him to win acceptance for his new self; that means he must break out of the cocoon of pity they spin around him, and shake himself out of his own self-pity. In the end, he does it not by angry speeches but by humbling himself, showing them what help he needs, patiently teaching them how to adjust to his disability.

Fred passively drifts back into his old pre-war rut because good jobs are not available, and he goes through stages of rebellion against the humiliating position the work puts him into. His wife humiliates him as well by demanding that he wear his uniform when they go out; she will accept him only as an officer and a gentleman, not a soda jerk. Lacking the education he needs for a middle-class job, he regresses to nostalgia for his action-filled Air Force days, when he expressed his real manhood—which is suppressed in civilian life. At the movie's end he sits in the pilot's seat of one of the rows of junked B-24 bombers parked outside town and hears in his head the sounds of aerial combat. It looks like he's headed for a human junk-yard, another obsolete bombardier. But he is jolted out of his nightmare by the man in charge of the junkyard, who asks what he's doing up there. He talks himself into a job converting the surplus planes into materials for postwar homes. Unlike so many real-life veterans, Fred needs no govern-ment help to improve his prospects. Instead, a chance meeting pulls him out of the muck of failure and impending poverty. He will work hard, rise in business, and climb socially by marrying the banker's daughter.

The Blue Dahlia's Johnny faces a tougher challenge, one more conso-nant with a crime story plot: he must prove he's not a wife-killer—or, more broadly, that's he's not a killer back from the war—before he can re-enter society. He sets off on a quest through the underworld for vindica-tion, helped by the girl (Veronica Lake) who picked him up hitchhiking and who is willing to trust him.

Like a good soldier, Joe Parkson in *Act of Violence* must carry out one last self-ordained military mission before *his* war is over. He must avenge his buddies and right a wartime wrong. The script gets around the prob-lem of murder by showing the informer taking the deadly bullet from pur-suing cops' guns rather than from Joe's. In *Cornered,* Dick Powell must finish the job of killing fascists by avenging the murdered Resistance fighter. In other words, his war against fascism isn't over.

The nightclub tout Harry Fabian in blacklistee Jules Dassin's *Night and the City* represents another noir character, a total opposite. Apparently he missed the war; now he has no trade, no profession other than being a pro-moter. He's "an artist without an art" who just "wants to be somebody." He has no home to return to. He has spent his whole life running away—from foster homes, from cops, from prisons. He's still running, this time for his life, desperately fleeing the mobsters he double-crossed. But for him there is no refuge, not even with his wife, whom he's cheated on. She brings him money and tells him, "I don't know how to help you. Nobody could love any man as I love you. You worked hard, but it was the wrong thing, always the wrong thing." He reminds her that he's promised her a life of ease and plenty; he'll make good—he tells her to turn him in and collect the $1,000 price tag the mob put on his head. Sickened, she refuses.

He keeps running, fleeing deeper into an urban labyrinth from which there's no way out, and runs into the embrace of the wrestler he cheated in his scam, who strangles him and throws his body into the Thames, like so much garbage. The reptilian mobster Kristo, watching Harry's death from the bridge, tosses his cigarette contemptuously into the river and walks away.

The new vogue for psychiatry seeped into the postwar noirs, often in plots revolving around troubled heroes who are set right by psychotherapy. This trend was started by Alfred Hitchcock's artistically filmed, highly successful *Spellbound* (1944), a kind of Freudian noir in which a young doctor (Gregory Peck) is freed from a recurring nightmare by a beautiful analyst (Ingrid Bergman). In real life, many veterans were undergoing the same torments from war traumas.

The popularity of film characters who are suffering psychoneuroses, whether conflict-related or not, was not surprising when one considers that combat units averaged 23 percent casualties attributable to psychological stress; more than a million soldiers suffered symptoms serious enough to make them unfit for combat. And contrary to the conventional wisdom, it didn't get any easier with experience. Studies showed that the longer a soldier fought, the greater the likelihood of his psychic breakdown—200 days was considered the outer limit for most men. Uncounted thousands were sent home with their traumas undiagnosed, untreated.

One Red Oak veteran, who had spent most of his war in German prison camps, had a case of "nerves" when he returned, his son recalled. Sudden noises, like fireworks, would set his synapses crackling. He was plagued by nightmares and haunted by memories of the time the German guards shot a friend of his who said he was too sick to work and left him lying on the ground as an example to the other prisoners. Eventually, the veteran connected with a hospital in Missouri, which provided the therapy that the VA didn't give him. For twenty years he regularly visited a group of veterans in Kentucky who shared his prison experiences. With them he was able to talk through his emotions, and this informal therapy brought him some peace, at last.

A VA study from the nineties of men who had been prisoners during World War II or the Korean War revealed that one in six needed treatment for post-traumatic stress disorder and physical problems attributable to the conditions of their captivity. The physical problems triggered by extreme deprivation, mistreatment, and humiliation in prison camps caused delayed psychological eruptions as well, including nightmares and anxiety attacks. And these problems recurred as the vets grew older, sometimes triggered by the loss of a spouse or other shocks. Yet there was no program addressing the specific needs of former POWs until 1981.

A radio show called *Reunion U.S.A.* specialized in short plays that realistically dramatized the problems facing homecoming veterans. The show gained 10 million listeners and ranked among the top five programs on ABC. It was created by the Hollywood Writers Mobilization, which comprised leftish, social-minded screenwriters interested in making more responsible films and radio plays. One of the most effective scripts was *The Case of David Smith,* by Abraham Polonsky, later a blacklisted Hollywood writer and director. It tells the story of a psychoneurotic veteran who organized native guerrilla fighters on an island in the Pacific. Captured and tortured by the Japanese, he returns home deeply scarred, hardly speaking, and slowly starving to death. A psychiatrist finds a note he wrote before he died. It reveals that the cause of his psychoneurosis was the betrayal of his promise to the guerrillas that after the war they would be granted freedom. Instead they got the return of the old colonial system.

The real story here, according to the commentary by psychology professor Franklin Fearing that followed the radio play, is what happens to a soldier who returns to civilian life and cannot "find meaning in the world that he now confronts." Fearing goes on: "He now seeks some evidence that the world of civilians in which he finds himself understands, if only faintly, the reasons for which the war was fought and the price which must be paid for peace. If, instead, he finds a complacent willingness to return to the past or glib talk about our enemies in the next war, he will retreat in horror and revulsion."

But the psychoneurotic vet's chances of making a successful readjustment to civilian life were not helped by the stigma still clinging to mental illness or by the VA's failure to deal adequately with combat neuroses. Nor was civilian sympathy for the troubled ex-GI's plight helped by sensationalistic stories in the press that warned of "The Coming Veteran Crime Wave" or asked, "Will Your Boy Come Home a Killer?" Tabloids relished gory headlines: "Veteran Beheads Wife with Jungle Machete"; "Sailor Shoots Father."

The most famous "berserk vet" was Harold Unruh, who exploded into a murderous rampage in Camden, New Jersey, in 1949:

BERSERK VETERAN KILLS 12

A 26-year-old war veteran went berserk today and shot and killed 12 persons. . . . Detectives said the street where the killings took place looked like a battle field. . . . Bodies were strewn all over the street. . . . Killed in the 45-minute blast of bullets were two small boys, five women and five men. . . . Harold Unruh used a German Luger, barricaded himself in a second floor room and exchanged fire with 50 cops. . . . As they dragged him away they had to fight off a mob of 1,000 who screamed "Lynch him" and "Hang him now."

Unruh, a loner, hated his neighbors and harbored a grudge against the VA for denying him care. He was judged insane and spent the rest of his life in a mental institution.

Like Unruh, some readjusting vets had negative images of the home front. While overseas they read news reports in the military press about profiteers and striking war workers and 4Fs who'd made a pile while others faced bullets. Barrack-room or foxhole bull sessions eventually came around to stories about this or that guy's wife cheating on him. Buddies received Dear John letters. As a result many vets returned with images of lazy civilians who had devoted themselves during the war to making money and seducing soldiers' wives.

A War Department survey found that one in five vets felt "completely hostile" to civilians. "When they come back they treat you like scum," was a typical plaint. A 1947 Gallup survey showed one-third of vets feeling estranged from civilian life, and 20 percent "hostile" to civilians. The redoubtable Agnes Meyer, wife of the publisher of the *Washington Post,* found on a reporting swing around the nation a pervasive mood among vets of "appalling loneliness and bitterness." The unemployed vets were "floating in a vacuum of neglect, idleness and distress." By 1947 half of ex-servicemen were saying that the war had been a useless experience "that left them worse off than before it."

Of course, many of the ex-GIs were feeling low about their own civilian circumstances. One vet's view was fairly typical: "A lot of things are disgusting right now. Everything you buy is sky-high and hard to get, and a place to live is almost impossible to get." A VA survey concluded that 64 percent of married vets and 80 percent of singles were squatting with friends and relatives. As one said, "We are running out of relatives."

Indeed, alarmed psychologists warned that the growing number of young families doubling up was becoming a threat to marital stability. Wives needed to break with their parents to create a home of their own; sons needed to sever parental ties and become financially independent; living with in-laws had built-in tensions. Charles Brown, chief of the New York Mental Hygiene Service, called the housing shortage and its attendant worries "one of the biggest factors in making many veterans mentally sick."

Some of the veterans' bitterness found its way into Mauldin's cartoons after his own discharge in early 1945. Mauldin brought a noirish style to his cross-hatched civilian cartoons. Biographer Todd DePastino called them "redolent of the betrayal, isolation and bewilderment felt by many who fought for a better world."

Inspired by his own experience of being ripped off while buying a car, Mauldin did sardonic cartoons featuring sleazy car salesmen who sold clunkers at Office of Price Administration ceiling prices while tacking on "extras" that amounted to bribes. In one of these he shows Willie at a used car lot inspecting an ancient wreck with a sign reading "Pre-war Quality

O.P.A. Ceiling Price $250." The salesman is saying, "Of course, the steering wheel costs $750, but we knock off fifty bucks for ex-soldiers."

He satirized the lurid headlines about violent veterans in a cartoon of a man sitting with his wife and staring at a tabloid headline, which reads, "Veteran Kicks Aunt." The woman is saying, "There's a small item on page 17 about a triple ax murder. No veterans involved."

Mauldin had left-wing sympathies, and in one picture he made a dig at right-wingers who thought it would have been better if Nazi Germany had defeated Communist Russia. According to DePastino, an anonymous FBI researcher clipped this cartoon and used it to start what became a voluminous file on Mauldin's political activities. The antiauthoritarian attitude that made him the bane of brass hats and endeared him to GIs set him on a collision course with conservative opinion back home. He ditched Willie and Joe and parlayed his anger into a career as an editorial-page cartoonist, ending up with a Pulitzer Prize.

After a vet reacquainted himself with his wife, kids, parents, and hometown, his next readjustment worry was finding a job or trying to reclaim his old one, which was guaranteed him by the Servicemen's Readjustment Act, passed in 1944 and expanded in 1945, and better known as the GI Bill.

Rather than futilely trying to reconvert their military specialty to a job on the civilian market, many vets preferred to seek training in civilian fields or study for a college degree—both alternatives financed by the GI Bill. "Magnanimous" was the operative word for this centerpiece feature of the bill. The colleges implementing it were so thrilled by the tuition money the new students brought in that they welcomed them despite the dislocations, crowding, inconveniences, and teacher shortages they created. Veterans received special consideration both in admission requirements and courses they were allowed to take. This policy seems to have held throughout the life of the World War II bill. For veterans, enrollment was a breeze: once an institution accepted them they signed some papers and drew $75 a month to live on, while their tuition bills were handled directly by the government.

The $3.9 billion in direct tuition payments during the life of the bill gave a tremendous boost to higher education in America. The VA was good for up to $500 in tuition and picked up other costs such as room and board, allowing state universities to make additional money by charging local vets out-of-state tuitions. The colleges invested their endowment money in new buildings; they launched ambitious expansion programs to meet new student demands—for a dental college, for example.

When all was said and done, 5.6 million vets enrolled in VA-approved training, learning practical skills from commercial art to chicken sexing. For many, this timely boost was the key to a future laden with better-paying prospects than they had in the Depression years. Another 2.2 million aimed even higher—for something few Depression-scarred kids dared even dream of before the war: a college education, and with that a good job or a profession. According to the 1989 World War II Veterans Survey, an average of 75 to 90 percent of those who had graduated from various colleges and universities called the bill a "turning point in their lives." As one newly minted BA recalled to Studs Terkel, "The war changed our whole idea of how we wanted to live when we came back. We set our sights pretty high. All of us wanted better levels of living. I am now what you call middle class."

The bill proved to be a socially liberalizing force as well. True, although black vets were eligible for aid, the law did not guarantee their acceptance at segregated Southern universities. They could, of course, attend black colleges, and these institutions saw their enrollments climb well over 50 percent above the 1940 figures. But more black veterans attended Northern universities than ever before (a goodly number stayed in the North). The traditional quotas for another minority group, Jewish students in the Northeast, gradually eroded as well. Women vets, however, were the program's biggest failure. Facing pressure to marry and make a home, along with discrimination in professions like law and medicine, they didn't participate in large numbers; only about 40 percent of female vets availed themselves of the program. Suzanne Mettler writes that these women "thought of the G.I. Bill as targeted primarily toward males, and perceived themselves as fortunate secondary beneficiaries" (i.e., as the spouses of upwardly mobile college grads). Generally, colleges favored male vets over women in allotting their scarce openings.

At the years of peak enrollment (1947–48), vets sometimes made up more than half of student bodies. Harvard, one of the nation's most elite universities, was greatly transformed by the GI invasion. The 1946 student body of three thousand, largely made up of Harvard veterans whose education had been interrupted by the war, was known as the Great Return. Admissions standards were lowered, setting the school on the road to becoming more democratic, less class-bound; vets would go for an interview and be admitted the next day. Because of the faculty shortage, joint classes were held with all-female Radcliffe College for the first time, thus dissolving the seemingly impregnable sex barrier between the two institutions.

The service experience that affected so many members of this generation even influenced the attire of the corporate soldiers. The ultimate business uniform of the fifties, celebrated in the title of Sloan Wilson's best-selling book, was the gray-flannel suit. Richard Horn describes it: "a three-button, single-breasted, charcoal gray flannel suit, with narrow shoulders, narrow, small-notched lapels, flaps on the pockets, and pleatless, tapering trousers. A white or pale blue cotton broadcloth shirt with a button-down collar and button cuffs, trim ties with regimental stripes and small knots, and trim black leather shoes that rose at the ankle and the toe."

Before the gray-flanneled corporate male appeared, men's fashions, like women's, celebrated the end of fabric shortages—or, more accurately, men's and women's clothing manufacturers did. In 1949 men were extended the "bold look," which the fashion-conscious *Esquire* heralded as a more macho style than traditional business attire. It featured porkpie hats, broad-shouldered jackets, spread collars framing fat Windsor knots on wide big-patterned ties, and thick-soled cordovan brogues. It was a look fit for a private eye in a film noir.

If men's fashions were aimed at the new company man, women's fashions affirmed the glamorous but nonworking wife. Because of fabric shortages, women's wartime fashions had been comparatively simple, eschewing frills and furbelows. The iconic padded shoulders of the thirties career-girl movies were out, replaced by natural shoulders or the bare-armed look; large fancy hats were replaced by turbans, which had proved more practical in factory work because they kept long waves of hair from being snarled in drill presses. For the same reason, tight sweaters were in vogue, being both sexy and machine-resistant.

But after the war the image of the patriotic, cloth-saving working woman who still looked pretty for her soldier boy gave way to conspicuous consumption, decked out in the "new look," a style created by the Paris designer Christian Dior. He swathed women in voluminous fabrics, long skirts with amphora waists that proclaimed her postwar role of wife and child-bearer, but also the glamorous accessory wife an upwardly mobile organization man could display on evenings out.

The thrifty ex-GIs who took advantage of the GI Bill spurned the Joe College look. They attended classes wearing their old field jackets and khakis. They crammed their wives and kids into narrow Quonset huts, studied amid squalling babies, and let off steam in weekend beer blasts.

College under those conditions was a grind. Like the war, it was something you got through. Yet like other sentimental grads, most GI grads looked back on college as the high point of their lives. As a Penn State graduate told Suzanne Mettler: "We were driving out of State College after I graduated and got the job in Washington, and I stopped the car. My wife asked why. . . . I said I just wanted to look [back] at the college. We'd been there for four and a half years, I said, 'Those have been the best years of our lives.' She said, 'You're right!'"

A June 1947 survey of vets counted 15.8 million of them; their average age was twenty-nine; 80 percent were under thirty; three-fifths of them were married and two-thirds lived in urban areas; 33 percent had gone into service directly from school, the Army being their first job; 14 percent were college graduates, and 25 percent had finished high school. All told, veterans and their immediate families made up nearly one-fourth of the US population.

This cohort's most significant *statistical* impact on society was to give a major bump to the national divorce rate in 1946. During 1945–46 the divorce rate shot up to more than twice what it was in 1939—an average of thirty-one divorces for every hundred marriages, the highest rate in the world. And the divorce rate among veterans was twice that of civilians. Some 53 percent of 1944 marriages in Los Angeles County landed in divorce court by 1945. Those cold postwar figures represented the shakeout of how many desperate grabs for passionate love between wartime strangers. In New York between January and August 1945, 2,500 servicemen got divorces for adultery, which was the only legal ground for divorce but now easier to claim.

The war accelerated a longstanding trend eroding the Victorian social stigma of divorce. In the Depression people stuck together, come hell or high water, for economic as well as morality reasons, because breaking up was costly. By the late forties the money and opportunity was there to get out of a hasty marriage to someone you hardly knew at the time, let alone after four years of separation, and look for a new mate. Greater economic independence gave more women the courage to bail out of failed marriages. There was also a rise in infidelity among long-separated spouses, though opportunity was as much a cause as separation (availability of lonely members of the opposite sex in transient communities, whether military or factory).

Yet the divorce boom was paralleled by a compensatory spike in the marriage rate. In 1946 it was 16.4 per 1,000, up from 13.2 in 1942. The birth rate in 1946 soared to 24.1, compared with 18.8 in 1939, the last Depression year. Four million children were born in 1946.

This upsurge in births after a decade's decline was the natural result of women marrying at the peak of their fecundity—younger on average than in the thirties. The average marriage age dropped one full year during the war years, the steepest drop of the past fifty years. The trend started in 1942 with the rush of wartime marriages, and it continued after the war.

Sexual need did not always lead to marriage. The religious-inspired moral code buckled under the strain of greater mobility and painful separations and the fatalism war engendered. It was a time when "I'll be seeing you" was a catchphrase among young people who were so often on the move, meeting and parting. A young dancer with the New York Ballet Theatre named Janet Reed caught the frenzy of the times in her memoir of touring the country: "We were uprooted and though we had a very carefree attitude, we were also very tentative about relationships. We were all so very young . . . innocent and rather lonely . . . wanting so much to be close to one another and knowing it couldn't last." (As it happens, Reed danced the part of one of the girls chased by sailors in the 1944 Leonard Bernstein/Jerome Robbins ballet *Fancy Free.*) "Tentative" was a polite way of saying you didn't want to get too involved with a guy who might never come back to you.

After the war, the rising incomes of young men subsidized by GI home loans and veterans benefits, combined with an improving job market, countered a major cause of the high marriage postponement rate of the thirties—lack of money.

Possibly related to the astronomical rise in the 1946 divorce rate was the spike in homicides that same year to more than seven per thousand. Indeed, the homicide rate climbed between 1943 and 1950. Demographer Fulano de Tal wrote that a bump in murders typically correlated with "indicators of social disorganization such as high divorce rates," among other factors. "Perhaps some men did not take the 'Dear John' letters peacefully," de Tal added. Or perhaps the veteran came home to the surprise discovery that his wife had a roommate who was sharing her allotment check and wearing his civilian clothes, as happened to one hapless guy. Or supporting her in a handsomer style than he could on a private's pay and allotment.

Then there was the issue of the high number of women who did their bit in the war plants. On the popular radio series *Reunion U.S.A.,* among the leading marital "problems" was a veteran's adjustment "to a wife unwilling to give up her employment and return to the drudgery of the kitchen." The alleged Amazonian traits acquired by these women became a social problem worthy of analysis by serious magazines like *Harper's,* where Anne Leighton wrote, "Many American war veterans are silently bearing some unexpected . . . difficulties in returning home to what used to be a pleasantly pliable and even appallingly incompetent little woman and finding a quietly masterful creature recognizing no limits to her own endurance." Perhaps the real-life equivalent was expressed by one Red Oak couple, Gil and Dorothy Schrage. They had to rejigger their pre-war marriage after he came home from the war. "While Gil was away I was used to making all the decisions," Dorothy said. "After he came home I had to stop doing it." Gil said, "I didn't know who was the boss in the family." It took a while for both to revert to their traditional roles.

This popular fear was fanned by articles like one in the *New York Times* by Victor Dallaire headlined "The American Woman? Not for This GI." Dallaire, a former *Stars and Stripes* reporter, took a wild swing at the "business Amazon." American women, he declared, were no longer nice; they elbowed their way through crowds, swiped your seat at bars, and bumped and pushed their way around. A popular 1947 book, *Modern Woman: The Lost Sex*, held that a woman could find fulfillment only in motherhood. It revived the myth that women must "defeminize"—that is, become more masculine—to succeed in the business world.

The nightmare vision was of "'domineering' women and economic insecurity, all waiting to overwhelm the returning veterans hoping to get their jobs and their 'girls' back," writes the feminist historian Elaine Tyler May. This negative image infiltrated popular culture. In films noir she is a femme fatale; while in the best-selling adventures of Mickey Spillane's private eye Mike Hammer, she is the sexy temptress who turns out to be a Communist spy, whom Mike must viciously beat up before shooting her.

The increase in extramarital sex was dispassionately documented in *Sexual Behavior of the Human Male,* a statistical compilation of the various sexual "contacts" of young men interviewed during and after the war by Alfred E. Kinsey, a biology professor at Indiana University. Despite being about as passionate as an actuarial table, the tome was hot stuff in 1948, selling 225,000 copies.

Religious moralists, confusing descriptive science with prescriptive morality, leapt on Kinsey, accusing him of undermining the nation's sexual morals. The Rev. Billy Graham, a young evangelist emerging as a prominent voice of Christian fundamentalism, proclaimed that it was "impossible to estimate the damage this book will do to the already deteriorating morals of America." Even a mainstream voice, the president of the Union Theological Seminary in New York, discerned in the book "a prevailing degradation in American morality approximating the worst decadence of the Roman era. The most disturbing thing is the absence of a spontaneous ethical revulsion from the premises of this study."

Sexual Behavior in the Human Male and its sequel, *Sexual Behavior in the Human Female,* revealed that the rate of marital infidelity among Americans was considerably higher than what the moral guardians were prepared to admit. Out in the real USA, infidelity was very much a concern of returning vets who had left behind wives or girlfriends and who lacked Kinsey's scientific detachment about the sexual behavior of *their* particular female. The common occurrence was dramatized in *The Best Years of Our Lives* in this charged exchange between Fred Derry and his wife, Marie:

> MARIE: What do you think I was doing all those years?
> FRED: I don't know, babe, but I can guess.
> MARIE: Go ahead. Guess your head off. I could do some guessing
>   myself. What were you up to in London and Paris and all those places?

Society condemned more harshly the straying wife who took up with a 4F, whatever the circumstances, than her straying GI husband overseas. Stories about soldiers who had sacrificed arms, legs, or sanity fighting for their country and returned to find their wives shacked up with another man were common, and drew popular outrage. The courts soon became clogged with "alienation of affection" suits brought by aggrieved husbands.

The alleged strayings of Chicago's war wives set State's Attorney William J. Tuohy's blood aboil. He announced he would prosecute them for adultery, something hardly ever done. A divorce court judge seconded that: "These women deserve the limit. And I mean a term in jail or prison and not just a small fine." A Newark judge raised the ante: he proposed that unfaithful wives be sentenced to wear a scarlet letter.

Still, the consensus of the clergy, psychologists, and women's magazine experts was that war wives should forgive their men's overseas lapses. *Ladies' Home Journal* told wives not to be jealous because those "short-lived adventures were unsatisfactory substitutes for the deeper, more meaningful life he has known with you. . . . Your chief rival is—the image he has created in his memory of you." *Women's Home Companion* advised unhappy wives to give their marriages "a year's honest effort." In a story on the rising divorce rate, the *New York Times* evoked, rather rakishly, husbands fraternizing "enthusiastically and impartially with frauleins, mademoiselles and signorinas," but the writer assured readers that those soldiers had all the while continued to idealize their wives. At any rate, the majority opinion was expressed in the smug words of *Good Housekeeping:* "Marriage is a sacred affair, for all the growing divorce rate. . . . You took your soldier, young woman: he's yours. In heaven's name stick with him."

This admonition seems to place the responsibility on the wife's shoulders, and indeed, this is where it usually ended up in the advice courts— i.e., the women's magazines and pop-psychology books of the day. Betty Friedan writes in *The Feminine Mystique* (1965) that psychoanalysts frequently blamed women for veterans' readjustment problems on the ground that they were not performing their traditional woman's role of comforting their spouse. The historian Susan Hartmann found that a persistent theme in popular advice articles was urging wives to put their husbands' needs above their own. (Such advice was dramatized in *The Best Years of Our Lives,* as we've seen.) In another study, Sonya Michel found that movies of the immediate postwar era usually showed wives nursing their troubled veteran husbands back to wholeness (not incidentally providing a happy ending to what was sometimes in real life a serious and wrenching problem calling for professional help).

For all the marital unrest, this was a hyper-domestic generation; witness the high marriage rate running neck and neck with the divorce rate. Veterans' lives had been tossed about by the angry seas of depression and war, and many vets had developed a yearning for stability, which society told them came through marriage and the family. The Harvard sociologist Philip Slater judged postwar hyper-domesticity to be "part of a general postwar retreat from the world." He attributed this to a "more generalized desire, born of Depression and war, for the tranquility of home life." In *Children of the Great Depression* the sociologist Glenn Elder quotes a psychologist on this attitude:

We youth, all of us, men and women alike, needed to replenish ourselves in goods and spirit, to undo, by an exercise of collective will, the psychic disruptions of the immediate past. We would achieve the serenity that had eluded the lives of our parents; the men would be secure in stable careers, the women in comfortable homes, and together they would raise perfect children. Time would come to a stop. Call it what you will—a mystique, an illusion, a myth—it was an ideology of sorts, often unspoken but perhaps for that very reason most deeply felt.

"Tranquility," "serenity": the Crisis Generation becomes the Peace of Mind Generation. "The important thing," Tom Rath, the man of *The Man in the Gray Flannel Suit,* tells himself, "is to create an island of order in a sea of chaos—somebody very bright had said that, somebody whose name he had forgotten. . . . And an island of order obviously must be made of money, for one doesn't bring up children in an orderly way without money. . . . Money is the root of all order, he told himself, and the only trouble with it is, it's so damn hard to get."

And painful. For Tom, the former paratrooper, becomes unhappy in his demanding civilian job as an assistant to the hard-driving president of a broadcasting company, which he took for the money. Wilson raises questions typical of the organization man, but he never really faces them. By giving up ambition for a promotion, Tom ends up having it all—a good job at which he doesn't have to work seven days a week but still makes enough money to keep his wife and kids in middle-class comfort, living in a suburban castle and inheriting land that he will sell in a lucrative real estate deal. Wilson's novel appealed to a wide audience because it explored, if it did not seriously challenge, the high value the Crisis Generation placed on creating a money-lined haven in a world clamorous with competition for status and also a psychological haven, in the veteran's case, from the tormenting memories of combat. A much deeper-probing novel about a returned veteran trying to negotiate a balance between work, success, family, and self-realization is Richard Yates's artfully written, coruscating *Revolutionary Road* (1961), set in 1955. The hero, encouraged by his wife, rebels against his corporate job, but he is shown to be a phony intellectual whose fine talk about throwing it all up to go to Paris and write the big novel burning in his soul is empty rhetoric. He is curiously like the protagonist in Jules Dassin's film noir *Night and the City*—"an artist without an art." The author wrote it as a criticism of "a general lust for conformity all over this country, by no means only in the suburbs—a kind of blind, desperate clinging to safety and security at any price." Indeed, the worries about conformity were already bubbling up in the forties and would congeal in best-selling sociological studies of straitened corporate and bureaucratic life like *The Lonely Crowd* (1950), *White Collar* (1951), and *The Organization Man* (1956). In the fifties the corporation would become a symbol of standardization and group-think like small-town conformity and provincialism, epitomized in Sinclair Lewis's *Main Street,* had been to the *après guerre* generation in the twenties.

After the war, marriage was, in the reigning cliché of women's magazines, a "full-time job" that replaced the one a wife had left in an office or a war plant. The despairing woman isolated in a suburban housing tract would be lectured that she was the mainstay of society because a stable happy family was the bulwark of American life.

In *Children of the Depression,* Elder seems to conclude from his interviews that the strongest supporters of the traditional wife's role were "women who grew up in deprived households" with a strong mother at its center. In such families the oldest daughter had an important, responsible role to play helping her mother. She was likely to internalize the idea that a woman's primary task was to serve her family.

Economic reasons loomed larger than patriotism to many women who went out to work during the war. Even if they were paid on average only two-thirds of what men got, factory jobs were much more lucrative than the traditional women's positions like teachers and secretaries. Reasons for needing more money very likely included a husband in the service, on whose meager allotment it was difficult to support a family. Still, as feminist historian Elaine Tyler May writes, "For all the publicity surrounding Rosie the Riveter, few women took jobs that were previously held exclusively by men, and those who did earned less than men."

Yet moralists steadily inveighed against the whole idea of women working. Lifelong bachelor J. Edgar Hoover, for example, blamed war-working moms for the rise in juvenile crime and "perversion." "There must be no absenteeism among mothers," he thundered, as if it was any of his business. "Her patriotic duty is not on the factory front but on the home front!" Women workers were not immune to this kind of social shaming, which went all the way up to Congress: a senator suggested passing a law that would "force wives and mothers back to the kitchen," opening up their jobs to worthy veterans. And to corporate boardrooms: the chair of the National Association of Manufacturers advised, "From a humanitarian point of view, too many women should not stay in the labor force. The home is the basic American unit." Forcible discharges and layoffs duly hastened the patriotic task of herding women to the exits.

The upshot was that within a year of VJ Day, some 2 million women had left their jobs permanently. The director of the Women's Bureau of the Labor Department told a New York trade union conference that the 2 million figure included "many who had left their jobs voluntarily," suggesting that many others had been fired. Only sixty thousand were said to be seeking reemployment. In one survey 75 percent of working women said they wanted to do the same job after the war, but by that they meant lower-paying "women's jobs"—secretaries, sales clerks, stenographers, typists—in which most women were employed during the war, contrary to the image of Rosie the Riveter. Thus the number of women employed in 1946 equaled that in the war years; but 90 percent had taken a pay cut. Overall, the average weekly pay of all working women fell by 26 percent.

Younger women with families could no longer afford to work—or had the energy to. This explains why the ranks of working women between age twenty and thirty-four fell by 1 million. Yet the long trend was toward more and more working wives; their number rose from 3 million in 1940 to 10 million in 1960. These employed spouses toiled because their family needed the money rather than because they were seeking a fulfilling career or professional advancement. Routinely relegated to part-time or subordinate jobs, they neither challenged their husband's paternalism at home nor their foreman's sexism at work.

Even those women who took the higher-education path (including veterans who used the GI Bill) tended to drop out to marry rather than graduate and seek a professional career. And of those who *did* graduate, two-thirds would marry three to six years after college. Only half of the female graduates found the kind of jobs for which college prepared them.

By the fifties a new trend emerged: most women went to college hoping to meet an upward striver who would be their ticket to "affluent domesticity"—in, yes, suburbia.

The promarriage ethic so prominent among the Depression-bruised youth who went to war cast a long shadow into the next decade. Elaine Tyler May discerned in the postwar generation's need for stability the seeds of the cold war consensus that settled upon America in the fifties. As she writes, this family-centered generation had always "looked toward home as a way to bolster themselves against potential threats." One husband described domesticity in cold war terms: his family gave him "a sense of responsibility, a feeling of being a member of a group that in spite of many disagreements internally always will face its external enemies together."

On the cover of the paperback edition of May's book is a 1961 *Life* photograph of an all-American family—husband, wife, two kids—proudly seated in their fallout shelter. Nuclear family indeed.

Voices

"Sit down, sit down," he said. "Sorry to have kept you waiting but I've had trouble on my hands since three o'clock this afternoon. The bastards've pulled a strike on me."

"That's too bad," I said.

"Too bad for them," he said. "I'll have 'em in the bread line in a week. I've got a police department that's specially trained in breaking strikes and a National Guard that's specially trained in picking up the pieces. And a few patriotic organizations that'll wave the flag while they do it."

—HORACE MCCOY, *KISS TOMORROW GOODBYE* (1948)

We know there is a national and international conspiracy to divide our people, to discredit our institutions, and to bring about disrespect for our government. No country on earth, and no government can long endure this vicious attack.

—ATTORNEY GENERAL TOM C. CLARK, JUNE 1946

5

THE BIG WALKOUT

BARELY TWO MONTHS AFTER VJ DAY, picketers were marching outside factory gates carrying signs with the slogan "Fifty-two for Forty." The workers were demanding a 30 percent hike in hourly pay so that their compensation for forty hours of work would equal what they had earned for fifty-two hours at wartime rates including overtime.* A September Gallup poll asking if autoworkers should get raises to recoup what they had earned during the war showed 56 percent opposed and only 31 percent in favor. This hinted at trouble ahead for labor's demands.

The demands were not new. In September 1944, the *New York Times* reported that at a War Labor Board hearing, representatives of the AFL and the CIO called for immediate abolition of the wartime cap on wages because they feared prices would rise unchecked after the war. "These hearings showed," wrote reporter Louis Stark, "that the unions were apparently suffering from a case of 'conversion jitters.'" That is, they were thinking ahead to the return to peacetime production and the end of high earnings inflated by overtime. Stark summed up the mood of labor in this mathematical problem: "How can I, a wage-earner now paid fifty-two hours' pay for forty-eight hours' work, get along if cutbacks reduce my earnings to pay for forty hours at straight time?" Those picketers were saying, in effect, "Fifty-two for forty or fight."

---

* In other words, forty at straight time plus eight at time and a half, or twelve at straight time. Thus: 40 + 12 = 52.

Henry Fonda played one of the postwar era's few working-class heroes in *The Long Night* (1947). Directed by Anatole Litvak, it symbolically expresses workers' need to fight for dignity and justice. It came out just after the 1945–46 strike wave and before HUAC and the blacklist made impossible pictures taking the worker's side. *Everett Collection*

Average workers' pay had risen from $27 per week in 1941 to $45.50 in 1945, mainly because overtime was necessary as war plants raced to meet the military's voracious demands. Workers in heavy industry were averaging even more with overtime. Philip Murray, president of the steelworkers union, said that in April 1945 his people were pulling down $56.32 per week. By January 1946, though, a steelworker putting in a forty-hour week averaged only $43 and change—a drop of nearly $50 a month since VJ Day. That would have bought a lot of groceries.

Thus the seeds of the great postwar strike wave of 1945–46 were planted.

The year 1946 marked the high-water mark of American labor's political influence. During the war, prodded by an unceasing demand for workers, union membership had swelled to 30 percent of the workforce. Labor's clout was demonstrated in the 1944 presidential election when the doorbell-ringing and pamphleteering of the CIO's Political Action Committee (PAC) boosted FDR to a fourth term.

A labor-friendly administration and Congress were ensconced in Washington. Interior Secretary Harold Ickes told the 1944 CIO convention, "You are on your way and you must let no one stop you or even slow up your march." The CIO PAC proclaimed an ambitious agenda for postwar America: "We must move forward to a broad program of social and economic security for the men and women of this nation."

But even as labor was girding its loins for the greatest wave of strikes in US history, the country was slowly swinging to the right.

In November 1945, United Auto Workers vice president Walter Reuther, chesty, red-haired, hungrily ambitious, led 177,000 GM workers out, shuttering eighty auto plants. Bolstered by a strike fund of $600,000, these workers would remain out for 113 days. The union demanded a 30 percent wage increase, from $1.12 per hour to $1.45. In keeping with Truman's hold-the-line policy, Reuther stipulated that the wage boost not be accompanied by a price hike for cars, which would send inflationary currents rippling through the economy, shrinking the raise. He insisted that GM could well afford to requite the union's just demands without raising auto prices. If the company disagreed with him, he challenged it to open its books and prove otherwise. Management immediately dismissed the proposal as one more step toward Leninism in the workplace.

Polls showed that 44 percent of the public approved of the UAW strikers' demands for pay equity and 35 percent condemned them. But there
was ominous portent in another survey that had 42 percent blaming the
UAW for the strike against 19 percent holding GM culpable.

With UAW members treading the picket line, the Great Walkout of
1946 was launched. For the next days and months, strikes would course
through the great underbelly of American industry in peristaltic waves. All
told, between VJ Day and June 30, 1946, there were 436 work stoppages.
By the end of 1945, 3.5 million workers had hit the bricks; and by the summer of 1946, some 5 million had been out. A total of 50 million working
days were lost. In several cities, general strikes shut down all commerce.
It was the biggest national strike in US history.

The various unions involved demanded wage raises ranging from 10
to 30 percent. The big industrial unions wanted the largest pay hikes, jus-
tifying them as covering, at least in part, their members' lost overtime. In
the nonwar industries, where overtime was not as prevalent, pay demands
were correspondingly lower.

Management dug in, determined to take back prerogatives that had
slipped away during the war; they regarded the fight as "part of a long-term,
irrepressible struggle for power," labor historian Jeremy Brecher writes.
"Business was resolved to 'restore efficiency' and raise productivity . . . by
breaking the de facto control of production won by workers during the
war." In other words, this was more than a squabble over 30 cents: it was
a fight to preserve capitalism itself, which management identified with its
own autonomy.

Public sympathy quickly shifted; people were craving—demanding—
new cars and refrigerators. With savings and a brightening economic horizon, they wanted the material abundance that the ads had promised them
during the war years. As *Time* reported, "The plain fact was that the people
everywhere, not caring much who got what, sensing that both higher
wages and higher prices were in the air, wanted labor and industry to get
back into production on almost any terms." The unions were one of the
Democratic Party's important constituencies, so the president said workers deserved a raise now that the war was over. Privately, however, he was
more ambivalent. He regarded John L. Lewis, who had led his coal miners

out three times in 1945 and would take them out twice more in 1946, as a traitor, and was suspicious of other union bosses. As the strikes dragged on through 1946, the public grew angrier and Truman's approval ratings dropped—from 82 percent in November 1945 to 63 percent in February 1946 to 50 percent in April of that year.

A lot of the defectors told pollsters they disapproved of Truman because they thought he was "moving left." Their number grew from 10 percent to 44 percent in February 1946. Nearly 50 percent wanted him to move back "in the middle." On the question of which party could better handle strikes (i.e., get tough with the strikers), the Democrats dropped from 41 percent in October 1945 to 23 percent a year later.

Management waged a propaganda war against unions in newspaper ads. GM executives assailed Reuther's demand that the company open its ledgers. This was not a mathematical issue; it was a fundamental ideological one: was the American economy "to be based on free competition or . . . to become socialized, with all activities controlled and regimented?" The corporation sounded the tocsin: "American business must be free to pay the going rate rather than have its pay scales set by a political bureaucracy." (Never mind that during the war, business was quite happy to have the government cap wages.) In their standing-at-Armageddon posture, GM executives also claimed that the union's erosion of management's control over production schedules, work rules, and the shop floor posed a threat to "private capital and free enterprise."

The giant corporation was under no immediate pressure to settle; it could afford to rest comfortably on its cushion of wartime profits and postwar tax rebates, while letting labor draw the public's ire for holding up production of much-coveted new cars. When some GM executives said that the company could afford a raise because the war had enabled it to improve production techniques and greater productivity, top management sidestepped, insisting that control over production, not the bottom line, was the issue—thus hardening its position.

Reuther, his future ambitions riding on the strike, disagreed with Philip Murray that the union should bow to management's demands in return for hefty wage raises. As Nelson Lichtenstein writes, "He understood that only a direct assault on a key corporate adversary would blunt industry resistance and prod the government into putting some backbone into the OPA's postwar price guidelines." Reuther's troops were in a combative mood, energized by the idea of challenging the company in a strike rather than leaving their fate to a government board, as they had during the war.

As if underscoring the union's readiness to fight, some 50,000 World War II vets in the UAW's ranks donned their old uniforms and marched on the picket line in a patriotic display designed to win public sympathy and boost morale. There was a strong spirit of working-class unity; after their strike vote, UAW members spontaneously burst into the old Wobbly anthem "Solidarity Forever!" Lichtenstein sums up: "The war, with its legacy of full employment, patriotic entitlement and democratic expectation, had offered millions of workers an emancipatory vision." Alas, like many hopes of the common people aroused during the war, this vision would wither in the postwar chill.

President Truman was quite aware of the unions' vital role in the old New Deal coalition. But when fighting for workers and for liberal values might mean alienating party conservatives, he equivocated. On civil rights issues, for example, such as renewal of the Fair Employment Practices Commission (FEPC), he made noises pleasing to liberals and then backed off a bit to placate the Southern Democrats. An administration official complained, "The strategy was to start with a bold measure and then temporize to pick up right-wing forces." Political reporter Samuel Lubbell called Truman "a man of persistent irresolution" with a "faculty for turning two bold steps into a halfway measure."

Truman realized he was acquiring an image of vacillation. To counter it, he made public displays of furious decision-making designed to show he was fully in charge. Biographer David McCullough quotes a journalistic description of him racing through his day, in "the decisive style that is now recognized as typically Truman," editing speeches with "hurried" strokes of the pen, ticking off at a press conference in the space of five minutes a series of major reorganizations and appointments. By November a skeptical *Life* story would blur that image: "People began to suspect that his confidence might be based on naivety; that his ability to make decisions fast reflected a failure to weigh them carefully."

Truman had begun moving away from the New Deal, which he had once strongly supported. He still did, but partly out of insecurity he wanted the old New Dealers put out to pasture and his friends brought in. By late 1946 he had stacked his administration with a cadre of loyal conservatives, most of them from his home state of Missouri.

Among these was the banker John Snyder, who now headed the Office of War Mobilization and Reconversion (OWMR). Consider Snyder in action. When the steel strike became a test of what price increases the new Wage Stabilization Board (which came under the OWMR) would tolerate, he caved in to the industry, which said it would grant an hourly raise of 18.5 cents if it was permitted to jack up its prices by $10 a ton. Staffers with the OPA and the OWMR, engaging in some independent fact-finding, determined that if the industry upped its price only $1 to $2 a ton it could still make a decent profit. Big Steel signaled to Snyder that it could live with a $5 raise. Alarmed, OWMR counsel Thomas Emerson prepared a legal memo stating that a $5 increase without OPA approval would violate the law. Snyder glanced at it and said, "I don't want to receive this memorandum. If it is ever stated that I received this memorandum I will deny it."

Shortly thereafter, Snyder announced he had granted the $5 increase. The OPA and the Wage Stabilization Board approved it. The thumb was out of the dike. Between March and November the Cost of Living Index rocketed up 14 percent.

After the steel settlement was announced, a host of other industries followed suit. A fact-finding panel appointed by Truman to solve the auto strike recommended that GM grant the UAW a 17.5 percent raise, or 19.5 cents an hour, in return for a price increase. The company, however, insisted on its absolute right to pay the "going rate" rather than what the government proposed. It offered 18.5 cents. Reuther blasted the panel's finding, but his UAW rivals at Ford and Chrysler, whom he was challenging for control of the union, grabbed the 18.5 cents. Leaders of the United Electrical workers, some of whom had Communist ties and disliked the socialist Reuther, accepted a comparable offer from General Electric. Reuther called these settlements a "betrayal."

When James Dewey, the federal mediator, urged Reuther to accept 18.5 cents, the UAW leader told him, "I will be God damned if I will compromise a compromise. We are not going to take less than this, and this is all horse shit about going back to work." He insisted on a penny more to save face, but GM was set in stone. On the 113th day the union gave in, settling for 18.5 cents, though Reuther rationalized that some vague fringe benefits he had negotiated were worth a penny more, netting a raise of 19.5 cents.

Some scholars argue that the union could have achieved the same result at the bargaining table. But Reuther wanted member muscle behind him when he sat down at that table. True, he had his own future to consider. Leaders of other unions, their position and perks at stake, would have preferred to work things out with management. But the workers were burning with grievances built up over the war years and itching to strike. As the economist Peter Drucker concluded, "It was on the whole not the leadership which forced the workers into a strike but worker pressure that forced a strike upon the reluctant leadership; most of the leaders knew very well that they could have gained as much by negotiations as they finally gained by striking. And again and again the rank and file of the union membership refused to go back to work."

A final act remained in the drama, and it would bring Truman center stage. Two major unions were still holding out: the coal miners and the railroad brotherhoods, both of them perpetrators of wartime strikes. With them, the administration had an even more dangerous situation on its hands. Workers in these two key sectors could tie up the entire nation, which was heavily dependent on coal for heat and power and on trains for public transportation.

Truman promptly signed an order calling on the government to seize the railroads (a leftover wartime power). This bought a five-day postponement. Frantic negotiations ensued; Labor Secretary John Steelman and even Secretary of State James Byrnes leaned on the two brotherhood leaders who were still holding out.

The May 23 deadline passed, and the union leaders ordered the engines back to the yards, blocking the country's arteries of commerce. In New

York suburban trains stopped at the height of rush hour, forcing commuters to wangle alternative rides home. Reporter Meyer Berger described the eerie calm in the great railroad yards of the metropolis: "No rolling stock moved, no locomotives hooted. In the terminals the long platforms were empty and strangely silent. Behind closed gates, the long lines of trains stood dark and gloomy."

The next day alarmed telegrams from businesses and ordinary citizens flooded into the White House. Truman retired to his study and composed an angry message to Congress, calling for drafting the strikers if they refused to return to work. His diatribe, McCullough writes, was "one of the most intemperate documents ever written by an American President." He damned home-front slackers and traitors who had sabotaged the war effort, among them John L. Lewis, who had called two coal strikes in wartime, "which were worse than bullets in the back to our soldiers." He said the railroad unions "held a gun at the head of the government." Yet their members were already earning "from four to forty times what the man who was facing the enemy fire on the front was receiving." And their fat cat leaders raked in "from five to ten times the net salary of your president."*

The union leaders had lied to him, he charged; a "weak-kneed" Congress lacked the guts to pass his cooling-off bill. "Mr. [Philip] Murray and his Communist friends had a conniption fit and Congress had labor jitters." The president was "tired" of being "flouted, vilified and misrepresented." On the spot he called for volunteers to defend the Constitution. He specifically exhorted "you men who are my comrades in arms, you men who fought the battles to save the nation just as I did twenty-five years ago, to come along with me and eliminate the Lewises, the Whitneys, the Johnstons, the Communist [Harry] Bridges [head of the longshoremen's union]." By inviting ex-servicemen to take action against the traitorous union bosses, he evoked, perhaps unintentionally, the spirit of the American Legionnaires' assaults on Wobblies in 1919.

---

* Here his figures were a mile off: railway workers earned nowhere near forty times what a soldier got; Lewis drew $25,000 a year, and the brotherhood leaders earned comparable amounts—well under Truman's salary ($75,000).

Truman's aides were appalled by his language; his suave new counsel, Clark Clifford, another Missourian, quickly confiscated the notes. Advisers huddled and offered suggestions. Then Clifford retired to the Cabinet room, where he rewrote the radio speech Truman was scheduled to deliver at 10 p.m. that night.

In his address to the nation a calmer Truman bluntly declared a crisis and announced he would call out the Army if necessary to get the trains running again. But he had not given up his intention to draft the strikers. In his address before Congress the following day, he requested "temporary emergency" legislation "to authorize the President to draft into the Armed Forces of the United States all workers who are on strike against their government." As he came to those words in his speech, the secretary of the Senate handed him a note, which he hastily scanned before reading aloud: the holdout unions had capitulated; the railroad strike was over. This unintended bit of theater drew wild cheers from the legislators. But Truman's speech left a lingering bad taste. His advisers, including Attorney General Tom Clark, Secretary of State Byrnes, and Judge Sam Rosenman, doubted the constitutionality of drafting strikers.

The House passed the measure 306 to 13 after two hours of debate, but the bill was defeated in the Senate 70 to 13. The constitutional conservative Senator Robert Taft led the opposition, declaring, "I am not willing to vote for a measure which provides that the President shall be a dictator." It was perhaps the finest hour for "Mr. Republican"; it was certainly one of Truman's worst. The liberal *PM* dubbed the striker draft "military fascism." AFL president William Green warned that "fascism may grip America unawares." Richard Strout, *The New Republic*'s Washington columnist, exclaimed, "Draft men who strike in peacetime, into the armed services! Is this Russia or Germany?"

In a kind of flashback, Truman yielded to what historian Michael Sherry calls an "impulse to apply wartime reflexes to postwar problems."[*]

---

[*] In a September 1945 diary entry Truman flashes back to 1918, when, he writes, civilians "forgot the war" and "began to talk of disarmament. . . . They became fat and rich, special privilege ran the country—ran it to a fall." Truman, although nearly overwhelmed by the heavy responsibilities of his new office, was in a sense still fighting the last war—or rather the last postwar.

In her newspaper column, former First Lady Eleanor Roosevelt implored the president not to backslide "into a military way of thinking."

Meanwhile, Lewis's striking miners became Truman's next challenge. The conservative press called him a coward for bowing to the arrogant Lewis. Under such pressure (and perhaps recalling the polls criticizing him as too prolabor), Truman ordered a government seizure of the mines. Lewis defied the order, and rather than set the Army on the miners the government granted his demands for an owner-financed welfare and retirement fund (which would grow into a comprehensive healthcare plan).

Lewis led his miners out again in November, demanding still more welfare contributions plus vacation pay. They remained absolutely loyal to him. Between 1939 and 1949, he had won an increase in their average weekly pay from $22.16 to $76.84—$703 in 2010 purchasing power. Truman blasted the strike as an insurrection against the US government, and federal lawyers got an injunction ordering the miners back to work. While the president vacationed in Key West, Lewis was hauled before a federal judge, who lectured him that his strike was "an evil, demoniac, monstrous thing that means hunger and cold and unemployment and destitution and disorganization of the social fabric." The judge fined the union $3.5 million, and, as Truman wrote to his mother, "John L. had to fold up."

By mid-March 1946, confronted by government pressure, hard-nosed management, and a hostile public, the strikers were losing heart. Most of the remaining unions followed the steelworkers and the miners, and agreed to an hourly raise of 18.5 cents. Many smaller unions had to live with an average of 10 cents an hour. The best face *The Nation* could put on it was that labor had held its own in the fight. And indeed, the strikes could be seen as a holding action against industry's determination to push down real wages and reclaim its prerogatives in the workplace.

But even that last stand was ultimately a failure. First, the OPA, which unionists counted on to keep inflation in check, had been mortally wounded by Snyder's cave-in to Big Steel. An OPA historian later wrote, "From this point on a really firm price policy was no longer possible, either administratively or politically." Prices lurched upward by 16 percent between June and November 1946. OPA granted GM alone three more increases in car prices that year. Workers' average weekly earnings dropped 8 percent below what they were in 1945. The unions would bargain for a second round of raises in 1947. With management anxious to pump up peacetime production, those raises were generally granted. In return, the unions accepted one-year no-strike contracts. By May 1947, though, auto-and steelworkers were averaging 25 percent less in real wages than they had in 1945.

The public backlash against the strike created the favoring wind conservatives needed to pass antiunion legislation. On their first try, a harshly punitive piece of legislation known as the Case bill, actually written by the National Association of Manufacturers, they struck out. After polling his Cabinet, Truman heeded the New Dealers and vetoed the bill with a reasoned message pointing out that its main purpose was punitive, not preventive. The liberal/labor coalition in Congress mustered enough votes to defeat any attempt to override, but antiunion sentiment dominated the Seventy-Ninth Congress.

Senator Kenneth Wherry, a Nebraska Republican, spoke for rural and small-town America when he blasted "unionists who fatten themselves at the expense of the rest of us" and asked how long America would tolerate "big labor's use of the strike bludgeon to win the . . . inflated, unrealistic pay scales that hamper productivity, slow reconversion and deny goods to the Average American. . . . Big labor beware, the people are tiring of your arrogance, and your increasing privileged position."

The rising antiunion tide would sweep away the Democrats' majorities in both houses in the 1946 midterm elections and carry to passage the Taft-Hartley Act of 1947, which made unions legally liable for strike-related damages, allowed states to ban union shops, barred secondary boycotts, and required union leaders to sign loyalty affidavits. Truman would veto that too, but he was overridden by the Republican Congress.

And so, as the historian Alan Derickson writes, "the outcome in the postwar labor wars was that management defeated demands for greater industrial democracy." In the years ahead, unions would agree to the multiyear contracts and reduced economic power management demanded in exchange for higher pay, job security, pensions, life and disability insurance, and health insurance. The result was the emergence of what Lichtenstein and others have dubbed the "private welfare state," a sort of anti–New Deal in which corporations rather than the state provided social benefits. Under this grand bargain, workers prospered into the sixties—until rising global competition enabled the corporations to cut back on their benefits.

Another negative outcome of the 1946 strikes was the forced entry of red-baiting into the house of labor. The drive to purge Communists, started by Reuther and others and buttressed by the Taft-Hartley Act, drove leaders of most unions to embark on a red hunt, triggering internal factional fights and challenging leftist leaders of local unions in representation elections. It also opened the way to raids on the more militant unions by anti-Communist internationals. In 1949–50 the CIO, once known for its militancy in the sit-down strikes of the thirties (led by Communist organizers), purged its ranks of eleven unions considered Communist-dominated and merged with the AFL.

This action was supported by the rank and file, a majority of whom were hostile to Communists and feared that continuing to tolerate them would damage labor's cause. But the purges sanitized unions by leading to a kind of "depoliticization," which resulted in their withdrawal from campaigning for political goals such as the expansion of New Deal social welfare programs. Instead, union leaders concentrated on winning fringe benefits for their members. The UAW's 1947 contract openly discouraged political action. The shift to pure economic bargaining would become, in Nelson Lichtenstein's view, a "strait jacket that restricted the social views and political strategies once advocated by the laborite left." Such a truncated vision had no place in it for groups on the left, not only Communists but progressives who advocated social and foreign policy positions outside the hardening cold war consensus, including talking with the Soviets.

Without this ballast to port, labor's ship would list to starboard, and in the fifties its political influence would diminish even as its numbers held strong and its members prospered.

A MORE DECISIVE DEFEAT of the union movement at this time, now mainly forgotten, had long-term reverberations. This was a CIO organizing drive in the South called Operation Dixie. Launched in 1946, it was primarily aimed at bringing Southern mill workers into the Textile Workers Union of America (TWUA). During the war, under a sympathetic NLRB, union membership in the South had for the first time risen to the low five figures. But the CIO and the Textile Workers were really taking a stand in Dixie against capital flight to that region, which had been going on since the mid-twenties but had accelerated after the war. The textile industry was only one of the industries moving to the South in search of cheap, nonunion labor. Such major corporations as RCA, Thompson Products, Swift, Armour, J.C. Stevens, and Ford joined the exodus.

The unions had a long-range political goal as well—mobilizing an interracial coalition of poor people, blue-collar workers, farmers, and others who had been deliberately excluded from New Deal protections by the Southern power structure, and energizing white liberal Democrats to speak out more strongly against segregation. This coalition, if it grew, could in time outvote the segregationist Democrats who returned racists like Theodore Bilbo and John Rankin to Congress and Gene Talmadge to the governor's mansion with machinelike regularity. These retrograde Democrats had long been a drag on the party's progressive ambitions— even opposing (in order to keep white supremacy in place) federal aid to the region aimed at reversing its deep-seated poverty.

At a press conference in April 1946, CIO and Steelworkers president Philip Murray launched the drive with some cocky rhetoric. But his words suggest that he underestimated the dangers the racial issue posed to organizing in the South. Rather than hurl a challenge to segregation (although he had supported the FEPC and established the Committee to Abolish Racial Discrimination inside the CIO), he insisted the union had no racial agenda. This drive's goal, he said, was limited to the "economic emancipation" of 1 million unorganized workers in the South by winning higher wages for them. He said that the general goal was the end of "all forms of discrimination in industry." In other words, eliminating job and pay discrimination rather than the political, social, and educational kind. (The campaign called for one modest step in that direction: ending the poll tax, which discouraged African Americans and poor whites from voting.) "To Secure These Rights," the 1947 study by President Truman's commission on racial discrimination, reported that average wages of black war veterans in twenty-five communities in the South ranged from 30 to 78 percent of the average for white workers in those places. Unemployment among blacks in April 1946 was three times that among whites.

Some labor chroniclers have criticized the CIO for its naïveté about the potency of racial politics and for its lack of familiarity with local customs. To be fair to Murray, during the war and after, Negro leaders like Roy Wilkins and A. Philip Randolph were gradualists in their strategies for bettering the lot of their people. A testimonial to that fact was that none of the prominent black leaders who contributed to the important anthology *What the Negro Wants,* published in 1944, called for overthrowing segregation. Rather, they ranked the end of segregated education as one of their "ultimate, long-range proposals." In the meantime, they agreed, blacks should fight discrimination in jobs and schools rather than wasting their "energies struggling for integration."

Militant black leaders like Ella Baker and Thurgood Marshall chastised the somnolence of Southern branches of the NAACP, which served mainly as social clubs and concentrated on sponsoring lawsuits challenging black teachers' low salaries. But Southern blacks were stirring. Dr. Mordecai Johnson, president of Howard University, pointed to the growing number of African American college students who were seeking admission to state universities. He believed that the walls of Jericho were starting to tumble down, as the old spiritual had it.

His optimism gained credence when the Supreme Court in 1950 ruled in *Sweatt v. Painter* that Herman Sweatt, an African American student on the GI Bill, must be admitted to the University of Texas law school on terms of full equality. To keep him out of the main school, the state had rented a suite of offices in Houston for a "campus" and hired two black lawyers as faculty, with Sweatt their only student; there was no library. When his lawyer, Thurgood Marshall, put him on the stand, Sweatt testified: "I don't believe equality can be given on the basis of segregation."

The Supreme Court ultimately agreed with him, even though in the meantime the Texas legislature had appropriated $3 million to set up a more commodious, though still separate, law school with a full-time five-member faculty.

Sweatt had prevailed in the courts, but some blacks believed that more militant, if nonviolent, tactics were needed as well. Here the labor militancy of Operation Dixie made a contribution by advertising mass action such as strikes to protest injustice. The stage was being set for the use of nonviolent tactics by CORE and other groups, which challenged Jim Crow where it lived rather than just in the federal courts, as the NAACP was doing.

Yet for the CIO and the textile workers union, Operation Dixie was a resounding defeat. By the campaign's close in 1952, union membership in the South had actually dropped from 20 to 10 percent of all workers. Contributing to the failure was the growing ideological split inside the CIO, which came to a head with the anti-Communist purges that hit hardest the most militant Southern-based unions, such as the tobacco workers and the meatpackers, both Communist-led and racially integrated. Also to blame were the obstacles created by the Taft-Hartley Act; the antilabor climate in Washington, which had stiffened resistance in the South; and the NLRB's dilatory enforcement of the Wagner Act, which guarantees workers' right to join a union.

The CIO's poor planning also contributed to the debacle. For one thing, the campaign lacked adequate resources—people, money, allies. Another hindrance was the Northern-based leadership's cultural blindness to conditions in Southern mill towns. The CIO mistakenly chose to follow a Northern strategy, which stressed the importance of transformational victories like the 1937 sit-down strike in Flint, Michigan. That strategy was better suited to auto plants in Detroit than to Southern towns, where the mill owner virtually owned the local government and the police.

As for the organizers, there simply weren't enough of them. The "flying wedge" of 200 unionists dispatched in the first wave looked pretty puny when spread out over twelve large states. And because of the shallow pockets of contributing unions, cash ran dry and the CIO had to cut operations in half after the first year.

Finally, the Northerners did not fully appreciate the cultural wall between white and black workers; they did not know how to counter the race-baiting tactics of the owners or the determined, sometimes violent opposition of local citizens (some of them Klan members) and the hostility of local cops. As one organizer recalled to Barbara Griffith, "They mobilized the towns against us. They controlled most of the churches in the towns. Even the black churches they sometimes controlled too, with donations. They owned practically everything else. . . . And they mobilized them."

The main tactic was harassing the union's organizers in various ways, including violence. The organizers showed great courage (some seventeen of them were beaten up in the first year). J.P. Mooney, who had been an organizer for the Communist-led Mine, Mill and Smelters Union, was mauled by police while distributing leaflets at the textile mill in Avondale, Alabama. Mooney returned the next day with bruises and black eyes and resumed handing out leaflets. The cops arrived and stomped him, landing him in the hospital for six weeks. The police chief visited his bedside, praised his guts, and told him that the next time he showed up at the plant gate he would be shot dead. As soon as he was discharged, Mooney returned to his post. His presence was so inspiring that the workers signed union pledges en masse and the plant was unionized.

Rival AFL organizers made fierce red-baiting attacks on the CIO as they competed with the TWUA and other unions for new members. But the most militant and effective unions in the South were Communist-led ones like the Food, Tobacco, Agricultural and Allied Workers of America (FTA), which adopted a "race-conscious radicalism" to unify their people around race and gender grievances.

One can only speculate what might have evolved out of Operation Dixie if it had succeeded in greater measure. Perhaps the power structure based on segregation would have been shaken. Perhaps unions would have acquired political power in the South, neutralizing the die-hard segregationists who ran the Democratic Party, injecting new blood into it. But those changes would not have borne fruit in time to avert the drubbing Democratic liberals suffered of the 1946 midterms.

IN THE FALL OF 1946, an angry anti-Washington attitude gripped the land. The 1946 Republican campaign slogan, created by an ad agency, resonated with the mood: "Had enough? Vote Republican." People *were* fed up, though some were fed up with some things and others were fed up with other things. Some, probably most, were fed up with the rise in the cost of living—up 20 percent over the previous twelve months and 8 percent in a single month. (For example, washing machines, which cost an average of $91 in 1942, sold for $112 in 1946; refrigerators shot up from $155 to $207 over the same period.) Some were irritated by soaring food prices, primarily of meat, which had become scarce. Indeed, House Speaker Sam Rayburn grumbled that the upcoming test was going to be a "damned beefsteak election."

What Americans were really fed up with were conditions they believed were blocking the way to the promised land of postwar security and prosperity—a general "public disillusionment with the evaporation of their postwar dream," as pollster John Fenton writes.

Rather than promising to do anything much about it, Republicans dusted off the red-baiting tactics used in 1944 against FDR's run for a fourth term:

> *Item.* Senator Taft charged that the Democratic Party was "so divided between Communism and Americanism that its foreign policy can only be futile and contradictory."
> *Item.* GOP national chairman B. Caroll Reece said the election was "a stark choice between Communism and Republicanism."
> *Item.* A *Washington Post* reporter traveling across the country found "hatred of communism rampant."
> *Item.* Business organizations like the National Association of Manufacturers and the Chamber of Commerce compiled dossiers on the red infiltrators undermining the nation.

Item. J. Edgar Hoover warned that one hundred thousand Communists were active in America and infiltrating respectable groups.[*]

Item. The American ambassador in Moscow, Averell Harriman, told a group of journalists in May 1945 that there were unbridgeable differences between Russia and the United States on long-term policies.

Former British prime minister Winston Churchill added his orotund eloquence to the swelling anti-Communist sentiment in a March 5 speech at Westminster College in Fulton, Missouri, as President Truman watched onstage. "From Stettin in the Baltic to Trieste in the Adriatic an iron curtain has descended across the Continent," he rumbled. A week after the speech, the Gallup poll found only 19 percent agreeing with Churchill's central plea for stronger military ties between the United States and Great Britain (aimed at preserving the British Empire people rightly suspected), but some 50 percent pronounced the US-Soviet wartime alliance dead. And 60.6 percent agreed with the proposition that the United States was "too soft" on Russia.

In May, the administration pushed through Congress an urgent $4.4 billion loan to Britain, which was deeply in debt to the United States and short of dollars to buy essential goods. John Maynard Keynes himself had resorted to warlike hyperbole to warn the British government that it faced an "economic Dunkirk." But Congress was cool toward the proposal. Keynes finally negotiated the loan, but Washington extracted painful concessions, including cessation of London's longstanding policy of giving preferred treatment to imports from former colonies, a system that was the commercial backbone of the British Commonwealth. It was the best deal Keynes could get at the time, given the hostile temper of American domestic

---

[*] I retain a boyhood memory of a newsreel in which Hoover, his bulldog jaw cocked defiantly, railed against alien forces that he pronounced *"commonusts."* These newsreels matched the stark tabloid look of crime films of the time, like *The Naked City*. Director John Frankenheimer caught this atmosphere perfectly in a hearing scene in his 1962 film *The Manchurian Candidate*.

politics. As Richard M. Freeland reports, "The argument that proved decisive was the anti-Soviet one."

Around the same time, a Soviet request for $6 billion in aid was brushed off by Congress—though it made sense on humanitarian grounds and as a potential lever to influence Soviet conduct and possibly even cool the growing tensions with Moscow. But such a loan was out of the question in a Congress controlled by politicians who exploited those tensions for electoral gain. (Whether Stalin would have accepted the aid is another matter.)*

The British loan imbroglio showed that Republican help was needed to push through any serious foreign policy measure, and that the only way this help could be obtained was by successfully framing the measure as anti-Communist policy.

Also, anti-Communism offered tactical advantages for GOP candidates. First, stressing one's fierce opposition to Communism enabled one to call for the support of like-minded patriots of both parties. Second, it appealed to on-the-fence ethnic and religious groups like Polish Americans, who were traditionally Democratic but infuriated by Soviet dismissal of the pro-Western London government in exile, and other ethnic Catholics mobilized by their church's militant anti-Communism, which included covert opposition to left-liberal candidates. Catholic blue-collar workers were aroused by church directives denouncing alleged Communist infiltration of unions and mobilized by the Association of Catholic Trade Unionists, an active participant in campaigns to oust allegedly Communist-dominated unions in bargaining elections.

---

* In the Soviet Union signs of famine appeared in the summer of 1946. During the "hungry winter" of 1946–47 there was significant loss of life from malnutrition. The historian V.F. Zima estimated "that in the USSR as a whole about 100 million suffered malnutrition after the war and that from 1946 through 1948 it caused about 2 million deaths. At least half a million people starved to death in the Russian Republic." A war-impoverished citizenry faced price increases for bread. Stalin's policies were largely at fault. His government confiscated a greater-than-usual share of grain from collectives, leaving workers little or nothing, and shipped grain to Eastern Europe even after harvest losses in 1945. The government overcompensated in building up the grain reserves.

Anti-Communism comprised many voices, from the philosophical and moral anti-Stalinism in intellectual circles to the patriotic animus of union members to the visceral hatred of the Soviets among Polish Americans. But it was in the air, everywhere, and well suited by tradition, political experience, and proven results to political manipulation. The GOP's anti-Communist strategy was to cripple the Democrats' strong left arm—organized labor. Fittingly, in his run for a House seat in California, Richard Nixon revived the GOP war on the CIO's political action committee, saying that a vote for him was "a vote against the Communist-dominated PAC with its gigantic slush-fund." His people spread rumors that the Democratic incumbent, Jerry Voorhis, was a fellow traveler. Perfecting the talent for guilt by innuendo that would propel his early career, Nixon announced, "Jerry is not a Communist but not many members of the House have voted against more measures the Communists vigorously opposed than he."

Meanwhile, the Truman administration was quietly tilting toward a more hardline stance vis-à-vis Moscow. While avoiding direct denunciations of the Soviets, with whom it was attempting to negotiate the fate of Europe, the administration fanned the anti-Soviet flame. For example, as a way of taking a stronger anti-Soviet posture without seeming to do so, the administration publicized its confrontations with Moscow in negotiations over such flashpoints as Turkey, Iran, and Greece, which up to then had been kept confidential. These efforts, however, won few points among congressional Republicans, who had no desire to give Truman credit for any achievements.

That year people were also aggravated by a familiar blanket complaint: the "mess in Washington," of which an incompetent and too-liberal president had become the symbol. The domestic issues on which FDR had regularly campaigned—economic royalists, greedy businessmen, hunger, poverty, joblessness, the Axis, fear itself, etc.—no longer resonated with these restive voters. Truman's image problem, according to the political scientist William Lydgate, was that "he was more popular as a substitute Roosevelt than as a real-life Truman." When he stepped into the Oval Office, most people hoped he would make good—that is, stand in for the dead president. But he brought to his new role precious little political capital of his own.

By October, the polls were registering a strong pro-GOP trend; by November Truman's approval rating slid to a new low of 32 percent. The popular tide was flowing in a Republican direction. A low turnout at the polls on Election Day—35.2 million out of a potential electorate of 60 million—favored the GOP. Many potential voters had new addresses and were ineligible to mark a ballot. Most of these people—Southerners who'd moved to California or Detroit war plants, young blue-collar families seeking new jobs, ex-GIs—would likely have marked them in the Democratic column.

Demographics aside, a conservative counterrevolution was under way. The Democratic vote total shrank from 25 million to 15 million—mainly because some of the party's loyal constituencies jumped into the Republican column. For example, a stunning 51 percent of all blue-collar workers and 49 percent of all union members voted Republican.

When the dust settled, the Republicans had grabbed fifty-five House seats from the Democrats, giving them a fifty-nine-seat majority, the largest since 1928. In the Senate they snatched away thirteen seats, upending Democratic control; now the balance stood at fifty-two Republicans to forty-four Democrats.

Suffering the most grievous losses were the certified liberals. Thirty-seven of the sixty-nine most liberal House members were ousted. Voters fired precisely half the 116 representatives who had voted for Truman's Employment Act.

The conservative upsurge brought seven ultra-right-wing voices to the Senate, including Indiana's William Jenner, Ohio's John Bricker, California's William Knowland, and Wisconsin's Joseph McCarthy, all of whom had played the Communists-in-government issue fortissimo.

The American people—inspired and shaken by the war years, still projecting memories of the Depression on the future, no longer unified by the cause of Victory, feeling Arctic winds from the Soviet Union, feeling themselves leaderless in the first year without FDR—panicked.

New Deal historian James Boylan contends that the 1946 election returns were a warning to the party in power: "the Depression was over, the war was over. The emergency politics of the Depression—welfare-oriented, radical in flavor if not in content—had to be reappraised. . . . In the 1930s, the majority had been the poor; in postwar politics the majority had become, if not affluent, at least no longer poor." As Jordan Schwartz writes, the New Deal built the modern middle class by opening up the old middle class "to admit new ethnic groups and integrat[ing] much of the working class into capitalism through protected bargaining rights and a credit revolution that made home ownership desirable, through afford-ability. New Deal state capitalism generated untold number of jobs in transportation, construction and electrical-related industries."

Historian Allen J. Matusow discerned a more immediate trend: a shift "from the politics of need to the politics of greed." The sociologist Glenn Elder, following a similar train of thought but putting it more benignly, concluded that the hard times many of the Depression generation had known in the thirties, which had "enhanced the value of material goods and the desire for children, [were] soon followed by an economic up-swing that often turned these values into reality. In a single life span, Americans had moved from scarcity to abundance, from sacrifice to the freedoms made possible by prosperity."

War and Depression meant hard times and pessimism; Americans were in a mood to move on to prosperity and hope. They believed that the industrial Prometheus that had helped win the war should be unbound to produce the promised good life abounding in family happiness, material satisfactions, and mass entertainment. They wanted the war to be truly over so that the country could move toward a secure future, free of fear of Depression, liberated from New Deal bureaucrats, safe from subversion at home and aggression abroad.

Voices

Writers I consider intellectuals . . . most of them can take care of themselves. I am interested more in workers.

—HERBERT SORRELL, PRESIDENT OF
THE COUNCIL OF STUDIO UNIONS, 1937

You also have to realize that we were in the film business not to change the world but to make films. To change the world we were involved in other kinds of things, like the labor struggle in Hollywood, against the studios and against the right-wing union, the IATSE.

—ABRAHAM POLONSKY, WRITER/DIRECTOR,
EX-COMMUNIST, 1997

Why does the Communist Party want to control Hollywood? . . . Because in Hollywood we have the greatest medium of propaganda that has ever been conceived in the world.

—JACK TENNEY, CALIFORNIA STATE LEGISLATOR, 1945

Alien-minded communistic enemies of Christianity are trying to take over the motion picture industry and spread their un-American propaganda as well as their loathsome, lying, immoral and anti-Christian filth before the eyes of your children in every community in America.

—REPRESENTATIVE JOHN RANKIN,
ON THE FLOOR OF THE HOUSE, JULY 17, 1945

I am a witch hunter if the witches are Communists.

—ADOLPH MENJOU, TESTIMONY BEFORE HUAC, 1947

Q. When you wrote this short story, "Night Shade," were you a member of the Communist Party?

A. I decline to answer on the ground the answer may tend to incriminate me.

Q. Did that story in any way reflect the Communist line?

A. That is a difficult—on the word "reflect" I would say no, it didn't reflect it. It was against racism.

Q. Would you say that it resembled—whether it reflected or not—the Communist line with respect to race problems?

A. No, I couldn't pick out. . . . Did it reflect that more than, say, other political parties, I would have to say no. I think the truth would be that it didn't reflect it consciously or solely.

—DASHIELL HAMMETT, EXCERPTS FROM SECRET SENATE TESTIMONY BEFORE SENATOR JOSEPH MCCARTHY'S SUBCOMMITTEE

I would prefer, if you would allow me, not to mention other people's names. Don't present me with the choice of either being in contempt of this Committee and going to jail or forcing me to really crawl through the mud to be an informer.

—LARRY PARKS, TESTIMONY BEFORE HUAC, 1951

6

RED DAWN
ON SUNSET STRIP

HOLLYWOOD, THOUGH KNOWN AS A COMPANY TOWN, did not escape the great postwar strike wave of 1945–46. Indeed, in some senses it led the way, for it was also a labor town, organized top to bottom by unions representing the creative talent as well as the behind-the-scenes craftspeople, from cameramen to script editors to grips.

Three talent unions were born in Hollywood during the turbulent thirties that would play significant roles after the war: the actors, writers, and directors guilds. The first two initially leaned left, like most unions formed amid the bursts of labor militancy of that time. According to historian Michael Denning, although they were small in membership, the talent unions made their members "feel directly connected to the union struggles of American working people. Moreover, since the idea of white-collar and professional unionism had been largely confined to the left, and since the union activists were often the alumni of the proletarian avant garde, the culture unions were often led by Communists and Popular Front leftists."

Most motion picture crafts workers belonged to the International Alliance of Theatrical Stage Employees, Moving Picture Technicians, Artists and Allied Crafts of the United States (IATSE, or IA for short). Founded in the 1890s by stagehands, it evolved to comprise an array of unions serving the film industry (including the all-important projectionists in the studio-owned movie houses). These disparate elements were held together by a

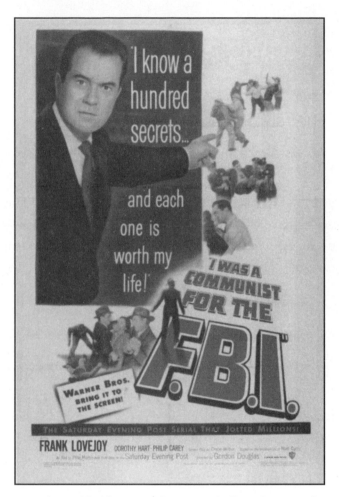

One of many blacklist-inspired propaganda films, the story of an FBI informant who exposes a Commie union. *Everett Collection*

strong central leadership, which had the power to override locals' votes for a strike or whatever, leaving them with little autonomy.

Movie-making tasks were subdivided among a bewildering variety of craftspeople—electricians, carpenters, cameramen, publicists, painters, set decorators, script readers, office workers, and others—around twenty in all. Given this structural maze, jurisdictional disputes abounded. But it would be wrong to believe that labor in Hollywood did not have real bread-and-butter issues of pay and working conditions.

The IA, however, was not always active in resolving these issues. Its parent union, the conservative, business-oriented American Federation of Labor, had little power or will to intervene in, let alone settle, jurisdictional squabbles—not to mention major differences over working conditions, wages, and other fundamentals.

Moreover, the IA's Hollywood local had been run like a combined protection racket and money laundry by the Chicago mobsters George Browne and Willy Bioff (henchmen of Al Capone's heir, Frank Nitti). Their main activity was selling the studios labor peace in exchange for payoffs, skimming the union treasury, and exploiting any business "opportunities" the studio bigs steered their way. In 1941 Bioff went to prison for extorting $500,000 from studio bosses in exchange for calling off a strike. Browne was also convicted of various crimes.

A dissidents' movement within IATSE had dropped the dime on the pair to the California State Assembly and the attorney general. One of the movement's leaders was Irv Hentschel, a slight, self-educated machinist and ex-Communist. The new head of the Hollywood local, Roy Brewer, had been a vice president under the old regime and had colluded with others to shield Browne and Bioff from nosy inquiries by the dissidents. Another member of the old guard, Richard Walsh, now headed the international union.

The change thus had been mainly cosmetic. As Mike Nielsen (a film scholar) and Gene Mailes (a union member and supporter of Hentschel) write in *Hollywood's Other Blacklist,* after the corrupt leaders' departure the union remained in the hands of "the entire official family who had helped them maintain their jobs, using the same tactic that the mob had used so successfully—rabid and incessant anti-communism." Brewer joined forces with Eric Johnston, head of the Motion Picture Producers Association of America (MPAA), who was using the Communism issue to undercut workers making wage demands the producers considered inordinate.

Studio workers were angry at the bosses and the IA. The rank and file resented the way their tainted leaders ignored the workers' bread-and-butter issues. Many of them would rally behind the cause of "union democracy," a term that meant giving the various craft locals the power to determine their own bargaining goals rather than following headquarters' pro-management dictates. The industry provided extremely desirable jobs, paying on average $80 a week, but their continuing prosperity was threatened by cost-cutting pressure from management as the wartime boom in ticket sales faded.

Moreover, the widespread cancellations of defense contracts after VJ Day created a pool of skilled unemployed people in the LA area eager to compete for the good-paying studio jobs. Finally, the unions wanted to preserve wartime gains, just as most unions involved in the postwar strike wave did. But the rebellious IA members got little support in their quest for justice from a leadership so tight with the bosses. Hence, the attraction of a more democratic body, known as the Conference of Studio Unions.

The CSU, a constellation of nine craft unions with nearly ten thousand members (compared to IA's fourteen thousand), had been founded in 1940 by Herbert Sorrell, a muscular ex-boxer who had been a set painter, a picket captain, and a brawler in the ongoing skirmishes with strike breakers that characterized Hollywood labor relations. He was now a business agent for Painters Local 644 and, for all his tough-guy reputation, considered "the closest thing there was in Hollywood to an honest labor leader." Sorrell was a hero among IA dissidents because of his outspoken opposition to the Browne-Bioff machine and his handiness with his fists against imported goons.

IN MARCH 1945, the CSU declared war on IATSE. The casus belli was the demand of Sorrell's painters union to be recognized as the exclusive bargaining agent for a group of seventy set decorators who had formed a small independent union and signed a contract with the producers a few years earlier. Unable to get satisfaction from management, Sorrell threw up picket lines around the major studios on a rotating basis. Other craft unions joined him, and the strikers' ranks swelled to seven thousand. Thus began the studio strike.

After six months tempers on both sides combusted. On October 5—known as "Black Friday"—hundreds of IA members and management goons armed with chains, rubber hoses, and blackjacks formed a flying wedge to break the picket lines at the gates of the Warner Bros. complex. CSU men and women fought back in what became a bloody melee. Local law enforcement agencies, from city police to county sheriff's men, waded into the fray. A stinging fog of tear gas swirled about the combatants. Cars full of "substitute workers," as the *New York Times* called them, crashed into the scrum, injuring many before they were surrounded by a mob of strikers, who dragged out the occupants and rocked the vehicles over on their sides, blocking the entrances. The Warner Bros. security police tossed tear gas bombs from the roofs of buildings at the entrance, as executives watched. Cops sallied forth and bashed heads with their clubs; the company fire department blasted sheets of water into the ranks, knocking strikers off their feet like tenpins. A witness described a huge truck emerging from the studio lot carrying "fifty goons . . . stripped to the waist, with leather bands." Another witness saw a "large open cattle truck" pull up and disgorge "fifty muscular men" swinging chains. A Warner Bros. employee witnessed cops and scabs smashing "people's heads, faces, bodies; deputy sheriffs and cops knocking down men; a girl wearing a white hardhat and Red Cross arm band pushed down on the pavement; three cops beating up a bleeding man lying on the ground."

That day the CSU picket lines held, but skirmishes raged on into the ensuing days and weeks, spreading to other studios. On October 23, there was a major clash at Paramount in which fifty were injured and thirteen arrested. It was a small-scale war, and it yielded bizarre scenes slightly reminiscent of the recent, bigger war. Veterans on the picket line wore their uniforms; one day after battling the sheriff's men, they formed a column led by a flag bearer and marched past the gates. The lawmen lined up in a single rank and saluted the flag. Air-raid warden helmets were pulled out of closets and worn as protection or wielded as weapons.

The picketing shut down filming for a time, but the studio won injunctions against the strikers. Sorrell was prosecuted and sentenced to prison early in 1946 for violating an injunction against mass picketing at Warner Bros. He served sixteen days, and emerged to enter negotiations for a new contract. Contrary to studio executives' insistence that the strike was jurisdictional and involved no issues of wages or working conditions, the two sides negotiated a new contract with a 25 percent wage increase. But the truce didn't last.

In December AFL president William Green (who believed, as he had been told, that the CSU was composed of Communists) appointed a three-man arbitration panel to investigate still another jurisdictional dispute that had cropped up between the carpenters in Local 946 of the CSU and the grips belonging to IATSE. The arbitrators issued a Jesuitical finding distinguishing set "erection," the province of the carpenters (meaning they built the sets), from set "assembly," the domain of the grips (who only set them up or took them down). The powerful head of the CSU-aligned carpenters complained, and the panel was prevailed upon to reverse itself in favor of the CSU. That act only muddied the waters. The studios ignored the ruling, and the CSU ordered the carpenters not to work on "hot sets"—meaning those that had been "erected" by the IATSE members. This move played into the hands of the producers and shattered the July truce.

According to Pat Casey, a disaffected lawyer for the producers who attended their secret meetings, IATSE international president Richard Walsh and his Hollywood lieutenant Roy Brewer were colluding with the studio heads in a strategy under which the studios would send home any CSU carpenters who refused to work on hot sets. The studios would not fire them (thus making it impossible for them to collect unemployment insurance and forcing them to look for other jobs). IATSE members would then replace them, effectively breaking the strike. Nielsen describes how it worked in practice: "In the third week of September 1946, the producers began assigning members of Carpenters Local 946 to work on 'hot' sets.

As each group refused to do the work, they were dismissed. One hundred painters and carpenters at Universal demanded pink slips. The studio refused to give the workers the slips and called upon studio police to escort them off the premises."

As the *Wall Street Journal* had previously reported, and as Casey's notes confirmed, the producers' strategy all along had been to portray the strike as a jurisdictional squabble over arcane work rules. This, they figured, along with labeling the CSU a Communist pawn, would discourage support from the talent unions, particularly SAG, with its famous and wealthy members. And that is indeed what happened.

The studios obtained a court order banning more than eight pickets; Sorrell challenged the edict by sending in 1,500 of his members to march around the Columbia studios. Some 610 men and sixty-nine women were arrested; by the end of November 1946, 802 CSU supporters had been jailed on various charges from contempt to dangerous conduct. Their trials stretched out over months, crippling the CSU's campaign. Management and IATSE had the law on their side.

Next, the Teamsters entered the fray, overriding a vote by their Los Angeles local to honor the picket lines. The Teamsters' corrupt leadership was behind this action. The local Teamster leader, Joe Tuohy, was in cahoots with Joe Schenck, the Twentieth Century Fox executive who had been implicated with Willy Bioff, sent to prison, and pardoned by President Truman in a shady deal. Schenck had dealt Tuohy a cushy job on the studio payroll at $400 a week and a seven-year contract guaranteeing a raise to $500.

By now the strike was doomed, as IATSE members steadily replaced recalcitrant CSU men and women. The Painters International, acting for the AFL, ousted Sorrell from the leadership of Painters Local 644. When the local voted to defy the ruling, the AFL canceled its charter—and the CSU gradually faded away. The locals constituting it allowed their members, who were by then hurting financially, to go back to work—those who still had jobs to go back to. For management had fired those considered "insubordinate," meaning those who had stuck by the union on the hot-set issue. Some would never work again in the movie industry. An old tactic was reborn: the blacklist.

CSU supporters would criticize Sorrell for not trying hard enough to mobilize natural allies like the CIO, but that union had waited until after the war to endorse the strike (because it violated the wartime no-strike pledge). The AFL convention would adopt a resolution denouncing Sorrell as "an important stooge and tool of the Communist party design for the destruction of AFL unions in Hollywood." They had nothing on him except daring to start a rival union; the Communism charge, which management was already bandying about, was their only alternative. And as with most such charges, instead of having to prove it, they placed the burden on the accused to prove his innocence.

The talent guilds split internally along left-right lines. A well-publicized show of support by their famous members would have helped gain a fairer shake for CSU in the court of public opinion (it had been relentlessly bashed in the LA press). Some marquee names like Katharine Hepburn, Charlie Chaplin, Edward G. Robinson, Gene Kelly, and others joined the picket lines—and for their pains were accused of sympathizing with the reds. Their union leadership gave them no moral or legal support.

Sorrell was also blamed for not reaching out to minority workers, who had a dog in this fight—they suffered discrimination by racist studios like Warner Bros. Still other critics complained that he was too prone to use brawn rather than brains. He had said, "If they want it bloody, we'll make it bloody," and bragged to Ben Dobbs, labor secretary of the CP's LA branch, "I love to hear the cracking of bones on a scab's legs." Dobbs said Sorrell "lacked leftist grounding. He was a terrible tactician."

THE DEFEAT OF THE CSU crushed all chances of establishing democratic unions in the movie industry. Disunity in Hollywood labor's ranks and the superior muscle of the studios, backed by the LA police, shattered this dream.

The debate over supporting the CSU generated schisms within the talent guilds, with Communism the wedge issue. The conservative faction in SAG, which included Robert Montgomery and most of the board, favored neutrality in the strike, on the ground that it was solely over jurisdictional issues—which, of course, was IATSE's and the studio executives' position. Montgomery resigned in March 1947, and the guild chose board member Ronald Reagan to replace him. Reagan was a New Deal liberal but growing more conservative. His right turn became clear in a speech he made to SAG members at a mass meeting in October 1946, in which he argued that the union historically had not taken sides in jurisdictional strikes and therefore should remain neutral in this one. The speech was instrumental in his being chosen president, a post he would hold for seven one-year terms. It would serve as a springboard for his subsequent career in politics— becoming a spokesman for General Electric, winning election as governor of California in 1966, and becoming president in 1980.

In the end, Reagan's liberal ideals dissolved like sugar in hot coffee. By late 1946, the FBI had recruited him as confidential informant T-10. Soon he was furnishing information to the Bureau about SAG's leftist faction. He later wrote that he had become a strong anti-Communist after being outraged by the rough tactics the party used in trying to take over the American Veterans Committee's Los Angeles branch. He was also on the scene when the party engineered a coup to gain control of the Hollywood Independent Citizens Committee of the Arts, Science and Professions (HICCASP), a group of liberals searching for a compass to guide their postwar political activism.

Biographer Edmund Morris says these events caused "an identity crisis" in Reagan, from which he emerged, according to historian Larry May, a convert to the brand of anti-Communism espoused by Eric Johnston—an evangelical vision of Hollywood wielding the propaganda weapon of film to defeat the Soviet Union in the ideological war to secure "the American century." The CSU strike became the tipping point.

THE CSU STRIKE HAD profound effects. Mailes estimates that, counting the craftspeople who were blacklisted during the strikes and the members of the talent guilds who were politically blacklisted during the HUAC probes, a total of 2,500 people lost their livelihoods. With a company union—IATSE—in place, it was not necessary even to allege a Communist connection. Anyone the employers didn't like—including accused reds but also dissidents and CSU sympathizers—could be charged with disloyalty to the company union and expelled from it, and thus their job.

Blacklisting the carpenters who refused to work on the hot sets paved the way for blacklisting writers, actors, and directors who were alleged to have Communist ties. "The weakening and corrupting of the unions and guilds made it easier to get at the leftist intellectuals," Nielsen and Mailes write. "It revealed how easy it was to frighten and stampede people with the cry of 'Communism!'"

The CSU strike was also a template of the postwar management-labor struggles. According to historian Dennis Broe, "Hollywood labor history, more than mirroring that of the nation as a whole, actually established the pattern that was followed by other industries." The strike was widely covered in the press and shown on newsreels. The scenes of violence on the picket lines gave Republican members of the new Congress the impetus they needed to pass the antilabor Taft-Hartley Act. One member called it "a very, very important consideration when we were drafting" the bill.

The studio strike clamped down a new code of political morality— anti-Communism—on the industry, just as the Fatty Arbuckle scandal of the twenties had prompted adoption of religious morality. And the tactic of the Communist smear against obstreperous unions was adapted to create a big flap about Communist and progressive writers and directors who were allegedly smuggling red propaganda into their movies. Cue HUAC!

It also influenced the content of the postwar crime films. In his book *Film Noir and Postwar Hollywood,* Broe identifies a new breed of antihero in these films: "The main action of the film consists of the protagonist's attempt to prove his or her (or his *and* her since men and women were as frequently class allies as antagonists) innocence almost always against a foe whose class position was that of someone in charge, in control." Broe ties this proletarian Lone Ranger to wildcat strikers who walked out in defiance of labor's no-strike pledge and to their postwar successors who found themselves subjected to condemnation by Congress, antiunion Republicans, and the public. Since Hollywood was dominated by the left during and immediately after the war, the workers' cause attracted widespread sympathy. Films about labor were rare, however, being considered noncommercial. So the screenwriters depicted working-class heroes as private eyes like Sam Spade and Philip Marlowe, or as wrongly accused loners who must fight the system in order to win justice. Writing in the late forties, the producer John Houseman (*The Blue Dahlia*) noted the recurrence in postwar crime films of an "outsider figure lacking confidence and alienated from the values and aspirations of mainstream society."

A rare film with an identifiable working-class hero was *The Long Night* (1947), directed by Anatole Litvak with a script by John Wexley, a veteran noir writer with leftist views. It was a remake of French director Marcel Carné's 1939 film *Le Jour se Lève (Daybreak),* which evoked the defeat of the French working class and the rise of Nazi collaborators in the thirties. The central figure is François, a solid proletarian played by Jean Gabin, the great leading man of the era who frequently embodied this type in films like *Pépé le Moko*. François is tricked and his girlfriend stolen by a dog-show illusionist, Valentin, who represents the bourgeoisie. He kills Valentin in a rage, and as the police close in on him he commits suicide. The American version is set in small-town Ohio. Rather than simply reviving Carné's saga, however, Litvak revealingly transformed it into a story of hope and (very subtly) struggle.

In Litvak's version, Joe (Henry Fonda) shoots the Valentin figure (Vincent Price) because he seduced the girl Joe loves, Ann (Barbara Bel Geddes). Joe is trapped in his room as the police close in. But the crowd that forms in the town square around a statue of a Civil War veteran (an "earlier GI Joe") roots for Joe, the veteran and blue-collar worker.

Rather than committing suicide at the end, Joe goes away peacefully with the cops. When he takes out a cigarette, a black man steps out of the crowd and gives him a light, asking, "You gonna make it, Joe?" "Yeah," he replies. "I think we're just about going to make it." This was as far as a mainstream Hollywood film could go in expressing sympathy with the veterans, the working class, and minorities.

In his history of Popular Front culture, Michael Denning sums up:

The 1947 congressional investigations of Hollywood (which led to the imprisonment of the Hollywood Ten) were largely provoked by the postwar strikes led by the Conference of Studio Unions against which studio executives launched the tactics of blacklisting and anticommunism that would tear Hollywood apart and halt the trend toward social content. In the immediate postwar years the movies sometimes tackled contemporary issues, or symbolically probed the impact of the war on the American psyche. The blacklist sparked a reaction against these movies and nurtured pressures for blander fare or pure entertainment.

AN INVITATION TO THE House Un-American Activities Committee to probe Communism in the film industry had been extended by the Motion Picture Alliance for the Preservation of American Ideals (MPA), founded by Adolphe Menjou, Ward Bond, John Wayne, King Vidor, Hedda Hopper, and other conservatives. The MPA contended that leftist influence in Hollywood—exercised by New Deal agencies during the war, especially the Office of War Information's Bureau of Motion Pictures, and the Communist Party afterward—had undermined an industry that had once made wholesome movies whose only purpose was to entertain and uplift the masses and transformed it into one that spewed out agitprop dramas intended to brainwash audiences into accepting Soviet world dominance.

After inviting HUAC the MPA provided it with dossiers it had compiled on filmland leftists as fodder for their interrogations. Another list was generated by the CSU strike, which had opened up a liberal-conservative schism in the talent guilds. According to the actress Karen Findley, "The people who didn't choose to cross the Writers Guild picket lines provided HUAC with a ready list of targets to investigate in its upcoming grilling of Hollywood."

The FBI pitched in as well. It furnished HUAC with hundreds of names, although it did so *sub rosa* because it was barred by law from sharing classified information with unauthorized people. The law held few terrors for J. Edgar Hoover, however; not when "Commonism" was the enemy. The FBI scholars Athan Theoharis and John Stuart Cox write that he ordered the Bureau's field office in Los Angeles "to extend *every* assistance to this Committee." The office opened its files, and Washington funneled in additional information. In the end, the Bureau handed over a wealth of data, including two lists: one identifying Hollywood artists who were or had been members of organizations characterized as Communist-controlled or Communist-influenced and the other identifying non-Communists who "may possess information of value re infiltration and would probably be cooperative and friendly witnesses." This timely trove included an April 12, 1947, briefing by confidential informant M-10 on the activities of the "two cliques in the Screen Actors Guild that 'follow the Communist Party line' on all policy questions" and the names of their members. Also sent to HUAC was a summary of "Communist activities in Hollywood."

Another source of names was the ex–union leader Roy Brewer, who in 1947 was appointed to serve with Reagan as cochair of the AFL's Film Council. Among his many patriotic services, he commissioned the booklet *Red Channels,* which would become a key reference work for investigative bodies deciding on their next witness and what to ask him or her. Once the blacklist was in place, Brewer served his community as a "clearance" expert—advising accused actors of how to go about cleansing themselves of the Communist taint.

HUAC's anti-Hollywood crusade also had an agenda of its own: not only cleansing Hollywood of Communists but of Jews as well. One of HUAC's loudest mouths, John E. Rankin, was a notorious hater of Jews and Negroes, as were several other committee members. On the committee's early list of people of interest was a who's who of Hollywood's Jewish émigré community—artists who had fled Nazism like Bertolt Brecht, Hanns Eisler, Paul Henreid, and Peter Lorre.

American Jews on the list included producer Adrian Scott and director Edward Dmytryk. As Jennifer E. Langdon writes in her biography of Scott, one of the Hollywood Ten, "Scott and Dmytryk appear to have been specifically targeted by HUAC not because they were Communists— though that certainly didn't help their case—but because of their work on *Crossfire,* a very dangerous film in the eyes of HUAC." *Crossfire* (1947) was made in the style of a film noir, but as Scott had said, the intention was to combat anti-Semitism in the United States, which was growing despite the defeat of Nazism.

The prejudices driving HUAC's investigations were never challenged except by the unfriendly witnesses, who were not allowed to introduce their prepared statements or were gaveled into silence when they made the point orally. "Communists" were scapegoated to conceal the committee's true colors—its hatred of unions, Jews, minorities, liberals, and the New Deal.

The red hunters had only trivial success in identifying and exposing party-line dogma sneaked into films by traitorous alien Communist writers and directors. (An exhaustive 1956 study of movies written or directed by Hollywood reds by Dorothy B. Jones, former chief of the OWI's reviewing and analysis section, demolished the notion that any such thing had occurred.)[*]

Of course, propaganda is in the ideology of the beholder. An FBI agent previewing *Crossfire* for his boss found it "near treasonable in its implications and seeming effects [*sic*] to arouse race and religious hatred." Similarly, a Bureau critic found *Body and Soul* suspicious because it showed "the rich and successful man in a bad light." Also suspect was the fact that the movie's most exemplary character was a boxer played by the African American actor Canada Lee. Enough said, apparently. *The Best Years of Our Lives* did not pass the ideological test, either. Not only did it criticize bankers; a section of dialogue associated criticism of Russia with "anti-Semitism, Jim Crowism [and] Ku Klux Klanism." Even a light comedy like *The Farmer's Daughter* was suspicious because it "threw mud at the political factions known to oppose Communism."

Little of this came out in the HUAC hearings. The committee's main effort was concentrated on badgering film workers about their political beliefs and associations. Those who ended up on the blacklist got there not for the content of their films but for the content of their dossiers—for their associations with groups on the attorney general's list.

---

[*] The study was originally published in an appendix to *Report on Blacklisting* by John Cogley, reprinted by Arno Press in 1956.

At first, the liberal colleagues of the nineteen original suspects rallied behind them. Members of the Committee for the First Amendment (CFA), a star-studded cast of politically aware actors, traveled to Washington to lend moral support to those being grilled by HUAC. Once there, they watched with distaste the Representatives' bullying and badgering of witnesses, but the angry harangues of some of the "unfriendlies" shocked them as well. The noncooperative witnesses' seemingly devious testimony was actually part of a legal strategy designed to avoid having to name names of friends and associates without invoking their Fifth Amendment right to remain silent. Instead, they challenged the committee's power to inquire into their political beliefs.

The director John Huston, one of the CFA's leaders, called the unfriendlies' testimony "a sorry performance. You felt your skin crawl and your stomach turn. I disapproved of what was being done to the Ten, but I also disapproved of their response. They had lost a chance to defend a most important principle." Some, like Humphrey Bogart, felt that those who were Communists but refused to admit it had betrayed their supporters. (If they had admitted their membership, they could have been compelled on pain of contempt to name names of other party members.) The disgusted CFA contingent who had ridden in like the cavalry to support their fellow workers turned tail and headed home, to discuss with agents, managers, lawyers, publicists, spouses, whoever how to protect their own careers.

Thus, while commendably uniting to show their support for freedom of speech on the screen and in one's personal life, the CFA abandoned another important principle—namely, that advocacy of unpopular doctrines like Marxism, even membership in the Communist Party, was not illegal. The unfriendlies' constitutional right to inject their political ideas into films was strongly protected by the First Amendment, as was the right of conservative screenwriters like Ayn Rand (whom the producers would commission to write a pamphlet on politically correct screenwriting) to advocate her radically right-wing ideas of free enterprise in films like *The Fountainhead* (based on her novel). Darryl F. Zanuck piously replied to reviewer Bosley Crowther's criticism that his opportunistic anti-Communist thriller *The Iron Curtain,* a recounting of the Gouzenko spy case in Canada, contained propaganda: "Has the screen less right to freedom of expression than books or newspapers?"

True enough, but Zanuck's purity of heart is open to question. And in reality freedom of speech on the screen belonged to the people who owned the studios. What is more, the industry quickly threw overboard the First Amendment when its bottom line sank. Zanuck and other studio executives, most of whom had been opposed to the government's challenge to their right to hire whoever they believed could make the best picture, nevertheless adopted a policy that made "loyalty"—political orthodoxy—a prime criterion for hiring and firing.

WHAT IS GENERALLY CALLED the blacklist—referring to a policy of not hiring Communists or Communist sympathizers—was adopted by the eight largest studios in a meeting at the Waldorf-Astoria Hotel in late 1947 presided over by Eric Johnston, head of the Motion Picture Producers of America. According to Jon Lewis's *Hollywood v. Hard Core,* the studios' New York offices—which held the purse strings (they dealt with the bankers who provided credit to make a movie) and thus had the final say in picture-making—had pressured the Hollywood executives into establishing a blacklist. New York, reflecting Wall Street conservatives, favored predictable product; and they wanted politically neutered "entertainment." Their motive was primarily financial, not political: noncontroversial movies were safer bets.

The big eight studios adopted a form of self-censorship that called for using the political blacklist to stop films expressing social criticism or political views by taming the writers and directors of the talent unions, which harbored so many leftists. This followed the precedent of the economic blacklist set up after the studio strike to purge pro-CSU workers, which was meant to make the studios' labor force more docile—thus holding down costs.

The new era of ideological conformity spread soon enough to the foreign export market. MPAA president Eric Johnston set up a separate organization to vet movies for export, acting as an ideological enforcer and discouraging controversial movies (for example, those that seemed to oppose racism and anti-Semitism or were sympathetic to labor—or dealt with some social problem). Foreign revenues were increasingly vital as the domestic market declined—by 1949 they would make up nearly 40 percent of the studios' gross revenues—so the power to deny an export license to a movie could hurt a studio's bottom line. An idea of Johnson's standards can be gleaned from his statement to a group of screenwriters not long after the 1947 HUAC hearings: "We'll have no more *Grapes of Wrath,* we'll have no more *Tobacco Roads,* we'll have no more films that deal with the seamy side of American life. We'll have no more films that treat the banker as a villain." Films noir were also on the list.

All this had an effect on screen content. According to Lary May's *The Big Tomorrow,* movie plots became more reactionary. By the fifties, the proportion of films that were critical of bankers or depicted big business or the rich unfavorably (two primary ideological litmus tests) dropped from 50 percent of the total to less than 5 percent. The number of films with stories that involved social reforms also diminished. And the number of anti-Communist movies warning about the danger of internal subversion grew from 10 percent of all films made during World War II to 25 percent of all made between 1945 and 1955. Gangster movie plots now involved psychotic, individualistic killers; crime no longer had social causes, as was articulated in the gangster movies of the early thirties; nor was organized crime tied to civic or corporate corruption.

As Nora Sayre writes in *Running Time,* in the films of the forties and fifties "personal relations became far more important than public concerns. . . . Like the Broadway theater, movies focused on the rewards or miseries of intimacy. . . . And the fact that most of our films, like our culture, became apolitical was a political statement in itself."

A signpost of change was the increase in "police procedural" films (crime films made from the point of view of the police). American films noir of the 1945–50 period had generally depicted crime "from the inside, from the vantage point of the criminals involved," as Borde and Chaumeton write, rather than society's or the law's perspective. The transgressor—

even a murderer—might be sympathetic; often he was innocent, like the falsely accused loner heroes. Although an outsider, he was basically a good man with a beautiful, sympathetic woman who worked by his side in his quest for justice.

By the fifties, however, as political conformity took hold, the pro-authority police procedural film became the dominant genre. Dennis Broe calculates that nearly half of the police procedurals made between 1950 and 1955—ninety in all—featured an "informer cop" as a hero and criminals whose "secret activity could be read as Communist or union activated." The police procedural portrayed the city as a sinkhole of crime and deviance, the cops as the forces of authority, and the criminals as part of a larger conspiracy against order and decency.

By 1948, shrinking box-office revenues, inflation, and an economic slump drove studios to economize; they began firing people left and right—but mainly left, for the blacklist provided a handy excuse and ready-made list of candidates for the axe. The paranoid multimillionaire Howard Hughes, who purchased RKO Pictures, had a convenient test for determining which lefty contract writers to fire: he had them assigned to work on the script of a violently anti-Communist picture in the works called *I Married a Communist.*

This propaganda film was part of a new wave of anti-Communist crime films—*films rouge,* so to speak. These were the right-wing propaganda melodramas in which the villains were Communists and the heroes were cops or investigators, like John Wayne in *Big Jim McClain.* (Someone quipped at the time that even the Communist writers were writing anti-Communist movies.)

These performed poorly at the box office; they were too heavy-handed, doctrinaire. That the studios turned out so many of them raises deeper questions about the soundness of the studios' response to the HUAC hearings with the blacklist strategy. A Gallup poll taken on December 17, 1947, after HUAC's Washington hearings had run their course, showed that only 50 percent of the respondents had been following the hearings closely. Of these who had, about an equal number approved (37 percent) as disapproved (36 percent) of the committee; many of the latter denigrated the hearings as a "political publicity stunt." As Jennifer Langdon writes, "The raw data seems to suggest that the executives' concerns about a public backlash were exaggerated."

Pollster-in-chief George Gallup figured that although the HUAC circus had "some adverse effect" on Hollywood's image, it would have "little immediate effect on the box office." The most negative impact on ticket sales would occur among conservatives who were stridently anti-Communist. These people were mainly to be found among the over-thirty group, comprising some 40 million people. This older group also had the lowest rate of movie attendance. The majority of ticket buyers were thirty-and-under.

Did this mean that Hollywood should pander to a vocal segment of the older folks by publicly clamping down on artistic freedom with a blacklist and other drastic measures aimed at alleged Communists or sympathizers? If the industry catered to the older folks, would it lose the patronage of the younger demographic, which, after all, represented the future of the industry? In light of the greater liberality of the latter cohort on issues of sexual morality as well as politics, was it smart for the industry to abandon its steps toward issuing more movies on mature themes, including contemporary problems like racial prejudice?

To answer these questions executives would commission more polls and analyses of box-office figures. Actually, some evidence was already in hand. Between 1946 and 1949 total box-office receipts plunged 14 percent from the all-time high of $1.7 billion. Average weekly attendance also fell from its 1946 peak of 90 million. In that year an average of 80 percent of the public attended a movie at least once weekly; that number would decline to around 36 percent in 1950. This was partly the result of rising competition from television, but in 1950 there were only 3.6 million sets in homes. More prominently, it was caused by higher ticket prices, fewer theaters, a suburbanizing population, and so on. The studios were forced into a cost squeeze as a result of inflation, which resulted in rising costs.

STILL ANOTHER DELETERIOUS impact of the HUAC hearings was the effect of the blacklist on Hollywood's creative community. Hundreds of people accused of harboring subversive tendencies by HUAC or other self-appointed red-hunting groups were denied the right to make a living. Even people who had never had Communist Party ties, like the actresses Marsha Hunt and Karen Findley, were "graylisted" and saw their careers cut short by the professional anti-Communist network.

These people also found themselves shunned by colleagues. The sight of former friends crossing the street to avoid him inspired screenwriter Carl Foreman to write the anti-blacklist parable *High Noon* (1952), in which the craven townsfolk of Hadleyville (a name perhaps inspired by Mark Twain's dark tale "The Man Who Corrupted Hadleyburg," about a village that sold its soul for money) are afraid to help their sheriff (that old anti-Communist Gary Cooper), preferring conformity and security. One might add to that genre the exiled director Jules Dassin's *Night and the City* (1950), a story about a nightclub tout hounded by gangsters, and of course the numerous crime films whose protagonists must prove their innocence or who are victims of informants.

Like several other Hollywood leftists, Dassin went into exile when HUAC subpoenaed him. Foreman stayed and testified that he had left the Communist Party, then took the Fifth rather than name names. He had been a partner of producer Stanley Kramer in an independent company that made four films with strong social content, such as *Home of the Brave,* which focused on racial bigotry. But after Foreman was subpoenaed, Kramer—under pressure from executives and his distributor, Columbia—accused him of lying about his party membership and canceled their partnership.

For some writers among the Ten, the bitterest pill was that the Screen Writers Guild refused to come to their support. Certainly it was a slap in the face to John Howard Lawson, who had been among the founders of the Guild. This failure of traditional solidarity was a betrayal of the ideals of the labor movement. Moreover, it marked the end of the 1930s idea of unionized actors, writers, and directors feeling empathy with other working people. Now the studios were virulently antiunion as well as anti-Communist.

Also, the studio strike inspired Congress to pass the Taft-Hartley Act, with its requirement that union leaders swear they were not Communists.

Such oaths spread to other sectors, including academia, public education, and federal, state, and local governments. In a preemptive strike against HUAC, President Truman issued Executive Order 9835, which required background checks on all federal employees. Those who had belonged to or sympathized with the CP and a variety of organizations included on the attorney general's list were fired. This established the principle that employees could be discharged for political associations, even if they had resigned or disowned them years before. Such membership supposedly indicated subversive or traitorous tendencies. "Tendencies" were enough; no overt actions need be proved. An elaborate government "clearance" bureaucracy grew up to administer the program, which entailed FBI background investigations of clerks and supervisors alike. Many innocent or harmless people were sucked into the gears of this machinery and spit out stripped of their jobs and reputations.

The loyalty-oath mania spread. Conservatives in the talent unions demanded that not just their leaders but all their members take them, even though Taft-Hartley required only the former to do so. The Screen Directors Guild, led by Cecil B. DeMille, actually pushed through such an oath, which created a de facto blacklist of anyone who did not take it. (The oath was declared unconstitutional by the Supreme Court in 1966.)

ANOTHER EFFECT OF THE STUDIO STRIKE was the revelation that certain studio bosses had been in bed with the mobbed-up leadership of the IATSE. This news may also have contributed to the crime-film boom after the war. The private-eye novelist turned screenwriter Raymond Chandler sensed it in the air when, in 1944, he sent a friend this description of a group of movie executives returning from lunch: "They looked like a bunch of topflight Chicago gangsters moving in to read the death sentence on the beaten competitor. It brought home to me in a flash the strange psychological and spiritual kinship between the operations of big money business and the rackets. Same faces, same expressions, same manners. Same way of dressing and same exaggerated leisure of movement."

Chandler no doubt had contracted some of his social views from his private-eye hero, Philip Marlowe, who took the cynical view that law enforcement was riddled with corruption and who regarded business as not much better. "That's the difference between crime and business," a cop tells Marlowe. "For business you gotta have capital. Sometimes I think it's the only difference."

Marlowe, like Dashiell Hammett's Sam Spade, was a tough but honorable man in a violent, chaotic world with the sensitivity to feel its pain and the moral compass to navigate between corruption and chaos and law and decency. He was a sort of tarnished knight-errant in a time of war, killing, and greed. It is no wonder that films featuring these paladins—*The Maltese Falcon* and *Murder, My Sweet,* among others—are key examples of the noir sensibility.

Crime narratives have traditionally attracted creators and readers alike because they purge forbidden wishes and fears. In Hollywood they attracted filmmakers with leftist views who were criminalized by the anti-Communist repression, making them outlaws. Some cases in point: Jules Dassin, Joseph Losey, and Orson Welles, all of whom moved to Europe rather than face punitive grilling by HUAC. In London, Dassin made perhaps his greatest noir, *Night and the City*. Another exile, Welles, who was never officially blacklisted but deported himself, returned to the United States to make *Touch of Evil* (1957), a belated postscript to the postwar noir cycle, and also one of the most interesting in the canon.

In *Night and the City,* the nightclub tout Harry Fabian (Richard Widmark) dreams the American dream—a life of "ease and plenty"—and concocts a scheme to take over professional wrestling in London. But he comes up against the big-time gangster Kristos (Herbert Lom), who controls the business and crushes the interloper. In the end Harry flees into a shadowy world where he could be betrayed at any time by stool pigeons and informers. Hounded by the gangsters whom he tried to cheat, he ends up lost in the urban labyrinth like a man in a nightmare. Dassin sets this scene with stark images of bombed-out London, which evoke the paranoia and fear driving.

The atmosphere of suspicion and distrust created by HUAC and the blacklist also played a role in the rise of Hollywood noir. *Naming Names* author Victor Navasky commented, "The blacklist itself has a noir quality since there was no literal, physical blacklist, and you can add in the role played in enforcing it by ex-FBI guys and clearance mechanisms, *Red Channels*, etc. and the so-called graylist." Organizations like the MPAA and SAG denied there was a blacklist even as they tacitly collaborated in it. Film historian James Naremore writes, "During the 1950s, the congressional hunts for communists in Hollywood were themselves based on a kind of noir scenario." They encouraged suspicions and fear and left those accused in a purgatory of culpability for political activity that had once been legal and even patriotic. In short, the blacklist injected into the Hollywood community a sense of anonymous forces behind the scenes pulling the strings with the power to destroy people's lives. Sometimes studios hid the political reasons for not hiring them, telling them they were too tall or too old for the part. Writers were informed that the rejection of their scripts had nothing to do with their politics—that they just weren't writing well. Such rejections had a debilitating effect on many writers' morale and self-confidence.

Although the marriage of blacklist and black film was made in hell, it did for a brief time stimulate creativity. Historians Paul Buhle and Dave Wagner write in *Radical Hollywood* that for some of the industry's beleaguered progressives, film noir, "a genre that seemed to thrive on political and personal disappointment," proved a port in the storm because it "expressed the artists' political world view and the politics of contemporary film production."

The critic Carlos Clarens suggests that socially conscious liberal writers and directors were drawn to making crime films because they served as an alternative outlet for political dissent: "It was easier to instill a feeling that all was not perfect in American society by way of the ambiguities of the film noir than to take on the system [directly] and risk the cooptation of any subversive message."

In the 1995 documentary *Red Hollywood*, the historians Thom Andersen and Noel Burch point out that both liberal and conservative writers used crime movies as vehicles for social commentary (subject, of course, to commercial considerations dictated by studios) and were just as critical of society: "The right portrayed crime as a symptom of social disintegration, the left presented it as a form of capitalist accumulation." Speaking for the Marxists, the writer/director Abraham Polonsky asserted, "All films about crime are about capitalism, because capitalism is about crime."

In *Force of Evil* (1948), Polonsky went beyond existential dread to depict a city of corruption exemplified by the numbers racket but represented by the street sign flashed at the film's beginning: Wall Street. In the ending, Joe (John Garfield) climbs down the great stones beneath the George Washington Bridge to find the body of the brother he betrayed, tossed there like garbage by the thugs who shot him. Symbolically, he has descended to the ninth circle of his personal hell, shedding all pretenses to decency or honor. Yet at the rock bottom of existence, he finds in himself a nub of humanity and starts climbing back up to redemption. He will break with the gangsters, go to the DA, and turn state's evidence.

As Polonsky told interviewers Eric Sherman and Martin Rubin, "Having reached the absolute moral bottom of commitment, there's nothing left to do but commit yourself. There's no longer a problem of identity when you have no identity left at all. So, in your next step, you must become something."

FILMS NOIR, MORE FAITHFULLY than other kinds of films, reflected the personal anxieties of the late forties. They vacuumed up the psychological detritus swirling in the air, the velleities, secret wishes, criminal thoughts, unspoken fears, dream images of the times. "Noir etched a metaphor of light and shadow into the popular psyche," writes the feminist film scholar B. Ruby Rich, "rain-slicked streets, feelings of loss, fear and betrayal, male bonding, femmes fatales, postwar malaise, atomic pressures, Communist threats, melodrama and gangsters all coalesced under its banner." At their peak in the late forties, these crime films comprised as much as 16 percent of Hollywood's annual output, depending on one's definition. Many of these were cheapo B pictures, made to fill out a double bill; yet because of their low budgets, the "Bs" often flew below the studio radars, freeing their younger directors to experiment with new themes and techniques.

The panic-driven political cleansing of films after the HUAC hearings set back this creative ferment, which had produced a wave of realistic, socially critical pictures (and not only films noir) and artistic experimentation after the war. The studios hunkered down to weather the political and the economic storms, even as the ground shifted under them. Getting back to business, playing it safe, they stifled the flow of serious ideas; the artistic community, torn apart by distrust, lost the spirit of idealism that had inspired it just after the war. Those short years that were the heyday of American film noir were a time of ferment and experimentation, realism and political commitment, which was prematurely silenced by politicians, some of whom held the kind of fascist and racist views that many Americans believed their GIs blasted from the earth.

Voices

I felt all dead inside. I'm backed into a dark corner and I don't know who's hitting me.

—*The Dark Corner* (1946)

I had become a zombie. The world was dead and I was living.

—*Night Has a Thousand Eyes* (1948)

Do you look down on all women, or just the ones you know?

—Gloria Grahame to Humphrey Bogart,
In a Lonely Place (1950)

You're like a leaf that the wind blows from one gutter to another.

—Robert Mitchum to Jane Greer, *Out of the Past* (1947)

The story of our time is not the war nor atomic energy but the marriage of an idealist to a gangster and how their home life and children turned out.

—Raymond Chandler

7

URBAN NOIR

FILM NOIR WAS BORN at the end of the war, the product of a confluence of several social, political, and artistic developments, as we have seen. These converged to create the climate in which such films could thrive. But the films themselves were made by a culturally diverse group of individuals—screenwriters, directors, cinematographers, technicians, who contributed their variegated talents and cultural knowledge.

Beginning in the late thirties, some ten thousand European artists, scientists, professors, writers, and other intellectuals, many of them Jews, sought refuge in America. The historian Peter Gay writes that "the exiles Hitler made were the greatest collection of transplanted intellect, talent, and scholarship the world has ever seen." California welcomed many of these. The Western historian Henry Nash writes, "As no other single event, the coming of the émigrés to Los Angeles during World War II transformed southern California from a principal and local cultural center to one of national and international dimensions."

Generally, the motion picture industry vouchsafed these émigrés a chance to practice their talents. At the same time, they were seen by the FBI primarily as enemy aliens and potential subversives. One might think that their flight from Nazi persecution would have given them some kind of "home free" card. To the contrary, the FBI, sizing up the liberal or socialist ties inevitable among this staunchly antifascist group, invented a subversive label for them—"communazis." The bureau shadowed a number of the exiles, including literary giants like Thomas Mann, Klaus Mann,

In blacklistee Jules Dassin's *Night and the City* cheap hood Richard Widmark runs out of places to hide. *Everett Collection*

Bertolt Brecht, Erich Maria Remarque, Lion Feuchtwanger, and Hermann Broch. They were subjected to surveillance; agents interrogated them about their politics and sex lives; they were threatened with deportation. In his book *Communazis,* Alexander Stephan reports on this surveillance program, concluding that the FBI watch was an "absolute waste of time."

And yet, most of them were hired by the studios (or given "lifeline" contracts paying them a stipend until they found film work). Despite cultural and linguistic barriers, not to mention the taboos imposed by studio bosses and the Breen Office, many succeeded in making significant contributions to American cinema. The majority practiced their art or craft and made a variety of films, from anti-Nazi propaganda to films noir.

Jewish directors like Curt and Robert Siodmak, Edgar G. Ulmer, Douglas Sirk, Billy Wilder, Fritz Lang, William Dieterle, and Otto Preminger had apprenticed on films shot at the Ufa studios in Berlin in the twenties. They gravitated toward the themes of war, violence, psychosis, amnesia, alienation, fear and flight that recurred in the Weimar cinema. They favored stories about characters wrenched from their homes, as the émigrés had been, or loners bounced about by the blows of fate.

The long shadow of Weimar stretched over time and distance, between Berlin in the twenties and Hollywood in the forties, from *Caligari* and *The Blue Angel* to *Scarlet Street* and *Double Indemnity.* As the film historian Gerd Gemünden writes,

> The sensibility of the films which would later be labeled noir certainly entertains close affinities to the sense of loss and cultural despair which many German language exile filmmakers experienced in 1930s and 40s America. These films frequently revolve around questions of (war) trauma, psychosis, memory, and amnesia, split or doubled identity, featuring men driven from their home, outsiders who cannot comprehend the political and social forces that determine their existence. . . .
>
> Important predecessors to noir thus include Expressionism with its subjective camera, distorted angles, chiaroscuro lighting, and elongated shadows; along with the urban realism, moral decay, and sexual temptation of the so-called [street films]; and the German femme [*sic*] fatales of

the 1920s such as Lya de Putti, Louise Brooks and Marlene Dietrich . . .
film noir . . . allow[ed] German directors to reclaim a cultural heritage
long believed to be lost, but also to regain an auteurist vision and personal creativity.

Starting with Fritz Lang, one of the master filmmakers of Weimar
Berlin, author of the silent classics *Metropolis* and *"M,"* the German émigrés had to varying degrees fallen under the influence of German Expressionism and the "objective," or documentary, style that followed it.
Leading directors like Billy Wilder, Curt and Robert Siodmak, Edgar G.
Ulmer, and Fred Zinneman—all had served apprenticeships at the end of
the Weimar era.

In his book on Wilder, Gemünden imagines the empathy that the culturally displaced director felt for James M. Cain's very American hard-
boiled novel: *Double Indemnity.* "This image of southern California as a
sterile and culturally shallow place populated by disenfranchised, discon-
nected, and dishonest people is what must have appealed to Wilder," who
despite his success in Hollywood still felt himself to be an exile.

In *Double Indemnity,* Wilder and his German cameraman, Charles Seitz,
drew from a battery of standard Ufa techniques, such as chiaroscuro lighting and the documentary-style realism that the great Lang had used in
"M." The former illuminates the climactic shootout between Walter and
Phyllis in a room dimly lit by Venetian blinds. Other parts of the film were
so darkly lit that critics wondered if the set budget had been miserly. Seitz
would go on to shoot several black-and-white noir classics, including
Wilder's *Sunset Boulevard* and *The Lost Weekend,* and John Farrow's *Night
Has a Thousand Eyes* and *The Big Clock.*

The Big Clock, adapted from the poet Kenneth Fearing's novel, features
a tyrannical publisher, Earl Janoth (Charles Laughton), who bears a not-
coincidental resemblance to Henry Luce—and a distant one to Adolph
Hitler (the mustache). The devilishly intricate plot is powered by paranoia
and fear. A just-fired reporter, George Stroud (Ray Milland), is rehired
to investigate the murder of Janoth's mistress. Stroud is a driven organization man who has no time even for a honeymoon. But Janoth—the real

murderer—intends to frame Stroud because he was the last person to see the woman alive. *The Big Clock* transforms a corporate milieu into a Macbeth's castle seething with intrigue while the huge clock in the main lobby ticks away the workday hours.

THE EARLY EXPRESSIONIST MOVIES of the Weimar era, and the other kinds that followed, were frequently shot on studio sets. During World War II outdoor shooting was banned along the coast for security reasons, so indoor shoots were popular. At the same time, the studios, like other American businesses, had to put up with material shortages; the set makers had to reuse materials, so their props tended to be shabby and the lighting was dimmed so this wouldn't show. The film scholar Sheri Chinen Biesen writes in her book *Blackout:* "Many of these material limitations accentuated attributes that would be considered characteristic of film noir style: rain, fog, smoke, mirrors (rather than ornate sets), resourceful angles, night locations, and tented or tarped back-lot shooting." In his history of Hollywood in the forties, Otto Friedrich provides a variation on this theme: "At Warners, a studio so frugal that some of its employees called it 'San Quentin,' shooting a film in moody darkness and rain tended to disguise the cheapness of the sets." Dark lighting also became a hallmark of psychological thrillers, signaling menace and fear. As the director Howard Hawks explained when asked why his films were so darkly lit, "It's more dramatic."

When Edward Dmytryk, director of *Crossfire,* was asked about his movies, he said the "look" was all in the lighting—the use of shadows, chiaroscuro, hot lights, no light. To get the look he wanted he showed his cinematographer, Harry Wilde, a book of chiaroscuro paintings to emulate. Wilde outdid his expectations.

Prime examples of the Expressionist style in contemporary movies were Lang's *The Woman in the Window* (1944) and *Scarlet Street* (1945). Both were financed by an independent company founded by the liberal producer Walter Wanger, in which his wife, the cameo beauty actress Joan Bennett, and Lang were partners. Lang's films were Americanized variations of the German street films like *The Blue Angel,* which typically hinged on a plot showing a solid bourgeois citizen lured to his destruction by a seductive femme fatale. The studio-set New York in *Scarlet Street* becomes an Expressionist nightmare out of the Weimar era, with elongated shadows, rain-slick pavements, flashing neon lights, and ghostly voices. It is the story of a prostitute, her pimp, and the bourgeois who falls for her. Of course, these seamy facts (in the French original) were not mentioned in the American film. Johnny Prince (Dan Duryea) has no visible job; he is simply the prostitute Kitty's conniving boyfriend. (Yet the relationship was obvious enough to offend New York's movie censors, who banned the film.)

In *Scarlet Street*, Chris Cross (Edward G. Robinson), a hen-pecked bank clerk, falls for Kitty (Joan Bennett) and embezzles money to lavish gifts on her. He is the underdog in the relationship, like the martinet schoolteacher in Josef von Sternberg's *The Blue Angel* (and like the hero of *Detour,* as its director, Ufa graduate Ulmer, confessed). Chris wants to marry Kitty, but she dismisses him: "You're old. I'm sick of you. Johnny's a man." This rubs a nerve; he's less than a man. He goes crazy and stabs her to death with an ice pick. Johnny is arrested for the murder and dies in the electric chair. Haunted by guilt, Chris disintegrates and lands in a flophouse. Lying in bed in his shabby room, he sees the neon sign flashing like a supernatural visitor and hears Kitty's voice saying, "Jeepers, I love you, Johnny."

Chris will be tormented by guilt to his potter's field grave. But Lang denied that his fate was Production Code retribution for his sins. He said that Chris "suffers only from a jealousy which cannot be assuaged even by the death of the two people involved. He still hears their love talk, is tortured by it, and this is what turns him into a bum."

Biesen suggests that the jealousy theme appealed to veterans in the audience, who carried home a general suspicion that their wives or girlfriends had cheated on them while they were away. Here the family-unfriendly values of noir are bared. They are typically expressed by the femme fatale in *Criss Cross* (Yvonne De Carlo), who betrays her lovesick ex-husband (Burt Lancaster) for money: "Love, love. You have to watch out for yourself. That's the way it is. I'm sorry. What you want me to do?

Throw away all the money? You always have to do what's best for yourself. That's the trouble with you. It always was, from the beginning. You just don't know what kind of world it is."

In *Scarlet Street,* Chris is haunted at the end by the voices of Kitty and Johnny, his victims. But many films noir told the entire story through the hero's voiceover. This came into style with *Double Indemnity,* which is ingeniously told through flashbacks as Walter Neff dictates his confession. Wilder said he chose voiceover because it was an efficient narrative device for feeding plot information to the audience. The suspense comes not from discovering whodunit but from learning how he will be caught and punished; instead of an intellectual puzzle like the standard murder mystery, we see the protagonists caught in a downward spiral driven by personal flaws. The audience becomes complicit in the crime; it feels sympathy for the narrator as an ordinary guy with recognizable, if unsavory, motives. The postwar crime film managed to flout conventional morality not by condoning murder but by suggesting that inside many an ordinary guy lurks a killer, just as many ordinary guys became soldier-killers during the war.

Ulmer knew the horrors of war, having fought in World War I. He started his movie career as a designer in the twenties before immigrating to the United States, where he collaborated with the director Max Reinhardt on Broadway. He found work in Hollywood as a set designer, became a director, and had a hit with the 1934 horror picture *The Black Cat.* In this metaphoric antiwar story, Bela Lugosi and Boris Karloff play mortal enemies, an architect and a psychiatrist. The Bauhaus-style mansion in which Karloff's mad architect character keeps on display a gallery of his dead ex-wives (one of whom he stole from Lugosi, who now seeks revenge) preserved in life-size glass cylinders sits on a hill that was the epicenter of one of the bloodiest battles of that war and became the tomb of thousands of unclaimed dead.

Ulmer told Peter Bogdanovich that he took this vision from a novelist who wanted to write a play based upon Doumont, which, according to Ulmer, "was a French fortress the Germans had shelled to pieces during WWI; there were some survivors who didn't come out for years. And the commander was a strange Euripedes figure who went crazy three years later, when he was brought back to Paris, because he had walked on that mountain of bodies."

Ulmer apparently was referring to Fort Douaumont, one of several French forts around Verdun, site of the bloodiest battles of the war. In February 1916, the Germans captured Douaumont and held it for several months. Then a fire broke out, setting off stored explosives and killing hundreds of German soldiers (who were buried in the basement of the fort, now a tourist site). The French finally shelled and retook the place in May, using three divisions to do so. Thousands of men were killed in the fighting over an obsolete fort that had apparently acquired a psychological rather than strategic value to both sides. To Ulmer the Douaumont legend may have symbolized the murderous futility of the Great War.

QUITE A FEW OF THE ACTORS who emerged as stars in the forties launched their careers in noir because, unlike the famous Gables and Tracys and Davises and Crawfords, their personalities and acting styles were better adapted to projecting its terse "tough" dialogue. Humphrey Bogart, who had played criminals in the thirties and was the romantic leftist soldier of fortune turned saloon keeper in *Casablanca,* has been called the "iconographic figure in all of film noir." His characters usually showed "a combination of bitterness and amusement at a world of duplicity"; they were men "whose great expectations had been defeated by events." Bogart's face was a mask, a carapace "meant to cover the psychic injuries of a decent man trying to forget the past," as biographer Stefan Kanfer writes in *Tough Without a Gun.*

Other actors who vaulted to prominence in crime films included Robert Ryan, Kirk Douglas, Robert Mitchum, Dan Duryea, Richard Widmark, and Gloria Grahame. A popular noir team was Alan Ladd and Veronica Lake, who costarred in adaptations of Graham Greene's *This Gun for Hire* (1943), Dashiell Hammett's *The Glass Key* (1945), and Raymond Chandler's *The Blue Dahlia* (1946). They had a quality of "flatness" that seemed tailored to speaking the cynical, clipped dialogue of these films. As

Foster Hirsch writes, "Their faces barely move. Their dry, tight voices, monotonous in rhythm and intonation lack any music or coloring . . . suggesting, beneath their masks, a weakness and vulnerability that the noir stories require of them, as they get pushed about by bizarre turns of fortune."

Feminist critics would later celebrate the noir woman—the iconic femme fatale—as a lioness of empowerment and sexual freedom. Janey Place articulates this view when she writes that the noir era "stands as the only period in American film in which women are deadly but sexy, exciting, and strong . . . active, not static symbols . . . intelligent and powerful if destructively so." The femmes fatales were certainly more than just sexpots; they were apolitical rebels against the traditional female role. Depression babes ambitious for a materially richer life but lacking education or business ambitions, they rejected domesticity (unless they wanted to negotiate a marriage of convenience to a wealthy man) and used their sexual wiles to undermine patriarchal power—to "unman" a man and thus control him. (Note that the so-called New Woman—the German version of the twenties American flapper—was prominent in Weimar society; her cinematic counterpart could be found in the femmes fatales of "street films," like Louise Brooks in *Pandora's Box*.)

The rise of the femme fatale in films noir reflected male ambivalence and anxiety about World War II women, those Amazons unleashed by the war who worked at men's jobs, had sex with whomever they wanted, and rejected home and motherhood. In one of the rare films about a career woman who achieves business success, Hollywood resorted to a noir plot to sell the postwar message that women belonged in the home, not in the factory—let alone in the boss's office (except as his loyal secretary). Intentional or not, this was the effect of Michael Curtiz's *Mildred Pierce* (1946), the adaptation of still another James M. Cain novel. In the book Mildred's rise is the stuff of hard-boiled melodrama done the Cain way, with crosscurrents of self-destructive love affairs with handsome rogues and perverse mother love showered on a spoiled, treacherous daughter.

The movie opens with the sound of shots being fired in a chiaroscuro-lit living room. From the start, the audience is led to suspect Mildred (Joan

Crawford) of being the shooter. She turns out to have been innocent; the murderer was her daughter, Velda, whom she spoiled rotten. Cleared by the cops in the end, she and Bert, her first husband—a real man who's returned to her (she'd kicked him out because he was having affairs)—walk out of the precinct house together. They pass a scrub woman kneeling beside her pail, a final image suggestive of woman's true role. The implication is that Mildred will abandon her successful pie-baking business for Bert.

In Cain's novel there is no murder. It ends with Velda running off with Mildred's lover, Monty. Mildred is left alone, a victim only of excessive mother love: "The one living thing she had loved had turned on her repeatedly. . . . Her only crime, if she had committed one, was that she had loved this girl too well." Enter Bert with a bottle of whiskey: "In masterful fashion he sloshed it once or twice, then sat down on the bed," Cain writes.

"To hell with her," Bert says. Meaning to hell with perverse motherhood—not with her success as a professional, whose business did originate, after all, in her talents in the kitchen.

A NEW BREED OF CAREER WOMAN who was different from the high-spirited dames of the screwball comedies like Carol Lombard and Rosalind Russell emerged in the films noir in which women were involved at the production end. This was the wartime Amazon, physically as well as psychologically strong. Typical was *Phantom Lady* (1944), based on the Cornell Woolrich novel written before the war. The strong heroine more likely rose from the author's mother complex than from social realism. Still, the character was in synch with wartime American women. Strikingly filmed by Weimar graduate Robert Siodmak on dark, menacing city streets, *Phantom Lady* was produced by Joan Harrison, who trained as Alfred Hitchcock's assistant—and thus sympathized with the spunky secretary heroine (Ella Raines) known as Kansas, who follows a trail of possible witnesses through a series of sleazy urban venues trying to find the eponymous woman who can clear her boss, falsely accused of murdering his wife. At one point she flirts with a jazz drummer (Elisha Cooke Jr., the "gunsel" in *The Maltese Falcon*) who knew the mystery woman at the bar. "You like jive?" he propositions her. "You bet, I'm a hep kitten," she replies, adopting the lingo. When he takes off on a solo flight, she starts undulating and gyrating her hips in time. He beats away, sweating heavily, his eyes fixed on her in a vicarious orgasm. But Kansas is only pretending to be sexy, a virtuous femme fatale, so to speak. After meeting a gallery of sleazy urban types, she saves her boss's life (another weak male, incidentally). In gratitude he leaves an invitation on her Dictaphone to have dinner with him "tonight, tomorrow night, and every night"—a poor reward for all she's been through.

Perhaps the most strongly feminist crime film of the era, well ahead of its time, was *Outrage* (1950). Not only was it directed by a woman, the actress Ida Lupino (known for her tough, hard-bitten women in noirs like *Road House*), but it dealt with the subject of rape. Lupino sensitively explores the problems of a young woman (Mala Powers) after an attack. Her sense of violation and shame cause her to run away from family and fiancé. When a coworker in her new life tries to kiss her, she reacts violently and nearly kills him. Put on trial, she receives counsel from an understanding minister (Tod Andrews), who persuades the court that society has a responsibility to help such victims rather than condemning them.

A typical noir with a poisonous female, *Gilda* (1946) was produced by Virginia Van Upp, the foremost woman movie executive of the postwar years. Like many women in movies and journalism, Van Upp had been given a chance because of the wartime manpower shortage. Gilda (Rita Hayworth) is a femme fatale who flaunts her free sexuality but is tamed in the end. She has a stormy love-hate relationship with Johnny (Glenn Ford), whom she marries after her gangster-gambler husband disappears. Rebelling against his attempt to keep her in a gilded cage, she takes the nightclub stage and does a striptease, singing the femme fatale's anthem "Put the Blame on Mame." ("When Mame began to shim and shake/She caused the San Francisco quake.") Gilda and Johnny reconcile and return to the States for a new life. As he tells her, "Nobody has to apologize because we were both such stinkers." Such are the tarnished male-female relationships in films noir, where they are either partners in being stinkers or buddies righting a wrong (like Ladd and Lake in *The Blue Dahlia* or Bogart and Bacall in *The Big Sleep*).

Gloria Grahame was too willowy to be a sex goddess like the voluptuous Hayworth, but she brings off the role of sexy Laurel Gray in *In a Lonely Place* (1950), from a Dorothy B. Hughes novel about a serial killer. In the altered movie version, directed by the maverick Nicholas Ray (*They Live by Night, Rebel Without a Cause*), Dix (Bogart) is a troubled veteran with a violent temper. The film was made in the shadow of the blacklist, so it's no coincidence that Dix is a screenwriter who has become persona non grata with producers—blacklisted, as it were, but because of his hot temper, not politics. "Violence is as much a part of him as the color of his eyes," says a friend. Dix and Laurel fall in love, but in the end his uncontrollable temper frightens her. She leaves him, reaffirming the condemnation of violence against women that is the subtext of Hughes's novel. (The suppression of the serial killer plot in the movie actually eliminates the novel's chilling suspense.)

Grahame was perhaps the most distinctively "noirish" among the actresses of the late forties, with a hoarse voice and sultry eyes. She played types that were a hybrid of the scheming femme fatale and the bruised waif. Other femmes fatales, like Joan Bennett, Jane Greer, Ann Savage, Yvonne De Carlo, and Rita Hayworth, exhibited varying degrees of destructiveness as they used sexual wiles to manipulate men for material ends. The emergence of this type of woman (different from the usually good-hearted gold diggers of the thirties) was unique to films noir. The femmes fatales reflect male ambivalence toward independent working women, an attitude compounded of their insecurity upon finding themselves back in a competitive civilian world, becoming the provider again, perhaps working for a large corporation. Indeed, the character of the emasculated male was common in films noir. Al Roberts (Tom Neal) in *Detour* is a prime example.

In Otto Preminger's *Laura,* based on a novel by Vera Gaspary, the title character is described as a successful woman, though she is not complete until she finds the right man. She confesses this in voiceover: "My mother always listened sympathetically to my dreams of a career—and then taught me another recipe." Mr. Right turns out to be the detective played by Dana Andrews, whose rugged masculinity is highlighted by the contrast to Laura's ostensible fiancé, the epicene Clifton Webb, pushing the limits of the Production Code's ban on homosexual characters.

The archetypal noir femme fatale is the character Kathie Moffat, played by the dark beauty Jane Greer, in *Out of the Past* (1947). Kathie has no work; she is solely after money and will kill for it. She is literally a woman of the darkness. Her lover Jeff (Robert Mitchum) describes their affair in Acapulco: "I never saw her in the daytime. We seemed to live by night. What was left of the day went away like a pack of cigarettes you smoked. I didn't know where she lived. I never followed her. All I ever had to go on was a place and time to see her again. I don't know what we were waiting for. Maybe we thought the world would end." In the climax, like the transgressive lovers in *Double Indemnity,* they kill each other (with help from the cops at the roadblock Jeff drives Kathie into).

THE CRIME FILMS I've been discussing came out at a time when filmmakers were piously vowing to make more realistic, more mature, more *serious* pictures and to stop pandering to escapism and the censors. The producer Darryl F. Zanuck told the Writers Congress in Los Angeles in 1944, "We have radiated sweetness and light since the advent of pictures . . . [because] the profit motive in the final analysis has determined our course." Films, he continued, should portray "the grim and pressing realities before us in the world." Much of this was wartime idealism, but the war had rekindled in some a sense of working for a higher cause, a common purpose. The quote of the times was perhaps that of Rick in *Casablanca:* "In this crazy world, the problems of three little people don't amount to a hill of beans."

Speaking for the filmmakers on the far left, Abraham Polonsky hailed *The Best Years of Our Lives* as "a landmark in the fog of escapism" and posited a "struggle for content in films," meaning a fight for more realism, which he interpreted politically as "seeing through the false promises of peace and prosperity for all, made in return for past sacrifices and in response to the restlessness of postwar society." Polonsky called for greater freedom for artists of all persuasions to portray life as it is, and the moral conflicts and problems of real people. Agreeing, the liberal screenwriter Philip Dunne called for films that reflected "factual American themes" and expressed "the American and democratic ideals." James Agee, film critic of *The Nation,* proclaimed, "The time has come for a fully social cinema."

In fact, for a brief period, between 1945 and 1950, an increased number of realistic pictures about social problems, sometimes in the guise of crime films, *did* come out. These dealt with such topics as racial prejudice, alcoholism, rehabilitation of vets, juvenile delinquency, and political corruption. They emphasized strong stories filmed in a realistic style, which encouraged more location shooting (which was also cheaper). The documentary style came into vogue, pioneered by Louis de Rochemont in his *March of Time* series of short films on newsy topics. (This American realism coincided with the rise of so-called neorealism in postwar Italy, which had different origins—starting with the poverty of the filmmakers themselves—but resulted in powerful films like Roberto Rossellini's 1945 masterpiece *Open City,* which in turn influenced American directors like John Huston.)

Double Indemnity used a quasi-documentary style (Weimar's "objective" style) to tell a fictional story. "It was a picture that looked like a newsreel," Wilder said. "You never realized it was staged." The film had a cold, harshly lit immediacy, like a Speed Graphic tabloid photograph. In writing the script Chandler visited sites of scenes in the film, such as the Los Angeles supermarket where the two murderers, Walter and Phyllis, plot their future against a backdrop of canned goods. Wilder's cameraman, Charles Seitz, used the same techniques in other Wilder docu-noirs—*The Lost Weekend* and *Sunset Boulevard.*

This documentary "look" became characteristic of the crime films and police procedurals of the time. Because it was cheaper, many of these were shot on the streets of New York, creating a distinctive style of gritty urban realism: New York noir. In part this was because filming in the city was cheaper than in California, and studios started cutting costs as box-office revenues dropped. New York was also teeming with Broadway talent, and it had served as an entrepôt for artists fleeing the Nazis, some of whom settled in the city permanently.

The quintessential New York police procedural was *The Naked City* (1948), produced by Mark Hellinger, a former tabloid columnist, and directed by Jules Dassin, later blacklisted, from a script by Albert Maltz, a Communist Party member. It uses the low-key, flat, factual narrative style that would be travestied in television's *Dragnet*. The film's immediate inspiration, though, was the tabloid photographs of Weegee, whose real name was Arthur Fellig. He was a plump, cigar-chomping photographer who cruised the streets of New York listening to police calls and looking for murders to illuminate in the glare of his Speed Graphic. *The Naked City,* a collection of his photographs, had been published and sold well. It was full of photos of a Hogarthian gallery of New Yorkers, high and low, gangsters and hero cops, firemen and street urchins, hoods dead or alive—often in the latter state doing a perp walk, their faces covered with a fedora or handkerchief.

After *The Naked City* came urban noirs like *Kiss of Death* (1947), set in Little Italy, which displays the antiurban subtext in films noir. The hero (Victor Mature) and his wife move to Astoria amid suburban-like parks and streets; but they can't escape the claustrophobia of the city, with the Triboro Bridge and the Hell Gate railway bridge looming in the distance. William Keighley's *The Street With No Name* (1948) involved a brave FBI agent working undercover to expose a gang. Henry Hathaway's *The Dark Corner* (1946) focuses on a private eye whose seedy office features the Third Avenue El rattling by just outside the window.

California noir tended to show the visions of the German émigré filmmakers in Hollywood. The New York films, in contrast, emulated the de Rochemont documentary model. They were shot (in good part) on location rather than on studio sets. The city seemed ideally suited to filming in black-and-white with natural lighting in actual locations. The swarming streets served as a living backdrop. In making *Force of Evil,* Polonsky chose a similar but more expressionistic realism: he instructed his cameraman to study prints of Edward Hopper's urban types—detached souls floating in an urban limbo.

New York was more closely identified with the gritty urban realism of the late forties than any other city. Many of the films featured corrupt politicians and lawyers or hardworking ordinary people defeated by fate or chance. Their stories crisscrossed class lines, moving from soaring Park Avenue penthouses to shabby Lower East Side slums. A typical couple was Joe Norson (Farley Granger) and his wife, Ellen (Cathy O'Donnell), in *Side Street* (1950). Joe, a mailman, finds a briefcase containing a large amount of cash in an attorney's office. Tempted, he takes it but regrets doing so when he learns that the money was stolen. He is sucked into the underworld, trailed by the crooks who perpetrated the scheme and want their money back. In the end, a heartening triumph for the little guy, he confounds them. The film builds to a crescendo in a roaring, screeching car chase down real New York streets.

THE NEW YORK LOOK that inspired filmmakers did the same for contemporary artists like Jackson Pollock, Willem de Kooning, Robert Motherwell, and others who had migrated from the provinces or abroad and who would found the New York School of Abstract Expressionism, which dominated the postwar art world. They took their painting into subjective realms and away from the surface realism of the earlier Ashcan School. In their early work, at least, one can see the same visual values that the filmmakers perceived. In his history of the postwar era, *New Art City*, Jed Perl describes the chiaroscuro of the city that inspired them: "The black-and-white look of New York, which was telegraphed across the country and the world in movies, in magazines, in ad campaigns had a particularly urgent hold on the artistic imagination." Pollock, de Kooning, and others passed through a phase when they literally painted only in black and white, mingled with grays and browns.

It was fitting that New York, the new imperial city, would generate a new style of art, much as Paris had done in the first quarter of the century. Many of the painters associated with Abstract Expressionism had gravitated to New York in the thirties; others came after the war. They would find influential teachers like Hans Hoffman, émigré Europeans like Salvador

Dalí or Joan Miró, patrons like Peggy Guggenheim (who staked Pollock to $100 a month, the answer to an artist's prayer—indeed, to Robert Motherwell's Faustian bargain: "If somebody would give me $50 a month the rest of my life I'd give them all my art"). Also on the scene were prophetic critics like Harold Rosenberg of *ART News,* Robert Coates of *The New Yorker,* and Clement Greenberg of *The Nation,* who assiduously reviewed the latest shows and articulated sensitive, knowledgeable appraisals of the artists' attempts to make a new kind of art. Most important was the community of 200 or so fellow painters, who met and talked into the night at the Artists' Club on Eighth Street, the San Remo bar in the Village, or the Cedar Tavern on University Place, where one could nurse a 15-cent draft beer while watching Pollock grow more pugnacious.

During the Depression many New York artists had survived on stipends from the WPA's Federal Art Project. However, the city back then was not a happy place for artists. The German-born, Milwaukee-bred painter Carl Holty "hated the doleful half-empty cafeterias" where painters sat over cooling cups of coffee talking radical politics. Then came the war and military orders that revived the city's garment manufacturers. New York's bars, theaters, and nightspots were alive with soldiers and sailors in transit to Europe, and fast-spending war-rich civilians. In the wake of the boom, the drab social realism and the radical politics of the thirties gave way to an obsession with private visions.

The founding artists of the New York School largely belonged to a generation older than the one that went to war, and they had spent the war years in New York, hearing about it on the radio and reading about it in the papers and newsmagazines. Commercial art was thriving in the advertising shops on Madison Avenue, starting to prosper from the postwar explosion of consumer demand. To the dedicated New York School artists, however, working for an ad agency defined the term "selling out."

Politically quiescent in reaction against the failed radicalism of the thirties and chastened by the anti-Communism of the forties, they withdrew from social realism into a deeply subjective abstractionism. Shaping them as well was the enduring influence of the European schools. Cubism exercised a pull on Pollock, who was powerfully affected by Pablo Picasso's

Guernica, a portrayal of the terror bombing of civilians in a Spanish town during the Civil War that would become an enduring image of the horror of modern war. In 1939 Picasso had the painting moved from Spain to the Museum of Modern Art as a protest against the pro-Nazi Franco regime. Thus it was available to Americans for firsthand contemplation and study.

The names of émigré European artists—Marcel Duchamp, Fernand Léger, Max Ernst, Piet Mondrian, Joan Miró, Marc Chagall, Josef Albers, and others—were also swirling in the charged New York air. Americans knew their work from visits to Paris, but having them as neighbors intensified their influence. Pollock described it this way in 1944: "The fact that good European moderns are now here is very important for they bring with them an understanding of the problems of modern painting. I am particularly impressed with their concept of the source of art being the unconscious. This idea interests me more than these specific painters, for the two artists I admire most, Picasso and Miró, are still abroad."

Pollock's allusion to the unconscious reflected the strong influence of Surrealism on himself, de Kooning, and Motherwell, who said that the artistic process comprised three steps: "scribbling or doodling to coax the mind to release its sub-, pre-, or unconscious elements; reflecting on these improvisations to see what kinds of structures they suggest; and ordering all the elements into a composition that takes into consideration these structures and builds on them." Pollock and de Kooning practiced automatic writing as an after-dinner game.

Surrealism sought to release dream images into the conscious mind. In this it was akin to psychoanalysis, only it was not interested in deconstructing the meaning of dreams. Psychoanalysis also had a potent if indirect impact on artists. Pollock, an alcoholic, went into analysis in the thirties and continued it through and after the war (without much success).

Surrealism had emerged after World War I in the writings of the poet André Breton, who had been drawn to Dadaism, an anti-art movement celebrating the irrational. Like German Expressionism, Dadaism had risen in reaction against the mechanical murderousness of the late war.

But the New York School drew on a variety of influences in a fortuitous synergy of the times and the city. As Hans Hoffman, who conducted an influential art school on Eighth Street in Greenwich Village, said, "Every one of us has the urge to be creative in relation to our time—the time to which we belong may work out to be our thing in common." Prominent elements in the zeitgeist were the cold war and the rise of conservative political conformity, expressed during the war in patriotic unity and expanded after it into the cold war consensus. Such social and political pressures impinged on these artists' primary demand for freedom. They loathed standardized thinking, whether in government propaganda or Madison Avenue sloganeering, as the enemy of individuality, which the artists believed was essential to true creativity. Uninterested in or pessimistic about changing society, they looked inward for their subject matter, expressing their unconscious emotions rather than copying nature or street scenes, and concentrated on method, form, and color—the medium itself. They were repelled by scientists and social planners who "cannot understand how anybody is able to make anything, particularly a work of art, spontaneously or directly," as Barnett Newman put it. For these artists, spontaneity was the key that unlocked the private visions of the subconscious. As Pollock said, "I want to express my feelings rather than to illustrate them." His early masterpiece *Cathedral* was "a mind musing over its own operations," in Perl's phrase. Pollock adopted the drip technique and used ordinary paintbrushes as part of his method, which was dubbed "action painting" by the critic Harold Rosenberg because the artist moved about on the canvas as he dripped the paints.

It was as if these painters were retreating into the privacy of their minds from a world that war's horrors had transformed into a hell too grotesque to paint (as Picasso's *Guernica* had demonstrated even as he rendered it). As though they sought to go back to art's ground zero, to the origins of creativity, and begin anew . . .

Despite their aversion to political art, the Abstract Expressionists became tangled up in cold war politics. The CIA and the USIA sponsored exhibits of their work abroad as propaganda to show the greater freedom of American democracy compared with Soviet Communism. The art historian Erika Doss writes, "Abstract expressionism became . . . a weapon in the cold war . . . its abstracted anxiety was translated, ironically, into a symbol of uniquely American freedom."

But as Doss shows, the increased public recognition and higher prices that the Abstract Expressionists began harvesting for their work was not all to their liking. Pollock hated the invasions of his privacy sanctioned by his celebrity, which had been pumped up by the mass media. An article in *Life,* showing him painting with his drip technique, crowned him king of the new art, a title apparently earned by his freakish method of painting, not the merits of his art. It took the CIA's university graduates to decode American art and exploit for propaganda's sake its growing international fame, making abstract art a testmonial to American democracy and free enterprise. Ironically, the new artists who had subjectively rebelled against capitalist mass culture became prize exhibits of the bounties of free enterprise, while right-wing politicians railed against them as transmitters of bohemianism and Communism.

NEW YORK CITY'S ARTISTIC renaissance was echoed in other arts and entertainment forms, from dance and ballet to classical music and opera to Broadway shows. Jazz (Dixieland and bebop) thrived on Fifty-second Street at clubs like the Spotlight, the Three Deuces, Jimmy Ryan's, the Onyx, Tondelayo's, and the Hickory House, and in Greenwich Village at the Village Vanguard and the Five Spot. Birdland would become a jumping shrine to Charlie Parker, who lived on the Lower East Side for a time and played bebop with Dizzy Gillespie, Max Roach, and Charlie Mingus. Radio crooning as exemplified by Frank Sinatra and the big bands of Tommy Dorsey and Harry James packed them in at the Paramount Theater. And the city's nightlife flowered at glitter spots like the Latin Quarter, Copacabana, and the Stork Club, display cases for the war's new rich, who ogled the lavish floor shows and the celebrities who themselves came to be ogled and bold-faced in Winchell's column in the next morning's *Mirror.*

A wicked aura of gangsterism hung in the smoky bars that featured jazz artists (the critic Gene Santoro dubbed the atmosphere "jazz noir"). NYPD vice squad cops regularly raided them, acting on the presumption that they condoned drug use and race-mixing. At Café Society, Billie Holiday, a heroin addict and frequent target of the police, sang "Strange Fruit," one of

the most searing protest songs ever performed in a pop venue. It was written by Abel Meeropol, a Jew and a Communist: "Southern trees bear a
strange fruit / Blood on the leaves and blood at the root / Black body swinging in the southern breeze / Strange fruit hanging from the poplar trees."[*]

Holiday first sang the song in 1939, and her recording of it eventually
sold more than 1 million copies. Meeropol also wrote the words to perhaps the biggest Popular Front hit, "The House I Live In" (music by Earl
Robinson), as recorded by Sinatra. Despite (or perhaps because of) the
song's plea for tolerance and brotherhood, the record company excised
the original lyrics about black and white people living together. Another
popular black artist who clicked with the racially integrated audiences at
Café Society was Josh White, who had a hit with "One Meat Ball," a ballad about a shabby little man who enters a restaurant, orders with his last
15 cents a single meatball, and then meekly asks for bread with it. "You
gets no bread with one meatball!" the waiter yells for all to hear.

Blues composer Jerome Felder (Doc Pomus) remembered the synergism
of the racially integrated postwar night club crowds: "You felt great energy,
great vibes all over the place. I guess the band got 'sent' by the crowd, and
the crowd got 'sent' by the band. In those days, when people went out they
would always get dressed up. Not only that but they got along well with
each other. There was no racial problems—at least I wasn't aware of that;
there was no such thing as a club that was all black and all white."

Jazz engendered its own biracial subculture. After the war, there were
at least forty clubs in Brooklyn that featured jazz, blues, and boogie-woogie.
Many more were in Harlem, most famously the Baby Grand on 125th
Street and the Savoy Ballroom on Lenox Avenue, birthplace of the lindy
hop in the thirties. The dance step was, less acrobatically, copied by white
teenagers and spread by GIs overseas.

Other popular arts had their headquarters in New York. I have already
mentioned the mass-market paperback industry, which published the best
work of the noir novelists and created a mass audience for hard-boiled

---

[*] After the execution of Ethel and Julius Rosenberg, Meeropol and his wife adopted their
two sons.

fiction. New imprints like Gold Medal specialized in this kind of book, with their cover portraits of blondes whose breasts strained at flimsy blouses. The noir writers found the new format liberating and more lucrative than the fading pulps. Jim Thompson (*The Killer Inside Me, A Hell of a Woman, The Grifters*) came into his own under editor Arnold Hano, a former sportswriter who encouraged Thompson's violent, psychotic novels. Another noir writer, David Goodis, had started as a literary novelist and then tried screenwriting after a studio filmed his novel *Dark Passage,* about a vet (Humphrey Bogart) wrongly convicted of murder who escapes prison and, with the help of a woman (Lauren Bacall), tries to clear his name.

Unable to function in Hollywood, where one wrote only to please the studio bosses, Goodis returned to Philadelphia, where he lived at home and helped care for his mentally ill brother. He found his own voice writing novels about artists who fell off the success treadmill and ended up on Philly's waterfront skid row, one of his favorite haunts. In their masochism and weary withdrawal from life, the characters were beat down lower than the characters created by the Beat novelists in the early fifties. Turning out paperbacks for the racks in drugstores and pool halls freed Goodis to write honestly about the world he knew—the lower depths, a world of bums and winos, vicious hoods, and waterfront saloons—the street of no return (an actual street in San Francisco). He said he was able to write an "emotional autobiography disguised as fiction." His novels, mostly written in the late forties, included *Nightfall,* the best-selling *Cassidy's Girl, Down There, The Moon in the Gutter,* and *The Street of No Return.*

Horror comics, the closest equivalent to the film noir trend, ran into censorship when an outraged psychiatrist analyzed their emphasis on blood and gore as potentially criminalizing young people, their main audience. Exemplified by William Gaines's EC Comics, which published titles like *Tales from the Crypt* (featuring gross-out cover art from Al Feldstein and macabre and witty tales narrated by the Crypt Keeper), the comics would influence a later generation of filmmakers like George Romero and John Carpenter and novelist Stephen King. Yet they horrified Fredric Wertham, a Munich-born psychiatrist who had founded a free psychiatric clinic in Harlem. In a 1954 book sensationally titled *Seduction of the*

Innocent, Wertham claimed, "Our researches have proved that there is a significant correlation between crime-comics reading and the more serious forms of juvenile delinquency." After being grilled in Senate hearings in April 1954 (accidentally coinciding with Senator Joe McCarthy's probe of the Army), Gaines announced in September of that year that he was discontinuing all his horror and crime titles.

As David Hadju shows in his history of this bizarre episode, *The Ten-Cent Plague,* Wertham's evidence was overstated, but it sparked a congressional investigation that led to an outright ban of horror comics. Reading his accounts of the hearing in which the somewhat shady types in the comic-book industry were relentlessly grilled, one cannot help but notice an echo of HUAC's inquisitions and McCarthy's witch hunts.

Radio had become indispensable for bringing war news to millions, as it expanded its news divisions and sent reporters to cover world battlefronts. People's poet Norman Corwin practically invented the all-sound documentary, while Edward R. Murrow and colleagues brought on-the-spot eyewitness news direct to living-room Philcos. But after the war, the documentaries and plays written for the ear, and the portentous news programs presided over by such heralds of doom as Gabriel Heatter and H.V. Kaltenborn, would fade away. Local stations fought for survival by catering to young pop music fans.

Of course, that was mainly because television displaced radio from its central place at the American hearth. Television contributed to the decline of another wartime viewing habit—watching the newsreels and short subject reports like the *March of Time* at the local movie theater. *The March of Time*'s capsule documentaries thrived during the thirties and the war. In stressful times, it seemed, audiences actually welcomed the comforting omniscience of the narrator, Westbrook Van Voorhis, who sounded like God would sound if He ever chose to broadcast to a mass audience.* Van

---

* Actually, he could have been cast for that role in Dore Schary's strange 1950 movie *The Next Voice You Hear,* in which God preempts regular programming to tell Americans—and the world—how to live right, not be afraid of "their Father" and "do their Bible homework." The voice of God is never heard; it is relayed secondhand. The historian J. Hoberman analyzes the film as a response to a national psychological crisis after the Soviet atomic bomb test.

Voorhis's message that hope was real, that solutions for problems could be found, so welcome in hard times, was no longer needed in the prosperous postwar era, according to Raymond Fleming in *Hollywood Quarterly*. The booming confident voice, he writes, no longer appealed to "a citizenry that questions its own power to control the atom and command its own destiny."

As it emerged from depression and war, New York City was boastful and confident of its future. In her elegy *Manhattan '45*, Jan Morris writes that before VJ Day, "Manhattan already knew itself to be entering a splendid fulfillment. This was not only bound to be, in the postwar years, the supreme and symbolical American city. All the signs were that it would be the supreme city of the western world, or even the world as a whole."

The novelist Gore Vidal called those immediate postwar years New York's Golden Age:

> Between the end of the Second World War in 1945 and the beginning of the Korean War in 1950, there was a burst of creative activity throughout the American empire as well as in our client states of Western Europe. From Auden's *Age of Anxiety* to Carson McCullers's *Reflections in a Golden Eye* to Paul Bowles's *The Sheltering Sky* to Tennessee Williams's *A Streetcar Named Desire* to [Anthony] Tudor's ballets. . . . It was an exciting time. . . . *
>
> All the arts in America exploded. Unlikely arts like ballet. . . . Suddenly in music there's Lenny Bernstein. . . . We were producing many first-rate poets, starting with Robert Lowell . . . and Tennessee Williams in the theater. I mean it was a burst. In five years this happened. Everybody came along at the same time. Why? Because we'd lived through depression. We'd lived through World War II. Most of us had not been too frightened to get into the war, and so we went and got frightened once

---

* Anthony Tudor arrived in New York in 1939 and became artistic director of the Ballet Theater, creating notable new ballets like *Pillar of Fire* and *Romeo and Juliet*. His 1945 ballet *Undertow* was a murder story that dealt with male violence and sexuality. A young man with Oedipal problems murders a sexy woman. New York audiences found it too shocking.

we were there, naturally, but we felt that was what you had to do. So our reward was a golden age of five years in all the arts. And those of us who were in the arts, I mean it was a magical time. Then what happened? Korea.

It was no accident, perhaps, that all the names Vidal mentions save Lowell were homosexual or bisexual. The emergence of these artists was the first sign that gay people were "coming out" from society's shadowland. Their first organization for equal rights, the Mattachine Society, had been founded after the war by Marxists. Because of fear of persecution by the law and censure by the forces of religious morality, the society was organized into a loose network of discrete "cells" like the underground Communist Party.

On Broadway after the war gay artists found financial rewards and critical recognition of their talents, if not their sexuality. The postwar era produced a crop of playwrights and literary novelists like Tennessee Williams, William Inge, Truman Capote, and Vidal himself (though he considered himself bisexual). By 1960, it became a sport among Broadway critics to "out" contemporary gay authors, from Williams to Edward Albee, charging that their female characters were only queers in drag. This homophobia maligned a playwright like Williams, who created two or three of the greatest female characters ever to walk the American stage.

Streetcar gave Marlon Brando his first great role. Some speculated that Williams based the character of Stanley Kowalski on his male lover at the time; others named Jackson Pollock, exemplar of the T-shirted, hard-drinking machismo of the New York School painters, as his inspiration, which was highly unlikely. Williams had met Pollock at Provincetown one summer but hardly knew him. Among the gay illuminati Stanley was recognized as rough trade. But he had a broader symbolism as well. Williams saw Stanley as a cautionary figure, a type of fascist: "If you don't watch out, the apes will take over." Stanley is a knuckle-dragging emissary from a proletarian world dominated by violence and cruelty whose mission is to destroy the sensitive, vulnerable ones, the poets and poets manqué like Blanche DuBois, the character with whom Williams emotionally identified.

Streetcar marked the emergence of a new style of theatrical (and later movie) acting: the "method" school, of which Brando was an acolyte. This kind of training, incorporating techniques invented by the Russian director Constantin Stanislavski (1863–1936), reflected New York's cross-fertilization of the arts after the war. Method acting stressed drawing on deep-seated emotions and sense memories in creating a character, much as the analysand interprets his or her dreams through free association—or as the Abstract Expressionists sought to unlock their unconscious visions through automatic writing.

After the war Broadway burst out with new talent, unleashing a younger generation of dramatists who would dominate the American theater over the next decade—notably Williams and Arthur Miller, whose *All My Sons* (1947) touched a nerve of postwar guilt about home-front profiteering while American boys were dying, and whose masterpiece, *Death of a Salesman* (1949), showed the jungle cruelty of Darwinian free enterprise in its portrait of a self-deluding man who dreamed the American dream and is consigned to the human scrap heap at age sixty-three.

The forties also ushered in the age of the integrated American musical comedy, led by the theater veterans Richard Rodgers and Oscar Hammerstein II, whose maiden collaboration, *Oklahoma!* (1943), captured the creative ferment in dance and drama bubbling up. The show was integrated in the sense that it combined story, songs, and dance into a kind of musical play. But what made it such a popular hit (it ran a record 2,212 performances and won the 1944 Pulitzer Prize) was not only Rodgers's gorgeous melodies, Hammerstein's folk-poetic lyrics, or Agnes de Mille's innovative ballets (which transplanted the Freudian vogue into musical comedy). The muscular but unspoken patriotism of this story of the big frontier juiced the morale of wartime audiences. For people who only recently had thought of the state of Oklahoma in the image of the Dust Bowl and the Okies of the thirties, here was an optimistic, big-voiced celebration of a fertile land with a brawny future, foreshadowing postwar prosperity. As the actress Celeste Holmes, who played Ado Annie, recalled, "People in uniform were always in the audience. People have told me it was the last show they saw before they went overseas and how proud it made them feel to be an American." The sailors, marines, and GIs, after visits to the nearby Stage Door Canteen, obtained standing-room tickets. Hammerstein's daughter Alice, who had a job supervising the standees, remembered "the rowdy, noisy GIs" as a fresh element in the traditionally upper-class Broadway audiences.

Rodgers and Hammerstein's first postwar hit, *South Pacific,* based on James Michener's stories about American sailors on a Pacific island, celebrated Victory. There were two love stories intertwined in the plot, but each was clouded by the long shadow of racial prejudice reaching all the way back to the States. This inspired the liberal Hammerstein's most didactic lyric (doubly so): "You've Got to Be Taught to Hate." The roots of American racism reached far deeper than family upbringing, but at the time the words and the interracial themes were quite controversial. And the traces of social realism, particularly the character types, strengthened the musical's dramatic value. Rodgers and Hammerstein deserved commendation for injecting realism into the Broadway musical, once a haven of chorus girls and silly plots. Fittingly the only chorus girls in *South Pacific* were nurses in shorts and halter tops washing their hair onstage. Overall, as *Oklahoma!* celebrated the new frontier, *South Pacific* celebrated America's victory in the Pacific theater and promised a benevolent imperialism in which the natives would be adopted as our wards and raised up in democratic equality.

Rodgers and Hammerstein entered the postwar years in a noirish mood. Before *South Pacific* came *Allegro,* an experimental musical that might have revolutionized the genre once again, had it not been a flop. It was Hammerstein's attempt to portray the American success treadmill realistically, a premature venture into *Death of a Salesman* territory. The businesslike genius Rodgers wanted no more of this avant-garde stuff, so the two princes of Broadway turned to the positive realism of *South Pacific,* a story that nearly everyone in the audience who had lived through the war could relate to. The production rescued their foundering reputations. Then they crafted another success, though a lesser one, out of an even darker play with death as its theme. *Carousel* was based on Ferenc Molnár's 1909 play *Liliom,* about a roughneck carnie worker who kills himself after an aborted robbery. The heavenly powers give Liliom a second chance to redeem himself with the daughter he fathered by an innocent town girl. But he fails to perform the good deed required of him. He cannot escape the flaws of his character.

To make this downbeat vision palatable to Broadway audiences, Rodgers and Hammerstein sentimentalized Molnár's story in places, most prominently the ending. Although their protagonist, renamed Billy Bigelow, dies, he returns to earth to reassure his daughter that she'll "never walk alone," for at the end of the road lies "a golden sun and the sweet silver song of the lark." Billy is thus eligible for heaven. This optimistic message was Hammerstein's trademark, intended to end on a hopeful note and cheer up the audience from the sorrows of war.

Broadway was spared most of the blacklist hysteria that swept Hollywood and was free within commercial bounds to criticize the system. *Finian's Rainbow,* with its book and lyrics by E.Y. "Yip" Harburg (author of the greatest socially significant song of the Depression, "Brother, Can You Spare a Dime?"), espoused left-wing ideals in its satire of Southern racism and postwar consumerism. It is set in the fictional state of Missitucky. At one point, the Dixiecrat senator, who has been magically given black skin, realizes how badly black people are treated: "You can't get into a restaurant. You can't get on a streetcar. You can't buy yourself a cold beer on a hot day. You can't even go into a church and pray." One of Harburg's satiric lyrics comes in "When the Idle Poor Become the Idle Rich," which sends up American class distinctions and postwar consumerism—or as Harburg put it, "how consumption consumes the consumer."

Meanwhile, back in Hollywood, the postwar quest for realism was enhanced by the war service of so many Hollywood directors and actors. Like other veterans, some of them came home scarred by their service. George Stevens, whose Army photography unit had made the first films of the concentration camps, was deeply disturbed by what he saw and by his own unexpected reactions to the human skeletons—loathsome feelings of "arrogance and brutality" that welled up. "He didn't talk any more," recalled director Frank Capra, who partnered with Stevens and William Wyler in founding the independent company Liberty Films.

Capra believed his own career was set back by the four years he spent making training films with the Signal Corps, though the decline had started before the war.

The new realism surfaced in the private-eye films and crime films, which emphasized tough talk and violent action, giving them a veneer of verisimilitude. Their cynical dialogue was larded with working-class slang and irony. As Dennis Broe has written, the tough talk by an up-front guy like Sam Spade to the double-dealing Brigid O'Shaughnessy in *The Maltese Falcon* serves as an acid splash of reality on her two-faced romantic prattle.

But by the early fifties, crime films had fallen out of vogue. For one thing, churches and women's clubs had taken to criticizing their excessive violence. This triggered a running debate among critics about the nature of the films. The French critics, who discovered film noir after the Americans invented it, so to speak, praised the very qualities that the moralists found repugnant—violence; sexuality; obsession with fate, chance, and death; existential despair.

The French critics were speaking for themselves, of course. Intellectuals, particularly the existentialist philosophers, felt the heavy weight of the past, of corruption and defeat, and saw in film noir, as James Naremore writes, a reflection of their world—"a world of obsessive return, dark corners, or *huis clos*" (the phrase, which translates as "no exit," was the title of a play by the existentialist philosopher Jean Paul Sartre). Similarly, the astute American reviewer Barbara Deming, in her study of the films of the forties, saw the "no exit conclusion" as a recurring motif in films of this time. Whenever the hero and heroine try "to escape a condition of life in which [they] no longer believe . . . helplessness overwhelms them."

Deming and the German critic Siegfried Kracauer (now writing in America) diagnosed the crime film wave as a symptom of a deeper malaise afflicting American society. Responding, the critic James Agee wrote that films like *The Killers, The Big Sleep,* and *The Dark Corner*—now part of the film noir canon—were "nostalgic and amusing, if far from original melodramas," which Hollywood's creative artists, trapped in the studio system, "amused themselves" by making. It was wrong, he thought, to regard "such harmless little slumming parties" as if they were "a sinister mirror of American morals, psychology, society and art." Of course, Agee writes, all films have that nature, to a degree; but sociological analysis, though practiced sensitively by Kracauer and Deming, was becoming a new form of "priggishness," like the attitude of the church groups and club women who wanted crime movies censored. Even Agee, one of the finest film critics of his day, could, it seems, miss the significance of the "amusing" crime films.

The producer John Houseman, writing in the left-wing film journal *Hollywood Quarterly* in 1947, also found something morally repugnant about recent films like *The Big Sleep* and *The Killers,* which he called "tough" films. It was not the violence that was repellent, he said. Violence was "a basic element in American life and has always been an important element in American entertainment."

What offended Houseman were the private-eye heroes of these dramas, who have ambitions no higher than "a skinful of whiskey and a good sleep. In all history I doubt there has been a hero whose life was so unenviable and whose aspirations had so low a ceiling." Similarly, in *The Killers,* an expansion of Hemingway's short story, the main character, played by Burt Lancaster, passively accepts his fate when two hit men come after him. Houseman was repelled by these protagonists' "absolute lack of moral energy, their listless, fatalistic despair." This was a stark contrast to the gangster films of the thirties, which reflected moral values (crime does not pay) and featured a type of hero who fell "with a sort of tragic grandeur, paying the price of his sin."

Houseman found the moral passivity of the private eye and other heroes reflective of American society. "The 'tough' movie," he contended, "is without personal drama and therefore without personal solution or catharsis of any kind. It almost looks as if the American people, turning from the anxiety and shock of war, were afraid to face their personal problems and the painful situations." That is one of the best definitions of the alienation and despair of the most typical films noir, and it was written well before the French critics had exported the phrase to America. Perhaps this moral passivity was tied to the deadness of feeling, the callousness, that people develop when confronted by constant reports of death and suffering in the media. One is compelled to point out, however, that the hero in Hemingway's story is similarly passive, stoically resigned to his fate; and that private eyes like Spade and Marlowe have more character and decency than Houseman gives them credit for.

Mainstream newspaper critics like the *New York Times*'s Bosley Crowther tended to ignore the artistic merits of the best films noir, instead singling out their morally offensive stories and sleazy characters. A case in point: he dismisses Dassin's great *Night and the City* as a "pointless, trashy yarn" about a gallery of sleazy London underworld types among whom there is "only one character . . . for whom a decent, respectable person can give a hoot." Crowther concluded, "Mr. Dassin has a fine old time shooting his scenes from grotesque angles and generally working for a dark, malevolent mood."

But it took French critics like Borde and Chaumeton to locate the central emotions of true film noir—paranoia, fatalism, violence, dread. These elements linked noir to the psychological aftereffects of the recent war and to the dawning cold war. While the religious films and psychiatry melodramas popular during and after the war (discussed below) promised peace of mind, films noir held out no cure or hope of heaven here or hereafter, nor did they attempt to explain God's apparent absence in a time of such vast death and suffering. In that sense, they were perhaps the popular art form most closely attuned to the *après-guerre* mood, exemplified directly and profoundly in the existentialism of Camus and Sartre and the gloomy theology of Niebuhr. Films moved in a universe assumed to be tragic, violent, treacherous, contingent, absurd. Even man-made laws against crime and murder were flawed in films noir: the cops were corrupt or the heroes were a mixture of good and evil. And ultimately, violent death was the inexorable fate of those fated to be victims; its inevitability swept away love, ideals, honor.

The life and career of the novelist Cornell Woolrich best illustrates the spirit of the noir psychology—as much as any one writer could do so. He was not a filmmaker, but postwar Hollywood converted more of his books into films noir than those of any other American writer. Between 1942 and 1950, fifteen of his novels and stories—which were steeped in dread, a sense of the psychological terror of ordinary life, and the primacy

of chance or fate—were adapted into films, including *The Leopard Man,*
Phantom Lady, Black Angel, Fear in the Night, Night Has a Thousand Eyes, and
Rear Window.

Woolrich, a small, red-haired homosexual, lived most of his life in New
York with his divorced mother, Clare Woolrich, and liked to cruise the
docks for rough-trade sailors. He was a talented storyteller, a twentieth-
century urban Poe. In his best tales the crime was less important than the
suspense—the fear of death that haunted the characters. The mystery was
not whodunit; the mystery was life itself. Confessing his own psychology,
Woolrich expressed that of many noir characters: "A sense of isolation, of
pinpointed and transfixed helplessness under the stars, of being left alone,
unheard, and unaided to face some final fated darkness and engulfment
slowly advancing across the years toward me . . . that has hung over me
all my life." Not surprisingly, his stories (published in Gallimard's *Series*
Noir crime novels) were popular in France after the war. He projected his
own anxieties on his characters, psychologically torturing them by sub-
jecting them to exquisitely drawn-out ordeals of danger or menace.

Woolrich's theory of character was fatalistic: "The path you follow is
the path you have to follow; there are no digressions permitted you, even
though you think there are." He did not say who laid out the path, but he
seemed to have in mind the malign deity that toyed with his characters'
fates. His domineering mother may have been a model for his strong female characters. Perhaps as an embittered divorcée she had filled him from
a young age with stories of males' wrongs. For the intrepid women characters Woolrich created seem always to defeat the men who are always
trying to victimize them.

The heyday of films noir was brief, perhaps because Hollywood made
too many downbeat stories like Woolrich's as producers jumped on the
noir bandwagon. Executives complained that these depressing films were
turning off audiences; moreover, in the blacklist years any critical or even
pessimistic depiction of American society tended to be labeled unpatriotic
and thus subversive. Motion Picture Association president Eric Johnston
called for more pictures that "extolled virtue and 'the American way of
life.'" Accusing crime films of being too negative, he sought to ban some

of them for export. What was really subversive was their unprofitability amid the general economic downturn that hit the film studios in 1948. Also, the Supreme Court's decision that year that the movie companies must divest themselves of the movie theaters they owned, which the Court ruled constituted a vertical monopoly, ended the era of "B" pictures, which were made to fill out the double feature bills the studios forced on the exhibitors.

PROMINENT AMONG THE BIG-BUDGET "A" features, and more in the mainstream than films noir, were the religious films popular after the war. They were upbeat and consoling at a time when many anxious Americans were seeking peace of mind—which happened to be the title of an inspirational book by Rabbi Joshua L. Liebman that made No. 2 on the bestseller list for 1946 and No. 1 for 1947, selling some 580,000 copies. The same year that Liebman reached the top of the nonfiction list, Russell Janney's *The Miracle of the Bells,* which also had a religious theme, headed the fiction list. Liebman occupied No. 1 until 1949, when Fulton J. Sheen, who had a popular radio program, took over the religious franchise with *Peace of Soul.*

Catholic-themed movies were potent at the box office in the forties. Leading the trend was *Going My Way* (1944), a jaunty treatment of contemporary Catholicism. It led at the box office and gave birth to a sequel, *The Bells of St. Mary's* (1945). Both starred Bing Crosby, the most popular male actor of the time, as a breezy, crooning priest. He was teamed with Barry Fitzgerald, imported from Dublin's Abbey Theater with accent intact, as Crosby's lovable, curmudgeonly mentor. *Going My Way* was fortified with a wholesome social message by director Leo McCarey, a conservative Catholic who emphasized piety over politics. A social worker's vision of religion was about as realistic as the film got, expressed in the hit song "Swinging on a Star," in which Crosby exhorts the parish's budding juvenile delinquents "to be better off than you are" rather than being a pig by "swinging on a star." *The Bells of St. Mary's* dwelled on a homey parish issue: raising money for a new school. It was noteworthy for cloaking Ingrid Bergman in a nun's habit to play the un-romantic female lead opposite Crosby. The year's top moneymaker, it grossed $21.3 million.

In 1948 came another Catholic film, *The Miracle of the Bells,* based on Janney's novel. The film starred another crooner turned priest—the bad-boy idol of underaged girls, Frank Sinatra—and featured Fred MacMurray as a PR man promoting a film whose fatally ill star (Alida Valli) had died before its completion. The studio wants to withdraw it, but MacMurray's character goes to the actress's hometown in Pennsylvania and persuades Father Frankie to ring the church's bell throughout the day of her funeral. He then rallies the town's Protestant ministers to lend their bells to the chorus. This ecumenical concert causes a miracle: the statues in the church bow their heads in respect for the dead actress. Like *The Song of Bernadette,* the movie summons up a miracle to overcome fear of death. In films noir, no such consolation is offered.

There was also a wave of women's Gothic pictures that emerged at the time. The biggest hit in this trend was George Cukor's *Gaslight* (1944), which was set in Victorian England with Charles Boyer trying to drive In-grid Bergman mad. Another was *My Name Is Julia Ross* (1945), directed by Joseph H. Lewis, one of the ablest noir directors. In the latter a young En-glish woman (Nina Foch), desperate for money, takes a job as personal sec-retary to a widow in London. She is drugged and wakes up in a mansion along the seacoast of Cornwall, a virtual prisoner, the servants told she is mad. She is being used in a cover-up scheme, which involves abusing and brainwashing her so she can stand in for the murdered wife of the old lady's son, played by the sinister George Macready. Later critics saw the Foch character as a kind of composite of the victims of sadistic torture and the displaced persons who haunted postwar Europe's blasted landscape.

In the *Hamlet*-like plot of Edgar Ulmer's *Strange Illusion* (1945), a young man has a recurring dream in which his mother falls in love with a man whom he fears. A psychiatrist works with the young man on his dream, which is beginning to come true, as his mother falls under the influence of the man—who, it turns out, is a homicidal maniac who murdered his father, believed to have died in an auto accident.

Psychiatry thus served as the movies' secular alternative to religion, an alternate route to peace of mind. (Liebman's book draws on religion and psychiatry.) As depicted in postwar films it had an ambivalent image. Freudian analysis was extolled as a cure for personal ills. In Alfred Hitchcock's *Spellbound* (1945), Gregory Peck's problem represents the search for self and relief from postwar guilt. He is successfully treated by psychiatrist Ingrid Bergman, who interprets his nightmares (illustrated in sets designed by Salvador Dalí) to reveal that he is tormented by guilt for the death of a friend.

Riding this trend a kind of psycho noir appeared, marking the end of the society-made-me-a-criminal social-message films of the thirties. These were crime films with psychiatry in the plot; they usually showed analysts curing criminals of their murderous drives by locating the central traumatic event of their childhoods. In *The Dark Past* (1949), a rumpled, pipe-smoking shrink (Lee J. Cobb) is held hostage by an escaped convict (William Holden), who has a history of violence. Cobb cures him in situ by analyzing his recurring dream. At the end Cobb delivers a speech urging early treatment for all juvenile delinquents to divert them from future lives of crime.

Perhaps early intervention could have saved Bart (John Dall), the central figure in Joseph H. Lewis's cinematically dazzling *Gun Crazy* (1950). From boyhood on, he has been fascinated by weapons and has become a crack shot. After serving in the war, he meets a beautiful Annie Oakley named Annie Laurie (Peggy Cummins), and they run off together to launch a crime spree. Their mutual attraction to guns supplies the erotic (or phallic) subtext of their love. But Bart has an inhibition that prevents him from going all the way, so to speak: he does not want to kill. In contrast, Laurie is a true femme fatale. She craves luxuries and nags Bart to commit risky bank robberies. "I told you I was no good," she warns. "Well, now you know. I've been kicked around all my life, and from now on I'm going to start kicking back." The gun-crazy lovers are hunted down; they take refuge in a swamp. The sheriff—Bart's boyhood friend—calls on him to give up: "We're coming in, Bart. We know you won't kill us. You're not a killer." But Annie stands up and fires at him, crying, "I'll kill you!"

Bart shoots her before she shoots his boyhood pal—thus placing male friendship above heterosexual love.

One of the most effective of the psycho noirs was *The Dark Mirror* (1946), in which Olivia de Havilland plays twin sisters: one good, one evil. The good one wants to marry and settle down with a good man; the femme fatale wants to seduce and destroy him. The director, the German émigré Robert Siodmak, uses Expressionist techniques to establish the requisite dark moodiness. Thus did the Expressionist cinema of Weimar—launched with *The Cabinet of Dr. Caligari,* the first movie psychiatrist—reach American shores.

De Havilland excelled in psychological films, most famously *The Snake Pit* (1948), directed by Anatole Litvak. Reformist in impulse, it takes a humane view of the mentally ill, showing them suffering under a callous medical bureaucracy. Although feminists regarded it as preaching a conformist view of women's role, the heroine, Virginia Cunningham, is a working writer who lives in Greenwich Village with her husband and no children—hardly a Stepford wife. Like the novel by Mary Jane Ward on which it was based, the film painted a harsh picture of the care the author had experienced in New York's Rockland State Hospital. The initial script was by Arthur Laurents, a Communist and gay man (he was uncredited), who had done research by living in a mental hospital ward and talking to psychiatrists. Litvak had made his own firsthand observations and had urged his cast to visit similar institutions and attend therapy sessions. De Havilland became passionate about authenticating her Academy Award–nominated performance. Although the screenwriters, Frank Partos and Millen Brand, were progressives who later tangled with HUAC, they made the film a force for social reform without preaching. Its scenes show how the overcrowding and callousness in the hospital contribute to the patients' sense of hopelessness. The character of the compassionate Dr. Kik (Leo Genn), based on a real-life doctor at Rockland, makes a quiet stand for humane treatment. With a portrait of Freud looking on, he helps Virginia locate the origins of her illness in a father fixation.

In a late scene, all the patients—perhaps a hundred of them—are assembled for a dance. A young woman (the Broadway star of *Carousel,* Jan

Clayton, uncredited) stands up and sings the folk song "Going Home." Gradually, the patients join in, swelling to a chorus of yearning for home, family, ordinary life. The point is powerfully made that these lunatics are human beings who should be cared for as Dr. Kik cared for Virginia. *The Snake Pit* sparked reforms in several states. As a film set in an asylum, it had come a long way from *Dr. Caligari*.

The psychiatry vogue was one aspect of the greater realism of films released in the first postwar year. Typical were high-budget "A" films like *The Best Years of Our Lives* (discussed in Chapter Four) and Frank Capra's *It's a Wonderful Life*.

Capra desperately needed his film to score financially. He had recently formed the independent production company Liberty Films with the directors William Wyler and George Stevens. According to biographer Joseph McBride, Capra was "undergoing a secret metaphysical crisis, wondering whether he 'had put too much faith in the human race.'" Although only forty-nine, he feared "that he was reaching the end of his creative powers and that the time had come to make a definitive artistic statement." During the war Capra's populist political views had grown more conservative. A screenwriter who worked with him said the "Why We Fight" propaganda films he made for the armed forces "gave him a new sense of values, and then he was dead. He was working with the people who were the heavies in his own pictures, and it turned him completely around." Another friend thought he seemed dispirited: "He wasn't fighting like he used to . . . he was inclined to give up on things."

In films like *Mr. Smith Goes to Washington* and *Mr. Deeds Goes to Town*, Capra had thumbed his nose at big business, bankers, and homegrown fascists. But after the war, he was a politically divided soul. In searching for a new project he came upon a magazine story by Philip Doren Stern, in which the despairing hero is saved by angelic intervention. One of Capra's favorite books happened to be Dickens's *A Christmas Carol,* and this film provided a Christmas theme with a similarly inspirational ending.

Capra's divided soul is apparent in the alternative Bedford Falls that the angel Clarence (Henry Travers) conjures up to show George Bailey (James Stewart) what his hometown would have been like had he not lived. This city was actually a more truthful rendition of a contemporary upstate New York industrial city than the "real" one in the movie—a polluted, lawless place, its Main Street lined with saloons and dance halls. McBride calls this "a powerful vision of despair . . . shot in the fashionable *film noir* style." Capra's own mood swings between creative elation and despair made him spiritually at home in the nightmare city. The "real" Bedford Falls is a pleasantly nostalgic dream. Even the evil banker (Lionel Barrymore) drives a quaint horse and buggy instead of a Cadillac.

The movie's upbeat ending did not ease Capra's depression; nor did it solve his real-life crisis. Coming in nearly $1.5 million over budget and missing most of the holiday season, the movie flopped. Its failure dealt Liberty Films a fatal blow. The three directors had jumped too quickly on the independent trend that started before war's end but soon floundered in the treacherous postwar seas. Capra lost his nerve, to his later regret, and sold out his share.

Another shock awaited him. When the Korean War started in 1950, he volunteered to make films for the Army, as he had done in the last war. But he was denied a security clearance. He later learned to his horror that some of his transient involvements in liberal causes in the thirties, mixed with the usual innuendoes in his FBI file, had caused him to be judged a security risk. To the son of an immigrant, a man of deep emotional patriotism, being accused of disloyalty to his country was a shattering blow.

FILMS WITH SOCIAL MESSAGES had a strong appeal to the more serious postwar audience. Some delved into social realism to comment on class in America. In *The Strange Love of Martha Ivers*—a melodrama of murder and greed written by the leftist Robert Rossen, who made a number of realistic dramas—Martha (Barbara Stanwyck) owns the town's largest business. Her alcoholic husband, a childhood friend who knows her secret (she murdered her rich aunt), extols the "power and the riches that you'd learned to love so much, and that I'd learned to love too." Behind the public front of these leading citizens lurk twisted motives and unholy deeds. Martha's "strange love" of wealth and power is a corruption of real love.

Like many films of the time that employed critical realism, this one galvanized the conservative Motion Picture Alliance, whose reviewer charged that it contained "sizable doses of Communist propaganda."

Few postwar films contemplated the postwar landscape or the dawning cold war (except to emphasize the red menace in America). A rare exception was Billy Wilder's *A Foreign Affair* (1948), with its location shots of bombed-out Berlin and the comeuppance of an opportunistic German woman (Marlene Dietrich) who had been the mistress of a Nazi killer. Its scenes of GIs fraternizing with rumbustious Russian soldiers also drew conservative criticism. Dassin's *Night and the City* used location shots of bombed-out London as a backdrop to its story of a small-time criminal who falls out with the mob. And *The Third Man* (discussed below) showed the sometimes tense relations between Soviet and British military police in occupied Vienna.

I HAVE POSITED A PSYCHOLOGICAL link between the postwar noir trend and the late war. But few films of the time artistically or philosophically grappled with the true horrors of the cataclysm that was World War II: the mass civilian deaths, the Holocaust, the atomic bombing of Hiroshima and Nagasaki. Such catastrophes strike art and poetry dumb. Yet artists eventually feel they must somehow bear witness, and after World War II filmmakers were no exception. This seems fitting, since newsreel films were, after all, the first medium to reveal to American audiences the Nazi death factories and the Japanese atrocities in China.

The first postwar film to raise the subject of the Holocaust is nearly forgotten: *None Shall Escape* (1944), with a script by Lester Cole, a Communist who would become one of the Hollywood Ten, and Alfred Neumann, a left-wing German émigré. Shot in 1943, it is set at the fictional war crimes trial of an unrepentant Nazi functionary who ordered retaliation killings in a Polish village. Played by Alexander Knox, he is the stereotype of the cold, evil movie Nazi; the movies could not even conceive of a real one like Adolph Eichmann, the gray, obedient clerk of death captured after the war by Israeli commandos.

Orson Welles's *The Stranger* (1946) was also among the first films bearing witness to mass death, as was *The Third Man* (1948), in which he starred. With a mature script by the British novelist Graham Greene and brilliant direction by Carol Reed, the latter is set amid the ruins of a morally exhausted Vienna, where, as in Wilder's postwar Berlin, survival trumps morality. Welles plays Harry Lime, an American hustler who has gotten rich selling vials of diluted penicillin to hospitals through the black market. The children who are treated by the adulterated drug die painfully or are crippled for life.

High above the city in a Ferris wheel car, the elusive Lime greets his boyhood friend Holly Martin (Joseph Cotten), a hack writer of Western novels, whom Harry summoned to Venice to join him in his lucrative racket. Holly, who had been unaware of its nature until briefed by a hard-bitten British military cop (Trevor Howard), asks if Harry has ever seen pictures of the mutilated victims of his racket. Harry shrugs: "Victims? Don't be melodramatic. [He opens the door to the car.] Look down there. Would you really feel any pity if one of those dots stopped moving forever? If I offered you 20,000 pounds for every dot that stopped, would you really, old man, tell me to keep my money? Or would you calculate how many dots you could afford to spare? Free of income tax, old man, free of income tax. The only way you can save money nowadays."

Holly reminds him that he used to believe in God, to which Harry suavely responds, "Oh, I still do believe in God, old man. I believe in God and mercy and all that. But the dead are happier dead. They don't miss much here, poor devils." Greene, the Catholic convert who believed in the existence of evil, thus probed for it in the mind of a minor profiteer, whose thirdhand murders, motivated by cynical greed, are a simulacrum of the mass murders perpetrated by all sides in the war and witnessed by the survivors from afar.

In Vienna, Holly stumbles through a surreal cityscape searching for his old friend, only to be repeatedly told by the people who knew him that Harry is dead. Here we feel the Greene touch, his version of *Things are not what they seem*. He was a master of creating a real-life hall of mirrors with lurking menace and hidden conspiracies from banally ordinary people.

The Holly Martin innocent was a staple character in Greene's thrillers, as well as the pre-war European thrillers of Eric Ambler (*A Coffin for Demetrios*) and Hitchcock's early spy movies (*The Man Who Knew Too Much*).

Welles makes Harry boyishly charming and the most interesting character in the movie. As David Thomson remarks in his biography of Welles, *Rosebud,* we feel sympathy for the devil as he is pursued through the sewers. In the end Holly executes him, paying him back for his betrayal of their boyhood innocence.

During the filming, Welles asked Reed to allow him to write an addendum to his speech on the Ferris wheel in which Harry absolves himself of wrongdoing. "Don't look so gloomy," Harry tells Holly. "After all, it's not that awful. . . . In Italy for thirty years under the Borgias they had warfare, terror, murder, bloodshed—they produced Michelangelo, Leonardo da Vinci, and the Renaissance. In Switzerland they had brotherly love, five hundred years of democracy and peace, and what did that produce? The cuckoo clock." The point here is more histrionic than philosophical: Harry really evades the issue. Yet the speech provokes; it makes audiences think about, or at least flinch at, Harry's idea that after so many deaths in the recent war, what does it matter if one sacrifices a few score innocent children in the cause of money—"Free, of income tax, old man"?

The pessimistic side of Welles's imagination is a fascinating dimension of his artistry. He grappled in the thirties with fascism and nationalism, and with mass death after World War II. Even in 1939, as fascism was rolling over Europe, he planned to make it the subtext of his first Hollywood film, an adaptation of Joseph Conrad's *Heart of Darkness*. As James Naremore writes, Welles's intention in updating Conrad's anticolonialist tale was "translating the novella into . . . an 'attack on the Nazi system,' a 'psychological thriller' about a representative man thrown into the midst of 'every variety of Fascist mentality and morality.'" Welles altered Conrad's point of view to inject a more emphatic denunciation of the evils of colonialism in the Belgian Congo, on whose people King Leopold committed genocide and enslavement in the nineteenth century. But the central theme remains: the transformation of the civilized Western trader Kurtz into a monster, "as a result of his unlimited authority and will to power"—

and, one might add, alienation from the moral values that had made him in Conrad's tale an admirable figure at first who then deteriorates while living in isolation "where no warning voices of a kind neighbor can be heard whispering of public opinion."

The corruption of absolute power was a major theme with Welles, from *Citizen Kane* to *Macbeth* (1947), a reenvisioning of Shakespeare's murder drama as a film noir. Acting the title character, he probes the depths of megalomania.

Brooding along the same lines, in 1940 Welles outlined a script based on the case of the real-life French serial killer Landru, who murdered a series of rich widows. He called it *The Ladykiller,* and he saw it as a dark comedy and a perfect role for Charlie Chaplin. After that, accounts of what happened differ. Welles said Chaplin loved the idea but cooled to the project because he had qualms about being directed by Welles, which would have been true to Chaplin's ego. Ultimately, he bought Welles's script and rewrote it as *Monsieur Verdoux: A Comedy of Murders,* giving Welles credit for the idea. In Welles's version, set during World War I, the Landru character lures to his suburban cottage rich ladies who are frightened by the dirigible bombing attacks on London. Welles said that Chaplin updated the time to World War II and added "socially significant" newsreel scenes of Nazis on the march in the thirties—as well as the philosophical ruminations on guilt and innocence by Verdoux during his trial for serial murders. Welles told Peter Bogdanovich that in his ending, he had eschewed speeches and instead showed the Landru character drinking the traditional glass of rum condemned criminals are given. It is the first drink of his life, and he remarks, smacking his lips, that if he had known about *this* pleasure, he might never have turned to murder. (In Chaplin's version, Verdoux drinks the glass of rum but has no comment.)

Chaplin plays Verdoux as an elegant charmer, a veritable Cyrano in his flowery wooing, impeccably dressed in dandyish clothes, his fluffy white hair streaked with black—in short, the polar opposite of the Tramp, his only feature film character up to then. Verdoux explains to the authorities that he got into this business, as he pointedly calls it, after he was summarily fired from his job as a bank teller, which he had performed with exemplary efficiency for thirty-five years.

Desperate, he discovers a survival skill: a talent for seducing wealthy widows. Once he has stolen their hearts, he cajoles them into signing over to him their estates and bank accounts. In the opening scene, he is in the garden of the country cottage he shared with one such woman, cultivating his roses and ignoring the neighbors' complaints about the black plume of smoke emanating from the incinerator, which is consuming his latest wife's remains. The incinerator can be taken as a symbol of the crematoriums of the death camps. At any rate, this successful businessman has sent some twelve women up in smoke.

We learn he has a pretty wife, confined to a wheelchair, and a little boy who worships him. They know him as a father who is often away on international business. "Ten years, wonderful years," he tells his wife regarding their marriage, resuming his familiar chair and taking up his newspaper. His wife frets that he is working too hard. "These are desperate days," he tells her. "Not an easy task for a man my age to make a living." The world he shields them from with his money and love is a jungle in which only the strong survive.

Verdoux's best friend is the local pharmacist, who improbably experiments with poisons. He tells Verdoux about a new one he has formulated, which is capable of killing without leaving a trace in the victim's body. What could be better suited to Verdoux's modus operandi? Borrowing the formula, he mixes a batch, determined to test it on an anonymous denizen of the streets of Paris. If his or her death of unknown cause is announced, he can assume the poison is as undetectable as its inventor claims it to be.

In Paris, he meets a gamine (Martha Nash) who, he learns, was recently discharged from prison, where she served time for petty crime. He takes her home for a meal, planning to serve her a glass of wine spiked with a lethal dose. But she tells him a touching story about how she lost her husband, a soldier wounded in the war. It seems that he died while she was in jail; she had loved him "like a child" because he "so depended on me." He was her religion; she worshiped him. Indeed, she insists, "I'd have killed for him." This vow to kill for love impresses Verdoux, who fancies it is something they have in common—for does he not kill out of love for his wife and boy? Verdoux is so moved he substitutes another glass of wine for her poisoned chalice and lets her go with a gift of money. He tests the poison instead on a detective who has come to take him in for interrogation. (The police have discovered his connection to a series of rich widows who have mysteriously died.) The man drinks the doctored wine and dies in transit—the cause is later announced as a heart attack—and Verdoux slips away.

With his new secret weapon, he plans to put an end to one of his most annoyingly durable wives—a vigorous, raucous woman played by the unsinkable Martha Raye. A comic mixup of the poisoned wine by the maid spares her the deadly dose, and Verdoux's scheme to drown her by taking her out on the lake in a rowboat and overturning it collapses in a farcical misfire. This woman will not die and turns up to plague him again just when he is about to marry a very rich and handsome widow, whose resistance he has broken down with daily flowers delivered to her door and passionate speeches in person.

Trying to hide from his nemesis, he is forced to abandon ship. A financial panic strikes shortly after, ruining him. His wife and child die in the meantime, leaving him sadly wandering the streets, a shadow of the fastidious lady-killer he once was. One day a large chauffeured limousine stops near him; it is the gamine he helped years before. She tells him that in gratitude for his saving her life, she will take care of him the rest of his days. It seems she has married a wealthy munitions manufacturer who is a generous man when not pursuing his deadly business.

They go to a restaurant, where Verdoux is recognized by the relatives of one of his previous victims who call the police; Verdoux, by now weary of life, goes quietly to take his punishment.

At trial, however, he defends himself by playing a variation of Harry Lime's tune. He is, he insists, a small businessman. It's the big businessmen, the munitions makers, who kill on a grand scale: "Wars, conflict—it's all business. One murder makes a villain; millions, a hero. Numbers sanctify, my good fellow!" And: "As for being a mass killer, does not the world encourage it? Is it not building weapons of destruction for the sole purpose of mass killing? Has it not blown unsuspecting women and little children to pieces? And done it very scientifically? As a mass killer, I am an amateur by comparison."

Here Chaplin was making a direct attack on America's use of the atomic bomb: *Monsieur Verdoux* was completed just six months after Hiroshima. Still, there is a kind of quaint datedness in Chaplin's inveighing against the merchants of death, the munitions makers and Wall Street bankers who were castigated in the thirties as the villains who provoked World War I to fatten their own profits. World War II, however, was a more horrible one in terms of civilian deaths, dwarfing any notion of its having been provoked by profiteers, even if profit was certainly one of its collateral effects. The extinction of all those anonymous dots at Hiroshima and Nagasaki, Dresden and Cologne, London and Coventry, Nanking and Singapore, and on and on were inflicted by soldiers and airmen sent by sovereign states.

Reviewers were outraged by Verdoux's speeches of self-exculpation during the trial. One of the few to defend the movie was James Agee. Chaplin, he wrote, had abandoned his Tramp persona to play a "responsible" man, a solid bourgeois clerk who takes up killing to provide for his loved ones. Verdoux's career is ultimately a "powerful metaphor for war," with "the Verdoux home as an embattled nation, the wife and child as the home front, Verdoux as an expeditionary force, hero in the holiest of causes, and war criminal." Verdoux as defender of his own home front is like the soldiers going off to kill in battle, the pilot dropping his napalm bombs, the atomic bomb burning alive thousands in Hiroshima—all of them are doing it for the loved ones back home. Who could find them guilty of murder for doing their duty? In the defense of home and family, the end justifies the means. That, of course, is the logic of war.

Even a sympathetic Agee found flaws in Chaplin's thinking. How can the existence of corporate mass killers justify one man taking the lives of twenty love-befuddled women? Verdoux was not really a businessman; he was a serial killer, who killed as coldly as the pilot of the bomber. At the heart of the movie is a nagging question that Chaplin fails to answer: does Verdoux kill for love, or does he love to kill? If the former, he is guilty; if the latter, he is a monster.

Nevertheless, despite its philosophical contradictions and occasional windiness, *Monsieur Verdoux* was one of the most morally challenging films to come out of the war. There were few other movies that so earnestly tried to bear artistic witness to the mass civilian deaths that were the terrible hallmark of this war. Years later *Monsieur Verdoux* was shown in New York, this time to overwhelming critical acclaim. The *Times*'s Bosley Crowther wrote, "'Monsieur Verdoux' is an engrossingly wry and paradoxical film, screamingly funny in places, sentimental in others, sometimes slow and devoted to an unusually serious and sobering argument." Its central message is that while the self-styled "small businessman in murder" is executed as a loathed criminal, the big businessmen, the munitions manufacturers, the generals, and the politicians who indirectly commit murder on a mass scale reap honor and profits.

In April 1947, in New York, *Monsieur Verdoux* grossed an anemic $18,000 the first week, sagging to $12,000 by the fifth. It was picketed by the American Legionnaires, who had taken upon themselves the patriotic duty of imposing boycotts on filmmakers who, like Chaplin, were suspected of being reds. Chaplin withdrew it.

Chaplin had abandoned his beloved Little Tramp for the respectable-bourgeois killer, apparently in order to accomplish something rare at the time—making his art a moral statement. Yet his growing unpopularity, his reputation as an anti-American, and the lurid publicity stirred up when he was hit by a paternity suit ensured the most damaging reception of all: indifference. In the temper of the time, his message was impugned as Communist propaganda. HUAC subpoenaed him, and he told Chairman J. Parnell Thomas, "I am not a Communist; I am a peacemonger." Rather than face the inquisition, Chaplin exiled himself to a luxury chateau in Switzerland.

Welles, likewise facing summonses and public pillorying for his liberal views and unconventional lifestyle, joined the other Hollywood blacklistees in a general exodus to Europe, a sad reverse trickle to the great wave of freedom-loving intellect and talent that arrived on American shores in the late thirties. Thus two of the greatest artists Hollywood had produced were banished.

Voices

The twentieth century consists almost entirely of a state of mind tinged, and sometimes dominated, by wartime consciousness.

—MARIANNA TORGOVNICK, *THE WAR COMPLEX* (2005)

The fighting of two major and two minor wars in half a century has drained our national character incalculably; from expansiveness, drive, native generosity and unquestioning warmth we have been reduced to pettiness, caution, meanness and suspicion.

—VANCE BOURJAILY, *THE HOUND OF EARTH* (1964)

Many historians have noted an interesting phenomenon in American life in the years immediately after a war. In the councils of government fierce partisanship replaces the necessary political coalitions of wartime. In the greater arena of social relations—business, labor, the community—violence rises, fear and recrimination dominate public discussion, passion prevails over reason. Many historians have noted this phenomenon. It is attributed to the continuance beyond the end of the war of the war hysteria. Unfortunately, the necessary emotional fever for fighting a war cannot be turned off like a water faucet.

—E.L. DOCTOROW, *THE BOOK OF DANIEL* (1971)

And after the Japs would come the Russians and why the Russians? They couldn't tell you.

It was just accepted that would happen. . . . If you said no, not the Russians, they just looked at you.

—RICHARD BROOKS, *THE BRICK FOXHOLE* (1946)

The war isn't over by any means.

—CLARK CLIFFORD (1947)

Five percent of machine tools were to go to the Russians under Lend-Lease. This was violated again and again. There were always problems. Shortly after the end of the war, the question of a loan to Russia came up. Generals and ambassadors were all sending cablegrams: Don't do it without making demands. Along with the wartime alliance was an underlying antagonism, that these guys were bastards, that we're gonna have to tangle with 'em. Oh, I felt that cold war coming in my bones.

—JOE MARCUS, QUOTED IN STUDS TERKEL'S *THE "GOOD WAR"*

I used to say that every March the [Truman] administration has a crisis looking toward war—March 5, 1946, the Churchill speech at Fulton, Missouri; March 12, 1947, the speech about Greece; March 17, 1948, the Truman speech before Francis Cardinal Spellman to some Catholic group in New York which was a very warlike speech.

—HENRY A. WALLACE

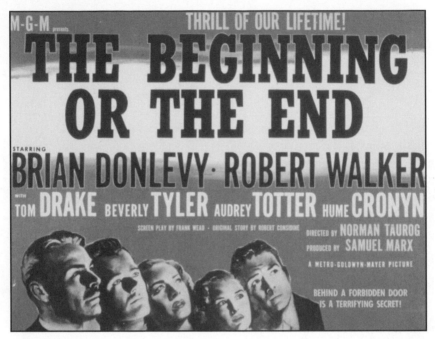

The *Beginning or the End* fed audiences a potted history of the making of the atomic bomb. *Everett Collection*

8

THE GUNS OF MARCH

BARELY A MONTH AFTER VJ DAY, Secretary of the Navy James V. Forrestal and others in the administration were so worried about a Soviet threat that they believed it necessary to scare the complacent American public. As Forrestal wrote to a friend, Americans were "going back to bed at a frightening rate, which is the best way I know to be sure of the coming of World War III." "Going back to bed" meant abandoning their World War II state of alert—indeed, believing that war was over. Not to Forrestal. He'd expressed these sentiments to fellow Wall Streeter Bernard Baruch, who agreed and pointed to the nation's experience after World War I, when it was lulled by pacifist dreams into dismantling the military. World War II had come about, he told Forrestal, because the United States allowed its military strength to decline.

An echo of Forrestal's view is found in the State Department's reaction to a 1945 Gallup poll showing 70 percent of all Americans *opposed* to a "get tough" policy with Russia. The department took the poll as a wake-up call. Undersecretary of State Dean Acheson began making speeches telling Americans they must be "on permanent alert."

By September 1946 polls suggested a shift in public opinion. Nearly two-thirds of Americans described Russian behavior as "less friendly" than it had been only a year ago. In a later poll 44 percent said that their feelings toward Russia had become unfriendly, against 35 percent who remained friendly.

Americans' growing distrust was revealed in their use of the word "Communism" (sometimes "world Communism") to refer interchangeably to the Soviet Union, the domestic Communist Party, and the ideology espoused by both. Most Americans thought that the central tenet of "Communism" was "anti-religion"; "government ownership of property" came a close second, thus pitting God-fearing America against godless Communism in a holy war. By the end of 1946, 43 percent believed Russia would "cooperate with us in world affairs"; by the end of 1949 that number had sunk to 20 percent.

In 1946, several events converged to influence opinion leaders: the failure of the Council of Foreign Ministers to negotiate various issues leading to a peace treaty—in particular with the governments of Eastern European countries; Foreign Service officer George Kennan's "long telegram" from Moscow warning of Soviet intransigence; Churchill's "iron curtain" speech in Missouri. These led policy-makers to forge a cold war consensus based on rivalry and confrontation with Moscow. For this policy the support of the American people was needed. And so government figures directed a harsher rhetorical fire against "Communism."

When Kennan wrote his famed Long Telegram in February 1946, he was the ranking Foreign Service officer at the Moscow Embassy in the ambassador's absence. His eight-thousand-word dispatch analyzing Soviet intentions and objectives was gobbled up by the national security establishment—particularly White House national security aide George Elsey and Navy Secretary Forrestal, who had copies run off and circulated among Washington influentials. Elsey's immediate superior, presidential counsel and speechwriter Clark Clifford, called the Long Telegram "probably the most important, and influential, message ever to be sent to Washington by an American diplomat."

Originally, the State Department had asked Kennan why a speech by Stalin in February 1946 had been so confrontational, so critical of the West, coming on top of other seemingly unfriendly actions by the Soviet Union. Kennan's analysis concluded, "In summary, we have here a political force committed fanatically to the belief that with US there can be no permanent *modus vivendi*; that it is desirable and necessary that the internal harmony of our society be disrupted, our traditional way of life be destroyed, the international authority of our state be broken, if Soviet power is to be secure."

But Kennan did not foresee war between the two rival systems. He said that the Soviet leaders do not "take unnecessary risks" and that they are "highly sensitive to the logic of force." In other words, most times they will back down in confrontations. Also, the Soviet Union was "by far the weaker force," and the Russian people were "emotionally farther removed from the doctrines of the Communist Party" than ever before. Washington's best course was to educate the American public to the realities of the situation. If this was done, said Kennan, a kind of latter-day Hamiltonian who feared the deleterious effects of political passions on foreign policy, "there would be far less hysterical anti-Sovietism in our country."

Those qualifications went unremarked. The hardliners were more interested in shocking the public than in educating it.

In early 1947, Senator Arthur Vandenberg, the main spokesman of the Republican Party's internationalist wing, and Secretary of State James Byrnes delivered speeches on consecutive days calling for a stronger stand against Soviet interference in Eastern Europe. The press dubbed the two speeches (which may have been coordinated) the "Vandenberg Concerto." The *Times* called Byrnes's speech a "new orientation" in American foreign policy.

The main new orientation was that Byrnes had publicly proclaimed a broader US commitment to oppose the spread of Communism, whether by invasion, subversion, or winning democratic elections. He also declared his department's intention to use the negotiating table as a forum for anti-Soviet propaganda. In the wake of the war, US views on issues between the two nations had been hushed up in hopes of resolving them through quiet diplomacy. Now, however, such disputes would be broadcast to the world. As Townsend Hoopes and Douglas Brinkley write in their biography of Forrestal, *Driven Patriot,* the Truman administration had "essentially ended its policy of seeking compromises on fundamental issues" with the Soviets.

How the new public diplomacy would play out in the real world was soon revealed. In March 1947, Truman decided to address the tensions with the Soviets over the future of Turkey and Greece. On the eve of the president's speech, Senator Vandenberg urged him to "make a personal appearance before Congress and scare the hell out of the American people." With that exhortation in mind, Clark Clifford drafted a speech intended to be "the opening gun in a campaign to bring people up to realization that the war isn't over by any means." By "the war" Clifford meant World War II; the president was summoning Americans to arms once again, fewer than two years after VJ Day.

Truman had been prodded into action by a report on hostile Soviet intentions—not the one written by Kennan in far-off Moscow but one crafted much closer to home. Although Clifford later claimed the credit for it, his assistant, George Elsey, had done the initial draft, basically a consensus of administration thinking on Soviet relations cobbled together from reports and memos issued by a variety of sources in the administration. The report conjured up an alarmist view of the Soviet threat, calling all American Communists potential Soviet agents and recommending a rapid defense buildup to foil the Soviet threat.

Truman read the document the very evening he received it. At seven the next morning he called Clifford to tell him it was "powerful stuff," which, if it got out, "would blow the roof off the White House; it would blow the roof off the Kremlin." He ordered his aide to collect all extant copies and lock them up in the Oval Office.

Only years later, when Clifford leaked a draft copy of the report to Arthur Krock of the *New York Times,* was it made public. Krock observed that it prophesied "the shape and thrust of Truman's subsequent great programs— the Greek-Turkish aid legislation, the Marshall Plan, the North Atlantic Alliance (including NATO), and what later became known as the 'Truman Doctrine.'" It was also, according to the historian Elizabeth Edwards Spalding, "a prototype for the most exhaustive Cold War report to the president, NSC-68," an April 1950 study drawn up by the National Security Council that laid out the blueprint and rationale for the cold war arms race.

Truman's address to Congress on March 12, 1947, indeed fired the opening gun in the cold war by proclaiming a worldwide doctrine of containment. The Turkey matter had arisen after the Soviets pressed the Turks to amend a 1936 treaty so as to allow joint Soviet-Turkish control over the Black Sea Straits; the Soviets' demand included the right to station Russian troops on Turkish soil, to which the Turks objected strenuously as a virtual invasion by an unfriendly power. Before Truman's speech, the United States had ruled out negotiations with the Russians on this matter. Dean Acheson informed the Senate Foreign Relations Committee that talks were impossible: "You cannot sit down with them."

In Greece, a Communist led rebellion was under way against the reactionary monarchy, propped up by a large military and British troops. Forrestal testified that if Greece fell and the Soviets got hold of the straits, the world would be "cut in half."

When the president addressed Congress and the American people by radio on March 12, he asked Congress to approve $400 million in military and economic aid to Greece and Turkey. To create the scare Vandenberg advised, Truman mustered a parade of horribles without directly implicating Moscow: "If Greece should fall under the control of an armed minority, the effect upon its neighbor, Turkey, would be immediate and serious. Confusion and disorder might well spread throughout the entire Middle East . . . we must take immediate and drastic action." (In November Truman would put it even more ominously: "If Russia gets Greece and Turkey, then they would get Italy and France and the iron curtain would extend all the way to western Ireland.") Then he unveiled his central message: "I believe that it must be the policy of the United States to support free peoples who are resisting attempted subjugation by armed minorities or by outside pressures."

The press called it the Truman Doctrine, and it had consequences. The United States would pour in arms, money, and military advisers and build a Greek army of more than 250,000 men to fight a Communist guerrilla force of 23,000. As the historian Robert Pollard writes, the United States in effect "adopted a military solution to the Greek problem, substituting the annihilation of the enemy for the reform of the social and economic conditions that had fostered the insurgency in the first place."

After he had made the speech Truman wrote one of his blowing-steam letters to his daughter, Margaret. It is of interest for the special attention he pays to former commerce secretary Henry A. Wallace and Florida senator Claude Pepper, now his chief critics on the left: "The attempt of Lenin, Trotsky, Stalin et cet., to fool the world and the American

Crackpots Association represented by Joseph Davies [former ambassador to Russia, author of *Mission to Moscow*], Henry Wallace, Claude Pepper and the actors and artists in immoral Greenwich village, is just like Hitler's and Mussolini's so-called socialist state. Your pop had to tell the world that in that impolite language."

Clifford would, in hindsight, express regrets about the speech, saying it was "too broad a statement of our country's policy" and placed too many responsibilities on the United States, theoretically committing it to aiding countries all over the world, large or small, that were deemed threatened by Communist aggression from without or Communist subversion from within. James Byrnes complained that the Truman policies were "only leading us to World War III."

Senator William Fulbright of Arkansas, later an opponent of the Vietnam War, wondered, "If we undertake the support of Greece and Turkey, how and when can we stop the lavish outpouring of our resources?" Many Republicans opposed the aid package on budgetary grounds, but Vandenberg supported it and pushed it through in the Senate, backed by Acheson's lobbying. The votes were 67–23 in the Senate and 287–107 in the House.

The capitalist-lining *Fortune* magazine approved of Truman's crisis stance: "The only way to avoid having American policy dominated by crisis is to live in crisis—i.e., prepared for war." Another Luce voice, lapsed Communist Whittaker Chambers, reviewing for *Time* Arnold Toynbee's erudite tome *A Study of History* (which became a surprise best seller in 1947—No. 4 for the year), proclaimed that the United States was "the champion of the remnant of Christian civilization against the forces that threatened it. . . . Our destiny demands a response to this [Soviet] challenge."

As the foremost defender of the faith and "Christian civilization," the Catholic Church had for years backed a hardline policy toward Communism. Most prominent among the church's American spokesmen were Archbishop Fulton J. Sheen (who had a popular weekly radio show) and Cardinal Spellman (who had a prominent pulpit in St. Patrick's Cathedral). In full spate, the latter would exhort his flock to "help save civilization from the world's most fiendish ghoulish men of slaughter" and urged them to read Mickey Spillane's latest novel, pointing out the "good parts" such as the passage in which private detective Mike Hammer says, "Don't arrest them, don't treat them with the dignity of the democratic process of the courts of law . . . do the same thing they'd do to you. Treat 'em to the inglorious taste of sudden death."

On the Protestant side, the Federal Council of Churches' Committee for a Just and Durable Peace, chaired by John Foster Dulles, joined the wake-up-America brigade. The committee announced in 1946 that "differences" with the Soviet Union "will never be removed by compromise," thus tacitly rejecting FDR's wartime policy.

Not long after promulgating his doctrine, Truman attempted to insulate his party from highly politicized Republican charges that the government was infested with Communists. The president's political advisers, though deprecating the idea that the government was being subverted, urged him to co-opt the issue before the Republican Congress took more drastic action. And so Truman issued Executive Order 9835, which established a federal loyalty program under which civil servants accused of having current or past ties, loosely defined, to a subversive organization, also loosely defined, could be fired with no opportunity to confront their accusers or challenge the evidence against them. There was a hearings procedure for employees under suspicion, but it was stacked against them. Using sometimes obsolete information, the Justice Department, under Attorney General Tom Clark, had compiled a list of subversive organizations, belonging to which would cost a government worker her job. The grounds for such a designation were secret, so a group on the list could not contest the damning label.

As the parties tried to outdo each other in toughness on Communism, Truman's order led the GOP to pass the McCarran Act of 1950, which Nevada senator Pat McCarran cannibalized from the 1948 Mundt-Nixon Bill. Its central aims were to require Communists to register with the government, to bar them from holding public office, and to deport aliens discovered to be Communists.

The Soviets had indeed recruited spies from the ranks of party members working in government before and during the last war. Now, however, these spies—including Klaus Fuchs, the Rosenbergs, Elizabeth Bentley, and Judith Coplon—had been caught. The people were scandalized by the extent of past Soviet spying and could not be mollified by the proposition that governments had always spied on one another and would continue to do so.

The loyalty security program was a blunderbuss that hit more innocent citizens than spies. Truman's executive order turned out to be the opening wedge of McCarthyism. It virtually codified the confusion of dissent with disloyalty and legitimized guilt by association.

In the paranoid atmosphere of the time, criminalizing dissent seemed prudent and reasonable. After all, *Reader's Digest,* HUAC, and FBI pamphlets told people that Communists were everywhere. They lived double lives; they *lied* about their party affiliation. They infiltrated and subverted. They could be your mailman, your grocer, your next-door neighbor. The Age of Anxiety became the Age of Distrust. Now you could be adjudged "disloyal"—and thus ineligible for a government job—if you thought, said, or even believed this or that; or associated with so and so; or once belonged to or had a "sympathetic association" (whatever that might mean) with such and such organization. You were penalized not for criminal actions but for "associations," which presumably revealed hidden *tendencies* to disloyalty that disqualified you from holding a "position of trust." The guilty associations proving these tendencies were culled from a secret database of membership lists, employee questionnaires, and hearsay and unproven assertions reposing in the secret files of the burgeoning security apparatus—the FBI, HUAC, loyalty boards, police red squads, corporate security people, the American Legion, etc. People could be deprived of their livelihood without visible cause, let alone due process of law.

Given the rise in rhetorical heat, the defense budget soon came under critical scrutiny. After the war, as we've seen, a great majority of Americans had favored drawing down the armed services and economizing on defense. Hearing their voices and giving social programs a higher priority than military buildups, Truman had allowed the peacetime defense budget to slip to $13 billion. Nevertheless, the United States, facing no imminent threat, maintained a military establishment many times larger than it had in the isolationist thirties, including an army of more than half a million, a national guard, the world's largest navy, a fleet of intercontinental bombers, and a far-flung network of bases. The Pentagon was relying on the threat of the nation's tiny atomic arsenal to halt the numerically superior Soviet army should it roll into Europe. Still, with its fleet of long-range bombers and its bases ringing Russia, the United States was in a sufficiently credible state of readiness to make the Soviets think twice about going to war—assuming they were even considering it, which was extremely unlikely given the vast damage they had suffered in the recent war.

Nevertheless, Congress moved in fits and starts to install a national security state. In 1947 it passed the National Security Act (amended in 1949), which reorganized the three service branches under the Defense Department and created the National Security Council and the Central Intelligence Agency. (The Air Force, thanks to its high-profile saturation bombing campaigns during the war and saturation lobbying afterward, had won status as a coequal branch of the military.)

In July 1947 Forrestal became the first defense secretary, and he worked hard to fight the economizing trend. An introverted, conscientious, deeply patriotic man, he was one of the earliest high officials in the administration to worry about a Soviet invasion of Europe. As his biographers Hoopes and Brinkley write, "At a time when major figures like Roosevelt, Hopkins, Stimson, Byrnes, Marshall, and Eisenhower were acting on the belief that nothing basic about Stalin's Soviet Union precluded a friendly relationship with it, Forrestal perceived in its nature and purposes a fundamental threat to the West and to the idea of free men." Forrestal would labor tirelessly to build a new anti-Soviet consensus.

By Forrestal's reckoning, the springs of Soviet conduct could be traced to Marxism, a doctrine in which its leadership religiously believed. This insight he acquired in talks with former ambassadors to the Soviet Union William Bullitt and Averell Harriman. Bullitt had a theory that Communism was "fundamentally a religion, based on a faith transcending rational calculation" (which would have been news to Karl Marx—and Stalin). Harriman analyzed Soviet conduct geopolitically. To him Soviet intentions were obvious: Moscow's demand for a "security belt" of countries on its borderlands camouflaged its true plan to conquer Europe.

As an ex–investment banker, employed for many years by the Wall Street firm of Dillon, Read, Forrestal was a passionate anti–New Dealer who regarded its economic and social programs as first steps on the road to Communism. Accordingly, he disdained devout New Dealers in FDR's administration like Henry Wallace and Harry Hopkins. Of Wallace, he remarked, "When Henry looks at me with that global stare, I really get frightened." When he heard Hopkins opine that Europe was moving left, Forrestal took the remark not as a valid observation prompted by the recent victory of the Labour Party in England but as a prophecy by a diehard New Dealer who fervently hoped that America would follow suit.

Forrestal, along with military commanders and lobbyists for the aircraft industry, now wasting away for want of military and civilian orders, plumped for "an ideology of preparedness," as military historian Michael Sherry calls it. Its premises were "to forge a permanent military-industrial-scientific establishment, to reorganize the armed forces, to institute a permanent system of universal [military] training, to acquire far-flung military bases, to occupy defeated enemies with American forces, to retain a monopoly of atomic weapons and to create a high-tech American Pax Aeronautica." At the time the Air Force was the most popular service branch. Not only was it more glamorous; the American people preferred dropping bombs on foreign cities to sending their boys to die on foreign shores. A 1949 poll found that 74 percent of respondents believed the US Air Force would "play the most important" role in winning a future war (only 10 percent assigned the Army or Navy an important role).

A 1948 *Newsweek* article, apparently based on leaks from high Pentagon sources, described a US plan for unleashing aircraft against a Soviet threat. It hypothesized a fleet of American superbombers dropping atomic bombs on major Soviet cities. The imaginative writers conjured up a scenario of the United States "closing the circle of air bases around Russia" in order to "make it smaller and smaller, tighter and tighter until the Russians are throttled." Several Pentagon generals freely talked about a preventive war against the Soviets, causing consternation at the State Department. Under Secretary Robert A. Lovett termed such talk "ill-advised in view of the international situation." Ironically, in 1946, *Life,*

Colliers, and other popular magazines had imagined the destructive impact of an atomic strike on the United States. Now the scenario writers were imagining the next war as likely, with the United States dealing a mortal nuclear blow to the Soviet enemy.

Privately, Forrestal showered the president with memos touting the need for more defense spending. On February 9, 1948, he told Truman that the "most critical immediate problem is the serious shortage of manpower in the Army. . . . I cannot overemphasize the importance of this shortage." Forrestal declared that he was "seriously concerned about the legislative situation respecting Selective Service," which was due for renewal. The nation needed a military draft to bring the Army back up to strength. He warned his chief about "a growing apathy throughout the country" to the Soviet threat.

Polls showed that when people were asked to choose between rebuilding America's military strength and handing over to a United Nations police force responsibility for keeping the peace, they opted by wide margins for a unilateral buildup. The inflated postwar hopes for the United Nations had faded; Americans opposed the idea of surrendering sovereignty to it. When a poll asked whether or not the United States, Britain, and Russia should "get together and do away with armaments and military training," twice as many respondents disagreed as agreed. Only 8 percent disagreed with the proposition that the United States "should come out of this war with more military bases outside this country."

Most Americans now believed in the ideology of preparedness. An October 1945 poll showed that 75 percent supported Universal Military Training (UMT), a program under which all young men were required to take a year of military-style training when they reached eighteen, followed by reserve service. Although UMT was heavily backed by veterans' organizations, public support for it waned, and Congress never passed it. Actually, Forrestal and other military leaders preferred a draft, since it could quickly assemble thousands of young men to augment the under-strength Army. In June 1948 Congress members, subjected to a drumbeat of dire warnings from the Pentagon, would pass a law reviving Selective Service, the first peacetime draft in the nation's history.

In February 1948, the leftist coalition government of Czechoslovakia was brutally overthrown by a Soviet-backed coup. This intervention shocked the American public to a more profound degree than previous crises because it stirred up memories of the 1938 crisis after Hitler marched into the Sudetenland and British prime minister Neville Chamberlain acquiesced to the invasion at Munich. Most believed that this appeasement had opened the door to further incursions by Hitler, leading to World War II. The Soviet coup in Czechoslovakia became a time warp in which not the Soviet Union but Nazi Germany was again marching into the Sudetenland as the first step in a plan to conquer all of Europe. The Munich Syndrome remained deeply embedded in American memory. It was operative in high policy-making circles, as well, from Forrestal, who saw Stalin as a new Hitler, down to the State Department official who said, "The Soviet Union's assault upon the West is at about the stage of Hitler's maneuvering into Czechoslovakia."

A *Newsweek* poll showed growing support for dropping a bomb on the Soviet Union, stoked by the preventive war talk of Air Force generals. Secretary of State George C. Marshall, who had opposed the Truman Doctrine as too warlike but had converted to distrust of the Soviets, warned that because of the "reign of terror" in Czechoslovakia the world situation was "very very serious." But his private hunch was that war was not likely, a view that echoed those of US intelligence officials and the State Department's Policy Planning Staff, led by George Kennan (who regarded Soviet moves in East Europe as defensive).

The anarchist-pacifist editor Dwight Macdonald commented that Americans were being told if Stalin weren't stopped immediately they were next on the list in Communism's agenda of world conquest. Such propaganda, he said, imposed on Americans a Hobson's choice between appeasement and containment, between disarmament and military strength—rather than rallying them to support diplomatic alternatives. But in these tense times no one had the leisure or the will to think about diplomatic alternatives.

Truman decided to state the administration's response to the Czechoslovakian crisis at the New York Democratic Party's annual St. Patrick's

Day dinner on March 17, 1948, usually a forum for mutually admiring speeches by the assembled pols. Secretary of State Marshall suggested to him that the subject was too grave for such a partisan forum, and that he should unlimber his message first to a joint session of Congress. Truman assented.

Rejecting a State Department draft as too tame, presidential counsel Clark Clifford pressed Truman to deliver "the strongest possible speech . . . on Russian relations." Clifford and his No. 2, George Elsey, then drew up an address that Marshall found inflammatory; he warned it might "pull the trigger—start the war." Clifford argued that Truman needed to speak bluntly to (i.e., scare the hell out of) the Republican-controlled Congress if he truly wished to convince them of the urgent need to pass the Marshall Plan, which had been stuck in committee. Marshall turned out to have been wrong, of course, but in rejecting his counsel, Clifford once again opted for the alternative of scaring the public.

The president's speech blamed the Soviets for creating the tensions in Europe: "The situation in the world today is not primarily the result of the natural difficulties which follow a great war. It is chiefly due to the fact that one nation has not only refused to cooperate in the establishment of a just and honorable peace but—even worse—has actively sought to prevent it." He criticized the Soviets not only for the economic crisis but for their repression of democratic movements in the Eastern Bloc and for backing subversion by Communist parties in Western Europe.

With the specter of Communism haunting Europe, the Republicans agreed to pass the Marshall Plan immediately. The wisdom of their about-face was borne out by history, which would declare it one of the greatest US foreign policy triumphs, a paragon of effectively delivered economic aid that not only bolstered the European market for American goods (crucial to US prosperity) but helped the Europeans modernize their industrial plants and revive their war-damaged economies. Each European nation designed its own reconstruction program; eventually, the United States dispensed $12.4 billion in aid. This was well short of the Europeans' request for $22 billion. Nevertheless, between 1947 and 1951 the combined gross national product of Western Europe rose by 30 percent.

Truman's St. Patrick's Day speech had a domestic political target as well: Henry Wallace, who had come to symbolize a faction of the far-left wing of the Democratic Party that believed peaceful coexistence with the Soviets was possible and desirable. Truman used the speech to link Wallace's criticisms of US policy to Communism. "We must not fall victim to the insidious propaganda that peace can be obtained solely by wanting peace," he intoned. "I do not want and I will not accept the political support of Henry Wallace and his Communists. If joining them or permitting them to join me is the price of victory, I recommend defeat." This was disingenuous, since Truman's recent firing of Wallace over basic policy differences demonstrated that he had no desire for his support.

Truman boasted of his rhetoric as "reading Wallace out of the Democratic Party." The speech also did double duty as an opening shot in the 1948 election. Clifford counseled that foreign policy was a handy issue on which Truman could distance himself from Wallace while making himself look strong in the bargain.

WITH THE 1948 presidential election looming, the crisis strategy was also ready-made for Truman's reelection campaign. As Clifford wrote in a November 19, 1947, strategy memo to the president: "There is considerable political advantage to the Administration in its battle with the Kremlin. The nation is already united behind the President on this issue. The worse matters get, *up to a fairly certain point—the real danger of imminent war*—the more there is a sense of crisis. In times of crisis, the American citizen tends to back up his President." (Italics added.) During 1946 Truman's hard line toward the Soviet Union would reposition him as a strong leader and counter Republican digs at his weakness and vacillation. Just so he didn't go past "a fairly certain point . . ."

Truman's St. Patrick's Day speech was the culmination of a gale of martial rhetoric that rattled windows in Washington like the winds of March. The historian Frank Kofsky argues in his trenchant *Truman and the War Scare of 1948* that the primary purpose behind the ominous speeches was to galvanize public support for a massive rearmament program.

The administration drive was sparked by a top-secret telegram from the US commander in Berlin, Gen. Lucius D. Clay, dated March 5, which Forrestal quotes in his diary. The general reports that he senses "a subtle change in Soviet attitude which I cannot define but which now gives me a feeling" that war could come "with dramatic suddenness." According to Walter Millis, editor of Forrestal's diary, Clay's cable caused "intense alarm among those in Washington who were aware of it," certainly Forrestal, and "its influence seems clearly traceable in the events of the next few days." Whatever "influence" it had seems to have been based on Clay's rhetoric rather than any than facts supporting it.

First, Forrestal publicly warned of a serious shortage of American soldiers, who were urgently needed to deal with "various potentially explosive areas" around the world, and of planes capable of dropping atomic bombs on the Soviet Union. He amplified his call for a revival of the draft and for supplemental hikes in defense spending, which was running around $14 billion. He also endorsed the calls by two independent commissions on airpower for significant investment in new planes, answering the shaky aircraft companies' prayers.

A day after Truman's speech, ex–Secretary of State Byrnes, coordinating with Forrestal, delivered a war-scare speech at the Citadel military academy in Charleston, South Carolina, warning Americans that they faced an international crisis in the next four to five weeks. He echoed Forrestal's appeal to expand the Army from its present "pitifully inadequate" 550,000 troops to 669,000. He also demanded approval of funding for the Marshall Plan while cautioning that economic aid alone could not curb Soviet expansion. And he recommended that the administration tell the Soviet Union that it intended to bring to the attention of the UN Security Council the latter's "indirect aggression" (meaning support for domestic Communist parties) in Italy, France, Greece, and Turkey. On top of that, he said, the United States should firmly state that it would "act immediately" (meaning militarily) to "preserve the status quo" wherever the Russians threatened to upset it. He also said that the nation must divert money from public works and social welfare programs into war spending. Appropriately, the nation's former top diplomat had "received a 19-gun salute on entering the campus."

New York Times columnist James Reston, a reliable Washington barometer, observed that the "Executive branch of the government in an effort to gain Congressional support of its policies has been talking a good deal about war lately." To manipulate Congress, the Truman administration had acquired the habit of "emphasizing and sometimes even overemphasizing the danger" from the Soviet Union. "We legislate, in short, in an atmosphere of crisis." That word again.

The bellicose outbursts prompted John Paton Davies of the State Department's Policy Planning Staff to warn that deteriorating US-Soviet relations could disrupt East-West trade and Marshall Plan aid. And Under Secretary of State Robert Lovett reported that "overexcitable statements, some by military people, on a preventive war" (he was probably referring to threats by Air Force generals) mixed with Henry Wallace's peace feelers left the Soviets baffled as to American intentions.

Eventually, cooler heads in the administration instructed Ambassador Walter Bedell Smith in Moscow to assure Soviet foreign minister Vyacheslav Molotov that the United States had "no hostile or aggressive designs whatever with respect to the Soviet Union" and that the door was always open for negotiations. In a violation of protocol, the Soviets published the confidential note and praised its "declaration of peaceful intentions," implying that the burden was on Washington to start negotiations. The Russians had been unscrupulous in revealing a confidential démarche, but the State Department had also been disingenuous in saying that the door to negotiations was open when it really wasn't.

Watching the dust devils dance, Reston wrote that backing and filling by the White House and the State Department made them look inept and inflexible. Because of "its decision to whip up a war scare the administration was thus compelled to pay a substantial price: first, by providing the Soviets with raw material for an embarrassing peace scare; and then by electing, once that new scare was under way, to calm the fears of the Western Europeans through a categorical repudiation of negotiations with the U.S.S.R."

NOW, WHEN GALLUP asked people what had become a recurring question, "Do you believe Russia is building up protection against being attacked in the next war, or is Russia trying to build herself up to be THE ruling power of the world?" only 12 percent said Moscow was acting out of security concerns, while 78 percent took the view that it was out to conquer the world. Another poll showed 71 percent disapproving of Soviet foreign policy.

Defense Secretary Forrestal monitored the papers daily, and on March 16 he noted they were "full of rumors and portents of war." He thought it "inconceivable that even the gang who run Russia would be willing to take on war, but one always has to remember there seemed to be no reason in 1939 for Hitler to start war, and yet he did, and he started one with a world practically unprepared." The United States must try to make the Russians understand "the folly of continuing an aggression which will lead to war." But if it was not possible "to restore them to sanity," then the United States must get ready for war so as not to be "caught flat-footed as we were in 1941."

Despite Forrestal's campaign, Truman did not swing behind defense spending on the scale the military had hoped for. The president called for increasing defense appropriations to $15 billion ($146 billion in 2010 dollars), but he worried that the added spending would necessitate deficit financing and generate inflationary pressures. He told Forrestal and the Joint Chiefs, "I want a peace program, not a war program."

Forrestal clung to his belief that the main obstacle to preparedness was public apathy. On April 21, he aimed for a shock effect in testimony before the Senate Armed Services Committee: "The tensions we are in are . . . permanent. . . . The problem [is that] we set up a plan last year based on the assumption of no immediate danger of war." This assumption was now invalid, he said, so the country must face up to "the possibility of war" and rearm accordingly.

On May 21, at a meeting with Secretary of State Marshall and other high officials, Forrestal told his colleagues that he was worried about "the changing tempo of the Congress and . . . the relaxation of tension." Marshall said that because of "the susceptibility of the American public to propaganda," they had lost sight of the deeper issues involved. Forrestal interposed that they must counteract the "American tendency to go from apathy to inertia."

On May 28 Forrestal wrote Truman that he was "seriously concerned about the legislative situation with regards to the resumption of Selective Service," which had still not been passed. He blamed "a growing apathy throughout the country" for Congress's slowness to act; the fading of the war talk had engendered "a dangerous complacency on the part of certain elements in this country."

BY 1948 "THE AMERICAN PUBLIC saw the Soviet danger in the way [Kennan in his Long Telegram] had wanted them to see it," writes cold war historian Daniel Yergin. "There could be no question that the anticommunist consensus had become firmly established in the country." By that time Kennan, the intellectual father of the containment doctrine, had become appalled at the way his analysis had been distorted by administration hawks to justify a dramatic rise in US defense spending. He wrote that he was against "intensive rearmament" because it would hurt the US economy and militarize the rivalry with the Soviet Union, sabotaging diplomatic efforts for peaceful coexistence.

Years later, he admitted to David Gergen in a television interview that his message from Moscow in the Long Telegram had been misinterpreted, though he blamed himself for this. He had meant political rather than military containment. So soon after World War II it was mad to think the Soviets wanted to go to war with the United States. What had impelled Kennan to use such stark language was his fear that the United States had been making "one concession after another to the Soviets." He thought those concessions were unnecessary and actually inflated Russian leaders' truculence because they gave the Soviets "the false idea of their own prestige." But tell this to the administration! "I found it easy to convince them that [the Soviet leadership] was a very dangerous group of men. But I couldn't persuade them that their aspirations were political . . . and not military. *They were not like Hitler.*" (Emphasis added.)

Kennan was but one man, but he was the best-informed Foreign Service officer on Soviet intentions, surely more worth listening to than the anti-Communists who were rending the air with their cries about a second Munich, another Hitler.

AFTER THE HUAC INCURSIONS into Hollywood, as we have seen, film noir gave way to film rouge. Whereas the films noir of the late forties were existentially paranoid and antiauthority, the films rouge—the rabidly anti-Communist films Hollywood rolled out in the early fifties (some fifty of them, including shorts and documentaries)—simply redirected that paranoia at Communism while upholding authority. The Communist agents allegedly infesting America made splendid villains. In these movies the "people" were depicted as childishly innocent about Communists and the threat they posed, which pretty much reflected what people in government (from Acheson to Vandenberg, Clifford to Forrestal) thought. In the films of the New Deal era, particularly Frank Capra's, the people, led by Jimmy Stewart, Gary Cooper, and other home-spun types, were a force for social justice, while big business and politicians were to be distrusted. The message of the postwar films was: distrust the people and trust authority figures. Now "government experts" were needed "to identify the spies, fight them and guide the immature American people toward safety," according to film scholar Saverio Giovacchini. In *Big Jim McClain*, John Wayne's character, a congressional investigator isolated by a complacent citizenry that has been duped by smooth-talking reds, must single-handedly wipe out the Commies.[*]

The anti-Communist thrillers did poorly at the box office, not so much because they flouted public opinion but because they were so heavy-handed and propagandistic. More successful at stirring up public opinion against the Soviet espionage menace was J. Edgar Hoover, who had a very

---

[*] During my service in Army counterintelligence I remember meeting a veteran agent who, like Big Jim, had fought Communists infiltrating unions in Hawaii. I still can see the intensity on his face when he said, "These guys were *bad!* Oh, I hated them!"

influential Washington audience in the palm of his hand. Congress granted his every request for increased funding to expand his Bureau. (Between 1947 and 1950 the FBI budget rose from $37 million to $50 million, accounting for nearly half of the total Justice Department budget.) The irony was that nobody asked why the FBI had failed to uncover the Soviet spy rings operating in the thirties and forties.*

Curiously, polls showed that Americans were less worried about spies than they were about Communist *infiltration*—nests of covert reds in government, schools, unions, movies, and radio, transforming them into bastions of pro-Soviet propaganda so subtle that the public wasn't aware of their influence, yet so powerful that the public would be brainwashed (a term that had not yet come into vogue).

According to the Harvard sociologist and pollster Samuel Stouffer, "the public tends to regard the internal Communist threat chiefly in terms of infiltration and influence, rather than espionage and sabotage." That is, they feared that Communists infiltrating schools, unions, and motion pictures would influence Americans to become party members and subvert the government.

Labor was especially suspect, which explains why two-thirds of Americans approved of the Taft-Hartley Act's requirement that officers of labor unions take a non-Communist oath. At the same time, only 3 percent of Americans said they actually knew a Communist, though 10 percent confessed to knowing someone they *suspected* of being a Communist. This leads to the conclusion that three times as many Americans *suspected* people of being Communists as actually *knew* any. But it also suggests the

---

The Nation magazine had a long record of being critical of the FBI, and it earned a 21,000-page FBI file for its efforts. "The F.B.I. also launched special field investigations of *Nation* contributors, pressured teachers who used the magazine in their classes and cooperated with government agencies seeking to discredit opponents of their policies—all in the name of Americanism," according to Penn Kimball. The roof fell in when a long investigative article by Fred Cook appeared on October 18, 1958. This article triggered a 180-page memorandum attempting to refute the article (a few minor errors were found)—presumably for Hoover's edification, because it remained classified until an FOIA request unearthed it. Cook himself suffered some minor FBI harassment and acquired his own file. (See Richard Lingeman, "The Files' Tale," *The Nation,* December 22, 2009.)

extent to which Communists tended to be seen as an alien "other" in the common consciousness of most Americans. Substantial majorities believed that there were "many" Communists in America, as opposed to the pollsters' other choice, "only a few." (The CPUSA had some 50,000–75,000 dues-paying members at its peak before World War II, plus 20,000 young people in the Young Communists League. Those numbers dropped precipitously after the war.)

RAISING THE ONLY CLEAR CHALLENGE to the calcifying cold war consensus was a handful of radical politicians and journalists and the loose community of pacifist and feminist antiwar groups.

Immediately after World War II, peace enjoyed a large share of public favor and media attention. Groups like the American Friends Service Committee (AFSC) and the Women's International League of Peace and Freedom (WIL) were respected. Contributing to this favorable image was the awarding of the 1946 Nobel Peace Prize to an American, Emily Greene Balch, who helped found WIL during World War I. The following year the prize went to the AFSC for its humanitarian aid projects in Europe.

But there was also a backlash against American pacifists because of their advocacy of disarmament between the wars. They were generally blamed for the country's unpreparedness, which had led to appeasement of Hitler and World War II. The isolationist politicians of the thirties were also blamed, but Republicans in Congress erased this stain on their party's image by adopting militant anti-Communism after the war.

The pacifists of the World War II generation were a different breed from those who emerged after World War I. The older generation, said A.J. Muste, general secretary of the Fellowship of Reconciliation (FOR), peddled a "sentimental, easygoing pacifism" and attracted people who "sat and talked pleasantly of peace and love," feeling that by doing so they were solving the problems of the world.

Most of the postwar anti-warriors, Dwight Macdonald wrote, practiced a new pacifism that was not simply "a passive refusal to go along with the warmaking State, [but] primarily a way of actively struggling against injustice and inhumanity." They were strongly influenced by the nonviolent tactics of Gandhi's liberation movement in India and condemned Stalinist totalitarianism and Marxist materialism. But they were also opposed to containment and preparations for a war with the Soviet Union.

Most conscientious objectors (COs) later said they emerged from the war with a stronger commitment to working for peace and equal rights. The inmates of the CO camps had mounted nonviolent protests collectively defying the authorities and pressing for change in prison conditions. They consciously borrowed the *satyagraha*[*] tactics of Mohandas K. Gandhi and followers in the nonviolent campaign for India's independence. Lawrence Wittner quotes one CO: "It is no longer necessary to look to India for examples of successful nonviolent resistance to tyranny. We can look right here in America at what has happened to the . . . camps."

Several thousand others refused to collaborate with the system and rejected CO status. They were sentenced to up to four years in federal prison. For the great majority of pacifists prison was a radicalizing experience. The federal penitentiary in Danbury, Connecticut, seethed with resistance in 1941 when about a dozen inmates who had been denied permission to hold an antiwar demonstration refused to report for their work assignments. They were placed in solitary confinement, but the warden eventually relented because one of them was the star pitcher for the prison baseball team.

The jailers' responses to future acts of disobedience grew harsher. When two Danbury pacifists launched a "fast unto death" to protest CO regulations, they were force-fed with their arms bound to keep them from making themselves vomit. Their protest continued for eighty-two days and inspired other pacifists. By mid-1943, the number of pacifists incarcerated at Danbury had grown to 200, and they struck against the segregation of black and white prisoners in the dining hall. After 135 days, the rebels were released from lockdown; the warden told them he was rescinding racial segregation, making Danbury the first nonsegregated facility in the federal system (and the site of the first nonviolent victory against racial

---

[*] Literally, "soul force" or "truth force."

segregation in the United States). In the wake of this "victory," the rebellion spread to other prisons, with many pacifist inmates going on permanent strike.

At the end of the war, several thousand pacifists "graduated" from prison schooled in protests. As Wittner writes, "Prison provided a vital fund of experience that pacifists drew upon in postwar struggles. Jim Peck and other veterans of the Danbury upheavals found themselves quickly caught up in the activities of CORE and other radical pacifist enterprises upon their release from prison." Peck, who became a leader in the postwar civil rights movement, recalled, "These demonstrations constituted our attempts to apply effectively on the outside the non-violent methods of protest which we had used in prison." He felt certain "that non-violence would prove as effective in combating racial discrimination on the outside as it had been in Danbury."

Ironically, those who refused on religious grounds to fight the war against fascism would be in the advance guard of the fight against domestic fascism (if the doctrine of white supremacy may be defined as such) after the war. Although the Allied armies killed fascists, they did not kill fascism. The pacifists refused on moral grounds to kill the fascists abroad, but they led a nonviolent attack on them at home.

In 1947 CORE paired with FOR to organize a Journey of Reconciliation. The purpose of this exercise in nonviolent activism was to test enforcement of the 1946 Supreme Court decision in the Irene Morgan case. In 1944, Morgan, an African American woman who worked in a war plant, was aboard a Greyhound bus bound for Baltimore after a visit with her mother in Virginia. When the driver ordered her to give up her seat to a white passenger and move to the back of the bus, she refused, thus anticipating Rosa Parks by eleven years. Angered by her treatment, Morgan sued the bus company; the case went all the way to the Supreme Court, which ruled that state Jim Crow laws placed "an undue burden on interstate commerce."

The first Journey for Reconciliation took place between April 9 and April 22. An interracial group totaling sixteen men traveled among fifteen cities in the Upper Southern states—Virginia, North Carolina, Tennessee, and Kentucky. Each journey was made by squads of eight to ten men. The whites were to sit in the back of the bus, the blacks in the front. They were engaged in an experiment in civil disobedience they hoped would not only challenge Jim Crow laws but help develop tactics for a wider campaign dealing with hostile responses by drivers, local cops, and the public. A report by protest leaders Bayard Rustin and Jim Peck said that "twenty-six tests of company policies were made and there were twelve arrests." (The FBI, alerted to the journey before it started, recruited an informer in FOR, who furnished the Bureau with the Rustin-Peck report.)

The responses to the interstate travelers varied from arrests and hostility to spontaneous expressions of sympathy by both Northerners and Southerners. One of the groups, led by Peck and Rustin, ran into trouble in Chapel Hill, North Carolina, where they boarded a bus bound for Greensboro. The driver ordered Rustin and another black man to move to the back of the bus. When they refused he called the police, and the two were arrested. They were bailed out by a local Presbyterian minister, who, according to the FBI, "has caused a split in the membership of his church as a result of his attitude on racial questions." Angry taxi drivers at the terminal moved in to harass the group; one of them hit Peck with a "hard blow" on the head and reprimanded him for "coming down here to stir up the niggers." According to the CORE report, "Peck stood quietly looking at them for several moments, but said nothing. Two persons standing by, one Negro and one white, reprimanded the cab driver for his violence. The Negro . . . was told: 'You keep out of this.' In the police station some of the white bystanders could be heard saying: 'They'll never get a bus out of here tonight.'"

After being released by the police the group was driven to the minister's home. Later, his phone rang. On the line, an anonymous voice ordered, "Get those damn niggers out of town or we'll burn your house down." The police were called and arrived in about twenty minutes. The interracial team felt it would be best to leave town, and they were driven to Greensboro. Later, an angry crowd gathered outside the minister's home and threw rocks at it.

In another incident, Peck and an unidentified African American sat together in the front of a bus departing from Asheville, North Carolina. The driver called the police, who arrested the black person, whereupon Peck said, "You might as well arrest me, too," and moved to the back of the bus. He was hustled out, and the two were tried in police court and sentenced to thirty days of hard labor.

So it went. No serious violence, and sometimes expressions of support from passengers, white and black. One white woman, asked by the bus driver to sign a card backing him up, told him, "You don't want me to sign one of those. I'm a damn Yankee and I think this is an outrage." A Southern white woman on the same bus gave her name and address to Rustin in case he needed a supporting witness.

Among the CORE report's conclusions was that women passengers were "more intellectually inquisitive, open for discussion, and liberal in their sentiments than men," which seemed counter to the Southern view that Negroes lusted after white women. Sometimes, as the report put it, Southern women gave in simply because they were weary of the inconveniences of segregation: "One white woman, reluctantly taking a seat beside a Negro man, said to her sister, who was about to protest: 'I'm tired. Anything for a seat.'"

The Journey for Reconciliation achieved little reconciliation, but the tactic would be used again in the Freedom Rides of the early sixties, producing better results though also drawing more violent retaliation. Reflecting Hoover's racist fears that black people demanding equal rights were dangerous subversives, the FBI kept a close watch on the FOR. Informants produced a steady stream of reports on its activities. One of these, by an unidentified informant, passes on chatty gossip about FOR leaders' activities: the "Racial and Industrial Department of the FOR is operated by a little Jewish fellow George Houser [Houser was a Methodist minister], and a little negro Bayard Rustin, operating as FOR interracial secretaries."

THE FBI'S INTEREST in the FOR and its adjunct, the War Resisters League (WRL), held steady through the forties. The WRL had been brought to Hoover's urgent attention by James Forrestal. In a 1948 "Dear Edgar" letter, the defense secretary enclosed a memorandum written by a member of his staff warning "that a broad organized pacifist movement may exist which advocates a subversive policy of 'non-violent direct action' and that this movement may be communist influenced or dominated." The staffer warned that there were some fifteen thousand FOR members, most of them socialists and some "possibly" Communists; others were radicals from the labor and pacifist movements. Among the "direct actions" they planned, the memo claimed, were strikes and picketing—"total civil disobedience" of "unjust statutes." To "some extent" the people involved in those actions "are in accord with and possibly subject to support from the Communist Party."

Forrestal requested that the FBI investigate the activities, influence, and funding of these extremists, who threatened to subvert the military with their demos. Hoover apparently sent back a bundle of information that his men had compiled on the FOR, for which "Jim" replied with his deep thanks, adding that it looked as though the Bureau had done a "pretty thorough job."

The FBI also took upon itself the task of collecting evidence that would help deport Communists and subversives. In February 1948, Hoover fielded a request from the commissioner of the Immigration and Naturalization Service for the FBI to look into whether a naturalized citizen's membership in the FOR constituted grounds for "cancellation of such naturalization."

No church was considered so holy that it was above subversion; on the contrary, churches were suspect. In November 1948 an "urgent" telegram to the FBI director reported that an unnamed minister of the Community Church in New York City had demanded in his sermon that the federal government free an Ohio college professor who had been sentenced to eighteen months in prison for advising a student not to register for the draft. The minister was the Rev. Donald Harrington (who would become a leader of New York's Liberal Party), and he was referring to a teacher at a Mennonite college in Bluffton, Ohio, named Larry Gara, a Quaker who told a divinity student who refused to register for the draft to stand by his principles. Harrington said he too had advised young men to "consult their consciences." Therefore, "if Gara is guilty,

I am guilty.":* Such was the conformist mood under the hardening cold war consensus that the *New York Times* took Harrington to task in an editorial, saying his conduct would "encourage the individual to obey only those laws that pleased him," which "could only result in chaos." The editorialist wound up with the standard message: supporting the armed forces was supporting peace because "the way to help preserve peace is to keep our nation strong."

FOR members joined with ministerial students and faculty at Lynchburg College in opposing US Marine Corps recruiters on the campus. They picketed a mortgage lenders conference in Houston to protest neighborhood segregation in that city. They demonstrated against a filibuster by Southern senators of an act to renew the Fair Employment Practices Commission and rallied against the Truman Doctrine. They picketed the Freedom Train (railroad cars containing historic American documents that toured the country in 1947–48) because it segregated visitors and called on the president to grant amnesty to Communist Party leaders who had been imprisoned under the Smith Act, and also some 900 young men in prison for refusal to register for Selective Service.

Decades ahead of their time, they protested segregation of the swimming pool in the Palisades Amusement Park in Cliffson Park, New York, with a "swim-in" by a racially mixed group. This effort triggered attacks and violence against the pacifists. And they demonstrated against the revival of the Selective Service Act in 1948 on the ground that by conscripting civilians as potential soldiers, it encouraged political and military leaders to wage war.

All these activities were monitored by the FBI. Although its reports routinely pegged the FOR and WRL as pacifist groups within the meaning of the law, the Bureau would often add a kicker to the effect that their policies reflected the Communist Party line. The Bureau went on alert when pacifists told young men how to become conscientious objectors, even though both the telling and the becoming were protected by law and the

---

* Harrington was not arrested. The FBI decided that the sermon did not appear to be a violation of any law, so no action should be taken.

Bill of Rights. In October 1948 a member of the St. Paul's Presbyterian Church in Cottage City, Maryland, informed the FBI that the FOR had offered to counsel young men of the congregation on resisting the draft, adding "this all sounds bad to me and I thought you might want to know about it." Hoover personally replied within a week: "I am instructing the Special Agent in Charge of the Washington office to have an agent to interview you."

The FBI was not the only Big Brother watching the FOR, WRL, and other peace activists. The red squads in the big city police departments cast suspicious eyes on antiwar demonstrations. Military intelligence units were also keenly interested, though more poorly informed than the FBI. An Army intelligence report dated January 30, 1946, for example, warned that the FOR was "at times profoundly subversive in its propaganda" and "very anti-Army and anti-United States government." The FOR, the report continues, "has a very strange internationalist ideology which is indicative of a certain connection with the Comintern." Just what that "certain connection" was the report did not say, nor did it explain how such a tie could be maintained with an organization that no longer existed.

The Office of Naval Intelligence summary on A.J. Muste dated March 16, 1956, calls him "a leader in the Communist-penetrated Fellowship of Reconciliation, a member of the National Committee of the American Civil Liberties Union, and a pro-Marxist who has a long record of Communist party adherence." None of this was more than half true, of course, except his membership in the anti-Communist American Civil Liberties Union.

The investigations of the FOR were typically activated by a presumption that any group advocating views that strayed outside the cold war consensus, which stood for containment of Communism at home and abroad by military strength, was suspect. Such views did not land these groups in the gulag, but they did put them on the FBI's list, which meant that any member who worked for the government or might want to work for the government in the future, or to teach in public school or college, had a problem, because past ties to a suspect group would, in one way or another, turn up in an FBI file check.

THE ONCE-RESPECTABLE Women's International League for Peace and Freedom was singled out by the FBI as a ripe target of Communist infiltration. The Bureau reported that some WIL chapters were attracting women who were alleged Communist Party members or wives of them. The Bureau opened cases on Communist "infiltration" of several branches; later, when asked whether the WIL was "subversive," Hoover would depart from his usual form letter to mention that while the group was a legal pacifist organization, some of its branches were suspected of being Communist-infiltrated or -influenced.

Politically radical women, some of them members or ex-members of the CP, did join the WIL. Unlike many liberal organizations of the time (such as the ACLU and the NAACP), the League's national board administered a policy under which Communists could be members so long as they followed the WIL's values of pacifism, disarmament, peaceful settlement of disputes among nations, and civil liberties.

This policy, as well as the League's pacifist advocacy, was costly. Membership skidded to a little over four thousand compared to more than fourteen thousand in the thirties. More harmful, though, was the toxic distrust such accusations injected into the organization. As WIL leader Mildred Olmsted reported to her national board in 1953, although the League had been fairly free from outside attacks by anti-Communist groups, it was being disrupted "from within, by our own members who have become frightened by the current hysteria and want us to start labeling members and changing our traditional tolerant attitudes." She warned that while outside attacks sometimes unite a group, "*internal* suspicions and lack of confidence, secret whisperings and the growth of cliques and factionalism can break down our organizations faster, can be more fatal to its spiritual life, to its health and to its usefulness than any number of outside attacks."

There was little evidence that the WIL was ever "infiltrated" in the way that the professional Communist fighters warned about—that is to say, reds joining, doing all the work, taking over, and dictating policy. Indeed, the WIL national board members valued Communists' commitment to the cause and used them so long as they supported WIL ideals. Where they caused a problem was by agitating the conservative members, who for ideological reasons—or social concerns—did not want them in the branch. Thus, in the Denver, Miami, Chicago, and Boston branches, divisive internal fights broke out over demands that the alleged reds be expelled, and the national board often had to intervene to restore peace.

The coincidence of one's views on this or that topic of the day with those of the CPUSA was considered prima facie proof of Communist leanings. After the world Communist movement launched a peace campaign, advocating negotiations with Moscow became suspect. Anti-Communism discredited those who, from varying viewpoints, opposed the hardening cold war consensus between 1947 and 1950. In America, the Great Syllogism ran: Communists favor peace. X favors peace. Therefore X is a Communist (read: traitor, subversive, liberal, disloyal American, etc.).

Peace had become a dirty word.

THE PEACE MOVEMENT'S rapid decline was not solely attributable to the red-baiters and the FBI. It was also the result of ordinary Americans' fears and distrust, stirred up by the actions of the Soviet Union as reported in their morning papers, causing them to favor rearmament. The Soviet coup in Czechoslovakia swept away whatever wartime goodwill toward the Soviet Union remained. Then came the Berlin Crisis, which had been building for months after the Soviets began stopping US trucks carrying essential supplies to Berlin in the spring of 1948.

Following a separate track in the peace effort was the antibomb movement. The facts about the destructive power of the atomic bombs dropped on Hiroshima and Nagasaki in August 1945 had slowly percolated down through American society. First reports of the bombs' effects had been heavily censored. After the war ended, reporters were barred from the bombed Japanese cities. Some sneaked in ahead of occupation troops and filed stories, but these were embargoed by General MacArthur's censors in Tokyo. Pictures showing the flattened cities appeared in newspapers, but there were few eyewitness reports describing the human toll or the effects of radioactivity. And after all, the only eyewitnesses were Japanese survivors, and their reports in the press were dismissed as propaganda. Japanese newsreels showing the human toll were confiscated; US Army films of the ruined cities were classified secret. The radiation issue did not emerge until the atomic bomb tests at Bikini Atoll in the summer of 1946 stirred press speculation about the subject, on which the government was not forthcoming.

These tests (officially known as Operation Crossroads) have been largely forgotten, except for their association with an abbreviated woman's swimsuit, but at the time they provoked controversy and also revealed the public's conflicting attitudes toward the bomb. First, polls showed that an overwhelming majority of the public believed that the United States should keep the atomic bomb "secret" (a lower percentage of the college-educated—who presumably understood that nuclear physics knew no borders—shared this opinion). Nearly two-thirds said that the representatives of other nations should not be allowed to witness the Bikini Atoll tests or be given scientific reports on their results, lest they discover the "secret." Although 70 percent favored a UN ban on production of atomic bombs, they were willing to let the United States destroy its atomic arsenal only if a way was found to keep *all* nations from manufacturing such bombs. As a Michigan University public opinion analyst concluded, "Those who want the secret kept are more likely to feel the existence of the bomb may tend to avert war. Those who favor turning it over to the UN were more likely to feel that it has made peace harder to keep." This belief in secrecy stemmed from the conviction that America must rearm—in essence, go it alone rather than support international control or collective security.

In the aftermath, pollsters asked people if they thought that the existence of the A-bomb made it easier to keep the peace and if it made them worry about the weapon's destructiveness. A majority answered yes to both. This state of uncertainty and ambivalence was caused largely by the curtain of government secrecy around the bomb combined with lack of information on its actual effects, as demonstrated in Hiroshima and Nagasaki. The enthusiastic response to John Hersey's article "Hiroshima," a

low-key, factual account of the lives of six ordinary Japanese on the day
the bomb dropped, showed that many Americans were hungry for information on the bomb's actual impact. The article, which took up an entire
issue of *The New Yorker* in August 1946, drew hundreds of letters. When
it was later published as a book it sold some 230,000 copies, plus another
2 million in paperback.

More graphic was the testimony of physicists like Philip Morrison, who
visited Hiroshima weeks after it was hit. Appearing before the Senate
Committee on Atomic Energy in December 1945, he described the bomb's
effects on human victims: "The blood does not coagulate, but oozes in
many spots through the unbroken skin, and internally seeps into the cavi-
ties of the body." Morrison's words were widely quoted at the time, and
he went on to become one of the most outspoken campaigners against the
bomb. He wrote a vivid scenario of the effects of atomic weapons dropped
on New York City, which appeared in *One World or None,* a collection of
essays issued in March 1946 by the Federation of American Scientists. The
collection was widely reviewed and sold more than 100,000 copies. Its
message was simple: read this book, learn the facts of death, discuss proposed solutions with friends, and put the pressure on your representatives
to take action. "Time is short. And survival is at stake."

Thus the urgent ticking-bomb language of the atomic era entered the
national dialogue. Antibomb advocates burst on the scene and presented
the situation as a countdown to unimaginable destruction, which Morrison and others would hypothetically describe in mass magazines like *Life*
and *Collier's*. Paul Boyer writes in his cultural history of the bomb that *One
World or None* "was the quintessential expression of the sense of desperate
urgency and febrile optimism that characterized the one strand of the early
reaction to the atomic bomb. 'If only the American people could be awak-
ened and informed,'" the scientists believed, "'surely they would rally behind enlightened internationalism.'"

The scientists were initially welcomed like latter-day wizards into
the halls of Congress and other public forums. The radio commentator
Raymond Gram Swing glowingly described the earnest young physicists:
"Their faces are open and clear, their eyes look steadily, and as witnesses

before the Senate and House committees, and in their newspaper conferences, they were quiet, modest, lucid, and compellingly convincing."

As Boyer writes, the scientists were riding a wave of public support during "the brief interlude when atomic scientists were looked to as gurus who would lead the world out of the valley of darkness and confusion." And brief it would be.

FEARS OF AN ATOMIC Armageddon were key in the rise of the world government movement. They were behind the formation in April 1947 of the United World Federalists (UWF), with Cord Meyer Jr. as its twenty-seven-year-old president. Meyer was something of a golden boy, born to a wealthy Long Island family; his father was a powerful Democratic politician. After graduating from Yale in 1942, he enlisted in the Marines and commanded a machine gun platoon. During the battle for Guam he lost an eye when a grenade blew up in his foxhole. Reported killed in action, he recovered only to learn after he came home that his twin brother, Quentin, to whom he was very close, had been killed in the battle for Okinawa. He emerged from the war determined to dedicate his life to working for peace. He later wrote in his autobiography, *Waves of Darkness,* "The only certain fruit of this insanity will be the rotting bodies upon which the sun will impartially shine tomorrow. Let us throw down these guns that we hate."

After the war Meyer was present at the creation of the progressive American Veterans Committee (AVC), which challenged the conservative Old Soldiers establishment. The young vets of the National Planning Committee who set up the AVC were all up-and-comers; reporters ritually identified them as "the leaders of tomorrow," with Meyer himself nominated by a New York civic group an "outstanding young man." Among them was Charles Bolte, the AVC's first president, who had volunteered early in the war. Meyer had met Bolte in San Francisco in 1945 at the conference founding the United Nations, where they served as aides to former Minnesota governor Harold Stassen, a liberal Republican who would challenge Thomas E. Dewey in the 1948 GOP primaries.

Meyer and Bolte quickly became disillusioned with the embryonic UN. They believed it would be paralyzed and unable to keep the peace because of the permanent powers' veto in the Security Council. Upon hearing about the atomic bombing of Hiroshima, Meyer decided that "peace was no longer merely desirable but absolutely necessary to the survival of a large proportion of the human race."

Given the UN's weakness, he thought what was needed was a supranational organization capable of overriding the sovereignty claims of individual nations, large or small—in other words, a world government. Meyer became active in the founding of UWF in 1947 and was chosen to be its first president. He was a somewhat glamorous figure with his black eye patch, good looks, bottomless energy. After the war he had married Mary Pinchot, daughter of the wealthy liberal lawyer Amos Pinchot and "one of the prettiest, most popular and most brilliant members of the class of '42" at Vassar, according to the novelist Merle Miller, who met Meyer through the AVC and UWF.

From whatever angle, some form of world government looked like an idea whose time had come. The logic seemed irrefutable: national sovereignty and the nation-state system itself were adjudged to be the prime cause of wars. World government became one of the planks in the Federation of Atomic Scientists' platform. FAS, the lively scientists' movement that published *One World or None* in 1946, had its initial stirrings on September 1, 1945, when several of the nuclear brotherhood from the Manhattan Project gathered for a lunch in Chicago to discuss their feelings of guilt over what they had wrought and fears that it might be catastrophically employed in a future war. The success of the project, the greatest collective scientific effort in history, encouraged them to believe that through a similar effort—a crash program for peace—the peoples of the world, racing against time, could cooperate in building a viable world state. At the start the FAS's focus was on alerting the public and their representatives to the earth-ending potential of nuclear warfare. The scientists' campaign was intended to frighten the American people into accepting the radical idea of international control of nuclear weapons. They spread the facts about the awful destructiveness of the bomb, in speeches, pamphlets, graphic magazine spreads, and even a Hollywood film.

MGM's portentously titled *The Beginning or the End* (1946), the first Hollywood feature film on the bomb, had a curious history. According to the journalist Greg Mitchell, the FAS approached MGM, which agreed to make a film that would dramatize the development of the bomb, with actors impersonating the actual people involved in the project, including President Truman. It would also give roles to a quartet of popular young actors including Robert Walker and Tom Drake.

As was common during World War II, the military, represented by Gen. Leslie Groves, director of the Manhattan Project, was given script approval. Truman, who was all for the idea and even provided the title for the movie, wanted control over how he was portrayed, insisting that the face of the actor playing him not be shown. And he demanded that the part describing how he made the decision to drop the bomb be changed to show how intensely he had agonized over his decision. The filmmakers readily agreed, regarding his involvement as a publicity bonanza; his endorsement would make the film "seem sort of official," Mitchell said.

General Groves's interventions were more insidious. Rather than simply advising on the history of the bomb's development, he demanded changes intended to rewrite that history. For example, he prevailed on the filmmakers to play down the danger of radioactive fallout, following the official line at the time. Even more egregious untruths included the claims that Hiroshima had been a major military base (the base was a small one, and more than 95 percent of the casualties were civilians, mostly women and children), and that the United States had dropped leaflets warning about the bomb for ten days prior to the date, which was false. "That's ten days' more warning than they gave us before Pearl Harbor," a character says in the smug way such characters in propaganda movies had.

NUCLEAR ANXIETIES were imaginatively reflected in the wave of science fiction films that crested in the early fifties. The first wave of these films presented terrestrials rocketing in to lecture America on the need for world government. Thus the heavenly visitor Klaatu (Michael Rennie) in *The Day the Earth Stood Still* (1951) tells earthlings that their atomic weapons endanger the universe, so they are now under extraterrestrial surveillance: "We, of the other planets . . . have an organization for the mutual protection of all planets and for the complete elimination of aggression. . . . For our policemen, we created a race of robots. Their function is to patrol the planets in spaceships like this one and preserve the peace. . . . The result is, we live in peace, without arms or armies, secure in the knowledge that we are free from aggression and war."

Klaatu is shot by waiting soldiers when he disembarks; the military shoots first, asks alien invaders questions later. After Klaatu is brought back from death by extraterrestrial remedies, he meets with a scientist played by an actor who has a hairstyle like Einstein's and who endorses Klaatu's message. But world leaders balk, and Klaatu warns the UN that his robot, Gort, who is invincible to earthlings' weapons, will destroy them if they do not comply with his recommendations. Thus *The Day the Earth Stood Still* was a world government parable with a bit of "If Christ came back in our time . . ." tossed in.

The "visitor from outer space" genre would become popular in the fifties, but minus any pro-peace message—probably an effect of the HUAC invasion. Like the anti-Communist films rouge, the later science fiction films seethed with paranoia and terror. In films like *The Thing* (1951) and *Them!* (1954), visitors from outer space are hostile and sinister. They bring no messages of peace but covertly infiltrate America, even entering the bodies of good citizens and transforming them into evil beings—for example, *Red Planet Mars* (1952), *Invaders from Mars* (1953), *Invasion of the Body Snatchers* (1956).

The films also unveiled a new strain of anti-intellectualism. As Nora Sayre points out in her book on the films of the cold war, *Running Time,* the anti-intellectuals had taken over: now scientists were shown as "obstructionists or troublesome idealists, hence they are the adversaries of the military." In *Them!* the annoying eggheads want to collect samples and study the atomically mutated giant ants, thus keeping the military from exterminating them.

The film *Walk a Crooked Mile* (1948) is said by cinema historian J. Hoberman to have been inspired by the case of Edward U. Condon, a distinguished scientist on the Manhattan Project who resigned in protest of the heavy-handed security politics of General Groves. Condon later fell afoul of HUAC; one of its reports, calling him the "weakest link" in nuclear security, haunted him for years. The movie obviously took the HUAC point of view, wildly exaggerating inflated rumors and false charges that Condon had been a spy.

Possibly the wave of extraterrestrial films had its origin, at least in part, in the real-life flying saucer mass delusion of the late forties. This started in 1947, when an amateur pilot flying over the Cascade Range reported seeing "saucer-like" airships, which gleamed brightly. This report went out on the AP wires. There followed some 850 reports of mysterious flying machines. The next step would surely be that at least one of the numerous strange craft that were swarming the earthly skies would launch an attack as the first step of an alien invasion. However, the only reported case of a saucer landing was in July near Roswell, New Mexico, where the Strategic Air Command's Eighth Air Force was based. A rancher reported finding debris from a "flying disc"—metal struts with cabalistic messages on them.

This discovery engendered a cottage industry of flying saucer stories, books, reports, lectures, and films. Thus did a legend grow up that the Air Force had found the corpses of actual spacemen amid the debris, and had spirited off the remains and concealed their existence. A later Air Force investigation, however, established that the debris actually came from an Air Force experimental balloon that had crashed. According to the September 1994 Air Force report the balloon was one of several launched from Almagordo, under a top-secret project known as Project Mogul. The purpose of the program was to test high-altitude atmospheric measuring devices, which would be used to detect Soviet nuclear tests. At the time, this was the best technology available for the purpose. The Air Force itself helped stoke rumors by declaring that the Roswell saucer had been a weather balloon.

The media missed the real story behind the saucer myth. *US News & World Report* reported that the saucers were actually experimental aircraft being tested by the Air Force. The *Miami Daily News* published photos of "a glowing, concave object," which the paper identified as "the saucer that flies." As late as 1952 *Life* ran a pictorial story showing that strange craft were regularly penetrating into earth's atmosphere.

The flying saucer hysteria of the late forties was a metaphor for anti-Communist paranoia that would be known as McCarthyism. Inflated rumors, half-truths, and officials' lies transformed Communism into a mysterious alien force that threatened to take over the country. Government secrecy, which contributed to the spread of false allegations against government workers, also contributed to the saucer panic. The prime example of this effect was the Air Force's cover story that the Project Mogul balloon was a weather balloon. Classified or not, the project could still have been more forthrightly discussed by the Air Force. But secrecy was another mania of the times.

Years later, as mentioned in the Prologue, I read a news story about a CIA operation that had released a fleet of balloons over China. They were officially described as weather balloons but had actually been rigged to take aerial photographs of military bases—silent, windblown counterparts of the U2 spy planes that overflew the Soviet Union in the fifties, one of which the Soviets shot down, provoking the cancellation of a summit meeting between Nikita Khrushchev and Dwight D. Eisenhower.

THE SCI-FI FILMS of the early fifties voiced the warning cries of the anti-Communists, who had taken over Washington. As Kevin McCarthy, playing a lone escapee from the aliens' takeover of a small town in *Invasion of the Body Snatchers,* cries, "You fools, you're in danger! . . . They're after us! You're next! You're next!"

These films also reflected an anti-intellectualism and distrust of scientists by politicians and the military. This was exemplified in the treatment of Robert Oppenheimer, the leading scientist in the Manhattan Project, who with Atomic Energy Commission (AEC) head David Lilienthal drew up a plan for international control of nuclear energy under the UN. It won the backing of John McCloy, Dean Acheson, and other establishment types, but when the report reached Secretary of State James Byrnes's desk he was shocked by the sweeping nature of the proposals. Byrnes had already warned the Cabinet, according to James Forrestal, that "undue emphasis was being given to the views of the scientists on this subject." While it was all very well for scientists to say as they did that science has no boundaries, "that certainly did not apply to either Mr. Molotov or Mr. Stalin," who he very much doubted would allow international inspectors to snoop about their nuclear factories.

Byrnes's comment about scientists reveals he assumed (like many of his countrymen) that scientists favored international control of atomic energy because of some starry-eyed idea that "science has no boundaries." Of course, the point the scientists were trying to make was that *physics* has no boundaries. The physical principles of the atomic bomb were well known; the manufacturing techniques less so. Soviet atomic scientists were engaged in their own crash program to build one (a program accelerated by Stalin after Truman told him about America's new weapon at the Potsdam Conference in 1945). Oppenheimer believed that Soviet scientists were capable of building a bomb and inevitably would succeed. While sharing US know-how with them might hasten this outcome, it could also ease distrust between the two nations and open the way for negotiations about international control. But the cold war minds of Byrnes and Forrestal were closed to such an idea.

Oppenheimer was driven in part by a sense of responsibility—or guilt, if you will. As the former scientific head of the Manhattan Project, he believed like the FAS that the bomb posed a future danger to the world. On October 18, 1945, after briefing a congressional committee, Oppenheimer and Commerce Secretary Wallace walked back to the latter's office. Wallace later wrote in his diary, "I never saw a man in such an extremely nervous state as Oppenheimer. He seemed to feel the destruction of the entire human race was imminent." Oppenheimer said that his ideas about placing the bomb under international control were opposed by Byrnes, who "felt that we could use the bomb as a pistol to get what we wanted in international diplomacy." Oppenheimer said "his scientists back in New Mexico were completely disheartened" because of their worries that the bomb would be used in a future war, killing millions of people. Oppenheimer's passion struck a chord with Wallace. As he later wrote in his diary, "The guilt consciousness of the atomic bomb scientists is one of the most astounding things I have ever seen."

Oppenheimer continued to fight for his plan, which he summarized in an article in *The New York Times Magazine:* "It proposes that in the field of atomic energy there be set up a world government. That in this field there be a renunciation of sovereignty." Privately, Oppenheimer saw that the Soviets would never buy the Baruch Plan (so called because Bernard Baruch introduced it to the UN) because the plan left the United States free to develop nuclear arms while blocking other nations from doing so. In a breathless monologue while furiously pacing the floor, he prophesied to Lilienthal the future cold war dynamic of mutual distrust: "Russia will exercise her veto and decline to go along. This will be construed by us as a demonstration of Russia's warlike intentions. And this will fit perfectly into the plans of that growing number who want to put the country on a war footing, first psychologically, then actually. The Army directing the country's research; Red-baiting; treating all labor organizations, CIO first, as communist and therefore traitorous, etc."

By 1947, the scientists in the FAS movement were feeling a growing pushback from political and military leaders to their ideas on world government. They were criticized or hauled before committees and boards, their loyalty and present or past leftist associations impugned. In June, HUAC chair J. Parnell Thomas accused all five civilian AEC commissioners of being Communists. Thomas's claim actually originated with Pentagon officials opposed to civilian control of the atom. Later, numerous scientists in and out of government became objects of disloyalty charges. Investigations within the AEC resulted in several firings, and the inquisition spread until it reached top scientists like Edward U. Condon, Linus Pauling, and Oppenheimer, whose opposition to development of the hydrogen bomb was perversely linked to his associations with left-wing groups in the thirties, would result in his losing his security clearance.

The Oppenheimer prosecution attained the dimensions of tragedy; it encapsulated the dilemmas of all scientists who felt a conflict between serving their country and obeying their conscience. Most of them had overcome any feeling of guilt with the rationalization that developing the bomb was necessary because the Germans were attempting to develop one and then because it was a weapon powerful enough to quash fanatical Japanese resistance *and* because only a real-time demonstration of the bomb's destructive force would convince people that it must be placed under international control.

ONE ARTIST PERCEIVED (somewhat hazily) the tragedy of Oppenheimer. That was the Communist playwright Bertolt Brecht, exiled in Hollywood. Before the war, he had written a play about Galileo, who was tried for heresy because of his scientific finding that the earth revolved around the sun and forced to recant what he believed to be the truth. After hearing about Hiroshima and Oppenheimer's doubts, Brecht rewrote his play to make a comment on the bomb. The revised version, which starred Charles Laughton (who worked with Brecht on the script), had a short run at a Hollywood theater. In the earlier version, Brecht had portrayed Galileo as a moral sellout, who recants his theory of the solar system before the Inquisition rather than lose his comfortable life. In the new version, Brecht has Galileo say, "I take it that the intent of science is to ease human existence. If you give way to coercion, science can be crippled and your new machines may simply suggest new drudgeries. Should you, then, in time, discover all there is to be discovered, your progress must become a progress away from the bulk of humanity." Brecht's thinking is not entirely clear (and what he thought about the Soviet bomb—he was living in East Germany when the revised Galileo was produced—is omitted), but he is apparently saying the science must be free to serve humanity rather than commanded to serve the church or the state or industry.

In Oppenheimer's case, as a physicist he knew well the power of the atomic bomb and that the H-bomb's only purpose—however "sweet" the science that solved the problems of making it—would be to inflict a holocaust rather than to "ease human existence." Still, feeling guilt for his work on the Manhattan Project, he expressed his opposition—at a high cost, it turned out: he was virtually declared a traitor to his country.

Just as the loyalty board silenced Oppenheimer and HUAC sent Brecht into East German exile, so did the AEC's red hunt drive many scientists away from the FAS and into political silence. FAS membership plunged from 3,000 in 1946 to fewer than 1,500 in 1950.

Oppenheimer's chief critic, Edward Teller, once an advocate of international control, played a major role in building the H-bomb. Now he lectured scientists that they had no business in the political arena and should confine themselves to understanding natural laws and doing the will of their government, embroiled in a nuclear arms race with the Soviet enemy. Many FAS activists heeded Teller's admonition that building better bombs was their scientific duty and rejoined the team working on the Superbomb.

THE RED SCARE was not the only cause of the silencing of dissent to the cold war consensus and the atomic arms race. Veterans who'd vowed to work for "no more war" became preoccupied with working for a living and raising a family. Young men and women of the Crisis Generation who had been politically active in antiwar causes during the thirties were "exhausted by their wartime experience," Lawrence Wittner writes. He quotes an ex-soldier saying that the war had served "to enervate socially-conscious inquiry." A member of the Fellowship of Reconciliation agreed that young people's engagement with "labor problems, economics, race tensions, and . . . war seems to be far below that of previous generations." Those pre-war idealists still clinging to the Communist Party oscillated from pro-war to pro-peace as the interests of the Soviet Union dictated.

As for Hollywood progressives, they were isolated. In the wake of HUAC's 1947 inquisition, pro-bomb sentiment grew in the executive

suites, with the result that movies became a propaganda organ of the national security state and called for developing atomic weapons to keep
America strong. After *The Beginning or the End,* only a couple of films dealing with the bomb appeared, and these supported the government's position of keeping it exclusively for American use.

The director Fritz Lang was caught in the shifting political winds not
long after the war's end. He had made a film called *Cloak and Dagger* (1946),
in which Gary Cooper plays an OSS man who goes on a secret mission to
rescue an Italian nuclear physicist. The ending shows the OSS man saving
the scientist with the help of the local anti-Nazi partisans. Waving goodbye
to his Italian girlfriend, he boards an Air Force plane that will take him
back to America.

In the original ending, however, Cooper's character is sent on a further
mission to deactivate a Nazi atomic bomb factory in a cave where Germans used slave workers. But, the Americans learn, they are too late: the
machines have been dismantled and taken away to some Nazi lair in Argentina or wherever; the corpses of sixty thousand slave workers lie buried
inside. After inspecting this site, Cooper walks outside and is met at the
cave's entrance by an American GI, who comments, "This is Year One of
the Atomic Age." Cooper then speaks the film's message: "God have
mercy on us if we ever thought we could really keep science a secret—or
even wanted to! God have mercy on us if we think we can wage other
wars without destroying ourselves, and God have mercy on us if we
haven't the sense to keep the world at peace."

When the picture was shown, however, this rather preachy dialogue
had been cut. Lang was stunned: conveying this message had been his
main reason for making the movie, he told Peter Bogdanovich. Only later
did he learn that the scene had been excised with the entire last reel by
Warner Bros. executives. He was never told why, he said, but the Cooper
character's denunciation of keeping the bomb secret would not have sat
well in high government circles.

Another film illustrates, in a mild way, how the official Pentagon line
linking peace to "preparedness" was becoming the dominant ideology. *The
Boy with Green Hair,* one of the more unconventional films of 1948, was a

gentle fantasy by the liberal producer Dore Schary, who was attempting, after the box-office success of *Crossfire,* to produce more socially conscious films at RKO; screenwriter Ben Barzman, who would be blacklisted; and director Joseph Losey, who would soon go into exile rather than appear before HUAC.

The Boy with Green Hair starred Robert Ryan as a psychologist who has been summoned to the police station to interview a runaway boy named Peter (Dean Stockwell), who is unaccountably bald. The story develops in flashbacks: Peter is an American war orphan; his parents were killed in England, where they worked with displaced European children. He was adopted by kindly Gramps, an ex-vaudeville hoofer (Pat O'Brien). One morning Peter's hair turns green, triggering all manner of hostility in his conformist small town. The other children tease him, and he runs away to hide in a forest. There, in a fantasy scene, he meets a crew of young people who have stepped out of the war orphan posters on display at his school. They urge him to tell everyone that there must never be another war. Inspired by this vision, he does so with an evangelical passion; but the social pressure to abandon his peace message becomes too strong for him, and he agrees to shave off his green hair.

The eccentric millionaire Howard Hughes, who had just bought RKO, hit the ceiling when he saw the script. As head of Hughes Aircraft, he was interested in more government spending for warplanes. According to Losey biographer David Caute, Hughes asked Stockwell to add to his line about war being unhealthy for children a codicil saying essentially, That's why we need the biggest, strongest military in the world. Unable to get any cooperation or to otherwise "fix" the picture, Hughes considered canceling it, but a conservative executive talked him out of that. Instead the script was amended so that the dialogue between two women about the need to talk about world peace conveyed the idea that America must first be militarily strong.

SOVIET DOMINATION of Eastern Europe affected peace advocates on the left as well—although differently from the anti-Communists in government.

The Socialist Party's quadrennial presidential candidate Norman Thomas, already hostile to American Communists and their doctrines, became a cold warrior minus the "war" part, since he continued to advocate nuclear and world disarmament (while ruling out unilateral disarmament by the United States). He opposed the Truman Doctrine, for example, predicting that "American intervention in Turkey [will] become more and more imperialistic, more and more tied to the politics of petroleum"; and although he opposed Henry Wallace's Progressive Party as another "Communist front," he warned against the political exploitation of "anti-Communist hysteria" by the right. Dwight Macdonald, the former anarchist and pacifist, declared that the best way to avoid war was for the West to "keep up its military strength and to be prepared to counter force, with force." The tragic theologian Reinhold Niebuhr declared in 1948 that Americans must give up naïve dreams of getting along with the Soviets and militarily prepare to confront them, even at the risk of war. He pointed out that Churchill's 1946 "iron curtain" speech had proved prophetic, and it was time to abandon "the sentimental hopes of yesterday." The anti-Communist liberals in the recently formed Americans for Democratic Action joined the cold war consensus and condemned the Soviet spheres of influence in Eastern Europe.

Around this time, a studio that was planning a film based on Henry Wadsworth Longfellow's poem "Hiawatha" canceled the project. The poem conveyed a subversive message: bringing peace among the Indian tribes.

IN 1955 APPEARED *Kiss Me Deadly*. This belated, idiosyncratic noir (considered by French critics Borde and Chaumeton to be one of the greatest) signaled the terminal decadence of a style that had reached its prime between 1945 and 1950. It was directed by Robert Aldrich and written by A.I. Bezzerides (who scripted one of the best of the "proletarian" noirs, *Thieves' Highway,* about racketeers taking over California's agricultural business). Ostensibly, it was based on the best-selling paperback of the same title by Mickey Spillane, whose red-bashing private eye Mike Hammer marked a regression from Raymond Chandler's tarnished knight Marlowe. Hammer was a detective without conscience or scruples, a self-appointed vigilante killer of Communists. Marlowe emerged in the Depression and World War II, Spillane in the postwar red scare.

Spillane's paperback novels enjoyed a vogue among college boys looking for a sexy read. (Actually, his sex scenes were mostly sadism; they usually involved Hammer shooting a sexy woman trying to seduce him after she turns out to be a Communist agent.) In the Aldrich and Bezzerides version, Mike (Ralph Meeker) is depicted as a sleazy private eye who, with his good-looking secretary, Velda, entraps straying spouses in divorce cases. He is a self-indulgent narcissist who drives a sports car, lives in a cool pad, and seems to be the proto-*Playboy* man.

In Spillane's novel, the McGuffin is a briefcase full of drugs; in the film it's an attaché case filled with radioactive uranium, which powerful criminal elements want to get hold of and sell at immense profit. After much hugger-mugger, beautiful Gabriella, the last femme fatale standing, shoots the criminal mastermind Dr. Suberin and grabs the valise. Saying "Kiss me" to Mike, she plugs him and, with a curiosity as deadly as Pandora's, snaps opens the case, revealing eerily glowing bars of uranium. Contrary to the laws of nuclear physics, a chain reaction seems to have been touched off, and Gabriella goes up in flames. Mike, who is only wounded, finds Velda, who had been imprisoned by the crooks, and they flee. In the final scene, we see them wading into the surf as the beach house blows up in a big mushroom cloud.

There is a certain fitness to this ultimate decadence of a form that in some hands had functioned as a medium of social criticism. After the war, after the postwar disillusionment, after HUAC, after the pro-bomb trend, the only thing left was a passive nihilism that fatalistically acquiesced in the bomb. This is the way the film noir world ends: a mushroom cloud over a Malibu beach house. The fascist thugs like Mike Hammer (who had a real-life counterpart in Joe McCarthy) have arrived to preside over Armageddon.

CORD MEYER JR. HAD once vowed that if world government weren't achieved by 1951, he would take his wife, Mary Pinchot, and two sons to Africa to live with the Pygmies. In 1951, Meyer jumped the United World Federalism's foundering ship. "After two years of itinerant speaking and organizing," he wrote in his memoir, *Facing Reality,* "I had ceased to enjoy my role as Cassandra. . . . I came to dislike the sound of my own voice as I promised a federalist salvation in which I no longer had real confidence."

But he did not move to Africa. He joined the new Central Intelligence Agency at the direct invitation of fellow Yale grad Allen Dulles, who would become its director in 1953. In the Agency he worked his way up to assistant deputy director of plans, the division in charge of covert operations. In 1967, the left-wing *Ramparts* magazine revealed that Meyer had been in charge of a program that provided covert funding for the National Students Association and the English literary magazine *Encounter,* financing anti-Communist propaganda through them. The Agency also paid the way of anti-Communist American students to represent our side at a Soviet-sponsored youth congress in Prague.[*]

Meyer's *Times Magazine* profiler, Merle Miller, who shared his liberal politics, had written a well-received novel critical of his generation, *That Winter* (1948). Focusing on three young vets, Miller evokes his generation's uncertainty, their compromises and sellouts and failure to hold on to their ideals in the postwar corporate world. As a character says, the story was about "the millions of us who had been away for a while and had returned. Without any bands, without any committees of welcome, without banners. We hadn't wanted those. We'd tried to think we hadn't wanted anything, yet we had, and the difficulty was that we didn't know what we

---

[*] As a member of the postwar generation who had grown up in a small-town closet-liberal, civic-minded doctor's household, I was an anti-Communist, though I was also an anti-McCarthyite—such were the fluid labels of the time. And I was quite willing to attend the Communist-sponsored world youth festival in Prague (though unaware that the CIA would be paying my way) after the possibility was suggested during a chance shared cab ride with a beautiful and intelligent young woman named Gloria Steinem. I never heard from her again. Later I learned she headed a CIA front called, incongruously, the Independent Service for Information. I have often thought that this chance Manhattan encounter—anti-Communist boy and cute girl meet—could have sparked a movie of the times. But the times changed.

wanted, and neither did anybody else. That was the difficulty." Not knowing what they wanted from the postwar world, they had to take what they got.

On August 31, 1953, Dulles telephoned Meyer to inform him that the CIA had suspended his security clearance. The Agency had received an FBI report containing charges that he was disloyal. Among his suspicious activities was associating with the journalist Theodore White and the poet Richard Wilbur, who were allegedly involved in Communist front groups. (White, a *Time* man, had defected and written critically of Henry Luce's hero Chiang Kai-shek in his best seller *Thunder Out of China,* offending the China lobby.) It was suspected that J. Edgar Hoover had supplied the dirt in the course of his covert campaign to undermine the CIA, which he hated because it had assumed foreign intelligence functions that he claimed for the FBI. Finally, Meyer's ties with liberals in the UWF and AVC had made him suspect to the Bureau and other anti-Communists.

Unaware of the source of the derogatory information, Meyer hired a lawyer to draw up a brief refuting the allegations. He said that during this dark time of his life he reread Kafka's novel *The Trial.* Perhaps he was hooked by the first line: "Someone must have been telling lies about Joseph K., for without having done anything wrong he was arrested one fine morning."

On Thanksgiving Day 1953, Dulles told Miller that his security clearance had been restored.

POSTSCRIPT. By then, Cord and Mary Pinchot Meyer had drifted apart, following the death of their son in a murky auto accident; they later divorced. In 1964, she was found shot dead on the towpath of the Chesapeake and Ohio Canal in Washington. The killer was never found. The CIA's counterintelligence chief, James Jesus Angleton, a functioning paranoid whose wife was a college friend of Mary's, was discovered searching her house for her diary by Ben Bradlee (later editor of the *Washington Post*) and his wife, who was Mary's sister. The Bradlees kept the diary; it described her love affair with President John F. Kennedy, whose wife, Jacqueline, used to walk with Mary along the canal. A Washington conspiracy without a mastermind, apparently.

According to celebrity biographer C. David Heymann, Meyer ended his days in a nursing home, growing increasingly infirm (he died of lymphoma). Once, someone asked him who he believed had murdered his wife. "The same sons of bitches that killed John F. Kennedy," he replied, screwing in his glass eye. Conspiracies within conspiracies . . .

Voices

The first casualty of the cold war was the debate on foreign policy. . . . It was simply assumed that the Soviet Union is the enemy. Let's go from there, why debate it?

—J.K. Galbraith

INTERVIEWER: What was it about the Progressive Party ticket that appealed to you? Can you talk a little bit about what was progressive about the party?

PETE SEEGER: Well, it was really carrying on Franklin Roosevelt's idea: "Let's have peace with the Russians and let's work with unions and little by little working people will get a better break from the bosses.

—*Henry Wallace*, documentary film

Tessie Hutchinson was in the center of a cleared space by now, and she held her hands out desperately as the villagers moved in on her. "It isn't fair," she said. A stone hit her on the side of the head. Old Man Warner was saying, "Come on, come on, everyone." Steve Adams was in the front of the crowd of villagers, with Mrs. Graves beside him. "It isn't fair, it isn't right," Mrs. Hutchinson screamed, and then they were upon her.

—Shirley Jackson, "The Lottery" (1948)

9

THE LONELY PASSION OF HENRY WALLACE

ON THE EVE OF VE DAY, Secretary of Commerce Henry A. Wallace wrote in his diary, "More and more it begins to look like the psychology is favorable toward our getting into war with Russia." In a later entry he wrote, "The people behind this kind of talk are the rankest kind of un-Americans," who are actually "anxious to see the United States and Russia come to blows." Even before the war was over, Wallace often found himself at Washington dinner parties arguing with officials and pundits who regarded it as almost preordained that capitalist America must clash with the USSR.

Wallace more or less followed FDR in believing that the Soviets could be dealt with peaceably and that, in effect, the wartime Big Three would continue into the postwar world as allies, and would become joint guarantors of the peace. That view was being repudiated within the new administration while being loudly challenged outside it by the Republicans.

As the Roosevelt era receded, Wallace was occupying an increasingly isolated liberal promontory in the administration, increasingly dominated by anti-Soviet hardliners. From his post at the Commerce Department, he watched with mounting uneasiness the Truman administration's regression (as he saw it) from alliance with to hostility toward the Soviets. At first, he communicated his objections directly to the president either in confidential memorandums or at personal meetings. When Truman

Shirley Jackson's terrifying story "The Lottery," in which villagers engage in a ritual of stoning a victim chosen by lot, can be read as a parable of political and racial intolerance. *Farrar, Straus and Giroux*

proposed universal military training, Wallace criticized the idea as a "prelude to World War III." He supported a loan to the Soviet Union, as well as one to Britain, only to meet opposition from the State Department, which opposed the latter because it believed it would lead to the former.

In July 1946, Wallace sent Truman a plea to try to walk in the Russians' shoes: "How do American actions since V-J Day appear to other nations? I mean by actions the concrete things like $13 billion [budgeted for] the War and Navy Departments, the Bikini tests of the atomic bomb and continued productions of bombs . . . the production of B-29s and planned production of B-36s, and the effort to secure air bases spread over half the globe from which the other half of the globe can be bombed." Such steps made it seem as though the United States was preparing "to win the war which we regard as inevitable or . . . trying to build up a predominance of force to intimidate the rest of mankind." How would we like it if the Russians stationed long-range bombers within range of our shores?

Wallace's warnings had little tangible effect on policy, though Truman remained friendly. But under the surface bonhomie, he probably resented Wallace's presumption in advising him, as though *he*, Wallace, should be the president. After all, Truman had edged him out of the job. Still, he needed liberals' votes and was not ready to throw Wallace over the side. So he tried to keep him onboard by expressing agreement with anything Wallace said.

Moreover, Wallace warmly supported Truman's economizing and emphasis on balancing the budget by cutting defense spending while continuing New Deal programs. He opposed Soviet expansionism but advocated economic aid rather than demonstrations of military power. All of these points he conveyed privately to Truman. When he made any public speech touching on any of these issues, he always cleared the text in advance with the president.

Nevertheless, Wallace's increasingly diverging views and his disapproval of Truman's conservative appointees to the administration, such as John Snyder, impelled him to make the speech that gave Truman the pretext he needed to break with him. In September 1946 Wallace was invited to speak at an electoral rally at Madison Square Garden in New York sponsored by the leftish Independent Citizens Committee of the Arts, Sciences and Professions (ICCASP) and the National Citizens Political Action Committee (NCPAC). A co-speaker would be another New Deal liberal, Senator Claude Pepper of Florida.

Generally, Wallace said little that was different from his previous statements on US-Russian relations. He warned that the existence of the atomic bomb, guided missiles, and airplanes that "will travel as fast as sound" meant that "another war would hurt the United States many times as much as the last war. . . . He who trusts in the atom bomb will sooner or later perish by the atom bomb—or something worse." He called on Russia to cooperate with the United Nations "in a spirit of like-minded and flexible give-and-take." He emphasized the importance of choosing a policy of peace rather than confrontation with the Soviets. Peace would be the big issue in the 1948 presidential race, he said. "How we meet this issue will determine whether we live not in 'one world' or 'two worlds'—but whether we live at all."

But Wallace also said things in his speech that seemed to clash with administration policy. For example, he criticized the Republicans for favoring a military alliance with Britain, as Churchill had called for in his "iron curtain" speech earlier that year. He went on to say that Americans should "look abroad through our own American eyes and not through the eyes of either the British Foreign Office, or a pro-British or anti-Russian press." After saying that he was neither anti-British nor pro-Russian, he fatally added, "And just two days ago, when President Truman read these words, he said that they represented the policy of his administration." This statement could imply that the preceding sentence or sentences or much of the speech had Truman's approval. And so it seemed, since Truman had read an advance copy and later—before all hell broke loose—told the press he approved it. But when State and Defense Department officials perused an advance text of the speech, they objected that Wallace was giving his own foreign policy a phony presidential seal of approval and tried to have the remarks excised just before Wallace began to speak.

In the aftermath of the Madison Square Garden address, Truman—embarrassed that he had told the press he approved the speech and under mounting pressure from Byrnes (who threatened to resign, since the United States apparently had two foreign policies: his and Wallace's) and Forrestal, a visceral anti-Wallaceite—decided he needed to fire Wallace to show he was still in charge of foreign relations. Hearing of this, Wallace promptly tendered his resignation, vowing to continue to work for peace.

The president's clumsy handling of the speech made him look bad, and he vented his anger in a diary entry that reveals his true attitude toward Wallace:

> [Wallace] is a pacifist one hundred percent. He wants to disband our armed forces, give Russia our atomic secrets and trust a bunch of adventurers in the Kremlin Politboro [*sic*]. I do not understand a "dreamer" like that. . . . The Reds, phonies and the "parlor pinks" seem to be banded together and are becoming a national danger.
>
> I am afraid they are a sabotage front for Uncle Joe Stalin. They can see no wrong in Russia's four-and-a-half million armed force, in Russia's loot of Poland, Austria, Hungary, Rumania, Manchuria.

Probably some of the same language was in a note Truman sent Wallace the night before he fired him. Wallace described it as "not abusive, but . . . on a low level." He said he called the president and suggested he destroy the note lest the press get hold of it. Truman agreed and dispatched a messenger to pick it up.

The Wallace dispute brought out Truman's provincial, nationalistic side. As an old soldier, World War I veteran, and patriot, he held in contempt people who preached peace and disarmament; he believed they had been guilty of weakening America's military after World War I. In September 1945 he penned in his diary a flashback to 1918, in which he distinguished soldiers like himself from the "home people," who "forgot the war" and "began to talk of disarmament. They did disarm themselves, to the point of helplessness. They became fat and rich, special privilege ran the country—ran it to a fall." Then, Truman went on, in 1933 a "great leader" [FDR] appeared and rescued the country from chaos. When the European war came the people feared getting into it, but the great leader

woke them to the danger. And now there was a new enemy, a new
Hitler, a new Munich. To Truman the lesson was clear: he must follow
FDR's example.

Wallace turned the other cheek, rationalizing that the president had
been under pressure from two powerful foreign policy voices in the Senate, Arthur Vandenberg and Tom Connally, who backed Byrnes. The following year Truman would replace the independent-minded Byrnes (who
believed he, not Truman, should have been FDR's vice presidential choice)
with Gen. George C. Marshall, whom Truman idolized.

Once Wallace was gone, Truman was free to side publicly with the
anti-Soviet, pro-rearmament faction in his administration. In doing so he
foreclosed further debate within his party on how best to deal with the Soviets. Not long after he left the government, Wallace assumed the editor-
ship of *The New Republic* at the invitation of its publisher, young Michael
Straight, whose father, Willard, and mother, Dorothy, had provided Herbert Croly with the financial backing to start the liberal weekly in 1914.
Straight, however, began to worry that Wallace would use the magazine
as a podium for a 1948 presidential run against Truman.

It was no secret that Wallace was under intense pressure to challenge
Truman from disaffected old New Dealers like Beanie Baldwin—former
head of the Federal Security Administration, who had urged him to make
the fateful Madison Square Garden speech—and Henry Morgenthau Jr.,
FDR's Treasury secretary. Baldwin, a Virginian, had been an aide to the late
labor leader Sidney Hillman and was head of NCPAC, a left-wing spinoff
of Hillman's CIO PAC.

In December 1946, just three months after NCPAC and ICCASP co-
sponsored the Madison Square Garden rally, the two groups merged. The
issue of that union was the Progressive Citizens of America (PCA), a liberal
lobbying group headed by Baldwin. The PCA held another rally at Madison Square Garden in March 1947, drawing many progressive speakers,
including FDR's son Elliott, Harvard astronomy professor Harlow Shapley,
and Wallace. This time, Wallace openly attacked the Truman Doctrine
and called for stronger support for the UN. He branded Truman's loyalty
program a "disgrace" and a "$25 million witch hunt." "Communists," he

averred, "should be treated as human beings rather than people who should be put in jail." The current loyalty purges "turn Americans against each other" and stir up a climate of intolerance and suspicion. "Every American who reads the wrong books," Wallace said, "every American who thinks the wrong thoughts, every American who means liberty when he says liberty, every American . . . would be under suspicion, even those who supported [Wendell] Willkie or Roosevelt." Such sentiments, how-ever fair-minded in hindsight, were rash even in that pre-McCarthy time.

Wallace would soon find himself in the eye of the disloyalty storm. That summer, on the eve of his departure for a speaking tour in Britain and France, some seventy American intellectuals conceived it to be their duty to issue a statement warning British foreign minister Ernest Bevin that Wallace did not speak for American liberalism. Rather, they said, he represented "a small minority of Communists, fellow-travelers and what we call here totalitarian liberals." The State Department warned the pres-ident that Wallace planned to make a speech in London criticizing the "bellicosity" of US foreign policy. At a Cabinet meeting Forrestal de-manded that the State Department suspend Wallace's passport. Truman objected that such a move would draw "severe criticism," but Forrestal said the government should take the gaff rather than allow Wallace to "in-terfere" with US policy. In the event, Wallace's passport was not pulled (this sanction would be used against future dissidents), and he made his trip.

In Britain, Wallace immediately got in trouble by again bashing Tru-man's loyalty program. "I believe," he declared, "that this witch hunt is part of a larger drive to destroy the belief, which I share, that capitalism and communism can resolve their conflicts without resort to war." Britons on the left who were unhappy with their country's role as a B-29 launch-ing site and, as one commentator put it, "atomic bomb absorber" ap-plauded Wallace.

Former prime minister Winston Churchill called Wallace a "crypto-Communist," then insisted he had been misquoted. The liberal columnist Walter Lippmann charged that Wallace was badly out of touch with real-ity, and the right-wing HUAC chair J. Parnell Thomas demanded that Wal-lace be prosecuted under the Logan Act, which forbade private citizens from trying to influence foreign governments. Truman held his fire but privately compared Wallace to another vice president, the traitor Aaron Burr. Eleanor Roosevelt told Beanie Baldwin she did not doubt Wallace's integrity but wished "with all my heart" that he had not made this trip and had not said the things he was saying.

Wallace moved on to France to address a delegation of peace advocates, most of whom turned out to be Communists, to his surprise. This news stirred up more rancor back home. The Texas legislature passed a resolution branding him "an outcast from all political parties of American origin." A January 1948 Gallup poll reported that 44 percent of the respondents associated the following phrases with Wallace: "Un-American—traitor to the Country; more sympathetic toward other countries than to the U.S.; policies he advocates are not in the best interest of our country; doesn't look out for the nation." In criticizing US policies abroad, Wallace had crossed a red line. His European trip became a negative augury.

Wallace experienced the backlash physically during an April tour through the Midwest. A speech in Evansville, Indiana, drew a crowd of 2,500 local folk bent on stamping out his alien presence in their fair city. The citizens broke down the doors of the auditorium and stampeded into the lobby, where they spied Baldwin and other staffers and started slugging them before police jumped in. Wallace was allowed to speak, but after he finished the cops had to convoy him to a car, where he was trapped for an hour by the mob screaming curses at him. It was a portent of things to come.

Perhaps traumatized by Wallace's incursion, Evansville legislators passed an ordinance forbidding Communists and their sympathizers to live or work in the city—one of many such measures at the time. A university professor who appeared onstage with Wallace was fired. An Indianapolis hotel canceled a scheduled lunch for Wallace supporters, and the Indiana National Guard refused to allow his people to use its armory for a concert by Paul Robeson. Even in his home state there was a backlash: the University of Iowa barred him from speaking on campus. He moved the venue to a Des Moines public park, speaking to three thousand students and interrupted by a barrage of eggs, another portent of future receptions.

Scheduled appearances at Wichita, the University of Missouri, and Stephens College were canceled because he was considered a radical.

Nor could Wallace find much encouragement in the early presidential-choice polls. In a Gallup survey asking respondents to choose among possible candidates, including Truman, Taft, Dewey, MacArthur, and Eisenhower, Wallace drew only 6 percent support. Another poll had 8.5 percent regarding Wallace favorably, 32 percent negatively. Two-thirds of respondents to still another survey answered no when asked if they would support Wallace if he ran as a third-party candidate.

Wallace later asserted that he had not seriously thought about running as a third-party candidate until late fall 1947; before then, he had been hoping to change the Democratic Party from within. "If the Democratic Party could be made into a peace party, I was for it," he explained. "If it finally turned out that it was a war party, in case it were legally feasible and possible, I would do what I could for a third party."

He loathed the turmoil and stress of political campaigning but was willing to swallow his aversion for the cause of peace. "What I was interested in," he said, "was not the campaign but the objective: I thought it would help peace; it would help understanding with Russia, which I looked on as the gateway to peace." He had no illusions he would win. He told himself that jumping into the muddy presidential waters would be a waste of time unless he could garner 3 million votes. If he drew fewer, the peace cause "would be damaged rather than helped." At a crucial time, encouragement came from California attorney general Robert Kenny, who formed a Democrats for Wallace group to give party supporters a real choice, rather than one between "Tweedledum and Tweedle Dewey." Beanie Baldwin, Wallace's unofficial campaign manager, worked to line up delegates to the Democratic convention, in hopes of blocking Truman's bid for reelection.

Truman's speech on Greece and Turkey convinced Wallace that the Democratic Party had become a "war party." He embarked on another US speaking tour, drawing standing-room-only audiences. Thousands rallied to hear him in Chicago; in Los Angeles, twenty-eight thousand packed Gilmore Stadium, with many movie stars on the dais, among them the auburn-haired Katharine Hepburn, in a brilliant red dress, who made a fiery speech: "Silence the artist and you have silenced the most articulate voice the people have." A United Press correspondent reported that Wallace drew more than three thousand in Portland, a record number for the Oregon city. In Atlanta, under the auspices of the Southern Conference for Human Welfare, a left-wing civil rights group, he spoke at an African American Baptist church before some four thousand people.

The FBI had an open case file on the Southern Conference for Human Welfare. According to a bureau informant who was at the event in Atlanta, Wallace criticized universal military training and told the audience that "America has nothing to fear from Communism but does face a danger from those who would violate the Bill of Rights in seeking out Communists and those who brand every liberal movement as Communist-inspired." Before a racially mixed crowd numbering 1,600 in Louisville, he attacked the FBI "thought police," the FBI plant faithfully reported. Before thirteen thousand people in Convention Hall, Philadelphia, he castigated the Bureau for conducting a campaign of terror against liberal government employees that was "reminiscent of the early days of Adolph Hitler."

Meanwhile, President Truman vetoed the Taft-Hartley Act and introduced the European Recovery Program, somewhat undercutting Wallace's rationale for a third-party run, since he had been calling for both actions (and had proposed a program similar to ERP three months before Truman did). When the Soviet Union declined to accept Marshall Plan aid, Wallace called the decision a great mistake, but he began to hedge his support for the ERP, which he now claimed was a tool of Truman's anti-Communist foreign policy rather than a visionary, altruistic plan for rebuilding Europe. He advocated a reorientation of US policy—abandoning the Truman Doctrine and placing the Marshall Plan under the auspices of the United Nations, which, of course, Congress would never permit. The PCA joined Wallace in attacking the Marshall Plan, and the CPUSA denounced it as a capitalist-monopolist ploy. On the other hand, many unions endorsed it and warned their members not to support any third-party movement.

WALLACE WAS BORED with his job at *The New Republic,* thought his boss, publisher Michael Straight, who knowingly hired him as a "non-working editor," meaning he mainly dictated editorials, which others rewrote, and lent his name to the masthead. Meanwhile, the pressure on him to run for president was building. Baldwin told him that the threat of a third party was the "only way we can make the Democratic bosses listen to us." Obviously, Straight opposed such a candidacy, since it would mean Wallace would have to resign, putting a crimp in Straight's business plan for raising circulation by making the magazine a more prominent liberal voice.

Straight decided to protect his investment by placing an ocean between Wallace and his PCA wooers. The two departed for Palestine, where Jews were seeking to found a nation and regather their scattered believers. There they visited holy sites and kibbutzim. Wallace called for a Jordan Valley Authority as a way of helping Jews and Arabs share the region's precious water, and he lambasted the HUAC hearings then beginning in Hollywood, where he had a following of PCA members.

A strong supporter of the partition of Palestine, creating a state for the Jews and for the Arabs in the British-mandated territory, Wallace met with the pope on his trip home and urged him to "do something" about the Palestine problem. (Truman would recognize the newly formed state of Israel the following year.) Back in the States, he said his junket to the Holy Land had fired him up for the cause of peace: "As long as every Foreign Office in the World is dominated by the doctrine of Machiavelli instead of the doctrines of Christ, we shall have war and the perpetuation of many kinds of dictatorships and falsehoods as each of the nations prepares for war."

On December 29, 1947, Wallace made a speech in which he informed his fellow Americans that he would be a third-party candidate for the presidency in 1948:

> We want this to be a genuine two-party country and not a country operated by a fake-one-party system under the guise of a bi-partisan block. . . . We shall never be against anything simply because Russia is for it. Neither shall we ever be for anything simply because Russia is for it. We shall hold firmly to the American theme of peace, prosperity and freedom. . . .

> If it is traitorous to believe in peace, we are traitors. If it is Communistic
> to believe in prosperity for all, we are Communists. . . . If it is un-American
> to believe in freedom from monopolistic dictation, we are un-American.

"Brave words," Wallace reminisced later. Downright foolhardy words in the current climate—which made it all the braver of him to say them.

Up until then, the apparatus for a Wallace campaign consisted of the PCA, which Baldwin had been operating as an advocacy group for progressive causes. The PCA had twenty-five thousand members at the time; by the fall of 1948, with Wallace as its presidential candidate, it would number around one hundred thousand, about half of them dues-paying.

Baldwin recruited other experienced organizers, most prominently Lee Pressman, former counsel of the CIO, and John Abt, who had been Sidney Hillman's chief lawyer at the Amalgamated Garment Workers Union. Former New Deal Brain Truster Rexford Tugwell became involved on the policy-making side, as did Frederick Schuman, professor of government at Williams College and an authority on international law, who would be Wallace's voice in the platform committee's deliberations.

Baldwin knew that in addition to raising money and hiring workers, the PCA faced the major task of getting its name on state ballots. He wanted Abt aboard to handle that chore, researching the election laws of each state and planning drives to collect enough signatures to qualify for the ballot.

In January 1948, the National Wallace for President Committee was born. It attracted a galaxy of liberal-left stars, including former Minnesota governor Elmer Benson, who became chair; Rexford Tugwell; Robert Lovett, a retired University of Chicago professor; Albert J. Fitzgerald, president of the United Electrical and Machine Workers Union (UEW); O. John Rogge, former assistant US attorney general; W.E.B. Du Bois, the black scholar; Charles P. Howard of the Des Moines newspaper family; and, representing the arts, the illustrator Rockwell Kent, the sculptor Jo Davidson, and the actor Paul Robeson. In April the committee held its first meeting, in Philadelphia, at which some 385 delegates from forty-three states laid the groundwork for a national convention in Chicago that July to nominate Wallace as its candidate for president and Senator Glen H. Taylor of Idaho as his running mate. The new party was temporarily named the New Party.

In November 1947, the CPUSA had received a heads-up from Rogge that the Justice Department was planning to arrest its leaders. This happened the following year. Twelve top Communist Party functionaries would be rounded up and tried for violating the Smith Act by being members of a conspiracy dedicated to teaching the violent overthrow of the US government.

On orders from party head William Z. Foster, the Communists mounted a legal defense based not on the First Amendment but on philosophical premises, which led to interminable courtroom debates, casuistry, and hair-splitting. Foster had, under orders from Moscow, led a coup to oust wartime CP leader Earl Browder, architect of the Popular Front. Now leading the party, Foster had been busily piling up a string of bad decisions. Among others, he decided that mounting a defense to the Smith Act on free speech grounds was an exercise in bourgeois legalism. The convictions were upheld. In 1957, after some conservative justices retired, the Supreme Court narrowed the interpretation of the Smith Act so that it became nearly impossible to convict under it. This came too late for the eleven CP leaders sentenced to prison (four of whom had gone underground).

Foster and his underlings had learned that the Cominform—the Communist Information Bureau, a Soviet-sponsored organization that replaced the more secretive Communist International (Comintern) as ideological enforcer of the international Communist movement—favored using any means to defeat Truman, rather than opposing the more reactionary Republican candidate. Moscow regarded Truman as too staunch an anti-Communist, and it was ready to take its chances with the Republicans. Also, it believed a third party would split the liberal-labor elements in the Democratic Party. Still another reason for this ploy, according to leftist editor and historian Philip Jaffe, was self-preservation: "Not only could the Communists continue to function without harassment after a large Progressive Party vote, but they would also be provided with a kind of 'cover' or 'umbrella.'" The CP leaders figured that Wallace would garner up to

10 million votes, which would make the third party a force to be reckoned with in future elections—and they would inherit its clout.

Party secretary Eugene Dennis was dispatched to parley with the CP's new favorite son. Wallace gave him five minutes and a lecture: "All I said was there were two things I wanted him to understand—that the Communist party does not believe in God. I do believe in God; the Communist party does not believe in progressive capitalism. I do believe in progressive capitalism."

Under Foster, the CP adopted what the historian Maurice Isserman calls a "last-ditch stand mentality," or, as it was known in party circles, the "five minutes to midnight" strategy. This assumed that a capitalist crisis combining depression, domestic fascism, and war between the United States and the Soviet Union would soon occur, opening up the way for the party to take over the country. (This fantasy reflected the thinking in the Kremlin.)

With the ousting of Browder the Fosterites torpedoed any remaining hopes that his Popular Front policies might broaden the party's popular support. And by hijacking Wallace's campaign, Foster & Co. ignored the negative impact their presence would have.

First, the Communists alienated the progressive labor unions by demanding their members pledge their vote to Wallace. For most this meant defying their leaders, as both the CIO and the AFL leaderships had decided to back Truman. The party members were also ordered to oppose the Marshall Plan: Stalin rejected the aid offered Russia and Eastern European countries because of its potential to pry open his closed society. The unions and the anti-Communist liberals enthusiastically supported it. The net result was to give the CIO a pretext for purging its Communist-dominated unions.

The decision of most of organized labor to snub Wallace dealt him a fatal blow. Only a few of the leftist unions affiliated with the CIO, most prominently the huge United Electrical Workers, worked for Wallace. (The UE's leaders reaped the whirlwind for their defection when the CIO chartered a rival union to challenge them in plant representation battles. The UE's leadership would be decimated by the Taft-Hartley Act's non-Communist oath provision and other harassment.)

The CP did provide the bodies Wallace needed. Thousands of volunteers rang doorbells, passed out literature, and circulated petitions to add his name to the ballot in the various states. Baldwin saw himself, Straight said, "as the [Democratic Party boss] Jim Farley of the Progressive Party; he believed that like John L. Lewis, he could use the Communist organizers as shock troops and then send them to the kitchen to peel potatoes." Thanks to the volunteers' efforts, Wallace's name appeared on the presidential ballot in all but three states.

In the Wallace army was a young Communist named Arthur D. Kahn. Full of vim and enthusiasm, Kahn jumped onboard the National Wallace for President Committee shortly after its founding. Then he watched in frustration as the party dithered about officially endorsing Wallace. He chalked up the lag to "dogmatic sectarianism."

By dint of his energy and enthusiasm, Kahn, at the age of twenty-six, was appointed director of nationalities for the Wallace for President Committee. A full-time activist, he snared his first paying job since he got out of the Army; it enabled him to rent a cheap tenement flat on the Lower East Side. He marched into battle, beating the drums for Wallace among nationalities groups across the land. He met predictable resistance from the Eastern Europeans, understandably suspicious of Communism in all forms, but by Election Day he had signed up a respectable number in the various ethnic communities. He took comfort during his labors, he said, from comrades who reminded him "good-humoredly" that "Joseph Stalin had won prestige as an authority on the national question."

As for the CP's influence on the Progressive Party, Kahn provides a rank-and-file eye view: "I had, indeed, from the start been aware that many among the nationalities leaders with whom I dealt as well as staffers at the Wallace headquarters were members of the Party, and I took it for granted that a Party coordinator should meet privately with the comrades. . . . No one at headquarters, however, ever mentioned Party membership or Party policies. We recognized each other by our dedication and by the way we talked about issues."

Later the party came out for Wallace, and though he denied he was a Communist, he never publicly renounced its support. Looking back, he explained that since he was running a peace campaign, it would have been hypocritical of him to turn away Communists. When hostile press people asked him about reds in his ranks, he would say, "I'm not following their line. If they want to follow my line, I say God bless 'em." He would also challenge criminal prosecutions of Communists as a threat to civil liberties. Finally, the only way to purge from his party's ranks overt, covert, past, or present Communists, not to mention "sympathizers" and "dupes" or whatever, would have been to screen everyone working for him. This would have entailed setting up machinery like that of the Truman loyalty security program or even demanding non-Communist oaths—not to mention firing Abt's troops, who were collecting signatures in the states. All these things he had publicly opposed, and he hadn't the stomach, let alone the time and staff, to conduct his own red hunt.

Wallace's most trusted behind-the-scenes adviser was his wife, Ilo, a small-town Iowa woman who kept a close eye on his campaign and shared her opinions when they were alone. Wallace once said that Ilo valued respectability above all. "She has always been very violently anti-Communist," he also said, "and I suppose she picks up gossip from her lady friends who are usually quite conservative." He admitted that she did not cotton to Baldwin and loathed Abt, whom she considered a radical. She thought the speeches Lew Frank wrote for Henry didn't sound like him; she was uneasy with blacks and Jews. The campaign staff resented her attempts to interfere in the campaign. Yet Wallace said, in the aftermath, "I would say she went along with my idealism in the campaign and was a good sport." Which seems, on balance, rather tepid praise.

On one occasion, Ilo relayed to him that a woman had told her "how important it was to get out the word that we were not Communist dominated." Wallace dutifully wrote a statement that he would repeat over and over when the question came up at press conferences:

> I am not a Communist, have never been one and never expect to be one. The Progressive party is not controlled by Communists, nor was its convention or program dictated by them. Communism and progressive capitalism differ fundamentally although we share many social objectives.

I welcome the support of those who believe in such social objectives. I welcome the support of those who are working for such understanding with Russia that both the United States and Russia will be willing to accept a strong United Nations with world police force stronger than the armed might of either nation. We believe that neither the U.S., nor Russia should ever dominate the world. I will never tolerate those whose purpose it is to destroy our government by force.

This was putting it as straightforwardly as possible, without giving offense to his Communist supporters. But he might as well not have bothered because no one listened. "I don't know if [the statement] was ever published in full" by any of the papers that were covering him, he said. "It was bound to be the case no matter what I said . . . that I should be dubbed a fellow traveler or a dupe of the Communists. There was nothing I could say that would change that."

MUCH LATER, in the perspective of time, Wallace concluded that the Communist Party had been using him. After the election, he believed, the CP leadership planned to ease him out and take over the Progressive Party as a front for its political activities. The CP was also using the PP as a vehicle to defeat Truman by siphoning votes away from him. Wallace later said that the CP's support had probably gained him an additional two hundred thousand votes, but that its endorsement cost him 3 million votes in the election.

But the red label was indelibly stamped on his back, and he made no effort to counter it by purging high staff members who were reported or rumored to be Communists or sympathizers in the McCarthyite rubric. For one thing, he really didn't know who they were. Second, if he had known, he might have been compelled to fire all of his top advisers—John Abt, Lee Pressman, and possibly Beanie Baldwin.

Reminiscing about this trio after the campaign in 1951, Wallace mentioned that Pressman had testified to Congress just the previous year that he and Abt had been CP members while they were working under Wallace at the Agriculture Department. Wallace had actually fired them in his "liberal purge" of the department in the early thirties. When he asked Abt about his party ties, Abt denied he was a Communist, though he didn't say he had never been one. He cautioned Wallace that his wife's ex-husband, the late Harold Ware, was the son of the famous radical Mother Bloor. Now his ex-wife edited a magazine called *American-Soviet Friendship*.

According to Whittaker Chambers, Ware had organized a CP cell of government workers and run an espionage ring. The historians John Earl Haynes, Harvey Klehr, and Alexander Vassiliev, drawing on KGB archives, claim that although Ware appeared to cooperate in his testimony before HUAC, he actually

> sidestepped most of his knowledge of the early days of the Communist underground in Washington and his own involvement with Soviet intelligence, first with Chambers's GRU network in the 1930s and later with the KGB. He had never been the classic "spy" who stole documents. Neither his work in domestically oriented New Deal agencies in the early 1930s nor his later role as a labor lawyer gave him access to information of Soviet interest. Instead, he functioned as part of the KGB espionage support network, assisting and facilitating its officers and agents. He gambled that there would not be anyone to contradict his evasions and that government investigators would not be able to charge him with perjury. He won his bet.

As for Abt's connection to the CP, years later he said at his eightieth birthday celebration that he had been a party member for fifty years. "I am sure that this announcement will surprise no one here tonight," he said. "But it seems to me a rather sad commentary on the state of the freedom of political association in this country that I had to wait for half a century after the event before I felt free, publicly and proudly, to confirm a fact which anyone who knows anything at all about me has assumed to be true for lo, these many years."

Wallace, for one, had apparently been oblivious to this supposedly well-known fact, though one might expect Abt to have informed him upon entering Wallace's employ, just as he had warned him about his wife's ex-husband. After the election, though, Wallace came to believe that Abt was a "continuous follower in every respect of the party line" and moreover that he was the "force behind Beanie Baldwin," who had hired him. It was a startling if belated admission: his own campaign manager had been led around by a person who followed the Communist line and had lied to him about not being a party member.

But Wallace always steered by his own compass and said the same basic things he had been saying for years. Plus the things that Lew Frank wrote for him. Because of his overloaded campaign schedule, Wallace was too busy to write speeches. Thus, "a very considerable number of speeches during that period were written by Lew. Frankly I scarcely know what's in them to this day," he confessed. In the campaign pressure cooker he simply read what he was handed. Frank, previously a staff writer at *The New Republic,* had been recommended by Michael Straight, who had met him while they were both working on the liberal American Veterans Committee. Straight would regret his choice: "Lew became an invaluable aide to Wallace—and an impassable barrier, isolating Wallace from liberals like myself."

THE COMMUNIST PRESENCE would badly damage Wallace's campaign, but at the time he needed them: "The word from the [state party organizations] was Communist people were the only ones who were working," Wallace recalled. The "top control" of the state branches "was in the hands of passionate Communist people." Eager rank-and-filers like Kahn had been invaluable when Baldwin was trying to start up a new political party and launch a nationwide presidential campaign within a short span of time. But the Communists' presence scared off any liberals who shared Wallace's views on peace and dealing with Moscow.

Wallace was swimming against an overwhelmingly powerful tide, from the hardliners in the Truman administration to the conservatives in the GOP to the segregationists in the South to the anti-Communists on the left. The FBI planted informants in his campaign. His fiercest rivals were the anti-Communist liberals, though. Their opposition was principled, but it followed the playbook of the Truman team drawn up in a memo-randum by Clark Clifford and a former New Dealer named James Rowe, who was a law partner of the former New Dealer and Washington rain-maker Thomas "Tommy the Cork" Cochran. Truman loathed Cochran, so Clifford took sole credit for the memo.

Clifford, who had panicked about the Wallace challenge after the American Labor Party's Leo Isacson was elected to Congress in New York, told Truman that his first priority should be to win over America's 15 mil-lion independent voters. "This should be done," he said, "by driving home to them the failures of the 80th Congress, by linking Dewey closely to the leadership of that Congress, and by presenting the President as a crusader rallying the people to save the tremendous social gains made under the New Deal and carried forward by his administration in a difficult post-war period over the opposition of a reactionary Congress."

Next, Clifford advised, Truman must rally the party's progressive base by making pointed appeals to its constituent groups: liberals (emphasize Wallace's Communist support), African Americans (remind them of his support for the Fair Employment Practices Commission and his executive order ending segregation in the armed forces), labor (cite his veto of the Taft-Hartley Act), and veterans (speak of his own war service and "suc-cessful administration" of the GI Bill).

Clifford advised Truman not to worry about alienating the South, pre-dicting that "the negro votes in the crucial states will more than cancel out any votes the President may lose" by supporting civil rights.

In another preelection memo, Clifford and Rowe proposed an "all-out effort . . . to identify and isolate [Wallace] in the public mind with the Communists. [The] Administration must persuade prominent liberals and progressives—*and no one else*—to move publicly into the fray. They must point out that the core of the Wallace backing is made up of Communists and fellow travelers." Truman would remain above the fray, while promi-nent liberals like Eleanor Roosevelt and Reinhold Niebuhr would paint Wallace in his true colors.

The GOP's use of the Communists-in-government issue had been highly effective in the 1946 congressional elections, as we have seen. This time around, they trained their biggest guns on Wallace, perhaps trying to make him a symbol of the hated New Deal. Illinois governor Dwight Green called Wallace the surviving leader of a New Deal coalition "held together by bosses, boodle, buncombe and blarney." Wallace voters were part of the "lunatic fringe" that had kept the New Deal in power. Congress member Clare Boothe Luce called him "Stalin's Mortimer Snerd," and his supporters "economic spooners and political bubbleheads . . . labor racketeers, native and imported Communists and foreign agents of the Kremlin."

THUS WALLACE MARCHED into the valley with cannons to the right of him and cannons to the left of him. Even the maverick Dwight Macdonald, once a peace advocate, was among those casting stones at the only avowed peace candidate in the race. To Macdonald, Wallace was spoiled goods. He devoted several issues of his little magazine *Politics* to attacking Wallace, calling him "unprincipled," "totalitarian," "a corn-fed mystic," a "demagogue," and an "apologist for Stalin." He was "an instrument of Russian foreign policy, really an agent of the enemy and thus all the more dangerous."

Such was the divided state of the left. By 1948, the dawning cold war had opened a gap between the Popular Front liberals and the anti-Communist liberals centered around Americans for Democratic Action (ADA). To varying degrees the former (whom the anti-Communists branded "totalitarian liberals") favored negotiations with the Soviets; the latter, confrontation and containment. This split was another bad omen for a Wallace candidacy, and labeling Wallace a Communist dupe was a good way to exploit it, as Clifford recognized.

THE DEMOCRATS HELD their convention in Chicago, nominating Truman after the Southern segregationists walked out in protest against the party's adoption of a civil rights plank, formed the Dixiecrat Party, and nominated Senator Strom Thurmond of South Carolina as their Confederate flag-bearer. In his acceptance speech, blunderingly aired in the wee hours of the morning, the president came out fighting. He pledged to call that "do-nothing Eightieth Congress" back into session to pass his progressive agenda. A week later, the Republicans picked the bland governor of New York, Thomas E. Dewey, a former prosecuting attorney who had sent up members of the Mafia.

The New Party's maiden convention was held in Philadelphia starting on July 23. Some 3,240 cow-eyed idealists and hard-eyed activists descended on the city. ("All the worst idiots in the United States," observed a journalist present, the acerbic H.L. Mencken, covering his last round of conventions.) They came in all ages, colors, and sizes, and from various backgrounds; nearly half were trade union members, and more than 25 percent were veterans. The party drew a healthy sprinkling of artists and intellectuals. There was a strong Hollywood and Broadway presence. The novelist Norman Mailer (whose 1947 war novel *The Naked and the Dead* had won the best war novel trophy in its weight class) worked on the campaign paper the *National Guardian,* with the journalists Cedric Belfrage and James Aronson, who kept it going after the campaign as the voice of the hard left. And there were intellectuals like the Harvard American literature professor F.O. Matthiessen and Frederick Schuman.

The Progressive Party (as the New Party was renamed) conclave was a small-d democratic event. The arguments started at the advance deliberations of the Platform Committee and never stopped till the final night. Far from being "controlled by the Communists," Wallace's biographers John C. Culver and John Hyde write, the Platform Committee seemed to be controlled by nobody. Perhaps it would be more accurate to grant that Lee Pressman, who indeed was a Communist, may have inserted language favorable to Russia in the foreign policy plank, though what that was is not readily discernible to this historian. Certainly, the hard leftists nailed down a plank calling for nationalization of certain basic industries, which was contrary to Wallace's frequent sermons about "progressive capitalism," subject to stepped-up regulation and antitrust enforcement rather than government ownership. Over Wallace supporters' objections, the platform called for the people to seize control of the "main levers" of the economic system. Wallace's man on the committee, Frederick Schuman, commented on the irony of "the only businessman and capitalist currently running for President of the United States" (referring to Wallace's family seed business, which held lucrative patents on varieties of hybrid corn). Schuman was able to push through a plank on world government, which Wallace favored and the CP opposed.

Overwhelmingly, though, the platform was a progressive document. If it was Communistic, then all of the following things are Communistic: desegregation of public schools, federal aid to education, public housing, national health insurance, women's rights, public day-care facilities, home rule for the District of Columbia, voting rights for eighteen-year-olds, admission of Hawaii and Alaska to statehood, and a $100 monthly stipend for everyone over sixty. Come to think of it, "prophetic" would have been a better description.

What drew the most criticism in the aftermath was the convention's failure to adopt the so-called Vermont Resolution, which stated that the Progressive Party would not automatically follow any other nation's (read: the Soviet Union's) foreign policy. Some felt, however, that existing language saying that both the Soviet Union and the United States bore blame for current tensions between them made the same point.

With the platform planks finally nailed down, the convention opened. In keeping with the rainbow hue of the delegates, the keynote address was delivered by Charles P. Howard, an African American lawyer and publisher from Wallace's home state of Iowa. He called on Truman to finally issue an executive order integrating the armed services (Truman, a liberal on racial issues, obliged in late July).

Wallace's running mate was Senator Glen Taylor, an Idaho cowboy who had once ridden his horse up the steps of the Capitol. He was an eloquent populist speaker who had spent most of the Depression earning a living as a roaming troubadour of country and folk ballads, sharing the stage with his wife. He was steeped in folk and union songs and could, on request, belt out "Yes We Have No Bananas" in Chinese. He and his wife and children serenaded the conventioneers with "When You Were Sweet Sixteen."[*]

---

[*] In 1947 Perry Como had made a hit recording of this 1898 ballad.

The convention climaxed on Saturday night with a huge rally in Shibe Park, home field for the Philadelphia Athletics. Everyone chipped in an admission charge of $2.60, with the money going into the party's campaign fund. The Progressive Party—which had formally adopted its new name —would continue this fund-raising device, raising more than $3 million from ordinary people.

"It was a singing convention," Wallace later recalled. "They were people who thought they were going somewhere, people with joy in their hearts. . . . I don't know which ones of them were Communist, and it really wasn't in my mind to ask that."

Pete Seeger and other balladeers led the crowd in made-up songs that, in the Woody Guthrie tradition, tacked politicized words to old tunes like "The Battle Hymn of the Republic." Seeger and Broadway lyricist E.Y. "Yip" Harburg contributed a couple of originals, "We Are Building a New Party" and "Friendly Henry Wallace." Wallace had a favorite among the many songs the delegates sang—a hymn called "Passing Through," which went:

> I saw Jesus on the cross
> On that hill called Calvary
> "Do you hate mankind for what they done to you?"
> He said, "Talk of love, not hate,
> Things to do, it's getting late
> I've so little time and I'm just passing through."

That was about as close as Wallace came to revealing the Christ complex some people accused him of having. Wallace sometimes seemed to be preaching his own gospel, separate and detached from his party. He was truly alone, he later explained: "My own slant was conditioned by my biblical upbringing—even though I'm all alone I'll go ahead with what I think is right. That's what determined me. When it comes to a supreme issue like [peace], what if the whole world would be against me."

("Passing Through," which resembles an old hymn, was actually written in 1947 or 1948 by Richard Blakeslee, a student at the University of

Chicago. Pete Seeger heard him singing it and learned it. He sang it during the Wallace campaign. Leonard Cohen recorded another version. It is included in *Songs for Political Action,* a CD set by Ron Cohen and Dave Samuelson. As Richard Silverstein writes: "The lyrics breathed the heady atmosphere of political liberalism and optimism that followed Allied victory in World War II and preceded the McCarthy era and Cold War freeze. In 1948, a hundred flowers bloomed and *Passing Through* epitomized this.")

At the final rally, the lights of the stadium were darkened and a spotlight followed Wallace riding in an open car and waving to the crowd. A roar of welcome met him, reminding cynical journalists of Hitler's rallies at Nuremberg, which said more about the eye of the beholder than the mentality of the candidate.

In his acceptance speech Wallace evoked the New Deal and the fallen leader: "Franklin Roosevelt looked beyond the horizon and gave us a vision of peace, an economic bill of rights; the right to work, for every man willing. . . . Two years later the war was over, and Franklin Roosevelt was dead. And what followed was the great betrayal. . . . Into the government came the ghosts of the great depression, the banking house boys and the oil-well diplomats."

He called for trust instead of conflict with the Soviet Union and said that the Berlin Crisis, which had come to a head the previous month, was caused by Truman's abandonment of sincere efforts to negotiate a German peace treaty with the Soviets and adoption of a get-tough policy. The Allies had encouraged the return of former Nazi officials to power and the rebuilding of German industry. He echoed the obsolete Henry Morgenthau vision of a "pastoral" Germany, explaining, "With a Germany groomed and muscled as the easternmost outpost of another war, we cannot make a peace. Nor can the world which watches hopelessly."

ACCORDING TO A GALLUP POLL taken the month before Wallace was formally nominated, 51 percent of the American people believed that he and his party were controlled by Communists.

Actually, if Wallace intended to rally a "peace vote" to his banner, he would have had to look hard to find it. By 1948, there was not much of a constituency for peace (which is not to imply that Americans were spoiling for World War III). There were the peace groups discussed in the last chapter, but they were minuscule in number. They might have been recruited into a non-Communist coalition in the 1948 election, but they were repelled by Wallace's CP backing. As Morris Milgram, a veteran socialist, wrote in the Fellowship of Reconciliation's magazine on the eve of election, "Those who participate in the Wallace Party will find themselves considered by many to be dupes of the Communists, will find their community leadership sharply weakened, and will find the Wallace Party reduced to nothing when the USSR finds a change of line requires its dissolution." Instead, the peace groups formed a "third camp" and threw their support behind the Socialist Party candidate Norman Thomas.

There was a vocal veterans presence in Wallace's army, but for the great majority of ex-soldiers and sailors peace was not a burning political issue. As a *New York Times* reporter concluded in a 1946 article on veterans' politics, "Veterans still lack . . . any dominant, overriding issue, which will unite them all under one banner." Most vets, including those affiliated with the liberal American Veterans Committee, favored rearmament; let the younger guys, who'd spent the war safe at home, fight the next one, many felt—they'd done their time in hell.

Wallace's difficulties in attracting liberal support were compounded by the charges that he was a Communist dupe. Liberals who were repelled by red-baiting were nevertheless reluctant to back Wallace for fear they too would be labeled dupes. Liberals who did not share that fear, like *Nation* editor Freda Kirchwey, worried that Wallace's third party would draw votes away from Truman and give the reactionary Republican candidate a victory. Truman's strategy of moving left—advocating civil rights and government health insurance, repealing Taft-Hartley, keeping the New Deal welfare state safe from the wrecking crew—sealed the deal with these folk. (Kirchwey and other liberals were also put off by the Communists' prominent role in Wallace's effort.)

Truman's people banked on the anti-third-party argument to corral most liberals. Truman admonished the "people with true liberal convictions whose worry over the state of the world has caused them to lean toward a third party" that the simple "fact that the Communists are guiding and using the third party shows that the party does not represent American ideals . . . and will not promote the cause of American liberalism but will injure it." Wallace had his own standard riposte to the don't-waste-your-vote argument: "Don't waste your vote on a candidate who defeated himself when he drove the New Dealers from his administration. A vote for Truman is a vote without meaning. I am against wasting votes."

Pete Seeger summed up the ordinary voter's sentiments about the third-party issue: "I had a sister-in-law that said, 'Pete, I know Wallace is a wonderful man, but I didn't want to see Dewey get to be president, so I voted for Truman,' she said. And she apologized to me."

AND THEN THERE WERE those liberals who distrusted Wallace or disliked him personally. The journalist Theodore H. White dismissed him as a "bitter man, eccentric, ambitious, self-righteous." He was an appealing figure, White admitted, "his light brown hair just turning silver, his clear, open face and muscled form instantly attractive to men and women alike, his personal kindliness well known." But beneath the surface "he was a self-intoxicated man with but two subjects of conversation—botanical genetics and himself." Philip Jaffe thought him a bitter man who bore a grudge against Truman for firing him. Michael Straight agreed that "Wallace's hatred of Truman was a virus that raged within his frame," which led to his extreme disdain for Americans for Democratic Action (ADA), the anti-Communist liberals who clamored onboard the presidential train.

It is hard to believe that Wallace went through all that he went through solely as a personal vendetta against Truman. Still, he was human; and personal anger, along with his political convictions, lent fire to his opposition to the president.

IN AUGUST, Wallace made his first campaign foray into Dixie. Blind to what awaited him, he and his staff made a swing through Durham, North Carolina; Jackson, Mississippi; and Shreveport, Louisiana. He drew large

crowds, most of them people who were not there out of political commitment or even curiosity but to express their hatred of the Yankee Communist carpetbagger. Beanie Baldwin insisted that Wallace not speak before
segregated audiences, stay in segregated hotels, or eat at segregated restaurants. The result was that Wallace sometimes depended on the hospitality
of black people, sleeping and taking his meals in their homes, eating his
lunch from a picnic basket supporters had made up for him. These examples of racial integration only inflamed Southern outrage.

Which is not to say that Wallace was wrong to follow this kind of
Southern strategy. Eleanor Roosevelt, among other liberals, refused to
patronize segregated facilities. Wallace thus set a precedent for future
Democratic campaigners not to defer to Southern racist customs. He
held rallies in courthouse squares, wading into crowds of people who
hated his guts. There were times when his campaign put his life at risk.
His supporters were stabbed and beaten; Senator Taylor was arrested in
Birmingham for refusing to use the "whites only" entrance—on direct
orders of the police chief himself, Eugene "Bull" Connor, of civil rights
era infamy.

When Wallace spoke in Durham, two dozen or so impassioned critics
threw eggs and tomatoes, and set off firecrackers and stink bombs. One of
his student bodyguards was slashed, and National Guard members had to
escort Wallace to safety. In another town he was showered with rotting
garbage; the stench was so strong that people fled. A reporter who followed Wallace wrote that he could wash off the garbage that sometimes
hit him, but he could not forget the "horrid faces of middle-aged women,
or red-necked, tobacco-spitting hillbillies who have hurled epithets all
along the route."

Audiences chanted, "Go back to Russia, you nigger lover!" They bar-
raged him with questions like "Did Stalin tell you to say that?" They pelted
him with more vegetables and eggs. To Wallace, however, these people
were the same ones the New Deal had tried to rescue from poverty in
the thirties: the farmers and workers. As he said, "The faces I have seen
distorted by hatred are of people for whom I have in my heart profound
compassion, because most of them have not had enough to eat."

He quoted the Bible, evoked patriotism to open common ground. He asked listeners of a radio speech to join him in the Lord's Prayer, and after saying "deliver us from evil," he added a gloss: "The scriptures read, 'God hath made of one blood all the nations to dwell upon the face of the earth.'" To no avail. During one speech when the crowd was drowning him out with jeers, Pete Seeger started playing "The Star-Spangled Banner" on his banjo, but the people ignored him. Not that Wallace was a meek martyr. At one rally, after being hit by eggs thrown by a little boy riding on his father's shoulders, he lost his temper, grabbed the man, and shouted, "Are you an American? Am I in America?" The man shoved him back.

Local police observed all this with their arms folded. Only in Mississippi, of all places, did the governor call on people to give Wallace the same fair hearing they would (or should) give to any other presidential candidate. This designation included the Dixiecrats, of course, whose secessionist campaign actually helped Wallace get on the ballot in the Southern states because officials there were anxious to help the pro-segregation party and eased regulations aimed at blocking third-party candidates.

Wallace's arc through the South won him few points with Northern liberals. The ADA sniffed that his stand on racial tolerance was "hypocritical," in view of the Agriculture Department's unequal treatment of blacks back when he was secretary a decade earlier. Others on the left recalled his department's refusal to deal with sharecroppers. Even organizations of African Americans did not warm to him. An NAACP leader said, "The black minority cannot afford the luxury of futile protest."

Yet if Wallace's Southern tour accomplished anything, it stimulated awareness in the North of the dimensions of racial hatred in the South and that region's resistance to any challenge to segregation.

In early September, Wallace limped to the end of his *via dolorosa*. Back on home ground in New York City, which harbored his largest contingent of supporters, he drew a cheering crowd of forty-eight thousand paying fans in Yankee Stadium. He had seen the face of fascism up close, he told them, literally tasted fascism's "ugly reality." He had witnessed the "ugly spewing of hate and prejudice." But he added that "the significance of our Southern trip lies in the two dozen completely unsegregated, peaceful meetings which we were able to hold." He blamed not the Southern people but "the owners of the mine and mill and the great plantations . . . who incite the violence."

But people in the mobs didn't need their bosses to tell them to come out and heave garbage and rotten fruit at the Yankee invader. They were responding to a tradition that stretched back to the last century and that was still practiced in the postwar South. They turned out for a symbolic lynching.

In his 1953 oral history interviews for Columbia University, Wallace said, "The thing I remember best about the campaign through the South . . . was one long succession of tomatoes and eggs." A man of ideals, a politician who used words to convert or inspire, a scientist who believed in reason, he could never fully comprehend mob violence, the hate seething in the hearts and minds of these crowds. He later mused, "I tried to talk of the economic welfare of the South and there wasn't anything I said that they could possibly have objected to. It was the same kind of thing I'd talked to Southern senators for years about, but I'd get about six sentences along and they started throwing." Many of these people had been helped by the New Deal to survive during the Depression; now they had turned on its most outspoken champion in the 1948 race.

On the first night of Wallace's campaign, after a young campaign worker was stabbed and Wallace received his baptism of rotten eggs, Baldwin asked him if he still wanted to go through with the Southern tour. "No one can intimidate me," he replied.

THE 1948 ELECTION SAGA has been told and retold. The script usually reads: scrappy underdog Harry Truman conducts whistle-stop tour of the Midwest, speaking to farmers and workers and common folk who identified with him.

I remember him speaking from the rear platform of his campaign train, which had stopped at the New York Central crossing on lower Washington Street in Crawfordsville, Indiana. A feisty, dapper man planted himself behind a lectern on the rear car of the train, talking with a nasal voice in clipped sentences peppered with folksy phrases, sawing his arms up and down for emphasis: "Those Republicans'll feed you a lot of soothy syrup, but don't you swallow it." He inveighed against "that do-nothing Eightieth Congress." He said, "They are going to tell you what a great Congress they have been. If you believe that, you are bigger suckers than I think you are."

In the archives of the Truman Library in Independence, Missouri, is a one-page profile of Crawfordsville, giving the names of the mayor, congressman, and Democratic politicians, along with brief summaries of local business conditions, farmers' income, and other facts for handy reference. It shows that Truman's victory was no miracle. It was a credit to his strategy, to his ground game, to his stubborn determination and his common touch. On his whistle-stop tour he addressed the people face to face, without the distancing of radio (which he never mastered). He came across as a feisty, sincere, down-to-earth politician who had traveled all the way from Washington to your town to tell you what was wrong with Washington—in a word, Congress. He labeled the Eightieth Congress "the worst since the first." He promised to make Washington work for the people. He branded the Republicans servants of Big Business who would take away from the people their gains under the New Deal. He appealed to the farmers, still a crucial swing vote.

He had the crowd eating out of his hand. "Lay it on, Harry!" they cried. "Give 'em hell, Harry!" To which he'd say, "They call it hell, I call it the truth."

As for "running left," he got the words to that tune straight from a liberal source—*The New Republic*. Michael Straight writes, "Week after week our editorials were teletyped to the whistle stops where Truman paused on his campaign tours. His ghostwriter, John Carter, copied our comments onto the pages that Truman read aloud to the crowds that gathered to cheer him on."

Truman campaigned as a defender of the New Deal, but the historian Robert A. Divine argues that foreign policy, more specifically the Soviet Union, was more important to voters that year. Paradoxically, Truman's hard line on negotiations with Moscow made him, rather than Wallace, the "peace candidate" in most Americans' eyes. They believed that talking straight and carrying a big stick were the best guarantors of peace. Paradoxically, Divine writes, "Reassured by his tough rhetoric, the American people slowly relaxed, despite continued signs of Soviet hostility" in the mounting Berlin Crisis.

By establishing himself as a strong national leader in a time of crisis, he rallied the people, just as Clark Clifford predicted, while putting the lie to GOP charges of weakness and indecisiveness. He studiously ignored the conservative wing of his party, the Dixiecrats, appealing to the black vote without directly challenging white Southerners, hoping to collect the loose change of Southern liberals who disliked segregationists or still re-membered what the New Deal had done for the South. And he again read his liberal opponent out of the Democratic Party. As Divine says, "Wal-lace's political significance would be primarily as Truman's lightning rod against charges of softness toward communism, the precise role that Clif-ford had cast for him." With this strategy the Republicans cooperated.

Thanks to Wallace's candidacy, Truman was able to neutralize Re-publican red-baiting, a strategy that had been so effective in 1946. Mean-while, Dewey felt he had such a lock on the presidency that he played defensive politics, saying nothing that would rouse more than a yawn during the entire campaign. More significant, he failed to make foreign policy an issue in a campaign year when a majority of voters said it was their number one worry.

Dewey was dutifully following Arthur Vandenberg's bipartisan foreign policy line when he might have taken up the more partisan "rollback" cries of conservatives like John Foster Dulles, who made an issue of the Yalta agreements. Truman also took back from General Marshall credit for his administration's most popular foreign policy initiative—the European Re-covery Program.

Truman managed to avoid the war scare talk. In the middle of June, when Soviet troops started blockading shipments to Berlin, he turned down General Clay's suggestion that the United States send an armored column to challenge the Soviets and chose a peaceful alternative—supply the city with a massive airlift. But he also ordered more atom-bomb-carrying B-29s to English bases, causing *Newsweek* to trumpet that Russia now faced "not just defeat, not just destruction, but obliteration." Truman later turned down the crisis meter further with calls for diplomacy, proclaiming that the chances for peace looked excellent—thus vouchsafing some relief to an American public that had been whipsawed by war and peace scares. By July 25 James Reston could write, "Peace is 'bustin' out all over' here this weekend." The war talk faded for a time but revived after the Berlin talks became stalemated and Truman dispatched sixty more B-29s to England. But ultimately the diplomats fashioned a settlement short of war.

The peaceful outcome was, as Daniel Yergin writes, a product of restraint on both sides. It meant that a "rule" was confirmed during the Berlin Crisis: Washington and Moscow recognized that whatever could be achieved by war would be less than the likely costs of that war. The end of World War II in Europe, of which the occupation of Germany was the key outcome, had "brought no peace, but rather an armed truce, a precarious balance, a crisis always short of catastrophe." Once Russia got the bomb, this precarious balance of forces would evolve into a balance of terror. This, rather than disarmament, would engineer a cold peace—but at what staggering cost in defense spending and nuclear buildup and at what dreadful risk of an accidentally triggered nuclear war?

Dewey's advisers felt that with the Berlin Crisis looming, any criticism of Truman's foreign policies would make Dewey look unpatriotic. Yet polls had showed in July that the public, now fully alert thanks to the Munich Syndrome, overwhelmingly believed that US policy under the Democrats had been "too soft." Moreover, people conceived that the Republican Party was better able to handle foreign policy.

Forgotten, however, are the questions Wallace raised. They deserved to be debated rather than dismissed as Communist propaganda. Actually, his call for negotiations with Stalin was not so far in front of public opinion: a poll showed 63 percent of Americans supported such a summit, though respondents were almost equally divided on the question of whether it would succeed or fail. Americans, thinking for themselves, decided that negotiations were worth a shot.

But when Wallace challenged Truman on Berlin from the left, no one heard him amid the din of Communist charges. (He had already hurt himself with hasty remarks about a conservative plot to oust the government in Czechoslovakia. His credibility was further undercut from another quarter when the right-wing columnist Westbrook Pegler published early in the campaign some weird letters that Wallace, in a spiritual phase, had written to a New Age–style guru years earlier.) And the neo-isolationist objections of Heartland Republicans like Robert Taft to the Truman Doctrine were also muted. As Divine concludes, "Instead, in the name of patriotism, the bipartisan policy sanctified the Cold War. . . . The ultimate consequence . . . was to create a Cold War consensus that stifled meaningful dissent on foreign policy for the next two decades."

Truman garnered 24,179,347 popular and 305 electoral votes, to Dewey's 21,991,292 and 189. Dixiecrat Strom Thurmond was next, with 1,169,032 votes. Wallace came in last with 1,157,063, most of them from New York State.

The polls predicting a Dewey victory were famously wrong because the pollsters stopped polling a month before the elections. In that momentous October an estimated 4 million people switched to Truman. Many of them were liberals who had been on the fence, disliking Truman yet skeptical of Wallace. In the end, most of the fence-sitters jumped right rather than left. And so Wallace failed to win the 3 million votes he thought necessary to make a decent showing for the cause of peace.

At Wallace's Manhattan headquarters, an ornate mansion on Park Avenue South built by a robber baron after the Civil War, John Abt drafted a statement for Wallace to give to Truman. Wallace told him, "Under no circumstances will I congratulate that son of a bitch." Abt's statement starchily called on Truman to live up to his New Deal campaign promises and "to repudiate the bipartisan foreign policy, to remove the military from the civilian branch of government, and the bankers from the State Department, and to return to the Roosevelt policy of friendship and collaboration among all nations through the United Nations for the establishment of one world at peace."

When Ilo Wallace heard the returns, she wept. "I told him so," she sobbed. "He should never have done it."

THE PROGRESSIVE PARTY limped on after the debacle of '48, but Wallace steadily grew more alienated from it. The trauma of his campaign left him bitter about the left, particularly the Communists and his staff. He blamed, for example, Baldwin's insistence that he avoid segregated hotels and restaurants for the hatred that lashed him in the South. It had been a "serious mistake," he said, to defy Southern traditions. "You can't change the customs of people that fast." Wallace was not really close to black people or their struggle, though he surely helped them by speaking out for equal rights in the South.

Months later, when a Paul Robeson outdoor concert in Peekskill, New York, was violently broken up by local American Legionnaires who called him a Communist, Wallace (who now made his home on a farm called Farvue in nearby South Salem) phoned Governor Dewey asking that state troopers be sent in to stop the violence (without success). But when Robeson and his backers decided to defy the fascists by holding a second concert and mobilized progressive vets and union men armed with baseball bats, Wallace refused to endorse the event, saying, "I thought they were deliberately courting violence and would get what they asked for."

ORIGINALLY, HE WOULD SAY, he had envisioned the Progressive Party as "a broad-based party . . . an American party through and through. Our inspiration was American history and we were not looking for inspiration abroad." But after the election, the "Americans" (he meant anti-Communists) began leaving the party. In the spring of 1950, a former CP member testified before HUAC that the Communists ran the Progressive Party in Pennsylvania; reading this, Wallace was shocked. He told Baldwin that the party simply could not afford to be beholden to the Communists. Baldwin clued him in that the Communists dominated the state branches. This probably confirmed Wallace's belief that the CP had used him to set up a front party, which they were now moving to take over.

As the Progressives prepared for their national convention in February 1950, Wallace told party leaders that his support was conditional on their adopting some version of the so-called Vermont Resolution affirming that they did not automatically endorse any nation's (i.e., Russia's) foreign policy. Furthermore, he wanted the party to toss the plank calling for nationalization of key industries and pledge its support for "progressive capitalism."

He got what he wanted—for what it was worth. In his keynote speech in Chicago, he emphasized that the Progressive Party must "stand before the American people as being Americans first, last, and always." He let the world know that the Wallace party was not based on Marxism or Leninism but on "reform by constitutional and democratic processes . . . progressive capitalism not socialism." The platform now stated that both the United States and Russia had made mistakes in foreign policy. Wallace pronounced that language "generally satisfactory."

The *New York Post* columnist Murray Kempton sensed that the convention delegates were tepid about the Wallace program. "This was not a Wallaceite audience. Its members were ready to concede him the right to distribute blame equally between Stalin and Truman, but their hearts weren't in it." I. F. Stone faulted Wallace for not working for a positive progressive-liberal program: "It does no good to proclaim that [the Progressive Party] is 'an independent indigenous American party.' And to disown the Reds. Independence is proved by day-to-day action not by frantic intermittent verbal efforts at disentanglement. If Wallace had done the hard work of hammering out party policy the party would be independent." After all, the entire basis of Wallace's opposition to the established parties had been that he *stood for something* and they didn't. He never gave a thought to whether the Communists loved or hated what he stood for.

His ties to the Progressives gradually unraveled over the next four months. Then, on June 24, 1950, the armed forces of the territory called the People's Republic of Korea, located north of the 38th Parallel, invaded the territory known as the Republic of Korea, south of the 38th Parallel (an arbitrary line drawn in 1945 by Allied and Soviet officers to stabilize the front between their troops). The Progressive Party responded to the war with a statement condemning US intervention. It also opposed UN involvement because the Communist government that controlled mainland China was excluded from membership in favor of the Nationalist Chinese, who had fled to Formosa (Taiwan).

Wallace strongly opposed the party's position. After the invasion he returned to Farvue, his farm in upstate New York, where he received a call from UN secretary-general Trygve Lie. They later met secretly, Wallace said. Lie showed him a document providing legal justification for the Security Council's decision to condemn the invasion as a violation of the UN Charter. Wallace announced his support for the UN and for sending in US troops under UN auspices to oppose the aggressor. In his statement Wallace asserted that the choice was clear: "When Russia, the United States and the United Nations appeal to force, I am on the side of the United States and the United Nations."

Like the Truman administration, he assumed that the Soviet Union had ordered the North Korean attack: "Undoubtedly the Russians could have prevented the attack by the North Koreans and undoubtedly they could stop the attack any time they wish."

Free at last; Wallace was liberated from a commitment that aligned him with the Communist rather than the "American" side. Thus did the 1948 peace candidate freely and uncritically support Truman's decision to commit US forces to war.

All things considered, he would be glad to go home—the only home he had, not in Iowa but Farvue. There he seemed content, growing tomatoes and breeding chickens to produce more eggs.

Meanwhile, as the inventor of hybrid seed corn that quintupled the number of bushels per acre farmers produced, Wallace had become very wealthy. The Pioneer Hi-Bred Corn Company, which he had founded in 1926, provided an ample income. It would be sold to DuPont for $10 billion in 1999.

THE 1948 ELECTION was the peace left's last real challenge to the cold war consensus for more than a decade. Wallace's failure to attract wider popular support meant, in effect, the ratification by default of Truman's cold war policies. As a candidate, Wallace became a scapegoat to a segment of the public whose accumulated fears and hatreds had been festering in the years since the war ended. They aimed not to kill him (well, most of them)

but to kill his message with jeers and taunts. Like the woman who is stoned in Shirley Jackson's famous story "The Lottery" (1947), he was the community's designated scapegoat for their fear. The Truman people joined the stone-throwers because that's where the votes were.

The peace groups' "third camp," which supported Norman Thomas, fell apart, and the peace movement lay dormant until the anti-nuclear campaigns of the sixties. In 1949, when Truman made his fateful decision to develop the H-bomb, he was cheered by most Americans, including a by-now chastened scientific community. Oppenheimer and others had opposed taking that giant step toward Armageddon and suffered the consequences. In Oppenheimer's case, as biographers Kai Bird and Martin Sherwin explain, a majority on the loyalty board "did not want his views represented in the counsels of government. Oppenheimer wanted to halt and perhaps even reverse the nuclear arms race. He wanted to encourage an open democratic debate on whether the United States should adopt genocide [i.e., dropping the exponentially more destructive hydrogen bomb] as its primary defense strategy." By punishing the most important dissenter, write Bird and Sherwin, all scientists were put "on notice that there could be serious consequences for those who challenged state policies."

By the early fifties, rollback rather than negotiations had emerged as the main alternative to containment. As Bruce Cumings writes, McCarthyism shunted centrists and containment advocates like George Kennan out of the mainstream, while rollbackers like Gen. Curtis LeMay and James Burnham were brought to the center. Thus in the fifties one could argue for preventive thermonuclear war and still command the US Air Force, but one could not argue for accommodation with Moscow and hope to hold a high position in government. A diplomat "could push for attacking North Korea and become a protected confidant of Americans in Seoul, or advocate recognition of the People's Republic and be sent home on an early ship." The rollback doctrine was gospel in higher conservative circles, while the coexistence doctrine became the latter-day equivalent of appeasement.

This tilt in the ideological balance was in part enabled by the bitter factional split among liberals, who became divided over the Communism issue while being harried by the red-baiters. Even as the anti-Communist liberals were defending principles that were the core of social-economic liberalism, they slid down a slippery slope to a place where socialism and even militant trade unionism were held to be the same as Communism. It was, as Godfrey Hodgson writes in his social history *America in Our Time,* "the triumph of liberals over the left." That meant "the end of ideology," in Daniel Bell's phrase, which in turn meant, as Bell's friend the neoconservative Irving Kristol writes, "the collapse of the socialist ideal." The common ideals of the socialist and New Deal left were superseded by an ideology of abundance, military Keynesianism, private welfare capitalism, and consumerism.

Wallace and the Progressive Party's "Communist problem" really stemmed in part from the US government's policy of criminalizing dissent, which gave the CP the bright idea to take over the Progressive Party. Perhaps Wallace should have pursued an anti-Communist strategy, which would have made him a more respectable peace candidate, except he would not have been a peace candidate. He would not only have compromised his principles, but the necessary screening would have been impossible to carry out in the short time available to him. He was squeezed in the vise of time and the times.

Wallace was the odd man out: a political Main Streeter who avoided back alleys; a religious man who sought salvation in service; a self-absorbed man operating on a higher astral plane than most politicians, yet an egoist like most politicians; a somnambulist walking in a dream, a dream of peace that either insulated or armored him from the world.

But for all that, he accomplished more than many historians begrudge him, putting his body on the line to raise issues that were ignored by the two major parties, opening up a debate on alternatives that had been squeezed out of the procrustean national dialogue. He undermined those alternatives by accepting the support of the Communists, but it could be argued that given his character and beliefs, flaws and virtues, in the context of his times he had little choice.

Wallace followed history's script, which assigned him a role in a tragedy. It was the tragedy of a good man. He once said that while FDR was alive he had a recurring dream in which he and the president were striding across a green meadow. In the dream Roosevelt was not crippled; he was walking unaided, young and vigorous. That was the ideal Roosevelt Wallace believed in—the activist who had pushed through the New Deal, not the man in the wheelchair who had dropped him from the ticket to pacify the political bosses, and not the aging commander who died as surely in the war as did four hundred thousand of the men and women he sent off to fight it.

$\mathcal{V}oices$

I mentioned that General MacArthur had re-marked to me at the Haneda airport, just be-fore I left at 12 o'clock Tuesday, June 27th (Japan time), that anyone who advocated [sending US forces to Korea] ought to have his head examined.

—JOHN FOSTER DULLES

Put no faith in those who parley with Commu-nists or those who wish to do so. They are all dreamers and dodgers of reality and some are cowards.

—MELVIN B. VOORHEES, SHOW ME A HERO (1954)

"Who's killin' our boys?" one of them shouted. Another: "What're we doin' over there?" And another: "Let's drop the A-bomb."

—WILLIE MORRIS, TAPS (2001)

That big eight-wheeler rollin' down the track
Means your true-lovin' daddy ain't comin' back
'Cause I'm movin' on, I'll soon be gone

—HANK SNOW, "I'M MOVIN' ON"
(NO. 1 COUNTRY SINGLE, 1950)

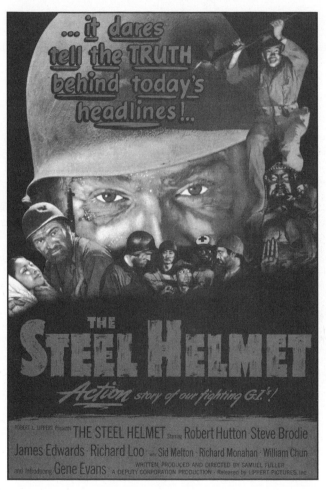

Samuel Fuller's antiwar *The Steel Helmet* (1951) was rushed out to exploit the Korean conflict. *Everett Collection*

10

KOREA— DRAWING A LINE

IN THE 1948 PRESIDENTIAL ELECTION Thomas E. Dewey, the Republican candidate, had not raised foreign policy issues, in deference to Senator Arthur Vandenberg's bipartisan foreign policy. As chair of the Senate Committee on Foreign Relations (1947–49), Vandenberg had pushed through Truman's programs, including the Marshall Plan and NATO. Now, however, he was seriously ill with lung cancer and absent from the Senate (he died the following April).

As Vandenberg faded away, a new voice emerged in the GOP, a louder, more strident one. It belonged to Senator Joseph McCarthy of Wisconsin. His entire focus was on foreign policy. He repeatedly castigated the Democratic architects of American foreign policy as bunglers and traitors. FDR and Truman represented "twenty years of treason."

Such charges resonated in the war-scare year 1948 and even more so in 1949, which was punctuated by a drumbeat of ominous developments in the Communist world, starting with the news that the Chinese Communists under Mao Zedong had driven Chiang Kai-shek's Nationalist army into exile on Formosa (Taiwan). This victory was followed by the Soviets' successful test of an atomic bomb.

Conservative Republicans like McCarthy, William Jenner, John Bricker, and others exploited these developments by amplifying the "Who lost China?" chorus. As for the Soviet spy scandals, they were portrayed as the result of lax security under the Democratic administrations going back to FDR, which allowed Communist spies to steal the "secret" of the atomic bomb, which in turn enabled their scientists to achieve their development of the weapon.* After Dean Acheson's January 12, 1950, speech, in which he placed Formosa and Korea outside the US defensive perimeter, Republicans cried "defeatism." General MacArthur in Tokyo was sympathetic to this viewpoint, calling Formosa "essential" to US security, allying him with the China lobby—Chiang's supporters in Congress. The China lobby stirred up hatred against Acheson as one of the "elite left-wing foreign policy experts favoring Europe and curtailing options in Asia" (apparently only effete Eastern Europhiles worried about a Soviet invasion of Europe, while real anti-Communists girded their nation for the Asian challenge). As the *New York Times*'s James Reston wrote, Acheson "seems to symbolize all the things about the State Department which congressmen distrust."

ON FEBRUARY 9, 1950, McCarthy, Acheson's nemesis, made an apocalyptic Lincoln Day speech in Wheeling, West Virginia, blaming traitors in the State Department for all that was going wrong in the world. At the outset McCarthy touched on a question tearing at most Americans' hearts: why had a great US victory in the last war failed to produce a secure and peaceful world? McCarthy intoned, "Five years after a world war has been won, men's hearts should anticipate a long peace—and men's minds should be free from the heavy weight that comes with war. But this is not such a period—for this is not a period of peace. This is a time of 'the cold war.' This is a time when all the world is split into two vast, increasingly hostile armed camps—a time of a great armament race."

Now, he said, America was in a "showdown fight." The difference between "our Western Christian world and the atheistic Communist world is

---

* How much help was provided by Klaus Fuchs, the Rosenbergs, and others is subject to debate, but the author recalls that while attending a conference in Moscow he heard a Soviet official crediting their information with speeding up the Soviet program. There is not the slightest doubt that the Soviet scientists were capable of discovering their own bomb.

not political," he went on. It is not a matter of competing economic systems. The real difference "lies in the religion of immoralism . . . invented by Marx, preached feverishly by Lenin, and carried to unimaginable extremes by Stalin." If the "religion of immoralism" (never defined) won out, the world would (presumably) suffer spiritual harm greater than the material damages that an economic or political system could inflict. "Today," McCarthy thundered, "we are engaged in a final, all-out battle between communistic atheism and Christianity. The modern champions of Communism have selected this as the time, and ladies and gentlemen, the chips are down—they are truly down." He dragged out some "figures" to underscore the danger that threatened the nation's very survival. Only six years ago the Communist world numbered some 180 million enslaved people, while the West harbored 1.6 billion free souls. In a mere five years—illustrating the "swiftness of the tempo of Communist victories in the cold war"—the number of people "on our side" had shrunk to only 500 million—changing the odds from 9 to 1 in the West's favor to 8 to 5 in the Soviet Union's.

McCarthy quoted an unnamed "outstanding historical figure" to the effect that democracy would be destroyed not by "enemies from without, but rather because of enemies from within." And then he got to the heart of the matter:

> The reason why we find ourselves in a position of impotency is not because our only powerful potential enemy has sent men to invade our shores . . . but rather because of the traitorous actions of those who have been treated so well by this nation. It has not been the less fortunate, or members of minority groups who have been traitorous to this nation, but rather those who have had all the benefits that the wealthiest nation on earth has had to offer . . . the finest homes, the finest college education, and the finest jobs in government we can give. This is glaringly true in the State Department. There the bright young men who are born with silver spoons in their mouths are the ones who have been most traitorous.

At that point, he brandished what he claimed was a list of the names of 205 people "that were made known to the Secretary of State as being members of the Communist Party and who nevertheless are still working and shaping policy in the State Department."

The senator was reprising the plangent chords of victimization, fear, and ressentiment that had coursed through the speeches of Father Charles Coughlin, Huey Long, and other fascist demagogues in the thirties. This time, according to McCarthy, the origin of the menace was not some evil cabal of financiers or bankers. It was a fifth column of privileged, college-educated young men who had been "born with silver spoons in their mouths" and who held "the finest jobs in government," the prime example being Alger Hiss. In a statement of truly staggering mendacity, McCarthy said that the greatest danger to America's security was not the Russian armies that threatened to overrun Europe and ultimately the United States; it was the Communists in Washington, boring from within and undermining the Republic's very foundations. Thus, his wild charges forged an iron link between the external and the internal Communist menaces.

McCarthy's speech had a wide impact. An April 1950 Gallup survey reported that 85 percent of Americans were aware of his words and more than two-thirds agreed that there was "something to" his charge that there were reds in the State Department. And 44 percent believed that the Communists wouldn't be in control of China if the US government had followed different policies, thus indirectly accepting McCarthy's and the China lobby's claim that the United States had "lost" China. A later poll found a plurality of 31.4 percent saying the senator was right, and 22 percent expressing disapproval. In other words, a plurality of Americans who were aware of the issues believed that (a) there were up to 205 Communists, more or less (McCarthy's figures changed), in the State Department, and that (b) they had traitorously connived in the "loss" of China.

The impact of McCarthy's inflamed rhetoric could be traced back to World War II, whose memory lingered in the national unconscious. The shock of the attack on Pearl Harbor had united the country around a common purpose. Not that this unity erased tensions among races and classes, for race riots and strikes broke out during the war. And Republicans harshly attacked FDR and some Democrats as soft on Communism, and Democrats fired back with charges that Republicans were covert fascists.

Nevertheless, the great majority of people on the home front during those times had a sense of participating in a common effort to which they were patriotically inspired to contribute. And they hated a common enemy. Once the war was over, people reverted to their primary loyalties—business, family, political party, union, church, and so on. Retaining some of the wartime demonization of the enemy, they transferred it to alternative targets after the war. This seemed to be truer of conservatives, who tend to be oriented toward religious values, opposed to New Deal–style programs helping the less well-off, and more ready to defend their country against enemies, both internal and external, real or fancied.[*]

In 1950 polls showed an equal proportion of Americans believing that the Communists were "winning the cold war" as believed the United States was winning it. McCarthy thus played on people's anxieties about America's "impotency" before the sinister Communist menace.

The senator's charges that the State Department was riddled with subversives who had caused the "loss" of China were, of course, fantasies. McCarthy named only nine Communists in the State Department, and that list was riddled with inaccuracies. The only name that persisted among those he cited was Owen Lattimore, a Johns Hopkins professor who was also a target of the China lobby. McCarthy tried to use Lattimore, a critic

---

[*] The social psychologist Jonathan Haidt compared the basic moral perspectives of liberals and conservatives. When the country has been attacked, he says, people's inbred tribalism intensifies, uniting a majority against the enemy, who is seen as starkly evil. In fighting this evil, the end justifies the means. Once the enemy is defeated, people revert to their own tribes. Then "the tribalism can ramp up, and reach really pathological proportions." One sees these reactions operative in the politics of the forties. People of the liberal and conservative tribes started demonizing each other and engaging in moral "wars" to defend their faith. This seems truer of conservatives, who felt frustrated and angry after being out of power for more than a decade. They demonized the long-dominant Democratic New Deal, which was inimical to their fundamental values of less government and less regulation of business, couched as individualism and self-reliance. Playing off the red-baiting tactics of 1944, they (or at least conservative Republicans like McCarthy) branded the Democrats as evil, the New Deal as "Communistic," and New Dealers in government as arrogant snobs living immoral lifestyles and becoming Communist spies or traitors. Thus, they believed that the New Deal threatened basic American values and the Soviet Union's actions in Europe and Asia threatened America's very survival. The end justified the means in opposing them. See Jonathan Haidt, *The Righteous Mind* (2012), for a fuller explanation of his theories.

of Chiang Kai-shek, to get at Acheson, whom McCarthy called "the voice for the mind of Lattimore" inside the State Department and champion of the "convicted traitor" Alger Hiss. Lattimore's sinister influence, McCarthy charged with no evidence, was behind Acheson's opposition to sending more aid to Nationalist China, causing its downfall.

ON JUNE 27, 1950, at 12:30 p.m., President Truman announced his decision to send Air Force and Navy units to bolster the army of the Republic of Korea (ROK), which had been routed by the North Korean invaders. Surveys after his announcement showed eight out of ten Americans backing him. The mood in Washington was almost ebullient that day. People felt they had been released from the tensions and uncertainties of 1948–49. Joseph C. Harsch, the *Christian Science Monitor*'s Washington bureau chief, a resident of the capital for twenty years, wrote, "Never before I have I felt such a sense of relief and unity pass through the city." James Reston observed in his *Times* column, "The decision to meet the Communist challenge in Korea has produced a transformation in the spirit of the United States government. . . . There have been some differences in the past seventy-two hours over how to react to the communist invasion, but . . . these differences have apparently been swept away by the general conviction that the dangers of inaction were greater than the dangers of the bold action taken by the President."

A front-page editorial in the *New York Herald Tribune,* a liberal Republican sheet, best conveyed the thinking within the administration: "It was time to draw a line—somewhere, somehow."

"Relief and unity" . . . "decision" . . . "communist invasion" . . . "differences" . . . "dangers of inaction" . . . "time to draw a line . . ." Nowhere in those words could be found a pithy definition of the precise threat this invasion posed to US security.

FROM THE BEGINNING, Truman saw the US response to the North Korean move in military terms. By Sunday, June 25, after Secretary of State

Acheson relayed the news to him in Independence, Missouri, where he was visiting the family home, he had made up his mind how to respond. For he told his daughter, Margaret, "Northern or communist Korea is marching in on Southern Korea and we are going to fight."

Acheson, who was a key influence on the president's decision-making, favored a military response. George Kennan, who advised Acheson as chief of the State Department's Policy Planning Staff (PPS), later recalled that "the course actually taken by this Government was not something pressed upon [Acheson] by the military leaders but rather something arrived at by himself, in solitary deliberation." (Actually, military leaders were, at first, reluctant to send troops into the war.) Acheson had also, on his own initiative, summoned the UN Security Council into Sunday session to confront the Korean crisis. This body would later pass a resolution demanding that the North Koreans withdraw behind the 38th Parallel and calling on members to take all measures necessary "to repel the aggression and restore international peace and security in the area." The Soviet representative (who surely would have vetoed such a resolution) was absent, boycotting the Security Council to protest its failure to admit Communist China as a permanent member replacing the Nationalist government.

US policy on South Korea had fluctuated as various elements inside the administration advocated different courses. In March 1949, the new National Security Council (NSC) warned that the Soviet Union intended to dominate all of Korea. That would endanger US interests in the Far East. Months later the president affirmed that the United States "will not fail to provide the aid which is so essential to Korea at this critical time."

Nevertheless, the Joint Chiefs of Staff had concluded that South Korea was not worth fighting for. In a speech to the National Press Club on January 12, Acheson himself had placed Korea outside the United States' defensive perimeter. According to Bruce Cumings in *The Korean War*, Acheson said that mainly to keep South Korean president Syngman Rhee in check. The South had guerrillas fighting in the North, and the North had its infiltrators in the South. The State Department wanted to make sure that Rhee did not get the idea that the United States would come to his rescue if he invaded the North.

The contingency plan in case of a Communist invasion drawn up by the NSC called for the United States to furnish military supplies but not troops. When the future of the 7,500-man contingent of US forces remaining in South Korea was being discussed, military commanders supported withdrawal. Their thinking was that "the U.S. should not become so irrevocably involved in the Korean situation that any action taken by any faction in Korea" could trigger US intervention and involvement in a war. The troops had been withdrawn, leaving a cadre of military advisers.

According to Cumings's history of the war, the US response "had little to do with Korea's strategic value, and everything to do with American prestige and political economy." Secretary of Defense Louis Johnson's biographers, Keith D. McFarland and David L. Roll, write that Truman, Johnson, and Acheson, with "little grasp of the real threats to U.S. national security," had magnified the North Korean invasion into one.

Truman, Acheson, and Johnson had pressing domestic reasons for coming to the aid of the South Koreans. Acheson and his allies in the foreign policy establishment had been locked with Johnson in a bureaucratic wrestling match over increased defense spending. A key internal document in this fight was NSC 68, a secret assessment of the Soviet threat written by National Security Council chair Paul Nitze that reached Truman in the spring of 1950. NSC 68 was a virtual declaration of cold war, portraying Moscow as bent on world conquest and calling for a dramatic upsurge in defense spending to counter the threat. The report had not been adopted as official policy at the time of the North Korean invasion, but Truman had come round to supporting its call for a boost in military spending well before the Korean War, according to cold war historian Benjamin O. Fordham.

The fiercest advocate for a lean defense budget was Johnson. In this he was reflecting Truman's original preference for a balanced budget along with continued social spending and reduced defense outlays. But Johnson's main reason was personal: he harbored ambitions to run for president as a Republican and was polishing his image as a penny-pinching conservative in line with the GOP's government-trimming agenda.

Acheson, however, wanted a bigger military to buttress his ambitious foreign policy. He and Johnson clashed several times, on one occasion almost coming to blows. According to McFarland and Roll, Johnson held a deep personal aversion to Acheson; the upper-class Harvard-educated secretary of state seemed condescending, and Johnson was jealous of his growing influence with Truman, whom Johnson counted as a friend. Whether Johnson knew it or not, Acheson considered him "nutty as a fruitcake" and encouraged aides to spread stories about his instability.

On policy grounds, Johnson opposed NSC 68's vision of national security entailing increased defense spending, so Truman's approval of it signaled a change in the president's attitude; it also meant that Acheson and his colleagues in the foreign policy establishment had won the battle. Now the administration was committed to an ambitious foreign policy, including arming NATO and defending Europe against a Soviet invasion. But such a program had yet to be implemented by Congress: something more was needed—Republican support.

Since conservative and isolationist Republicans remained the most stubborn opponents of higher defense spending, Acheson and his allies reached out to the GOP's internationalist wing. On one recorded occasion Acheson and his assistant, Dean Rusk, met with Massachusetts representative Christian Herter. At the meeting Acheson suggested using a future international crisis to stir up public support for armament spending. According to historian Fordham, Acheson described three possible scenarios that might sufficiently alarm the public: one of them was a Communist Chinese invasion of Formosa. Korea was not mentioned but presumably could have been. At any rate, as Cumings argues, "Acheson and other decision makers were awaiting some act by the Soviet Union that would help secure congressional support for an expansive rearmament program." Actually, the war scare of 1948 may already have done its job. A May 1950 Gallup survey recorded 63 percent in favor of higher outlays for the military. But a spike in the polls was not enough. A crisis was needed. Korea provided it.

THE PRESIDENT FLEW back to Washington on Sunday, June 25. Meeting him at the airport were Under Secretary of State James Webb and

Secretary of Defense Johnson. In a limousine returning to Blair House, Truman told them that he intended to "hit them hard," meaning the Communists.* "By God, I am going to let them have it." Johnson, in the front seat, reached back to shake the president's hand. "I'm with you, Mr. President," he said. Truman repeated like a mantra: "We can't let the UN down! We can't let the UN down!" Driving his thinking was a conviction that what he saw as a Soviet-instigated act of aggression would, if unchecked, lead to World War III. According to his own recollection, he was guided by the Munich precedent:

> If the Communists were permitted to force their way into the Republic of Korea without opposition from the free world, no small nation would have the courage to resist threats and aggression by stronger Communist neighbors. If this was allowed to go unchallenged it would mean a third world war, just as similar incidents had brought on the second world war.

Presidents, like generals, sometimes refight the last war.

Truman sat down with his diplomatic and military advisers on the evening of his return to Washington. Gen. Omar Bradley, chair of the Joint Chiefs, recalled that the unanimous sense of the meeting was: "We must draw the line somewhere" against Soviet-instigated aggression, so it might as well be in Korea. Bradley summed up the prevailing mood: "Underlying these discussions was an intense moral outrage, even more than we felt over the Czechoslovakia coup in 1948." As McFarland and Roll write, "The impact that the appeasement policies of the 1930s had on the decision makers was apparent in this session and others and throughout the crisis." On June 26, three prominent Republican senators, speaking for most of their party, specifically warned Truman against "appeasement" of the Communists, which would encourage the Soviets to invade other countries in Asia and Europe.

---

* As the White House was being renovated, the president was temporarily living across the street at Blair House.

The Truman Doctrine had been proclaimed to meet the challenge of Communist-backed internal subversion or rebellions like the Greek civil war; but it also mentioned "external" aggression. Korea was a case of the latter, Truman told reporters at his first meeting with the press upon his return to Washington: "The attack upon Korea makes it plain beyond all doubt that Communism has passed beyond the use of subversion to conquer independent nations and will now use armed invasion and war." His statement assumed that the ROK was the only legitimate government on the Korea peninsula. Moreover, the aggressor was identified as "Communism" rather than North Korea—thus implicating the Soviets without naming them.

Rather than reading North Korea's invasion as a unilateral attempt to reunite the Korean nation by force of arms, Truman framed it in Acheson's terms as the action of a puppet state carrying out the global strategy of its Kremlin master. Stalin's motives were variously seen as testing American resolve in South Asia or taking the first step of a grand design to expand Soviet hegemony in Asia and Europe by force of arms. Acheson worried that a Communist Korea would be a dagger pointed at the heart of Japan. As he framed the situation for the American public, there seemed to be no diplomatic alternative; it was war now or appeasement (and World War III) later. (Or as Churchill once said of Chamberlain: at Munich, faced with choosing between dishonor and war, he chose dishonor; in the end he got both.)

Finally, in line with Acheson's dictum that "Prestige is the shadow cast by power," Truman believed the United States must respond with force to the Soviet-backed challenge to avoid looking weak and diminishing its influence in the region. After all, America had been South Korea's patron—even though it had tried to shed that role more recently. Engaging with North Korea was not seen as a problem: the victors of World War II considered backward little North Korea, occupied for forty years by Japan, a pushover, despite its army of two hundred thousand supported by Soviet-made tanks and planes.

There was also a tangled skein of domestic political considerations. First, the poor showing of the outnumbered, ill-equipped South Korean army left the administration open to charges of having been caught unprepared (stirring long memories of the Pearl Harbor debacle). The administration had turned down the Rhee government's requests for tanks and other armaments, fearing an invasion by the South; Congress had only recently denied a similar request for aid.

Truman was under tremendous domestic political pressure when the Korean crisis exploded. Looming on the horizon was a midterm election in which the question "Who lost Korea?" would inevitably be raised by the GOP in the tradition of "Who lost China?" (A question no one would ask was whether those countries had ever been "ours" to "lose.") Although he castigated McCarthy as a demagogue, he still had to deal with McCarthy's power and influence, now in the ascendant. So domestic politics nudged him and Acheson toward intervention. Taking a military stand against the spread of international Communism, Truman decided, would immunize him from the senator's toxic charges.

Not that his decision was based solely on domestic politics. He was personally angered by what he saw as another Soviet betrayal, and in geopolitical terms he feared that Korea was another Munich; appeasement would bring World War III. But domestic politics was a potent part of the mix of motives driving his decision on how the United States should react.

Republicans had shifted to a different position since 1948, when Vandenberg's bipartisan foreign policy tamed their campaign rhetoric. With Vandenberg incapacitated by illness, they were freer to criticize the administration's choices. McCarthy was a sonorous new voice in the party's traditional anti-Communist chorus, a skilled demagogue. The Senate's leading Republican, Robert Taft, a principled conservative who had initially been queasy about the senator from Wisconsin, now found him useful. He was bolder and more reckless than past GOP spokesmen, and party conservatives and conservative Democrats like ethnic Catholics, along with independents (small-business people, for example), seemed in synch with his message. His wild accusations catered to fear and resentment, and stirring up these emotions gave his charges political purchase. As Senator John Bricker of Ohio told him, "You're a real SOB. But sometimes it's useful to have SOBs around to do the dirty work."

AT THE MEETINGS with his diplomatic and military advisers on June 25–26, Truman approved a show of force that fell short of sending in combat troops. At this stage, he feared a wider war. He had told his advisers at their second session on the night of June 26, "I don't want to go to war." He seems to have meant war not only in the sense of World War III with the Soviet Union but of mobilizing the home front as FDR had done after Pearl Harbor. He worried that a panicked public would start hoarding things they feared would be rationed. Truman had asked reporters covering his return to Washington from Independence not to file "alarmist" stories.

But after ominous reports of North Korean advances arrived from General MacArthur, Truman accepted Defense Secretary Johnson's recommendation that American troops, supported by air and naval forces, be transported to the southernmost port of Pusan, the only escape hatch for hundreds of US civilians trapped in South Korea. The decision was preceded by little debate, probably because, as McFarland and Roll write, the troops' deployment was to the rear areas of the fighting.

MacArthur upped the ante by urgently requesting the immediate dispatch of a Regimental Combat Team, which Truman approved. Then he raised it again, asking for two infantry divisions to mount a "counteroffensive." This request was also granted. Adding two divisions on the ground was, as Truman-era historian Arnold Offner points out, "committing the nation to more than a limited police action" (which was how Truman was characterizing the conflict in lieu of calling it a war).

Acheson had recommended that the president ask Congress for a resolution authorizing the dispatch of American troops, but Truman wanted to avoid a noisy partisan debate that would stir up war fever in the country, forcing his hand. (In this he may have been reflecting the old fear in the foreign policy establishment that public opinion oscillated wildly between apathy and belligerency.) Instead, he listened to Texas senator Tom Connally, chair of the Foreign Relations Committee and a political ally, who put the issue in language any son of the Lone Star State would understand: "If a burglar breaks into your house, you can shoot him without going to the police station and getting permission. You might run into a long debate by Congress, which would tie your hands completely. You have the right to do it as commander in chief under the UN Charter."

If he had asked Congress for authorization at the outset, the president might have laid a stronger foundation of public support for the war. Instead, he feared public opinion. And when the war went bad, as it would, Korea became "Truman's War." Failure to consult Congress also set a precedent that enabled future presidents to commit troops to foreign conflicts on their own initiative. As Senator J. William Fulbright later said, the Vietnam War started in Korea.

At this point, many Americans shared the view that it was time to "draw the line" after a series of unopposed Soviet "victories" in Eastern Europe. According to John Fenton of Gallup, the public approved of the Korean War because it gave them a "feeling of actually doing something about the Communist threat, after several years of seeing one country after another lost to them." It was almost as if the tensions fed by the war scares and cold war distrust had built up pressure to act to the bursting point. Korea was the opportunity to hit back at the Communists. Hence the heady mood in Washington and around the country.

ON SEPTEMBER 30, Truman publicly approved NSC 68 as the official national security policy of the United States. The document was largely the work of Paul Nitze, who now headed the State Department's Policy Planning Staff, from which the more moderate George F. Kennan had resigned. Like James Forrestal, Nitze was a product of the Dillon, Read Wall Street investment firm and a steadfast anti-Communist. NSC 68 set the United States on the road to ever higher defense spending in the coming years and decades. It defined the Soviet threat in dire language:

> The fundamental design of those who control the Soviet Union and the international communist movement is to retain and solidify their absolute power, first in the Soviet Union and second in the areas now under their control. In the minds of the Soviet leaders, however,

achievement of this design requires the dynamic extension of their authority and the ultimate elimination of any effective opposition to their authority. . . . The United States, as the principal center of power in the non-Soviet world and the bulwark of opposition to Soviet expansion, is the principal enemy whose integrity and vitality must be subverted or destroyed by one means or another if the Kremlin is to achieve its fundamental design.

NSC 68 characterized the conflict as one of opposing faiths. One preached freedom; the other, slavery: "The Kremlin regards the United States as the only major threat to the . . . idea of slavery under the grim oligarchy of the Kremlin. . . . The idea of freedom, moreover, is peculiarly and intolerably subversive to the idea of slavery. . . . The implacable purpose of the slave state to eliminate the challenge of freedom has placed the two great powers at opposite poles."

The language was not far removed from the rhetoric of Joe McCarthy— or of Harry Truman. For as cold war scholar Athan Theoharis contends, "Given the rhetoric of the Truman Administration, the McCarthyite attack was neither irrational nor aberrational so much as the logical extension of Administration policies and assumptions. On February 9, 1950, at Wheeling, West Virginia, the crows simply began coming home to roost."

WITH THE COMING of the Korean War, the clouds of fear and uncertainty hanging over the land lifted. The pro-war sentiment in June 1950 battened on the rallying-around psychology that war evokes.* It was not that they cared so much about the freedom of brave little South Korea or admired

---

* Recent psychological studies have revealed that in times when fear of death intrudes into the national consciousness, people will grasp cherished national or communal symbols that help restore their shattered confidence, such as the flag. This theory was brought out to explain why American flags broke out in such riotous profusion after the September 11, 2001, attacks on the World Trade Center and the Pentagon. See Jonathan Hyman's remarkable collection of photographs of such displays on billboards, signs, graffiti, clothing, etc., in *A Photographer's Journey: The Landscape of 9/11* (University of Texas, 2011).

President Syngman Rhee. Polls showed that less than 10 percent were will-ing to die for, or send their sons to die for, the freedom of South Korea; a considerably higher figure answered yes when asked that same question regarding Europe. (No one queried if they were willing to die for interna-tional law or the UN Charter.) Reflecting what the press and their leaders told them, Americans saw the attack as a major Soviet gambit on the cold war chessboard where the endgame was world conquest. Indeed, before the summer was out, some 57 percent of those buttonholed by Gallup said that America's entry into the war meant it was *now* engaged in World War III.

AMID THE INITIAL SURGE of public support for the Korean War, little dis-sent to the Truman administration's narrative was heard in the land. As we saw in Chapter Nine, Henry Wallace, the peace candidate, supported the war, as did liberal-left organs like *The Nation, The New Republic,* and *The Progressive.* And of course, the Americans for Democratic Action, now the dominant voice on the left after Wallace's defeat, enthusiastically en-dorsed the conflict. So did Kennan, who'd swung from containment to anticontainment and back.

Most of the peace organizations climbed aboard the war train. Some individuals perhaps felt the relief that Wallace did of being able to support their government in wartime and oppose the Communists like everyone else. The World Federalists (suspected by some of being willing to sell out the nation's sovereignty for a government run by foreigners) took out an ad declaring that they were "wholeheartedly behind our nation in this and every fight that may darken the nation's future." Influencing their decision was the conviction that the United States was acting collectively with other UN members as a kind of world policeman. As one World Federalist said, the "conception of a world police implies the right of intervention." On such grounds, the liberal-leaning Federal Council of Churches willingly flocked to the colors with Norman Thomas and the Socialist Party.

The pacifists, religiously opposed to all wars, were left talking among themselves. Only the Fellowship of Reconciliation (FOR) raised a vigorous dissent, saying that the real meaning of the term "police action" was that "a truncated UN has been conscripted as an ally of the United States in its struggle against the Soviet Union and world communism." By supporting the United States the UN had abandoned its role as neutral mediator and become a belligerent.

Even in its darkest visions the FOR could not have foreseen what lay ahead. By the war's third year American bombers would be napalming North Korean villages and breaking dams to flood cities, towns, and rice paddies. Air Force Gen. Curtis LeMay recalled that he had first been denied permission to napalm North Korean cities by the Pentagon. At that time, he claimed, killing a few thousand people might have made it possible to avoid killing many more thousands three years later. By 1953, desperate to put an end to a war that was now unpopular, the high command unleashed LeMay's B-29s. "We burned down *every* town in North Korea and South Korea, too," he said. (The Air Force dropped more bombs and napalm on North Korea than it had during the entire war in the Pacific theater.) On several occasions the United States seriously considered using atomic weapons. Nuclear capsules were transferred to the Ninth Bomb Group, and on April 6, 1951, Truman signed an order approving their use on Chinese and North Korean targets. Amid the confusion over MacArthur's firing, the orders were never sent.

AMERICA THUS ENTERED the war with little dissent. Some of the most trenchant objections to the Korean intervention came from conservatives like Robert Taft, who questioned the lack of congressional authorization for Truman's projection of US military power and doubted the president's constitutional right to unilaterally commit the nation's forces to a UN war. Others asked if it made sense to send American boys—many of whom had recently fought in World War II—to risk their lives in a distant civil war. Most of those so ordered went without protest.

Some of those veterans, whose reserve units had been reactivated, wondered what they were doing in a far-off place, taking up their M-1 rifles once again to fight against—whom? In his powerful novella *The Long*

March (1953), William Styron captured the shock and pain felt by a sensitive marine reserve officer who was rudely ripped from his comfortable civilian existence: "He had assumed he had put the war behind him—it was a fact almost mystically horrifying, in its unreality, to find himself in this new world of frigid nights and blazing noons, of disorder and movement and fanciful pursuit."

THE FIRST HOLLYWOOD movie about the war, *The Steel Helmet* (1951), reflected uncertainty as to just what we were fighting *for*. Directed by Sam Fuller, a conservative who had seen the carnage of war firsthand while fighting with the Big Red division in the Normandy invasion, *The Steel Helmet* was a bargain-basement quickie completed in ten days and shot in the studio with "Korean" exteriors at LA's Griffith Park. Its main character is a grizzled, cigar-chewing sergeant (Gene Evans), a World War II vet straight out of a Bill Mauldin cartoon. The North Koreans are all "gooks"—latter-day reincarnations of World War II–movie "Japs." (Richard Loo, of Chinese ancestry, who played many a "Jap" in World War II movies, returned in this one on the right side as a conflicted Japanese-American sergeant.) One soldier says, "They all look alike to me," whereupon Old Sarge tells him, "He's a South Korean when he's running with you, and a North Korean when he's running after you." Gooks and Russians are lumped together as one Communist enemy. The GIs are warned that the rice paddies are "crawlin' with Commies—just ready to slap you between two pieces of rye bread and wash you down with fish eggs and vodka!" Much of the action is centered in a phony-looking Korean temple the GIs have captured.

Fuller's hard-earned conviction that war is "organized insanity" drove the story. The inevitably brutal behavior of men at war overshadows the phony settings. One North Korean POW is shot by a GI; another taunts an African American medic who is treating him about the injustices suffered by his people, and spits on him. Even though the Commie has the best liberal lines, the point about racism is seriously made by Fuller, who was antiracist as well as antiwar.

What Fuller knew about the Korean War, which was just then unfolding, was not what he read in the papers but what he knew about the last one—what he had learned about war from the scenes of horror and death he witnessed on Omaha Beach. "Whatever the confrontation and wherever it's happening the underlying story is one of destruction and hatred," he later wrote. What he wanted to show in *The Steel Helmet* was not the nobility of the cause but the "confusion and brutality of war." He also presciently sensed that "if we started to fight in any corner of the world," it would be the start of "a repetitious cycle."

And so the first Korean War movie was an antiwar movie, made by a veteran who'd fought in the Big One. In a supreme irony, it was also a big box-office success. That's because, according to Fuller, it appealed mainly to young men who had been hooked by the distributor's ad campaign trumpeting the film as about the "roughest, toughest bunch of guys who ever called themselves U.S. Infantry!"

Right-wing anti-Communists branded it red propaganda. The Communist *Daily Worker* reflexively labeled it "reactionary," but praised the way it showed "what beasts the American soldiers were." The harshest political judgment came directly from the Pentagon, which summoned Fuller to Washington to explain himself. The military brass accused him of injecting subtle Communist propaganda into his film; they particularly objected to the spectacle of an American GI shooting a North Korean POW. Fuller told them this was what happened in war.

The conservative reactions to the picture, Fuller writes, caused him to doubt the cause he'd been fighting for in *his* war: "Soldiers were trained to fight the fascists during the war. Now the bigoted winds of McCarthyism were blowing across democratic America spreading the seeds of another kind of fascism. The only way to fight those people here at home was to expose their stupid, reactionary ideas."

THE ADMINISTRATION DID not offer or have much evidence supporting its views on why the North Koreans had breached the peace. That was not entirely its fault, for American intelligence agencies had no hard evidence on what Stalin was thinking or what his objectives were. The relatively new CIA had issued a stream of reports reporting on heavy North Korean troop movements to the border with the South indicating that an attack by North Korea was "possible" but "unlikely." According to an official CIA history, a June 1950 analysis of North Korean military capabilities concluded, "The DPRK is a firmly controlled Soviet satellite that exercises no independent initiative and depends entirely on the support of the USSR for existence." The CIA analysts believed that any invasion would come a cropper because the North Koreans did not have the strength to defeat the South Korean army without Soviet or Chinese assistance, which would not be forthcoming because the Soviets feared a wider war. Army, Navy, and Air Force intelligence all concurred with this view. MacArthur, surrounded by his imperial court in Tokyo, refused to believe that "Asian" troops would dare challenge the United States. He assured visitors that he could handle an invasion "with one arm tied behind my back . . . why heavens, you'd see these fellows scuttle up to the Manchurian border so quick, you would see no more of them."

The few independent academic experts on East Asia, who might have shed light on these matters, were nervous about providing views contrary to cold war consensus in light of Owen Lattimore's fate. Lattimore had questioned US backing of the repressive Rhee regime in South Korea and was attacked for it. Rhee, a Christian who was educated in the States and spoke excellent English, was viewed in conservative circles as a Korean George Washington. Even the Democratic administration believed that the ROK was an outpost of US interests in South Asia, along with Formosa and Japan.

In the early days of the war, US troops—most of them fresh from garrison duty in Japan—were badly roughed up by the advancing North Koreans. Reporters at the front filed stories about the Army's unreadiness and quoted GIs bitching about shortages of equipment, guns, and tanks, of World War II–era ammunition and weapons that wouldn't fire. The Republicans made hay with the reports. Rather than attack the commander in chief in wartime, though, they piled on his defense secretary, who ironically had promoted himself as an economizer so he could win the GOP nomination (but who had also worked efficiently to mobilize US forces to intervene in Korea). Republican legislators also reminded the citizenry of the State Department's "loss" of China, Acheson's exclusion of Korea and Formosa from the US defense perimeter, and Truman's failure to aid Chiang Kai-shek's troops during the civil war.

NOW TRUMAN WAS FREE to call for major increases in defense spending. On September 9, 1950, he proposed doubling the arms budget to $31 billion. He had already tapped Congress for emergency appropriations. By year's end he had requested a total of $16.8 billion in supplemental spending. As a result, actual defense appropriations for the year reached $47 billion, more than three times the $13.5 billion in Johnson's original budget. Acheson had his crisis. Later, he would say, "Korea saved us" by making the major increase in defense spending called for in NSC 68 politically possible.

And so while the US military budget tripled, outlays for social welfare programs shrank. Truman's bold call for a national health-care system, for example, was among the first to be scrapped. The Korean War and NSC 68 stalled Truman's Fair Deal in its tracks. The policy of world containment became militarized; it settled into a policy of permanent war for permanent peace.

At home the Truman administration stepped up its loyalty programs, gave the FBI free rein to take over these programs, and backed down from plans to respond to McCarthy's attacks on the State Department. Senator Pat McCarran's Internal Security Act (the former Mundt-Nixon bill, introduced in 1947), which had been languishing, was resuscitated. After all, the administration was selling the Korean War as part of the international Communist conspiracy. As Indiana's Senator Homer Capehart said, "I cannot conceive of anyone who would be opposed to passing the legislation necessary to control the Communists within our own ranks, particularly at a time when we are at war." The McCarran Act sailed through Congress in September 1950. Truman vetoed it with a ringing defense of civil liberties, but he was overridden. By that time, Benjamin Fordham writes, "the FBI already had drawn up plans to detain over 14,000 people in the event of an emergency [a provision in the act] and was busily recruiting informants in defense plants," where the presence of left-leaning unions was considered to pose a threat of sabotage or crippling strikes. These far-fetched scenarios were used to undermine radical unions, like the United Electrical workers and the Mill, Mine and Smelter workers, that were already under fire by mainstream labor leaders like Philip Murray and Walter Reuther, who were leading a drive to purge Communist-led member unions.

The war gave McCarthy more red meat and injected new vigor into the domestic red scare, acquiesced in by the administration and liberal anti-Communists (who "agreed with McCarthy's objectives but not his methods," as if the means could be severed from the end). And the rearmament program "established the military-industrial complex as a lasting feature of U.S. politics."

ON SEPTEMBER 27, after MacArthur's strategic victory at Inchon turned the war around, Truman endorsed the general's request to launch his troops across the 38th Parallel and accomplish "the destruction of the North Korean Armed Forces" and perforce the reunification of Korea. Although this latest decision of Truman's won the endorsement of the Joint Chiefs and the UN General Assembly, domestic political considerations also weighed heavily. Julian Zelizer writes in *Arsenal of Democracy* that Truman was aware "that Republicans could criticize him if he did not [allow MacArthur to cross the parallel], especially with polls showing that sixty-four percent of Americans wanted this course of action." With an election looming, it certainly made political sense for Truman to notch a big military victory in Korea. Also, he knew well that if he said no, Republicans would blast him for, yes, "losing" Korea.

Truman shored up his image by arranging a meeting with MacArthur on October 15. With midterm elections less than three weeks away, it would be, his advisers said, "good election year stuff" for the president to commune with his victorious general. The imperious MacArthur had declined to meet his president in the United States, so Truman flew all the way to Wake Island, a tiny dot of US territory in the Pacific. They had never met, and the interchange was cordial. Both men were savoring the prospect of an imminent victory that would bring American boys home by Christmas and end the Korean nightmare. MacArthur assured the president there was little chance the Chinese would intervene.

Contradicting MacArthur, the administration had numerous warnings—from the Indian ambassador, the British Labour government, and public statements from the Communist government itself—that the Chinese would meet a US invasion of the North with force. Official Washington dismissed all this as empty talk. Acheson said it would be "sheer madness" for the Chinese to enter the war.

FROM DECLASSIFIED SOVIET intelligence files, we now know that Stalin did not unilaterally "order" the North Korean invasion as part of a grand strategy to challenge the West. The main impetus had come from North Korean leader Kim Il-sung, who repeatedly complained to Stalin about provocations from the South, including guerrilla activities, and begged to be allowed to end the artificial division of his country, which had been occupied by the Japanese since 1905 but had existed as one nation for centuries. More or less the same motives animated Syngman Rhee, whose statements and provocations against the North fueled administration fears that he would start a war.

But Kim grabbed the initiative. His big mistake (and Stalin's) was assuming that the United States would not intervene. When Stalin learned that it had, he "was surprised and alarmed. . . . He evidently blamed Kim for having badly misjudged the situation," writes cold war historian Kathyrn Weathersby.

The Russian historian Evgeny Bajanov, working from Soviet archives declassified under Mikhail Gorbachev's *perestroika* policies, writes that Stalin's chief worry all along had been that Rhee might provoke Kim into rash actions. Accordingly, he stressed to Kim on March 5, 1949, that the 38th Parallel "must be peaceful. It is very important." Kim, however, kept begging Stalin for the go-ahead to "liberate the whole country through military means." He told Stalin he could not sleep nights worrying that if the unification of the country was not achieved, his people would throw him out. Kim sent Stalin forty-eight telegrams over this period.

Stalin feared that the North was too weak to defeat the South alone, so the Soviet Union could be dragged into a wider war. In January 1950, however, he relented and gave his tentative permission, adding, "it has to be organized in such a way there will not be a large risk"—of failure or of US intervention. According to Bajanov, Stalin changed his mind because of the Communist takeover in China, the successful testing of the Soviet atom bomb, the West's establishment of NATO (which the Soviets saw as provocative), and a conviction that Washington, wary of a land war in Asia, would not interfere.

At any rate, Stalin did not put the North Koreans up to attacking the South; rather, the DPRK, which was heavily dependent on Soviet economic aid, moved with Stalin's hedged permission. As another scholar writes, Kim won Stalin's approval on the condition that he could quickly overrun the weak South Korean forces and present the world with a fait accompli. Later, Kim said he had hoped to win the war within a month.

Once Stalin unleashed Kim, Soviet military support flowed. Russian generals wrote the battle plan for the attack; Russians provided tanks and ammunition. But Stalin vetoed Soviet air cover or troops on the ground and contributed a few thousand technical advisers instead. He may have enabled the invasion, but he was not about to invest Russian blood, treasure, or reputation in it.

When Truman sent in troops, Stalin quickly pulled out his advisers, presumably fearing their presence would trigger war with the States. After MacArthur's victory at Inchon sent the North Koreans into pell-mell retreat, Stalin attempted to salvage his bet by pressuring the Chinese to intervene (he had already insisted that Kim seek Beijing's approval for the invasion). He assured Chinese chairman Mao Zedong on October 5 that the United States "is not ready for a big war," so if the Chinese sent in five or six divisions they could easily halt the UN advance. Most historians believe Stalin was lying to lure Mao into the fight.

AS WITH NORTH KOREA, American intelligence believed that Mao was Stalin's puppet who would not act until told to. In fact, the reverse was true: although egged on by Stalin, Mao made his decision to enter the war independently. The decisive factor was MacArthur's move north across the 38th Parallel. Mao could not accept a reunited capitalist Korea on China's borders—a dagger pointed at Beijing's heart, so to speak, to borrow an American phrase relative to Japan. Of equal weight was a sense of obligation to the North Koreans. Thousands of DPRK soldiers had fought beside Mao's troops in the recent civil war. Indeed, several North Korean units were still in China, stationed along the border.

Mao's decision to attack came at an all-night Politburo meeting on October 13, 1950. After it, he cabled Foreign Minister Zhou Enlai: "I have consulted with Comrades in the Politburo. The consensus is that it is still advantageous to send our troops to Korea. . . . If we do not send off our troops, and allow the enemy to reach the Yalu River, the enemy will be swollen with arrogance. This will result in a variety of disadvantages to us, especially to the Northeast area. . . . To enter the war will be very rewarding; not to enter the war will be extremely harmful."

When Zhou met with Stalin in Moscow on October 9, 1950, to confirm delivery of the military aid Stalin had promised, the Soviet leader stunned him by reneging on his earlier promise to provide air cover, saying the air force was not ready. Zhou immediately cabled Mao and urged him to cancel the invasion, but Mao was determined to go ahead, and the Politburo backed him.

Stalin's broken promise opened a fissure of distrust between the two allies, argues the cold war scholar Jian Chen: "The Chinese desperately needed Soviet support in any form at this moment, and Mao had no other choice but to swallow the fruit of the Russian betrayal. Mao, however, would never forgive it. We have every reason to believe that a seed of the future Sino-Soviet split has thus been sowed in the process of China's intervention in the Korean war."

The United States' failure to anticipate Chinese intervention, based partly on racist assumptions of the superiority of Caucasian soldiers and partly on erroneous ideological preconceptions, was the greatest blunder

of the war. It caused thousands of additional casualties in the winter of
1950–51, during which US forces and ROK troops were driven back from
the Yalu River. As they retreated in the bitter cold, Chinese troops, blowing bugles and wearing quilted uniforms and plimsolls, struck from mountains lining the Americans' route of march, hitting their exposed flanks,
picking off isolated units, causing heavy losses. Only sacrificial resistance,
especially by the First Marine Division, enabled UN forces to withdraw
more or less intact.

Eventually, under Gen. Matt Ridgway, the better-led and now better-
armed US forces took back the lost territory up to the 38th Parallel, while
inflicting horrific casualties on the overextended, undersupplied Chinese
"volunteers" (perhaps three hundred thousand were killed, compared with
thirty-four thousand Americans killed in action in the entire war). As Korean War historian David Rees writes, General Ridgway had transformed
the Eighth Army into a professional army, "fighting not for the United Nations or against Communism, but fighting because it was ordered to." An
officer told *Time,* "The boys aren't up there fighting for democracy now.
They're fighting because the platoon leader is leading them, and the platoon leader is fighting because of the command, and so on up right to
the top." Professionalism—superior soldiering, watching out for one's
buddies—did more than anti-Communism to avert a US military defeat
in Korea. Indeed, anti-Communism had little to do with it. Despite indoctrination programs, most GIs wondered why they were defending this
"hellhole."* The virtues of an all-professional Army would become clear
in subsequent US wars.

THE WAR HAD LONG-TERM consequences. First, it planted the seeds of
distrust between the Soviet Union and the People's Republic of China. Sec-

---

* By the time I got in the Army, it was common for soldiers to refer to our ally as "Ko-fucking-rea."
A contemporary cartoon by Shel Silverstein—the Bill Mauldin of the Korean action—in an
Army paper showed a GI talking to another. He is gesturing at the wasted terrain all around
them: "What do you mean where's the latrine? This *IS* the latrine." Well, military inside jokes
often don't travel.

ond, it left a permanently divided Korea. Third, the adoption of NSC 68 opened up a flood of military spending that has continued to this day. (Ironically, a goodly proportion of the increased spending during the Korean War went to building new B-47 and B-52 bombers, capable of dropping atom bombs on the Soviet Union—which was under active consideration at times.) The military also improved tactical nukes, and by 1952 scientists had tested the first hydrogen bomb (the test emitted fallout that the Soviets analyzed, helping them develop their own superbomb). Thus the stage was being set for the next stage of the cold war: the balance of terror. It was also readied for taking over the French colonial war in Vietnam, after its troops were defeated at Dien Bien Phu. Finally, the war hardened US opposition to recognizing China and its right to a seat in the UN Security Council. Relations between the United States and the Soviet Union reached a new low of mutual distrust. They would not thaw until President Nixon sent Henry Kissinger to China twenty years later. By then the United States had come to understand that Soviet and Chinese Communism were not a monolithic force but rather separate powers with different interests.

THE WAR ALSO HAD devastating political consequences for the Democrats. Truman's approval rating had soared from 37 percent to 46 percent after his decision to go to war. By January 1951, only 38 percent of the public supported the intervention. By November 1952, it had dipped to 23 percent; two out of three Americans believed that the United States should pull its troops out of Korea.

As early as November 1950, shocked by defeats in North Korea, 45 percent of Americans supported dropping an atomic bomb on China; 37 percent opposed it. The following month, 51 percent said that if the UN got into "an all-out war" with China, the United States should also go to war against Russia; only 27 percent disagreed. Eighty percent believed that Moscow had ordered the Chinese to enter the war. The early defeats in Korea undermined Americans' sense of omnipotence after World War II. What the historian Tom Engelhardt called "victory culture" was replaced by the sense of impotence that McCarthy had evoked in his Wheeling speech. Out of this frustration sprang demands that Truman hit the enemy with atomic bombs (although such a weapon was tactically useless in the Korean fighting, as well as politically problematic). Failing that, he should bring the boys home.

Another result of the perceived Korean stalemate was that the public's attention swung back to Europe and the new NATO alliance. As John Fenton writes, "After the disillusionment of Korea, public opinion became even more convinced that the real battle, if it had to come, should be fought face-to-face with the Russians in Europe." Korea was a proxy war, an unpopular war. As such, it did not purge the complex anxieties and frustrations associated with the Soviet Union, the sense of threat that had burgeoned among people these past few years.

As Truman's popularity dimmed, that of Gen. Dwight D. Eisenhower, victor in Europe, rose. In 1950 Americans voted him the man they admired most in the world (Truman finished third). As Fenton writes, "The Korean dilemma chiefly served to pinpoint Truman's weaknesses and Eisenhower's strong points. The public agreed Truman was not up to the job, and that Eisenhower was the only man who could extricate the United States from the Korean mess."

In the election of November 1952, Eisenhower won a landslide victory over the Democrat Adlai Stevenson. He duly traveled to Korea but did not end the war. (Some scholars say that Stalin's death in 1953, rather than the US threat to use the atomic bomb, freed the Communist leadership, also tired of the war, to settle.) The Panmunjom talks had stalled on the issue of repatriation of all Chinese and North Korean POWs to their respective countries, which Truman opposed, perhaps recalling how unwilling Soviet prisoners had been sent back to Russia after World War II to their deaths or to Siberia. Finally, the dispute was resolved and the fighting, if not the war, stopped.

Korea was the wrong war for *some* right reasons. It could be justified as collective defense of a UN-recognized state against a rival regime's attempt to alter the status quo by violence. But it was so much an American show, with the British joining as best friend, and Australia, Turkey, and others providing fighting regiments, that the real precedent seemed to be that the UN would act against aggression if American interests were at stake. That was a long way from FDR's idea (or impossible dream) of the Five Policemen keeping the peace. Instead, the postwar world order became split by cold war rivalries.

ON JULY 27, 1953, a truce was signed at Panmunjom by the UN, North Korea, and China. (President Rhee refused to ratify a divided nation.) This was basically a cease-fire intended to gain breathing room that would enable the sides to work out a comprehensive peace treaty in further talks. That, of course, never happened.

The day the truce was signed, a reporter went to Times Square in New York looking for the celebration. Perhaps he anticipated bursts of Dionysian joy like those that attended VJ Day. All he found was people hurrying to work. They had probably long ago tuned out the Korean War and the tedious rhetoric at Panmunjom. And people may also have intuited that it ended only a phase of an ongoing war in which there could be no victory.

Voices

As life is action and passion, it is required of a man that he should share the passion and action of his time, at the peril of being judged not to have lived.

—Oliver Wendell Holmes Jr.

To the destructive element submit yourself, and with the exertions of your hands and feet in the water make the deep, deep sea keep you up.

—Joseph Conrad, *Lord Jim*

Seek and ye shall find.

—Matthew 7:7

WHY KOREA?
WHY NAGASAKI? CONFESSIONS
OF A COLD WARRIOR (II)

*WHY KOREA? WHOM DO YOU BLAME [the war] on? Whom? Joe Stalin? One man
screwing up the whole world is inconceivable. The greedy capitalists? They don't
have the guts. . . . The System? What system? The Forces? Perhaps, but that puts
us right back where we started from, trying to trap smoke in our nets.*

So I scrawled rather incoherently in my diary in July 1953, shortly before enlisting in the Army. I set down those lines while at home, where I
was spending a few weeks with my parents after graduation. At night I lay
in my boyhood bed wondering, Why Korea?

Eventually, I seem to have reached a conclusion. I announced in my
diary that I approved of the war after all. It was, you see, a fight for a
"world order" against "a nation [the Soviet Union] that does not act
through good will, only expedience."

In hindsight, of course, that's not very satisfying. It's appalling, actually.
My explanation—that it was all Stalin's fault—was simply parroting the
official explanations at the time. How pathetically ignorant we Americans
really were of Korea, its history, the causes of and alternatives to war!

But by then I was marching down a fatalistic path; there was no going
back. When the time came, I boarded the *Spirit of St. Louis*, one of the holiday trains of my college days, for Philadelphia, where I would rendezvous

Nagasaki: Year Zero + 10. Ruins of the Catholic cathedral in the Urakami district—Ground Zero. *Author photo*

with my college friend Mitch. On July 14 (Bastille Day), thirteen days before the Panmunjom truce was signed, we delivered up our bodies to the Philadelphia Army depot. After physicals and shots, we were bused to Fort Meade, Maryland, where we arrived very late at night, hungry and sleepy. A lanky, drawling sergeant was waiting for us with our introduction to Army life:

SARGE: You mens have a good trip?

RECRUITS: [Squeaks and mumbles]

SARGE: We'll get you some chow. Anybody here from West Virginia?

RECRUITS: [Mumbling]

SARGE: Nobody from *West by God Virginia*? (Suddenly angry) All right, yo' asses belong to *me*. You are trainees. You are lower than whale shit. Ain't *nothin'* lower than whale shit.

Welcome to the US Army.

After a couple of boring weeks spent "processing" at the "reception center" at Fort Meade, we were shipped to Fort Knox, Kentucky, for basic training in tank gunnery. Upon "graduation," Mitch and I moved on for special training at the Counter Intelligence Corps school, at Fort Holabird, Maryland.

"The Bird" exists now as a dim memory of an unhappy place. A cloud of fear hung in the air—the palpable threat that someone in G2 (intelligence) would confront you with derogatory information that had turned up in your background investigation. This, as I recall, was never told to us directly; it simply arrived somehow via the perpetual barracks-room rumor mill. There were stories of soldiers who suddenly "disappeared"— only later to resurface in Korea or clerking in a stateside post. The informal name for this procedure was "being G2-ed out," meaning that Army counterintelligence or the FBI had unearthed some damning information on you that raised doubts about your suitability to serve in a secret service. Once that was decided, there was no hearing, no appeal; you were immediately transferred.

The days passed in a drone of classes indoctrinating us in counterspy techniques, touch-typing, the history of Communism, and why we were fighting it (ominous music, hammer and sickle spilling into Eastern Europe, Asia, the world!). Nothing much else to do but hang out in the barracks or drink watery 3.2 beer at the PX. On weekends we sometimes went to Baltimore, hitting a seafood restaurant or touring the strip joints on East Baltimore Street or a clean Dixieland jazz place that drew college students and featured a piano player who channeled Jelly Roll Morton. More often, Mitch and I drove to Washington, where some of our classmates were stationed. There were parties in narrow Georgetown townhouses with creaking floorboards, packed to the gills with government girls, young lawyers, and fresh-faced naval ensigns.

Those hot muggy Washington nights swirled with noisy arguments about Senator McCarthy's latest revelations of the number of reds in government. Endless cavils, tiresome clashes over "facts," of which there seemed to be an abundance, only nobody knew whose facts were true, so the arguments deteriorated into Jesuitical distinctions. How many Communists were in the State Department, how many Marxists *could* dance on the head of a pin? Who promoted Peress anyhow?

That name, Peress, frequently came up in the McCarthy-Army hearings, which were at that time mesmerizing the nation on TV—in a kind of follow-up to Senator Estes Kefauver's widely watched hearings on organized crime, which was the new medium's first breakout hit (inspiring several films about the mob, like Fritz Lang's *The Big Heat,* in which the mob invades suburbia to blow up detective Glenn Ford's wife and Lee Marvin throws hot coffee in Gloria Grahame's face). I watched scraps of McCarthy's production on the rec-room TV at the Bird, totally unaware that it marked the beginning of the senator's downfall.

I can still hear McCarthy's droning voice, a kind of bullying lugubrious whine, harping on the Army's failure to deal with thousands (hundreds? a couple?) of Communists in its ranks. Peress was an ordinary dentist from New York City (ah, the banality of evil), who had been drafted and automatically promoted to the rank of major because of his professional skills. He was accused of concealing his membership in the American Labor

Party, which had supported Henry Wallace for president in 1948. But who knew what havoc a red dentist could wreak? Put in fillings that received transmissions from the Kremlin? McCarthy knew.

At one point the Army's attorney, a balding, bow-tied Boston lawyer named Joseph Welch, demanded that McCarthy come up with the names of the 130 Communists he had recently charged were planted in defense plants, ready to commit sabotage when the order came from Moscow. Refusing (probably because he didn't have them), McCarthy countercharged that a young associate in Welch's law firm named Jack Fisher was once a member of the National Lawyers Guild, an organization on the attorney general's list.[*] Welch chilled McCarthy with four chiseled Bostonian sentences: "Let us not assassinate this lad further, senator. You've done enough. Have you no sense of decency, sir? At long last, have you left no sense of decency?" The legal establishment takes care of its own.

By then, many Americans had grown tired of the man and the issue, and were receptive to this appeal to their basic decency. A June Gallup poll showed that after Welch's coup de grâce McCarthy's approval rating dropped from a January high of 50 percent to 35 percent, while his disapproval tally climbed to 45 percent.

ONE DAY WHILE I was sitting on my bunk shining my shoes in preparation for the weekly inspection, Mitch appeared, his face contorted like he'd taken a gut punch. "I've been G2-ed out," he announced in a strained voice. He didn't know the charges, and even if he did there was no way he could challenge them. He had been told only that derogatory information had turned up in his background investigation sufficient to make him untrustworthy, disloyal, a security risk, a potential traitor. He was immediately shipped out to a tank outfit stationed in Germany, where he put in

---

[*] The National Lawyers Guild was founded by dissident members of the American Bar Association who disagreed with the ABA's hardline anti-Communism. It defended CP members in court, which was an unpopular thing to do.

his time as a clerk typist. He told me many years later that he had learned
why it had happened:

> As for the recollections vis-a-vis my denouement at the Bird, it's a hard
> memory for me and contemplation of the emotions that attended it are
> dark feelings. Key words: injustice . . . fear . . . anger. As you know, no
> explanation attended that event, but using skills learned at the Bird, I was
> able to access my file information: [Major] Sweeney [his accuser] felt I
> might be undependable since I had lived in Czechoslovakia for 3 months
> in 1946 while my father was the UN rep there. I was 15 years old at that
> time. The trigger for my expulsion was that I had said, during a class dis-
> cussion, that the Bird would be a great target for the bad guys to infiltrate.*
> So ask yourself the question: could Sweeney have found me dangerous
> because he was a sleeper for the Evil Empire? We'll never know.

The last hypothesis was whimsical—cold war black humor (see *The
Manchurian Candidate*).

At the time I was tormented by the questions of what, if anything,
should I do? Protest this injustice to my friend? (Mitch, a lapsed Quaker,
was as much a Communist as Senator Taft.) Should I even continue serving in an organization that enforced a rigid ideology, in which we were
indoctrinated in our Americanism classes and which held that British socialism and Soviet Communism were one and the same, and that Communists were mere tools in a master plan for world domination? I realized
that I'd landed in a political theocracy whose beliefs were even then being
sung in the McCarthy follies playing on our TV screens.

Protesting was a concept unfamiliar to my generation. Especially
protesting the United States Army. As in World War II, if Uncle Sam
called, you saluted and moved out, however slowly and reluctantly. (Or
took steps as quickly and slickly as you could to avoid the call as the freer

---

* Lest there be any doubt, he meant that hypothetically, thinking like a security-conscious agent
should think.

thinkers did.) Once you were part of the great machine, there was no way out. You couldn't resign from the Army, for God's sake. Possibly I might have quit the CIC, but that course would have pushed me into security risk territory; it would have gone into my file, placed me under suspicion, while accomplishing nothing.

Maybe, if I'd been a really determined protesting type (like my ex-roommate Trev, who did try to do something), I might have stirred up a minor flap over Mitch's case in the press, but I doubt it, given the curtain of secrecy that hung over the Bird, the CIC, and the loyalty review system. Besides, this kind of treatment was common and widely approved. Such cases were a dime a dozen in the federal government, I heard during those Washington nights, and nobody I knew seemed to find the words or justification for protest.

What's more, I already had derogatory information in my file. At the close of basic training, we'd thrown a party in our barracks, and by bad luck or because of a tip, the battalion commander walked in and put us all on report, threatening court-martial. Eventually, we were let off with administrative hearings and proceeded to Fort Holabird. It was a relief, but I still believed in the back of my mind that I could be kicked out as a security risk and end up aiming my 76mm tank gun across the 38th Parallel.

Doubly inhibited, I did nothing. In the years since, I've occasionally wondered if I behaved ignobly. It came down to the question, How much do you go along with a system before you become complicit with it? How much do you put up with to "serve your country"?

AS FOR MITCH, as I said, he landed in Germany, more or less on his feet, clerk-typing. Not bad duty; it kept you out of the field and the tank turret. As he told me, "Hey, I still had PX privileges while camping out with the 40th Tank Bn. We were expected to stop the Russkies for approximately 15 minutes if they came at us. No, I wasn't told this—but I found out using the same Bird skills they taught me."

He met his first wife in Germany, who bore his children, some of whom I met for the first time at Mitch's memorial service in 2011. After

contracting prostate cancer about five years earlier and telling me and
other friends goodbye, he had a remission, and I visited him occasionally
in Philly. But in 2010 the cancer came back. The proximate cause of his
death was a terrible fall down stairs, probably while his mind was muddled
by pain medication. I learned all this secondhand from Natalie, his longtime loyal girlfriend. At the service someone showed a video of him at
a last dinner he had with friends. He wore such a sad, wistful smile, like a
man grieving at his own funeral. My God, he was entitled! Red-haired
Mitch, with his ripe sense of irony, talented bullshitter, charmer of
women, soul brother in arms.

I'll let Mitch have the last word. This is from his final e-mail to me:

Year 2011 has been rough—I'm struggling with enzyme issues relative to
my malignant carcinoid. Was close to death at one point only to learn that
my son Denis—the Vietnam USMC vet—had just been diagnosed with a
virulent form of CA with no cure. Managed to drive up to Rochester to
"say goodbye" shortly before he went into coma. Fourteen days later, I
attended his military funeral. Reality and non-reality all at the same moment. Pain that can only be characterized as exquisite and unremitting.

One lesson too late learned: Energy is not limitless—yet we waste so
much of life confronting minutia instead of dispensing the miracle drug
that is love. And in that I have been richer than I knew: much love is being
given me—and having folks like you as fellow travelers on my journey
has illuminated my path.

MITCH AND I and everyone in our World War II generation were the first
to grow up in the shadow of the bomb. Its presence, the possibility of its
being used, was always there—a constant omnipresence in our lives from
the time we were teenagers.

Of course, we didn't think of it constantly. Nor did we go through the
"duck and cover" atomic bomb drills in school that gave nightmares to
the kids who came after us. Our nightmares came from imagining the

bomb from the scraps of information and bits of newsreels we saw at the time. We were in a way the *beneficiaries* of the Hiroshima and Nagasaki bombs; it meant no war for me or my two-years-older brother. It meant the end of the war for our country and the older generation that had gone off to it. We came to adolescence in the very adolescence of the atomic age. We were the Children of Ground Zero, in a manner of speaking.

We grew up dimly aware that a nuclear war might end civilization; but that potential remained a fantasy, a scenario you read about in *Life* or *Collier's*. The possibility did not really come into concrete existence until the sixties, when we and the Soviet Union were locked in a serious nuclear confrontation, each bristling with real hydrogen bombs and real intercontinental ballistic missiles capable of delivering them. The balance of terror. The era of Herman Kahn and Dr. Strangelove and "thinking the unthinkable." The Cuban missile crisis.

Before that, the bomb did exist; it existed in our subconscious, our nightmares about what had happened at Hiroshima and Nagasaki, the actual nuclear Armageddons. We'd perhaps seen grainy news pictures of the two ruined cities, fields of ashes and human dots, but little else. We could only imagine what the suffering had been like at Ground Zero; there were no accounts (until John Hershey's *Hiroshima*, calm, cool, and recollected). We had, of course, read about the firebombings of the European and then the major Japanese cities, and had tried to see (or avoid seeing) what it was like to have been there. The atomic bomb was widely regarded at the time—and I remember thinking it—as a bigger, more terrible firebomb like those used on Germany that, of course, was intended to kill masses of civilians. Killing civilians, we knew without being told, had become the ultimate strategic goal of the war—killing as many of them as was necessary to finally end it without more bloody battles like at Okinawa. Miraculously, only one of these new bombs was needed to accomplish what squadrons of B-29s had wrought with thousands of firebombs over Tokyo. War had a bright future.

This, of course, was *good news!* The end of the war that we had so long hoped for was now only weeks or even days off. A few more of those babies was all it would take . . .

YEARS LATER, by a twist of fate, I landed in the country of my enemy, not really surprised to find the people friendly and not the apelike monsters I had read about and seen in propaganda movies. I worked with the men, embraced the women. After I was able to travel around the country and read the history, I began to grasp a bit of the real Japan, and I saw the ordinariness as well as the cultural beauty of these people I had once hated.

Still, for all my travels, a piece of the mosaic was missing. The empty piece was the nightmare cities, the cities whose searing destruction I could only imagine. The cities that had vanished in a few incandescent minutes, and the tens of thousands of people who had vanished with them from the earth.

So I suppose it was this unfilled picture that caused me to feel while in Japan an obscure but persistent pull to visit Nagasaki, which was fewer than a hundred miles south of Fukuoka, where I was stationed, in the northwest part of the island of Kyushu. The prompting rose from a deeper place than mere curiosity. After all, the city had been almost completely rebuilt; there were no ruins to see. And yet, only by going there could I recapture the fiery city that in my most macabre vision I saw reduced to ashes.

A phantom Nagasaki hovered in some corner in the back of my unconscious. A bundle of images, really, from photos of the time and my own imaginings and dreams. A vast gray field of ashes littered with rubble, reaching to the horizon in which a few lonely figures wandered. Thousands of people who had once lived on that ash plain had been incinerated in an instant, and their ashes and bones mingled with the greater ashes of their homes, their city. Ashes to ashes . . .

Perhaps those unconscious memories were part of what pulled me to Nagasaki—along with, to be honest, thoughts of pleasure. At any rate, in the spring of 1955, having accumulated some leave time, I bought a ticket there. It became the first stop on a tour that the very efficient Japanese National Railways laid out for me, which included the most scenic places on Kyushu: Onzen National Park; Beppu, where there were hot springs;

and Kumamoto, the southernmost place on the island, which stood in the shadow of a volcano.

I kept no diary of my Nagasaki stay, and it's faint in my mind now. I certainly didn't go around interviewing "victims" of the bomb. My Japanese wasn't up to that. I was a silent traveler; I saw no other Americans with whom to compare impressions.

I should add that another, completely romantic notion had drawn me. I knew, of course, that Nagasaki, a port, was the city where the Portuguese sailors had landed in the sixteenth century and established Japan's first trading relations with the West. They and seamen from other countries were tolerated by the ruling military government (shogunate) because of the rifles and gunpowder they brought to trade. The foreigners also imported ideas—primarily Christianity. St. Francis Xavier came to Nagasaki in 1549, and Catholicism spread like wildfire on Kyushu via the friars. Nagasaki was always the epicenter of the new faith, with perhaps half of Japan's three hundred thousand Catholics living there. But the shogunate had grown more xenophobic and decided that Christianity was a threat to its rule; it suppressed and persecuted its practitioners. In 1597 twenty-six Catholics (now considered martyrs) were crucified in Nagasaki's Urakami district, where a great cathedral was later built.

And so Christianity went underground for two centuries, and as the dark descended, the shogunate closed all its windows to the West, leaving it only open a crack in Nagasaki: a Dutch trading post confined to Deshima Island in Nagasaki Bay close to the docks.

Nagasaki was the focal point of Japan's opening to the West in the 1850s. Later, a novel was published about an American naval officer and his temporary "wife," a geisha known as Cio-Cio-San. From this legend was derived Puccini's *Madame Butterfly*.

I'd become entranced with this tale and once arranged a date with a geisha I'd flirted with at one of our "liaison parties" for Japanese officials. As it happened, a Japanese movie version of *Madame Butterfly* was playing, and I think that was part of my reason for hiring her services. Perhaps that's why she came. It was a fantasy on a fantasy. She arrived in a chauffeured car, with a chaperone, dazzling in a bright flowery kimono, taking mincing steps, her white-*tabi* feet in silver-and-blue *zori*. I could barely communicate with her in my inadequate Japanese; she seemed incredibly beautiful—like one of those elaborately painted plaster of Paris Hakata dolls, many of geishas, that were a product of local artisans.

During the movie's saddest scenes of Pinkerton abandoning Cio-Cio-San and her child to return home and her suicide, I glanced at my geisha: she was quietly sobbing. Across the divide of language and culture, we shared the romantic pathos of the legend, which had its origin in Nagasaki, where first met East and West. Indeed, there was a house still standing known as the Madame Butterfly House, though its official name was the Glover House, after the American trader who lived there in the 1860s and possibly took a Nagasaki geisha as a temporary wife, as Puccini's Pinkerton had done.

The city itself had not been wiped out, as Hiroshima had been; the bomb's full explosive force had been dissipated by mountains lining the valleys in the midst of which the city had grown. Ground Zero was located in the northwest part of the city, about two miles from the center and the adjoining harbor, a suburb called Urakami because it ran along the river of that name. The primary target, a large munitions plant, was located in the area.

As mentioned it was also the center of the city's ancient Catholic community. The Urakami cathedral, officially Our Lady of the Immaculate Conception, was considered the largest Catholic church in the Orient and could accommodate, it is said, six thousand worshipers. Some of them were inside praying when the bomb fell. The edifice burned and the roof collapsed and all those inside were killed. When I visited, only the cathedral's red brick façade remained. Nearby was a temporary museum, which had pictures and exhibits showing what the bomb had wrought. The rest of the area was still bare, not yet fully rebuilt.

Walking around the vertiginous city, sited among mountains on a lovely bay, I climbed ancient cobbled roads bordered by great lichen-crusted stone walls and came upon ancient Buddhist temples. At night I wandered down the twisty alleys of the pleasure quarter, drank and joked with the barmaids in little sake bars.

Save in the pleasure quarter this city did not *seem,* to me, a friendly place. Of course, knowing no one, how was I to judge? Still, I felt a deep sense of self-conscious isolation as apparently the only foreigner there. People in the streets hurried by me without looking, though I imagined I detected in their faces a tacit hostility. Perhaps I was merely projecting on them an inflated sense of my own complicity as the only American in the city. (The people, I suspect, paid me no attention. I found that most Japanese did not talk about the bomb, as though it was an unpleasant memory to be repressed. Of course, the political people loudly opposed the stationing of atomic bombs on Japanese soil.)

My first night there, the maid at the *ryokan* where I was staying served me dinner in my room (as is the custom in a *ryokan*), and I noticed that her face, which had been in a shadow, was suddenly illuminated by the lamp. I then saw that it was crisscrossed with cicatrices—pinkish wormlike scars pulling her mouth slightly awry. As she knelt beside me to give me a dish, I abruptly looked away. She was a *hibakusha,* a survivor. It would have been rude to ask her about what had happened to her. Yet her face, her scars, her expression seemed a living record of what the bomb had done. There was a sadness in her face, her eyes—her eyes were empty. No, her eyes were dead.

One of the books I'd read about the bombing before coming to Nagasaki—indeed, it probably added to my curiosity—was called *We of Nagasaki.* It was by Takashi Nagai, a doctor and professor at the medical school. At the time of the bomb he had been ill with leukemia, which came—ironically, I suppose, as one reflexively says—not from the atomic radiation but from working in the radiology lab at his hospital before World War II.

Nagai was a Catholic who lived in the Urakami district. The book tells the stories of eight people; or rather, they tell their own stories, in their own voices, though the doctor, a talented writer, edited and shaped their words. Several of the victims had been children at the time the bomb fell (some four years before the book was completed), including Kayano, Nagai's daughter, who was only four.

This modest book conjures up a Dantean inferno of images. Scenes of victims burned black, their skin hanging in shreds. A hospital where the dead and dying lay in a pool of shit and vomit that grew as more victims were brought there until it dripped down the stairs. Survivors who had returned to look for their homes and loved ones, finding this blank vast ash field, poking in the rubble to find a few fragments of a house or of bones, belonging, they could only guess, to a missing wife or child left behind because they, the survivors, had been lucky enough to have been away somewhere, up in the neighboring hills, perhaps.

What struck me about Nagai's book (which is about the length of John Hershey's *Hiroshima,* a similar reconstruction of survivors' tales), was not only the horrors described but his own conclusions about the impact of the bomb. Raised as a Catholic, he had taken quite literally the message of Christ, "Love thy neighbor" (which he gave, phonetically, to the new house he later built to replace his vanished one); he bemoaned the spiritual destruction wreaked by the bomb. What he regarded as its most destructive effect, beyond the survivor's guilt and apathy felt by *hibakusha,* their deadness of feeling (which Dr. Robert Jay Lifton explored in his book on Hiroshima, *Death in Life*), was a sense of guilt for sins of omission: what they had *not* done to help their neighbors in the midst of this unthinkable catastrophe. In the animal panic of fire from the sky, searing heat and unnatural winds, they had reflexively thought only of saving themselves—even before their wives and children or neighbors. Those guilt feelings, Nagai writes, were the bomb's most lingering effect, even beyond the radiation sickness. Here is Nagai prophesying what will happen in a future nuclear war:

> They are going to flee their cities and abandon their civilizations. They are going to dig into hillsides and hole up in mountain caves like beasts. They are going to go mad of fear without surcease.
>
> And the fact that they survived when friends and loved ones died; that, when faced by the grim choice, they left these to perish that their own skins might be saved; they loved not their neighbor—will press ever down upon their souls.

The bomb, some historians say, had been unnecessary; the destruction of Hiroshima, snuffing out eighty thousand lives, was sufficient demonstration of the lethality of America's superweapon. The Nagasaki plutonium bomb (known as Fat Man) was part of a plan in place to drop America's two working bombs on two densely populated cities. The second was used automatically without any further debate among the president's advisers. The only issues that gave pause were meteorological: bad weather forced the authorities to move up the planned date. And then clouds over the bomber's target, Kokura, caused it to go on to the alternate target—Nagasaki.

As I said, because of the city's site in a valley among hills, parts of it were shielded by mountains from the blast and survived intact. But the concentrated fireball instantly vaporized many, and left an estimated seventy-four thousand dead. The "atomic disease" would kill thousands more.

Looking back across the years, I like to think of my visit to Nagasaki as an attempt to *bear witness*—however superficially—for the sake of the sad woman at the *ryokan* and for the sakes of all the *hibakusha* and the dead.

In traveling to this city, I had come to Ground Zero, a place of cataclysmic misery. All its history and vitality had been reduced to a blank gray field of ashes like the surface of the moon. And the ashes became the reliquary of the ashes of thousands of lives. As I stood near the ruins of the cathedral (or so I retroactively believe), I had also reached my personal Ground Zero—the beginning of the search for understanding of my times. And the beginning of the end of illusion.

To live means to submit to the destructive element. There is no choice; you're thrown into the sea. If you let go of your life preserver, if you stop swimming, you are lost.

You try not to be complicit, but sometimes you must or risk not being part of your times, not having lived. Life is learned through the living of it. Being an actor in history, being part of your times.

How little I knew sixty years ago when making the choices I did. Awareness is all . . .

—August 2012, New York City

NOTES

CHAPTER 1: VICTORY DREAMS

17   *"This is a great"*: Quoted in David McCullough, *Truman* (New York: Simon & Schuster, 1992), 462–463.

19   *more than twenty*: Andrea Elliott, "V-J Day Is Replayed, but the Lip-Lock's Tamer This Time," *New York Times*, August 15, 2005.

19   *"The girls were grabbing"*: Robert Billian, Rutgers Oral History Archives, oral history.rutgers.edu.

19   *"a bunch of people"*: Roy Hoopes, *Americans Remember the Home Front* (New York: Penguin, 2002), 243.

20   *"Ordinary manners"*: Thomas I. Emerson, *Young Lawyer for the New Deal* (Savage, MD: Roseman & Littlefield, 1991), 309.

20   *"You know, soldier"*: Quotes from *Yank*, September 7, 1945.

20   *"No Mardis Gras was"*: Ibid.

22   *"not much of a churchgoer"*: Hoopes, *Americans Remember*, 232.

23   *New York City*: Milton Lehman, "Red Oak Hasn't Forgotten," *Saturday Evening Post*, August 17, 1946.

24   *"For all ordinary"*: Rick Atkinson, *An Army at Dawn* (New York: Holt, 2002), 35.

25   *"It was hard"*: Interview with the late Rex Holmes by author and Rich Sternberg, July 2008.

25   *"Your brother is missing"*: All Red Oak quotes are from author interviews, July 2008, unless otherwise specified.

26   *"Maybe it was just"*: "'Happiest Day of My Life'; 2 Sons, Son-in Law Alive," unidentified clipping, Red Oak World War II museum.

26   *"stoic but hopeful"*: "County's Casualty List Stirs National Publicity," undated clipping from *Red Oak Express*, quoting a story in the *New York Herald Tribune*.

26   *"as close to any town"*: Quoted in Atkinson, *Army at Dawn*, 398.

26   *"I was hopeful"*: Studs Terkel, *The "Good War"* (New York: Pantheon, 1984), 487.

27   *"People would be"*: Cable Center Oral History Collection, Barco Library, www.cablecenter.com.

27   *"It was a good"*: Quoted in Ronald Shaffer, *Wings of Judgment* (New York: Oxford, 1985), 155.

27   *"I know I would"*: Quoted in Judy Barret Litoff and David C. Smith, eds., *Since You Went Away* (New York: Oxford, 1991), 276–277.

28   *"the forging of national"*: Glen H. Elder Jr., *Children of the Great Depression* (Boulder, CO: Westview, 1999), 295.

28   *The CCC provided*: Michael Sherry, *In the Shadow of War* (New Haven, CT: Yale, 1995), 22.

29   *"martial virtues"*: Ibid., 380.

30   *"By building airports"*: Quoted by Stuart Rosenblatt, "The FDR Jobs Program that Saved the Nation," *EIR*, September 12, 2008.

30   *"a thundering flood"*: Alfred Kazin, *On Native Grounds* (New York: Doubleday, 1956), 393.

31   *"Suddenly, in the army"*: Clancy Sigal, "D-Day: Remembering the Back Story," *Guardian*, June 6, 2011.

32   *"division of the world"*: Clayton R. Koppes and Gregory D. Black, *Hollywood Goes to War* (New York: Free Press, 1987), viii, 113, 324–328.

33   *"This was to be"*: Bruce Catton, *The War Lords of Washington* (New York: Harcourt, Brace, 1948), 194.

33   *"a war to create"*: Gerald D. Nash, *The American West Transformed* (Lincoln: University of Nebraska Press, 1985), 182.

34   *"Roosevelt had committed"*: Quoted in Elbert Thomas, *The Four Fears* (Chicago: Ziff-Davis, 1944), 106.

35   *"The object of"*: Quoted in Richard Polenberg, ed., *America at War* (Englewood Cliffs, NJ: Prentice-Hall, 1968), 153–162.

36   *"worldwide revolution even"*: Quoted in Murray Kempton, *Rebellions, Perversities and Main Events* (New York: Times Books, 1994), 429.

36   if Roosevelt *"spoke to"*: Quoted in Richard M. Freeland, *The Truman Doctrine and the Origins of McCarthyism* (New York: Knopf, 1982), 21.

36   *"The American soldier"*: Quoted in John Morton Blum, *V Was for Victory* (New York: Harcourt, 1976), 89.

Voices

38   *Because hope and*: Alfred Hayes, *The Girl on the Via Flaminia* (New York: Harper, 1949), 70.

38   *"What did the lieutenant"*: Harry Brown, *A Walk in the Sun* (New York: Knopf, 1944), 14.

38   *There are some*: Jim Thompson, *Nothing More than Murder* (New York: Vintage, 1991), 86.

38   *"I'll get by"*: Fred E. Ahlert and Roy Turk, "I'll Get By" (1928).

CHAPTER 2: D.O.A.

41   *"Down in the lower"*: Meyer Berger, "400,000 in Silent Tribute as War Dead Come Home," *New York Times,* October 27, 1947.

41   *"The silence was awesome"*: Ibid.

42   at least four grieving people: See Fran Schumer, "After a Death, the Pain that Doesn't Go Away," *New York Times,* November 29, 2009.

42, 43 *"It took away," "are the ones"*: Charles M. Tuttle, *"Daddy's Gone to War"* (New York: Oxford, 1993), 46–47.

43   *"and it was too"*: Ella Leffland, *Rumors of Peace* (New York: Harper & Row, 1957), 51–52.

44   *"they, and their loss"*: Drew Gilpin Faust, *This Republic of Suffering* (New York: Knopf, 2008), 101.

44   *"'Tell me about my boy'"*: US Army Quartermaster Corps, 1946.

46   *"I remember the first"*: Rutgers Oral History Archives, oralhistory.rutgers.edu.

46   *"You realize," "Could you tell"*: Quoted in Litoff and Smith, *Since,* 233–235.

48   *"embarrassing," "that are contaminated"*: Quoted in Michael Sledge, *Soldier Dead* (New York: Columbia University Press, 2005), 229.

48   *"Yesterday a small"*: Lewis Mumford, *My Works and Days* (New York: Harcourt Brace Jovanovich, 1979), 400–401.

49   *"interferes with"*: Quoted in Sledge, *Soldier Dead,* 224.

50   *"Sweating American soldiers"*: Quoted in Steere, Edward and Boardman, Thayer M., "Final Disposition of World War II Dead 1945–51," US Army, Quartermaster Corps, QMC Historical Studies, series II, no. 4 (Washington, DC: Historical Branch Office of the Quartermaster General, 1957), 402.

51   *"betokened military might"*: Michael Sherry, "Death Mourning and Memorial Culture," in Mark C. Carnes, ed., *The Columbia History of Post–World War II America* (New York: Columbia University Press, 2007), 156–157.

51   *"the definitive collective"*: John Bodnar, *The "Good War" in American Memory* (Baltimore: Johns Hopkins, 2010), 88.

52   *"not only," "This memorial"*: Ibid., 91.

52   *"What kind of war"*: Ibid.

53   *"he who has not accepted"*: Mumford, 400.

53   *"in such monstrous infinity"*: David Nichols, ed. *Ernie's War* (New York: Random House, 1986).

53   *"The real war was"*: Paul Fussell, *Wartime* (New York: Oxford, 1989), 269.

55   *"realistic," "grim and grizzly [sic]"*: Quoted in Sheri Chinen Biesen, *Blackout* (Baltimore: Johns Hopkins, 2005), 192.

55   *"lusty-hard-boiled"*: Ibid., 192–193.

55   lurid Hollywood invention: John Houseman, "Today's Hero: A Review," *Hollywood Quarterly,* vol. 2, no. 2 (January 1947), in Eric Smoodin and Ann Martin, eds., *Hollywood Quarterly: Film Culture in Postwar America 1945–1957* (Berkeley: University of California, 2002), 259–262.

56   *"what everyone knew"*: Quoted in Biesen, *Blackout,* 68–69.

57   *"at bottom no one"*: Sigmund Freud, "Thoughts for the Times on War and Death," *Collected Papers*, vol. IV (London: Hogarth Press, 1925), 305.

58   *"knows and accepts"*: Quoted in John Costello, *Virtue Under Fire* (New York: International, 1987), 74.

58   *"The sadism of"*: David Thomson, quoted in Aljean Harmetz, "Richard Widmark, Actor, Dies at 93," *New York Times,* March 26, 2008.

59   *"radically different," "greed, criminality"*: Quoted in Lee Horsley, *The Noir Thriller* (London: Palgrave, 2001). One of the more subtle academic analysts of film and literary noir, Horsley writes, "Noir is 'the voice of violation,' acting to expose the inadequacy of conventional cultural, political and also narrative models. It expresses fears and anxieties but also has the potential for critique, for undermining complacency and illusions (the false promises of the American dream; the hypocrisy of the British establishment). The fact that film noir was created in the post-war United States is often attributed to an atmosphere in which American society 'came into a more critical focus.' More generally, the noir sensibility may come to the fore at any time of discontent and anxiety, of disillusionment with institutional structures and loss of confidence in the possibility of effective agency. . . . Literary like cinematic noir often moves towards a universal sense of absurdity—towards what Alfred Appel calls noir's 'black vision of despair, loneliness and dread—a vision that touches an audience most intimately because it assures that their suppressed impulses and fears are shared human responses.' But the immediate causes of pessimism and despair are grounded in the lies and corruptions of a particular milieu" (143–144).

59   *"Few cycles in the entire"*: Raymond Borde and Etienne Chaumeton, "Towards a Definition of *Film Noir*," in Alain Silver and James Ursini, eds., *The Film Noir Reader* (Popton Plains, NJ: Limelight, 1996), 19.

60   *"a world of obsessive return"*: James Naremore, *More Than Night* (Berkeley: University of California, 1998), 22–23.

60   *"no exit conclusion"*: Barbara Deming, *Running Away from Myself* (New York: Grossman, 1969), 131–132.

60   *"general sense of"*: Quoted in Paul Buhle and Dave Wagner, *Radical Hollywood* (New York: New Press, 2010), 359.

Voices

62   *Seldom, if ever:* Edward R. Murrow, quoted in Lynne Olson, *Citizens of London* (New York: Random House, 2010), 379.

62   *In a quaint:* Billy Reid, "The Gypsy" (1945).

62   *Detour, there's a muddy:* Paul Westmoreland, "Detour" (1945).

CHAPTER 3: RECONVERSION JITTERS

66   *"because it was"*: Quoted in Peter Bogdanovich, *Who the Devil Made It?* (New York: Knopf, 1997), 597.

66   *"In the absence"*: William S. Graebner, *The Age of Doubt* (Boston: Twayne, 1991), 104–105.

67   "Trav'lin down life's": Tex Williams, "Detour."

67   *"Yet once the war"*: John Gunther, *Inside USA* (New York: Harper, 1947), xii–xiii.

67   *"There's a lush"*: Quoted in James Boylan, *The New Deal Coalition and the Election of 1946* (New York: Garland, 1981), 20.

68   *"I began writing"*: Quoted in Elaine Showalter, *A Jury of her Peers* (New York: Knopf, 2009), 39.

69   *"After World War II"*: Linda Wertheimer interview, *Morning Edition* (NPR), October 11, 2010.

72   *"Our enormously productive"*: Quoted in Vance Packard, *The Waste Makers* (New York: McKay, 1960), 24.

72   "Hey everybody": Theard and Moore, "Let the Good Times Roll."

72   *The song:* Jim Daws and Steve Propes, *What Was the First Rock 'n Roll Record* (London: Faber & Faber, 1992).

73   *"the station was a major"*: John Broven, *Record Makers and Breakers* (Urbana: University of Illinois Press, 2010), 94.

73   *"The Honeydripper"*: Joe Liggis, "The Honeydripper" (1945).

76   *"If the threat"*: Abel Green and Joe Laurie Jr., *From Vaude to Video* (New York: Holt, 1951), 549.

77   *"after a conflict"*: Maurice Horn, ed., *The World Encyclopedia of Comics* (New York: Chelsea House, 1976), 27.

78   *"The business community"*: Russell Porter, "Business Booms in Middle West," *New York Times,* December 17, 1946.

79   *"in the pleasant"*: Quoted in Robert M. Hathaway, *Ambiguous Partnership: Britain and America 1944–1947* (New York: Columbia University Press, 1981), 23.

79   *average family incomes: Encyclopedia of Social History,* vol. I, 207.

80   *"After the demobilization"*: Robert Nathan interview, Columbia Oral History Collection.

81   *"by the hundred"*: Quoted by Henry A. Wallace, *Toward World Peace* (New York: Reynal and Hitchcock, 1948), 77.

81   *"an inflationary joy-ride"*: Chester Bowles, "Bowles Answers Six Vital Questions," *New York Times Sunday Magazine,* March 24, 1946.

81   *"The Congress are"*: Quoted in McCullough, *Truman,* 47.

82   *"The affluent went"*: Boylan, *The New Deal Coalition,* 56.

83   *"has opposed every"*: Barton J. Bernstein and Allen J Matusow, eds., *The Truman Administration: A Documentary History* (New York: Harper & Row, 1966), 84.

83   *"sucked livestock"*: Quoted in Boylan, *The New Deal Coalition,* 63.

85   *"It is questionable"*: John Fenton, *In Your Opinion* (Boston: Little, Brown, 1960), 5.

85   *"The general tenor"*: Ibid., 93.

85   *"a permanent war economy"*: Charles E. Wilson, "For the Common Defense, a Plea for a Continuing Program of Industrial Preparedness," *Army Ordnance,* vol. XVI, no. 143 (March/April 1944).

86   *"substantially exceeded"*: Ruben Trevino and Robert Higgs, "Profits of U.S. Defence Contractors," *Defence and Peace Economics,* vol. III, no. 3 (October 19, 2007).

86   *"become as political"*: Jordan Schwarz, *The New Dealers* (New York: Knopf, 1993), 284.

86   *"an apologist for"*: Emerson, *Young Lawyer,* 297–298.

87   *one called L-41:* Ibid., 315.

87   *"one of the first"*: Ibid.

88   *He preferred:* See Schwarz, *The New Dealers,* 325.

88   *Suburban Dream:* See Kenneth T. Jackson, *Crabgrass Frontier* (New York: Oxford, 1985), 237.

88   *Levittown:* See David Halberstam, *The Fifties* (New York: Villard, 1993), 134–135.

89   *"We can solve"*: Quoted in Jackson, *Crabgrass,* 241.

89   *"By the mid-1980s"*: Caroll Pursell, *The Machine in America* (Baltimore: Johns Hopkins, 1995), 282.

90   *"I've often said"*: Robert Nathan interview, Columbia Oral History Collection.

90   *"OWMR's mandated function"*: Emerson, *Young Lawyer,* 311.

90   *"Whenever an issue"*: Ibid., 313.

91   *"and was trying"*: Quoted in Nelson Lichtenstein, *The Most Dangerous Man in Detroit* (New York: Basic, 1991), 227.

93   *"Many people had"*: Nathan interview, Columbia Oral History Collection.

94   *"The free market"*: Kim Phillips-Fein, *Invisible Hands* (New York: Norton, 2009), 60.

94   *"The joining of New"*: Eric Goldman, *The Crucial Decade—and After* (New York: Vintage, 1956), 121.

95   *"a stringent but fair"*: "Chamber Opens Campaign to Oust Reds in U.S. Posts," *New York Times,* October 10, 1946.

96   *the FBI started using:* See Ellen Schrecker, *Many Are the Crimes* (Princeton, NJ: Princeton University Press, 1998), 42.

96   *"The situation changed"*: Quoted in Lyle W. Shannon, "The Opinions of Little Orphan Annie and her Friends," *Public Opinion Quarterly,* vol. 18 (1954), 169–179. In Bernard Rosenberg and David Manning White, eds., *Mass Culture* (New York: Free Press, 1965), 212.

96   *"Never forget the fact"*: Quoted in Ellen Schrecker, *The Age of McCarthyism: A Brief History with Documents* (Boston: St. Martin's, 1994), 123, 125.

98   *"The central role"*: Harold G. Vatter, *The U.S. Economy in World War II* (New York: Columbia University Press, 1985), 149.

98   *"in the direction of socialism"*: Lary May, *The Big Tomorrow* (Chicago: University of Chicago, 2000), 168–169.

99   *"was designed," "The 21-point program"*: Emerson, *Young Lawyer,* 325.

100   *"The 21-point program"*: Ibid., 327.

100   *"is really 'crisis'"*: Ibid., 329.

100   *"Without an economic"*: Quoted in Boylan, *The New Deal Coalition,* 22.

100   *"Personally, I think"*: Samuel Rosenman interview, Columbia Oral History Col-
        lection, 65.

100   *"laid out the"*: Alonzo Hamby, *Liberalism and Its Challengers: From FDR to Reagan*
        (New York: Oxford, 1992), 91–92.

101   *"Socialized medicine"*: Quoted in Stephen J. Whitfield, *The Culture of the Cold
        War* (Baltimore: Johns Hopkins, 1991), 23.

101   *"the bill offered clues"*: Boylan, *The New Deal Coalition,* 22–23.

101   *"was devastating"*: Emerson, *Young Lawyer,* 328.

101   civil rights–based liberalism: See Alan Brinkley, *The End of Reform* (New York:
        Knopf, 1995), 10.

102   *"the beliefs of the"*: Charles Bolte, *The New Veteran* (New York: Reynal & Hitch-
        cock, 1945), 76.

102   *"Giving each soldier"*: Dixon Wecter, *When Johnny Comes Marching Home*
        (Boston: Houghton, 1944), 523.

102   *"It was clear"*: James MacGregor Burns, *Roosevelt: Soldier of Freedom* (New York:
        Harcourt, 1970), 362.

103   *"The veteran who"*: Quoted in Glenn C. Altschuler and Stuart M. Blumin, *The
        GI Bill* (New York: Oxford, 2009), 29.

103   *"kind of entering"*: Ibid., 45; Samuel Rosenman, *Working with Roosevelt* (New
        York: Harper, 1952), 194–195.

104   *"never seen the veterans"*: Altschuler and Blumin, *The GI Bill,* 58.

105   *"consistently and perhaps"*: Suzanne Mettler, *The G.I. Bill and the Making of the
        Greatest Generation* (New York: Oxford, 2005), 77.

106   unskilled workers prospered: See Joseph Stiglitz, *The Price of Inequality* (New York:
        Norton, 2012), 55.

Voices

107   *"We kind of thought"*: William McGivern, *Heaven Ran Last* (New York: Dodd,
        Mead, 1949), 73.

107   *"There was a"*: Terkel, *The "Good War,"* 308.

107   *"After the whole"*: Sloan Wilson, *The Man in the Gray Flannel Suit* (New York:
        Simon & Schuster, 1955), 69.

107   *"He's stone cold"*: Wilmoth Houdini, "Stone Cold Dead in the Market" (1946).

107   *"Momma's on the"*: Lionel Hampton and Curley Hamner, "Hey Ba-Ba-Re-Bop"
        (1946).

CHAPTER 4: "HOME STRANGE HOME"

109   *"A General Electric"*: Richard Goldstein, *Helluva Town* (New York: Free Press,
        2010), 260.

110   *"It was no"*: Quoted in Godfrey Hodgson, *America in Our Time* (New York:
        Doubleday, 1976), 22.

113   *"He . . . has lost his"*: Quoted by Kaja Silverman, "Historical Trauma and Male
        Subjectivity," in E. Ann Kaplin, ed., *Psychoanalysis & Cinema* (London:

Routledge, 1990). Silverman quotes Siegfried Kracauer (of interest because of his study of the German cinema between the wars, *From Caligari to Hitler*) on the returning vets in *The Best Years of Our Lives*: "Visionless, at the mercy of any wind, benumbed even in their lovemaking, they drift about in a daze bordering on stupor. . . . It is as if those Innocents had been dragged out of their enchanted universe to face the world as it actually is—a world not in the least responsive to their candid dreams and hopes. The guise of the discharged soldier assures us that they are no average individuals, stunned by the shock of readjustment" (118).

113   *"I realized that"*: Eugene B. Sledge, *With the Old Breed at Peleliu and Okinawa* (Annapolis, MD: Naval Institute, 1981), 98.

114   *Others considered*: Ibid., 266.

114   *"We were under," "It took him," "in a different"*: Author interviews.

115   *half the respondents*: Fenton, *In Your Opinion*, 32.

115   *"The war was fun"*: Terkel, *The "Good War,"* 10.

115   *"After seeing this"*: James Agee, *Agee on Film* (Boston: Beacon Press, 1958), 236.

117   *"To a surprising extent"*: Bodnar, *The "Good War" in American Memory*, 157.

118   *"The trick is to"*: Wilson, *Gray Flannel Suit*, 164.

118   *veteran's journey of return*: Frank Krutnik, *In a Lonely Street* (London: Routledge, 1991), 65.

120   *Bob Moore*: See Stephen Buttry, "An American Story," *Omaha World Herald*, November 9, 1997. Villisca Review.com.

121   *"After the urgent"*: Lori Rotskoff, *Love on the Rocks* (Chapel Hill: University of North Carolina, 2002), 91.

126   *"find meaning in the"*: Abraham Polonsky, *The Case of David Smith, Hollywood Quarterly*, vol I, no. 2 (January 1946), Smoodin and Martin, *Hollywood Quarterly*, 134–135. See also Paul Buhle and Dave Wagner, *A Very Dangerous Citizen: Abraham Polonsky and the Hollywood Left* (Los Angeles: University of California, 2001), 77–78.

127   *"The Coming Veteran"*: Quoted in Thomas Childers, *Soldier from the War Returning* (New York: Houghton, 2009), 131.

127   *"12 Slain by Berserk Veteran"*: *Spokane Daily Chronicle*, September 6, 1949.

127   *"Bodies were strewn"*: *Tri-City Herald*, September 6, 1949.

128   *"When they come"*: Quoted in Joseph C. Goulden, *The Best Years* (New York: Atheneum, 1976), 47.

128   *"floating in a vacuum," "A lot of things," "We are running"*: Quoted in Childers, *Soldier*, 7, 210–211.

128   *"one of the biggest"*: Quoted in Rebecca Jo Plant, "The Veteran, His Wife and Their Mothers: Prescriptions for Psychological Rehabilitation after World War II," unpublished paper. Plant is the author of *Mom: The Transformation of Motherhood in Modern America* (Chicago: University of Chicago, 2010).

128   *"redolent of the betrayal"*: Tod DePastino, *Bill Mauldin* (New York: Norton, 2008), 220.

128   *"Pre-War Quality"*: Mauldin, *Back Home*, 134.

129   *"There's a small item"*: Bill Mauldin, *Back Home* (New York: Sloane, 1947), 54.

130 *"turning point in their lives"*: Mettler, *The G.I. Bill and the Making*, 68.

130 *"The war changed"*: Terkel, *The "Good War,"* 12.

130 *"thought of the G.I. Bill"*: Mettler, *The G.I. Bill and the Making*, 153.

131 *"a three-button"*: Quoted in *Time*, July 23, 1951.

132 *"We were driving"*: Mettler, *The G.I. Bill and the Making*, 63.

132 A June 1947 survey: See Blum, *V Was for Victory*, 339.

132 *one-fourth of the US population*: Ibid., 339; see also Altschuler and Blumin, *The GI Bill*, 8.

132 *divorce*: See Childers, *Soldier*, 114–115.

133 *"We were uprooted"*: Quoted in Goldstein, *Helluva Town*, 176–177.

134 *"Perhaps some men"*: Fulano de Tal, "Trends in Homicide Rates in the United States," Rutgers University. http://crab.rutgers.edu/~goertzel/FulanosPage.html.

134 *"Many American war"*: Anne Leighton, "The American Matron and the Lillies," *Harper's*, December 1946.

134 *"to a wife"*: Polonsky, "The Case of David Smith."

134 *"While Gil was"*: Author interview.

135 *"The American Woman"*: Victor Dallaire, *New York Times Sunday Magazine*, March 10, 1946.

135 *"defeminize"*: Ferdinand Lundberg and Marynia Farnham, *Modern Woman* (New York: Harper & Brothers, 1947).

135 *"'domineering' women"*: May, *Homeward Bound*, 90.

135 *"impossible to estimate"*: Quoted by Stephen J. Whitfield II, "The Culture of the Cold War," in Christopher Bigsby, ed., *The Cambridge Companion to Modern American Culture* (Cambridge: Cambridge University Press, 2006), 186.

136 *"These women deserve"*: Quoted in Goulden, *The Best Years*, 43.

136, 137 *"short-lived adventures," "enthusiastically," "Marriage is"*: Quoted in Childers, *Soldier*, 196–197.

137 *"We youth, all of"*: Quoted in Elder, *Children of the Great Depression*, 197.

138 *"The important thing"*: Wilson, *Gray Flannel Suit*, 165.

139 *"women who grew"*: Elder, *Children of the Great Depression*, 239.

139 *"For all the publicity"*: May, *Homeward Bound*, 75.

139 *"There must be*: Ibid., 74.

140 *"force wives and"*: Quoted in Krutnik, *Lonely Street*, 81.

140 *"many who had left," "Drop in Women Workers"*: *New York Times*, October 13, 1946.

141 *"affluent domesticity"*: May, *Homeward Bound*, 76–77, 79.

141 *"looked toward home"*: Ibid., 91.

Voices

142 *"Sit down, sit"*: Horace McCoy, *Kiss Tomorrow Goodbye* (London; New York: Serpent's Tail, 1949), 309–310.

142 *"We know there"*: Quoted in Boylan, *The New Deal Coalition*, 209.

CHAPTER 5: THE BIG WALKOUT

143   *"Fifty-two for Forty"*: *New York Times*, September 30, 1945.

143   *"These hearings"*: Louis Stark, "Labor's Mood Turns More Jittery," *New York Times*, October 1, 1945.

145   *Philip Murray*: "Text of Murray's Radio Address," Ibid., January 22, 1946.

145   *"You are on your"*: Quoted in Lichtenstein, *Most Dangerous*, 101.

145   *"We must move"*: Quoted in Steve Fraser and Gary Gerstle, *The Rise and Fall of the New Deal Order* (Princeton, NJ: Princeton University Press, 1989), 78.

146   *Polls showed that*: Lichtenstein, *Most Dangerous*, 238.

146   *"part of a long-term"*: Jeremy Brecher, *Strike!* (Boston: South End, 1997), 244.

146   *"The plain fact was"*: Quoted in Goulden, *The Best Years*, 118.

147   *"American business must"*: Quoted in Lichtenstein, *Most Dangerous*, 229.

147   *"He understood that"*: Ibid., 228.

148   *"The war, with"*: Ibid., 218.

148   *"The strategy was"*: Quoted in Nelson Lichtenstein, *State of the Unions* (Princeton, NJ: Princeton University Press, 2002), 116.

148   *"a man of persistent"*: Quoted in Lichtenstein, *Most Dangerous*, 227.

148   *"the decisive style"*: Quoted in McCullough, *Truman*, 471.

148   *"People began to suspect"*: Quoted in Boylan, *The New Deal Coalition*, 65.

149   *"I don't want to"*: Emerson, *Young Lawyer*, 318.

149   *"betrayal"*: Lichtenstein, *Most Dangerous*, 243.

150   *"I will be God damned"*: Ibid., 243.

150   *"It was on the whole"*: Quoted in Brecher, *Strike!*, 247.

151   *"No rolling stock"*: Meyer Berger, "Commuters Flee City Before Strike," *New York Times*, May 24, 1946.

151   *"one of the most"*: Quoted in McCullough, *Truman*, 500.

151   *"which were worse," "week-kneed"*: Ibid.

152   *"fascism may grip"*: Quoted in Boylan, *The New Deal Coalition*, 46.

152   *"Draft men who"*: Quoted in McCullough, *Truman*, 506.

152   *"impulse to apply"*: Sherry, *Shadow of War*, 123.

153   *"an evil, demoniac"*: Quoted in McCullough, *Truman*, 126.

153   *"John L. had to"*: Ibid., 127.

153   *"From this point"*: Quoted in Lichtenstein, *Most Dangerous*, 247.

154   *"unionists who fatten"*: Ibid.

154   *"the outcome in the postwar"*: Alan Derickson, "The United Steelworkers of America and Health Insurance, 1937–1962," in Sally M. Miller and David Cornfeld, eds., *American Labor in the Era of World War II* (New York: Praeger, 1995), 70.

155   *purge Communist*: Walter W. Ruch, "UAW Ousts Addes," *New York Times*, November 12, 1947.

155   *"strait jacket that"*: Lichtenstein, *Most Dangerous*, 261–262.

156   *"all forms of discrimination"*: Quoted in Walter W. Ruch, "CIO Will Seek End of South's Poll Tax," *New York Times*, April 11, 1946.

157   *"energies struggling for integration"*: Quoted in Howard Sitkoff, "African American Militancy in the World War II South," in Neil R. McMillen, ed., *Remak-*

  ing Dixie: The Impact of World War II on the American South (Jackson: University of Mississippi Press, 1997).

158 *resounding defeat:* See Willard Shelton, "Why 'Operation Dixie' Failed," *The Nation,* April 29, 1950.

159 *"They mobilized the towns":* Quoted in Barbara S. Griffith, *The Crisis of American Labor* (Philadelphia: Temple University Press, 1988), 88.

159 *"race-conscious radicalism":* William Jones, "Black Workers and the CIO's Turn Toward Racial Liberalism: Operation Dixie and the North Carolina Lumber Industry, 1946–1953," *Labor History,* vol. 41, no. 3 (2000).

160 *"damned beefsteak election":* Quoted in McCullough, *Truman,* 520.

160 *"public disillusionment with":* Fenton, *In Your Opinion,* 50.

160 *"so divided between":* Quoted in McCullough, *Truman,* 521.

160 *"a stark choice":* Quoted in Griffith, *Crisis of American Labor,* 144.

160 *"hatred of communism":* Quoted in McCullough, *Truman,* 521.

162 *"The argument that proved":* Freeland, *The Truman Doctrine,* 68.

163 *"a vote against":* Quoted in Griffith, *Crisis of American Labor,* 144.

163 *"Jerry is not":* Quoted in Boylan, *The New Deal Coalition,* 138.

163 *"he was more popular":* Quoted in Fenton, *In Your Opinion,* 46.

164 *"The Depression was over":* Boylan, *The New Deal Coalition,* 192.

165 *the New Deal built:* Jordan Schwartz, *The New Dealers,* 345.

165 *"from the politics":* Bernstein and Matusow, eds., *The Truman Administration,* 84.

165 *"enhanced the value":* Elder, *Children of the Great Depression,* 296.

Voices

166 *"Writers I consider":* Quoted in Gerald Horne, *Class Struggle in Hollywood* (Austin: University of Texas, 2001), 88.

166 *"You also have to":* Quoted in Paul Buhle and Dave Wagner, *Tender Comrades* (New York: St. Martin's, 1997), 488.

166 *"Alien-minded communistic":* Quoted in Jennifer E. Langdon, *Caught in the Crossfire* (New York: Columbia University Press, 2008), 7.

166 *"I am a witch hunter":* Quoted in Joseph McBride, *Frank Capra* (New York: Simon & Schuster, 1992), 244.

166 *"Q. When you wrote":* "Excerpts From Secret Senate Testimony Before Senator Joseph McCarthy's Subcommittee," *New York Times,* May 6, 2003.

166 *"I would prefer":* Quoted in McBride, *Frank Capra,* 244.

CHAPTER 6: RED DAWN ON SUNSET STRIP

167 *"feel directly connected":* Michael Denning, *The Cultural Front* (New York: Verso, 1998), 90.

169 *"the entire official":* Mike Nielsen and Gene Mailes, *Hollywood's Other Blacklist* (London: British Film Institute, 1995), x.

170 *"the closest thing":* Ibid., 92.

171 *"fifty goons," "people's heads":* Quoted in Horne, *Class Struggle,* 183.

172   *"In the third week":* Ibid., 150.

173   *Joe Touhy:* See Otto Friedrich, *City of Nets* (New York: Harper & Row, 1986), 281.

174   *"If they want," "lacked leftist grounding":* Quoted in Horne, *Class Struggle,* 17.

175   *"an identity crisis":* Edmund Morris, *Dutch* (New York: Random House, 1999), 231–35; May, *Big Tomorrow,* 190–191.

176   *"The weakening," "It revealed how":* Nielsen and Mailes, *Hollywood's Other Blacklist,* 167, 169.

176   *"Hollywood labor history":* Dennis Broe, *Film Noir, American Workers, and Postwar Hollywood* (Gainesville: University Press of Florida, 2009), 35.

176   *"The main action":* Ibid., xxiv.

177   *"outsider figure lacking":* Quoted, ibid., 49.

177   The Long Night: See Buhle and Wagner, *Radical Hollywood,* 357.

178   *"The 1947 congressional":* Denning, *The Cultural Front,* 89.

178   *"The people who":* Quoted in Buhle and Wagner, *Radical Hollywood,* 477.

179   *"to extend every," "may possess," "two cliques":* Quoted in Athan Theoharis and John Stuart Cox, *The Boss* (Philadelphia: Temple University Press, 1988), 254–255.

179   Red Channels: See Victor Navasky, *Naming Names* (New York: Viking, 1980), 97.

180   *"near treasonable," "the rich," "anti-Semitism":* Quoted in J. Hoberman, *An Army of Phantoms* (New York: New Press, 2011), 50–51.

181   *"a sorry performance":* Quoted in Friedrich, *City of Nets,* 326.

182   *"Has the screen":* Quoted in Hoberman, *Army of Phantoms,* 74.

182   *According to Jon Lewis's:* See Jon Lewis, *Hollywood v. Hardcore* (New York: New York University Press, 2000).

183   *"We'll have no":* Quoted in May, *Big Tomorrow,* 177.

183   *screen content:* Ibid., 204–205.

183   *"personal relations became":* Sayre, *Running Time,* 102.

184   *Broe calculates:* Broe, *Film Noir,* 96.

185   *"The raw data":* Langdon, *Caught in the Crossfire,* 78.

187   *"They looked like":* Quoted in Frank MacShane, *The Life of Raymond Chandler* (New York: Dutton, 1976), 121.

189   *"The blacklist itself":* Navasky e-mail to author, December 2010.

189   *"During the 1950s":* James Naremore, *More Than Night* (Berkeley: University of California, 1998), 104.

189   *"a genre," "expressed the artists'":* Buhle and Wagner, *Radical Hollywood,* 308, 321.

189   *"It was easier":* Carlos Clarens, *Crime Movies* (New York: Da Capo / Perseus, 1980), 195–196.

190   *"All films about":* Quoted in May, *Big Tomorrow,* 226.

190   *"Having reached the":* Quoted by Eric Sherman and Martin Rubin, *The Director's Event: Interviews with Five American Film-Makers* (New York: Athenaeum, 1969), 16.

190   *"Noir etched," "rain-slicked streets":* Quoted in Lisa Maria Hoagland, afterword to Dorothy B. Hughes, *In a Lonely Place* (New York: Feminist Press, 2003), 244.

Voices

192   "The story of our": Quoted in MacShane, *Raymond Chandler*, 103.

CHAPTER 7: URBAN NOIR

193   "the exiles Hitler": Quoted in Nash, *American West*, 187.

193   "As no other": Ibid., 198.

195   "absolute waste of time": Quoted in Dinitia Smith, "Book Details U.S. Spying on Wartime Exiles From Germany," *New York Times*, August 30, 2000.

195   "The sensibility": Gerd Gemünden, *A Foreign Affair: Billy Wilder's American Films* (Brooklyn/Oxford: Berghahn Books, 2008), 34.

196   "This image of": Ibid.

197   "Many of these": Biesen, *Blackout*, 51.

197   "At Warners, a studio": Friedrich, *City of Nets*, 82.

197   "It's more dramatic": Bogdanovich, *Who the Devil*, 343.

198   "suffers only from": Quoted, ibid., 172.

199   "was a French": Bogdanovich, *Who the Devil*, 343.

200   "a combination of": Quoted in Horsley, *Noir Thriller*, xi; see also Charles Higham and Joel Greenberg, *Hollywood in the Forties* (New York: A.S. Barnes, 1968), 37; May, *Big Tomorrow*, 229.

200   "meant to cover": Quoted in "Here's Looking at Him," *New York Times Book Review*, February 6, 2011.

201   "Their faces barely": Foster Hirsch, *The Dark Side of the Screen: Film Noir* (New York: Da Capo Press, 1981), 147.

201   "stands as the only": Quoted in Nicholas Christopher, *Somewhere in the Night* (New York: Free Press, 1997), 191.

205   "We have radiated," "the grim": Quoted in Nash, *American West*, 183–185.

205   "a landmark in the fog": Quoted in Buhle and Wagner, *Dangerous Citizen*, 293.

206   "factual American themes": Quoted in Broe, *Film Noir*, 43.

206   "It was a picture," "You never realized": Quoted in Biesen, *Blackout*, 108.

208   "The black-and-white": Jed Perl, *New Art City* (New York: Knopf, 2005), 70.

209   "hated the doleful": Oral history interview with Carl Holty, December 8, 1964, Archives of American Art, Smithsonian Institution.

210   "The fact that good": Quoted in B.H. Friedman, *Jackson Pollock* (New York: McGraw-Hill, 1972), 61–62.

210   "scribbling or doodling": Robert Hobbs, "Early Abstract Expressionism and Surrealism," "New York City in the '40s," chum338.blogs.wesleyan.edu.

211   "Every one of us": Quoted in Perl, *New Art City*, 61.

211   "cannot understand how": Quoted, ibid., 57.

211   "I want to express": Quoted on *The Fishko File* (WNYC), October 1, 2010.

211   "a mind musing over": Perl, *New Art City*, 191.

211   "Abstract expressionism became": Erika Doss, *Benton, Pollock, and the Politics of Modernism* (Chicago: University of Chicago, 1991), 216.

213   "Southern trees bear": Abel Meeropol (Lewis Allan), "Strange Fruit" (1939).

213   "You felt great energy": Quoted in Broven, *Record Makers*, 53–54.

214   *"emotional autobiography"*: Quoted in Bill Pronzini, foreword to David Goodis, *Nightfall* (Lakewood, CO: Centipede Press, 2007), 12.

216   *"a citizenry that questions"*: Smoodin and Martin, eds., *Hollywood Quarterly,* 114.

216   *"Manhattan already knew"*: Jan Morris, *Manhattan '45* (New York: Oxford, 1987), 7.

216   *"Between the end"*: Robert Scheer, "Gore Vidal: Living through History," *Truth Dig,* November 21, 2006.

217   *"If you don't watch"*: Tennessee Williams, Quoted in Joseph Wood Krutch, *"Modernism" in Modern Drama* (Ithaca, NY: Cornell University Press, 1953), 129.

218, 219   *"People in uniform were," "the rowdy, noisy GIs"*: Quoted in Goldstein, *Helluva Town,* 172.

220   *"He didn't talk"*: Quoted in McBride, *Frank Capra,* 508.

221   *"a world of obsessive return"*: Naremore, *More Than Night,* 22–23.

221   *"to escape a condition"*: Barbara Deming, *Running Away,* 326.

221   *"nostalgic and amusing"*: Agee, *Agee on Film,* 238.

222   *"a skinful of whiskey"*: Houseman, "Today's Hero," 259–262.

222   *"The 'tough' movie"*: Ibid.

223   *"pointless, trashy yarn"*: "The Screen: A Quartet of Newcomers Arrives," *New York Times,* June 10, 1950.

224   *"A sense of isolation"*: Quoted by Richard Dooling, introduction to Cornell Woolrich, *Rendezvous in Black* (New York: Modern Library, 2004), xv.

224   *"The path you"*: Quoted by Woody Haut, *Heartbreak and Vine* (London: Serpent's Tail, 2002), 116.

228   The Snake Pit: See Ben Harris, "Arthur Laurents' Snake Pit: Populist Entertainment in Post–WWII America," paper presented at the annual meeting of the American Studies Association, Philadelphia Marriott Downtown, Philadelphia, October 11, 2007. www.allacademic.com/meta/p186338 _index.html.

229   *"undergoing a secret"*: McBride, *Frank Capra,* 519–520.

229   *"gave him a new," "He wasn't fighting"*: Ibid., 504–505.

231   *"sizable doses"*: See Brian Neve, "The Hollywood Left: Robert Rossen and Postwar Hollywood," *Film Studies,* no. 7 (Winter 2005), 59.

233   *"translating the novella"*: James Naremore, "Orson Welles's *Heart of Darkness,*" *La Furia Umana* website.

237   *"the Verdoux home"*: Agee, *Agee on Film,* 25.

238   *"'Monsieur Verdoux'" is an"*: Bosley Crowther, "Charles Chaplin in 'Monsieur Verdoux' Returns for First Time Since '47," *New York Times,* July 4, 1964.

238   *Chaplin exiled himself:* See Carl Bromley, ed., *Cinema Nation* (New York: Thunders Mouth/Nation Books, 2000), 46–47.

Voices

239   *"The twentieth century"*: Marianna Torgovnick, *The War Complex* (Chicago: University of Chicago, 2005), 347.

239   *"The fighting of"*: Vance Bourjaily, *The Hound of Earth* (New York: Dial, 1964), 35.

239   *"Many historians have"*: E. L. Doctorow, *The Book of Daniel* (New York: Random House, 1971), 23.

239   *"And after the Japs"*: Richard Brooks, *The Brick Foxhole* (New York: Harper, 1945), 10.

239   *"Five percent of"*: Terkel, *The "Good War,"* 329.

239   *"I used to say"*: Henry Wallace, oral history, 5,071.

CHAPTER 8: THE GUNS OF MARCH

241   *"going back to bed"*: Walter Millis, ed., *The Forrestal Diaries* (New York: Viking, 1951), 100.

242   *Most Americans thought*: Samuel Stouffer, *Communism, Conformity and Civil Liberties* (New Brunswick, NJ: Transaction, 1992), 187.

242   *"cooperate with us"*: George H. Quester, "Origins of the Cold War," *Political Science Quarterly*, vol. 91, no. 4 (Winter 1978).

242   *"probably the most"*: Quoted in John Acacia, *Clark Clifford* (Lexington: University Press of Kentucky, 2009), 37.

243   *"essentially ended its"*: Townsend Hoopes and Douglas Brinkley, *Driven Patriot* (New York: Knopf, 1992), 257.

244   *"the opening gun"*: Quoted in Acacia, *Clark Clifford*, 67.

244   *"a prototype for"*: Elizabeth Edwards Spalding, *The First Cold Warrior* (Lexington: University Press of Kentucky, 2006), 59.

245   *"cut in half"*: Quoted in Arnold A. Offner, *Another Such Victory* (Stanford, CA: Stanford University Press, 2002), 204.

245   *"If Greece should," "I believe"*: Ibid., 207.

245   *"The attempt of Lenin"*: Quoted in Julian Zelizer, *Arsenal of Democracy* (New York: Basic Books, 2010), 70.

246   *"too broad"*: Quoted in Acacia, *Clark Clifford*, 70.

246   *"only leading us"*: Quoted in Spalding, *First Cold Warrior*, 91.

246   *"If we undertake"*: Quoted in Zelizer, *Arsenal*, 69.

246   *"The only way"*: Quoted in Robbie Lieberman, *The Strangest Dream* (Syracuse, NY: Syracuse University Press, 2000), 43.

246   *"the champion of"*: Quoted in Whitfield, *Culture*, 55.

246, 247 *"help save civilization," "Don't arrest"*: Quoted, ibid., 96.

249   *"At a time when"*: Hoopes and Brinkley, *Driven Patriot*, 259.

249   *"fundamentally a religion"*: Quoted, ibid., 262.

250   *"When Henry looks"*: Ibid., 263.

250   *"to forge a permanent"*: Sherry, *Shadow of War*, 124.

250   *"play the most important"*: David Thelen, "The Public Against the Historians: The Gallup Poll 1935–1971," *Reviews in American History*, vol. 4, no. 4. (December 1976).

250   *"closing the circle"*: Quoted in Frank Kofsky, *Harry S. Truman and the War Scare of 1948* (New York: St. Martin's, 1993), 27.

250   *"ill-advised in view"*: Ibid., 227.

251   "most critical immediate": Ibid., 29.

251   "a growing apathy": Ibid., 222.

252   Hitler was again: See Fenton, In Your Opinion, 68.

252   "The Soviet Union's": Quoted in Sherry, Shadow of War, 127.

253   "pull the trigger—start": Ibid., 73.

254   "reading Wallace out": Quoted in Robert A. Divine, "The Cold War and the
          Election of 1948," Journal of American History, vol. 59, no. 1 (June 1972).

254   "There is considerable political": Kofsky, War Scare, 92.

255   "a subtle change," "intense alarm": Quoted in Millis, ed., Forrestal Diaries, 387.

255   "various potentially": Ibid., 389.

255   "pitifully inadequate," "act immediately": "Byrnes Advocates 'Action on Russia,'"
          New York Times, March 14, 1948.

256   "Executive branch of the": Quoted in Kofsky, War Scare, 130.

256   "overexcitable statements": Ibid., 221.

256   "its decision to": Ibid., 221.

257   "full of rumors," "to restore them": Millis, ed., Forrestal Diaries, 394–395.

257   "I want a peace": Kofsky, War Scare, 166.

257   "The tensions we are": Ibid., 166.

258   "the changing tempo," "American tendency": Millis, ed., Forrestal Diaries, 444.

258   "seriously concerned about": Quoted in Kofsky, War Scare, 166, 222.

258   "the American public": Daniel Yergin, Shattered Peace (Boston: Houghton Mifflin,
          1977), 390.

258   "intensive rearmament," "one concession," "I found it": David Gergen, "Interview
          with George Kennan," MacNeil/Lehrer News Hour (PBS), April 18, 1996.

259   "government experts," "to identify": Saverio Giovacchini, Hollywood Modernism
          (Philadelphia: Temple University Press, 2001), 214.

260   "the public tends to" : Stouffer, Communism, Conformity, 18.

261   "sentimental, easygoing": Quoted in Lawrence Wittner, Rebels Against War
          (Philadelphia: Temple University Press, 1984), 63.

261   "a passive refusal": Ibid., 62.

262   "It is no longer": Ibid., 84.

263   "Prison provided a vital," "These demonstrations": Ibid., 92.

264   "twenty-six tests": Rustin-Peck report, FBI office memorandum, from SAC,
          New York, to Director, FBI, May 14, 1947.

264   "has caused a split," "Peck stood quietly": Ibid.

264   "Get those damn": FBI office memorandum, from SAC, Charlotte, NC, to Di-
          rector, FBI, April 23, 1947, 1–345–50.

265   "You don't want me," "One white woman": Ibid.

265   the "Racial and Industrial": Untitled FBI document, Pittsburgh, PA, April 4,
          1947.

266   "that a broad organized," "pretty thorough": Letters from Forrestal to Hoover,
          October 25, 1948, and November 16, 1948. FBI files.

266   "cancellation of such": Letter from Hoover to commissioner, February 9, 1949.

266, 267   "consult their consciences," "encourage the individual": Quoted in Wittner,
          Rebels, 187.

268   *"this all sounds"*: Letter in FBI files, October 5, 1948.

268   *"I am instructing"*: Memo from J. Edgar Hoover, October 12, 1948.

268   *"at times profoundly"*: US Army intelligence report, January 30, 1946.

268   *"a leader in the"*: Office of Naval Intelligence, March 16, 1956.

269   *"from within, by our"*: Quoted in Joanne Meyerowitz, ed., *Not June Cleaver: Women and Gender in Postwar America, 1945–1960* (Philadelphia: Temple University Press, 1994), 200, 134.

271   *"Those who want"*: Quoted in Lloyd J. Grabar and Ruth Flint Grabar, "America Faces the Atomic Age: 1946," *Air University Review* (January / February 1984).

272   *"The blood does not"*: Quoted in Paul Boyers, *By the Bomb's Early Light* (New York: Pantheon, 1985), 78.

272   *"Time is short"*: Ibid., 80.

272   *"was the quintessential"*: Ibid.

272   *"Their faces are open"*: Ibid., 60.

273   *"the brief interlude"*: Ibid., 81.

273   *"The only certain"*: Quoted in Merle Miller, "From a One-World Crusade . . . ," *New York Times Magazine*, January 7, 1973.

275   *"seem sort of official"*: Brooke Gladstone, interview with Greg Mitchell, *On the Media* (NPR), August 13, 2010.

275   *"That's ten days' more"*: Quoted in Boyers, *Bomb's Early Light*, 195.

276   *later science fiction films*: See Sayre, *Running Time*, 201.

276   *"obstructionists or troublesome"*: Ibid., 198.

277   Walk a Crooked Mile: Hoberman, *Army of Phantoms*, 84, fn. 11.

277   *A rancher reported*: Ibid., 44–45.

279   *"that certainly did not"*: Quoted in Millis, ed., *Forrestal Diaries*, 102.

279   *"I never saw a man"*: Quoted in Kai Bird and Martin J. Sherwin, *American Prometheus* (New York: Knopf, 2006), 330–331.

280   *"The guilt consciousness"*: Ibid., 331.

280   *"It proposes"*: Ibid., 347.

280   *"Russia will exercise"*: Ibid., 346.

282   *"exhausted by their wartime"*: Wittner, *Rebels*, 100–101.

283   *"This is Year One," "God have mercy"*: Quoted in Hoberman, *Army of Phantoms*, 27.

283   *Lang was stunned*: See Peter Bogdanovich, *Fritz Lang in America* (New York: Prager, 1969), 70.

284   *script was amended*: See Charles Highham, *Howard Hughes: The Secret Life* (New York: Putnam, 1993).

285   *"American intervention in Turkey"*: Quoted in W.A. Swanberg, *Norman Thomas* (New York: Scribner, 1976), 304.

285   *"keep up its military"*: Quoted in Lieberman, *Strangest Dream*, 40.

285   *"the sentimental hopes"*: Ibid.

287   *"I had ceased to"*: Cord Meyer, *Facing Reality* (New York: Harper & Row, 1980), 56–57.

287   *"the millions of us"*: Merle Miller, *That Winter* (New York: Sloane, 1948), 249.

288   *Hoover and the CIA*: See Mark Riebling, *Wedge* (New York: Knopf, 1994), 122.

289 *"The same sons of bitches"*: Quoted in C. David Heymann, *The Georgetown Ladies' Social Club* (New York: Atria Books, 2003), 168.

Voices

290 *"The first casualty"*: Quoted in Terkel, *The "Good War,"* 329.
290 *"INTERVIEWER: What was it"*: *Henry Wallace: An Uncommon Man*, dir. by Joan D. Murray (2011).
290 *"Tessie Hutchinson"*: Shirley Jackson, "The Lottery," in Joyce Carol Oates, ed., *Shirley Jackson: Novels and Stories* (New York: Library of America, 2010).

CHAPTER 9: THE LONELY PASSION OF HENRY WALLACE

291 *"The people behind this"*: Quoted in John C. Culver and John Hyde, *American Dreamer* (New York: Norton, 2000), 391, 397.
293 *"How do American actions," preparing "to win:"* Quoted, ibid., 417.
294 *"will travel as"*: Ibid., 421.
294 *"How we meet this"*: Ibid., 108.
295 *"[Wallace] is a pacifist"*: Quoted in McCullough, *Truman*, 517.
295 *"not abusive"*: Culver and Hyde, *American Dreamer*, 108.
295 *"home people," "forgot the war"*: Ibid., 519.
296 *"Communists," he averred, "should be"*: Ibid., 438–439.
297 *"severe criticism," "interfere"*: Quoted in Hoopes and Brinkley, *Driven Patriot*, 258.
297 *"I believe," he declared*: Culver and Hyde, *American Dreamer*, 440.
298 *"an outcast from all"*: Ibid., 441.
299 *"If the Democratic Party"*: Henry Wallace, oral history, 5065.
299 *"What I was interested"*: Ibid., 5089.
299 *"would be damaged"*: Ibid., 5079.
300 *"America has nothing"*: Memo from SAC, Atlanta, to Director, FBI, November 24, 1947.
301 *"only way we can make"*: Quoted in Michael Straight, *After Long Silence* (New York: Norton, 1983), 214.
301 *"As long as every"*: Quoted in Culver and Hyde, *American Dreamer*, 45.
301 *"We want this to"*: Henry Wallace, oral history, 5062.
303 *"Not only could"*: Philip Jaffe, *The Rise and Fall of American Communism* (New York: Horizon Press, 1975), 118–119.
304 *"All I said was"*: Culver and Hyde, *American Dreamer*, 452.
304 *"last-ditch stand mentality"*: Maurice Isserman, *Which Side Were You On?* (Middletown, CT: Wesleyan University Press, 1982), 246.
305 *"Joseph Stalin had won"*: Arthur D. Kahn, *The Education of a 20th Century Political Animal II* (Bloomington, IN: Author House, 2007), 36.
305 *"I had, indeed"*: Ibid., 43.
306 *"I'm not following their:* Culver and Hyde, *American Dreamer*, 464.
306 *"She has always been," "I would say"*: Ibid., 496–497.

306   *"I am not a Communist"*: Henry Wallace, oral history, 5091–5092.

307   *"I don't know"*: Ibid.

307   *Wallace later said*: Ibid.

308   *"'spy' who stole"*: John Earl Haynes, Harvey Klehr, and Alexander Vassiliev, *Spies: The Rise and Fall of the KGB in America* (New Haven, CT: Yale University Press, 2009), 427.

308   *"I am sure that"*: Joan Cook, "John J. Abt, Lawyer, Dies at 87," *New York Times*, August 13, 1991.

309   *"continuous follower in every"*: Henry Wallace, oral history, 5069.

309   *"a very considerable"*: Ibid., 5078.

309   *"Lew became an invaluable"*: Straight, *Long Silence*, 215.

309   *"The word from the"*: Henry Wallace, oral history, 5130.

310   *"by driving home"*: Clark Clifford, Memorandum, August 17, 1948, Clifford Papers, Truman Library.

310   *"the negro votes"*: Ibid.

310   *"all-out effort"*: Quoted by Culver and Hyde, *American Dreamer*, 465.

311   *"held together by bosses," "Stalin's Mortimer"*: Ibid., 479.

311   *"unprincipled," "totalitarian"*: Quoted in Richard J. Walton, *Henry Wallace, Harry Truman and the Cold War* (New York: Coward-McCann, 1968), 311.

311   *"an instrument of"*: Quoted in Michael Wrezin, *A Rebel in Defense of Tradition* (New York: Basic Books, 1994), 200.

314   *"It was a singing"*: Henry Wallace, oral history, 5124.

314   "I saw Jesus on the cross": Richard Blakeslee (1948).

314   *"My own slant was"*: Quoted in Culver and Hyde, *American Dreamer*, 478.

315   *"The lyrics breathed"*: Richard Silverstein, Tikun Olam website, www.richard silverstein.com/tikun_olam/.

316   *"Those who participate"*: Quoted by Liebermann, *Strangest Dream*, 56.

316   *"Veterans still lack"*: "Veterans' Direct Action a Minor Post-War Fear," *New York Times*, August 11, 1946.

316   *"people with true liberal"*: Quoted in Culver and Hyde, *American Dreamer*, 499.

317   *"I had a sister-in-law"*: Henry Wallace: An Uncommon Man.

317   *"bitter man, eccentric," "Wallace's hatred"*: Straight, *Long Silence*, 206.

318   *"horrid faces of"*: Quoted in Zachary Karabell, *The Last Campaign* (New York: Knopf, 2000), 223.

318   *"The faces I have"*: Ibid.

319   *"Are you an American?"*: Quoted in Culver and Hyde, *American Dreamer*, 494.

319   *"The black minority"*: Ibid.

319   *fascism's "ugly reality"*: Ibid., 495.

320   *"the owners of the mine"*: Quoted in Karabell, *Last Campaign*, 234.

320   *"The thing I remember," "I tried to talk"*: Henry Wallace, oral history, 5123.

321   *"Week after week"*: Straight, *Long Silence*, 224.

321   *"Reassured by his"*: Divine, "Election of 1948," 98.

322   *"Wallace's political significance"*: Ibid.

322   *"not just defeat"*: Kofsky, *War Scare*, 104.

323   *"Peace is 'bustin'"*: Ibid.

323   *a "rule" was confirmed*: Yergin, *Shattered Peace*, 392.

324　　*"Instead, in the name"*: Divine, "Election of 1948," 110.

324　　*"Under no circumstances"*: Quoted by Kahn, *Political Animal*, 51.

324　　*"I told him so"*: Quoted in Culver and Hyde, *American Dreamer*, 502.

325　　*"serious mistake"*: Henry Wallace, oral history, 5123.

325　　*"I thought they were"*: Quoted in Culver and Hyde, *American Dreamer*, 527.

325　　*"a broad-based party"*: Henry Wallace, oral history, 5120.

326　　*"This was not a Wallacite"*: Quoted in Culver and Hyde, *American Dreamer*, 507.

326　　*"It does no good"*: Ibid.

327　　*"Undoubtedly the Russians"*: Ibid., 508.

328　　*"on notice that there"*: Bird and Sherwin, *American Prometheus*, 542, 548.

328　　*As Bruce Cumings*: Bruce Cumings, *The Korean War* (New York: Modern Library, 2010), 80.

328　　*"could push for"*: Ibid., 82.

329　　*"the triumph of liberals"*: Hodgson, *Our Time*, 75.

Voices

331　　*"I mentioned that General"*: Quoted in Benjamin O. Fordham, *Building the Cold War Consensus* (Ann Arbor: University of Michigan, 1998), 118.

331　　*"Who's killin' our boys?"*: Willie Morris, *Taps* (Boston: Houghton, 2001), 85.

331　　*"That big eight-wheeler"*: Hank Snow, "I'm Movin' On" (1950).

CHAPTER 10: KOREA—DRAWING A LINE

334　　*"elite left-wing foreign policy," "seems to symbolize"*: Quoted in Zelizer, *Arsenal*, 94.

338　　*"Never before," "The decision," "It was time"*: Quoted in Goldman, *Crucial Decade*, 158–159.

339　　*"Northern or communist"*: Quoted in McCullough, *Truman*, 776.

339　　*"the course actually taken"*: Quoted in Cumings, *Korean War*, 12.

340　　*"the U.S. should not"*: Quoted in Fordham, *Consensus*, 70.

340　　*"had little to do with"*: Cumings, *Korean War*, 12.

340　　*"little grasp of the real"*: Keith D. McFarland and David L. Roll, *Louis Johnson and the Arming of America* (Bloomington: Indiana University Press, 2005), 301.

341　　*administration was committed*: Fordham, *Consensus*, 40.

341　　*Korea was not mentioned*: Ibid., 69.

341　　*"Acheson and other decision makers"*: Cumings, *Korean War*, 69.

342　　*"By God, I am going"*: Quoted in McFarland and Roll, *Louis Johnson*, 279.

342　　*"If the Communists were permitted"*: Quoted in McCullough, *Truman*, 776–777.

342　　*"Underlying these discussions," "The impact that"*: McFarland and Roll, *Louis Johnson*, 286.

343　　*"The attack upon Korea"*: Quoted in McCullough, *Truman*, 780.

343　　*"Prestige is the shadow"*: Quoted in Cumings, *Korean War*, 12.

344　　*"You're a real SOB"*: Quoted in Zelizer, *Arsenal*, 95.

345　　*the troops' deployment*: McFarland and Roll, *Louis Johnson*, 295.

345 *"committing the nation"*: Arnold Offner, *Another Such Victory*, 377.

345 *"If a burglar breaks into"*: Quoted in McFarland and Roll, *Louis Johnson*, 284.

346 *"The fundamental design of those"*: "NSC 68: United States Objectives and Programs for National Security," April 14, 1950, http://www.fas.org/irp/off docs/nsc-hst/nsc-68.htm.

347 *"The Kremlin regards the United States"*: Quoted in *Naval War College Review*, vol. XXVII (May/June 1975), 51–108.

347 *"Given the rhetoric of the"*: Athan Theoharis, "The Politics of Scholarship: Liberals, Anti-communism and McCarthyism," in Robert Griffin and Athan Theoharis, eds., *The Specter* (New York: New Viewpoints, 1974), 262–280.

348 *"wholeheartedly behind our nation," "conception of a world police"*: Quoted in Wittner, *Rebels*, 201.

349 *"a truncated UN has been"*: Ibid., 202.

349 *using atomic weapons*: See Cumings, *Korean War*, 156–157.

351 *"Whatever the confrontation," "if we started"*: Samuel Fuller, *A Third Face* (New York: Knopf, 2002), 256.

351 *"roughest, toughest bunch"*: Ibid., 262.

351 *"Soldiers were trained to fight"*: Ibid., 265.

352 *"The DPRK is a firmly controlled"*: K. Rose, "Two Strategic Intelligence Mistakes in Korea, 1950," Central Intelligence Agency, www.cia.org.

352 *"with one arm tied behind my back"*: Quoted in Cumings, *Korean War*, 14.

353 *doubling the arms budget*: McFarland and Roll, *Louis Johnson*, 315.

353 *stepped up its loyalty programs*: See Fordham, *Consensus*, 166.

353 *"I cannot conceive of anyone"*: Quoted, ibid., 161.

353 *"the FBI already had drawn up"*: Ibid., 165; see also Schrecker, *Many Are the Crimes*, 346, 348.

354 *"established the military-industrial complex"*: Quoted in Fordham, *Consensus*, 182.

354 *"that Republicans could criticize"*: Zelizer, *Arsenal*, 103.

355 *"was surprised and alarmed"*: Kathryn Weathersby, "New Findings on the Korean War," *Cold War International History Project Bulletin* 3 (Fall 1993), 1.

355, 356 *"liberate the whole," "it has to be organized"*: Evgeny Bajanov, "The Origins of the Korean War," alternativeinsight.com.

357 *"I have consulted with Comrades"*: Quoted in Jian Chen, "The Sino-Soviet Alliance and China's Entry into the Korean War," *The Cold War International History Project* (Washington, DC: Woodrow Wilson Center, 1992), 28–29.

357 *"The Chinese desperately needed"*: Ibid.

358 *"fighting not for the United Nations," "The boys aren't up there"*: Quoted in David Rees, *Korea: The Limited War* (Baltimore: Penguin Books, 1964), 190.

359 *the test emitted fallout*: Sherry, *Shadow of War*, 183.

360 *"After the disillusionment"*: Fenton, *In Your Opinion*, 93.

360 *"The Korean dilemma chiefly served"*: Ibid.

CREDITS

INDEX